W9-CLG-379

A HISTORY OF MUSIC IN AMERICAN LIFE

Volume II

THE GILDED YEARS,
1865-1920

A HISTORY OF MUSIC IN AMERICAN LIFE
Volume II

THE GILDED YEARS, 1865-1920

by
Ronald L. Davis

ROBERT KRIEGER PUBLISHING COMPANY
HUNTINGTON, N.Y.
1980

Original edition 1980

Printed and Published by
ROBERT E. KRIEGER PUBLISHING CO., INC.
645 New York Avenue
Huntington, New York 11743

Copyright © 1980 by
ROBERT E. KRIEGER PUBLISHING CO., INC.

Printed in the United States of America

Library of Congress Cataloging in Publication Data

Davis, Ronald L.
   A history of music in American life.

   Includes bibliographies.
   CONTENTS: v. 1. The formative years, 1620-1865.—
v. 2. The gilded years, 1865-1920.—v. 3. The modern era,
1920-present.
   1. Music—United States—History and criticism.
I. Title.
ML200.D3   780'.973   79-25359
ISBN 0-89874-003-7 (v. 2)

In Memory
of

BLANCHE M. MARTS
my own incredible Auntie Mame,
who showed me the meaning of
beauty and adventure

and

WALTER PRESCOTT WEBB
who loved the arts
as he loved the West,
and who affected many lives,
including mine

Introduction

Although immigrants came to the New World singing, frontier America had little time for the serious arts. Music, perhaps the most sensuous of Western Civilization's aesthetic expressions, was particularly neglected by a country whose cultural ideals emphasized hard work, material and social success, and emotional restraint. The Protestant ethic, reinforced by the wilderness experience, led the Puritans and other religious zealots to consider music a waste of time unless specifically contributing to the task at hand. The power of music to affect human emotions caused the Calvinist denominations especially to view it with more suspicion than fondness and therefore to restrict its role even in worship. An infant nation admiring reserve and control was far more comfortable with intellectual pursuits than with an art form prone to excite the senses.

With adolescence came an early nostalgia for vanishing innocence and a tendency to mistake sentimentality for honest feelings. As gentility was sought in the urban centers of the East, theaters and concert life slowly appeared as appendages of an aspiring commercial class who needed public arenas in which to display their newly acquired wealth and refinement. Serious music became prized as a demonstrable link with established civilization, an exotic and edifying experience that could be appreciated only with effort. Since men were consumed with economic and political matters, art in the young nation fell increasingly under the domination of women. Gradually the notion grew that serious music was not masculine. While music was essential for a sophisticated image, it was at the same time threatening to manhood if pursued in more than a cursory way. "I do not think," conductor Walter Damrosch would write, "there has ever been a country whose musical development has been fostered so almost exclusively by women as America."

Fawned over by the leisured classes, art music in the United States remained separate from life itself—an adornment imported from Europe for social purposes rather than an extract from the American experience. Until World War I serious music in America was dominated by immigrants and foreigners—first British, later Italian and especially German. Successful concert artists doted on the spectacular. John Philip Sousa at the turn of the century observed that life in the United States was more hurried than almost

VII

VIII

anywhere else; being restless, American audiences demanded variety and more in the way of showmanship.

By the middle of the nineteenth century vernacular music had been largely turned over to the minorities. Black entertainers, when outside the restrictions of the genteel tradition, often devised spontaneous expressions that were original, uniquely American, and frequently voiced the repressed emotions of whites as well as blacks, creating an idiom that would eventually develop into a national music. Even white performers in blackface could be less inhibited, less self-conscious, and therefore more honest about the issues and feelings that bothered or inflamed them. Later, with the advent of vaudeville and the rise of the commercial music business, the Jew came to dominate popular music in America, a phenomenon that continued at least until the end of the big studio era in Hollywood.

Meanwhile serious musicians were consistently being told they could not hope to win acceptance unless they had studied and been acclaimed in Europe. Since there were few symphony orchestras and no provincial opera houses in the United States, singers and conductors either went abroad to gain experience or turned to mass media, out of necessity spanning the gulf between vernacular music and the cultivated tradition. Eugene Ormandy, long the mainstay of the Philadelphia Orchestra, was first given a chance to conduct at the Roxy Theater in New York, one of the original movie palaces. Soprano Rosa Ponselle came to grand opera from vaudeville, whereas baritone Robert Merrill had worked in movie houses, the "borscht circuit," and radio before winning his Metropolitan Opera contract. Even then Merrill sought the best of both worlds—grand opera *and* popular entertainment— and was once fired from the Metropolitan for canceling performances to make a film in Hollywood. Beverly Sills, who made a sensational debut at the Metropolitan in Rossini's *The Siege of Corinth* after performing the same role at La Scala, began her professional career as Bubbles Silverman singing "Rinso White" commercials on radio. And American-born Klara Barlow, who made a hasty entrance into the Met as Isolde early in 1974, had been a cigarette girl in New York's Latin Quarter for a time.

While maturity and world leadership have brought increased sophistication, Americans have remained basically a vernacular people. The minstrel show, burlesque, vaudeville, Hollywood films, radio, and television have been the entertainment forms revered by the multitude, for whom musical comedy is high art. Symphony orchestras, opera, and recitals for most Americans suggest the unapproachable, the exalted, the tedious. Dynamic personalities—a Callas or a Bernstein—can occasionally break through this general reticence, but seldom does the music itself have such power. If the New Orleans opera company offers a nude Thais, as it did in 1973, *that* will make the national news. But barring the extreme, art music in the United States remains in the background—ardently supported by a select few, noticed in passing by the great majority.

American popular music, on the other hand, is heard around the world. Berlin, Kern, Porter, Rodgers, and the other giants of Tin Pan Alley wrote standards that are still performed wherever there is a piano or a dance orchestra. *South Pacific, My Fair Lady, Hello, Dolly!* and *Fiddler on the Roof* have played with immense success in London, Tokyo, and Tel Aviv, as well as year after year in dinner theaters and stock productions across the United States. Discos in Madrid or Rome or Mexico City throb with contemporary American hits, while Willie Nelson and Waylon Jennings have made their way from Texas to the Orient via Nashville, making those decades when American music was dismissed almost without a hearing seem quaint and long ago.

Yet there are those around who remember well when music that was considered any good at all came from Europe, and native works still have difficulty finding their way into American concert halls and opera houses. Music's dramatic struggle to take root in the United States has been far more than a story of art at war with barbarism, more than the determination of the creative spirit to triumph in the face of diffidence and even ridicule. When viewed collectively, the nation's history has been written in music, as vividly as it has been chronicled in words. So have its values and aspirations, its tensions and fears, its joys and yearnings for self-expression, along with the never-ending search for both personal and collective identity. What the historian has phrased in words, the musician has captured with notes, preserving the spirit and dimension of American life with accuracy and insight.

Dallas, Texas   RONALD L. DAVIS
March 28, 1980

Acknowledgments

A fourteen-year writing project carries with it innumerable frustrations and counterbalancing rewards. High among the latter has been the opportunity to meet an assortment of helpful, talented people. My gratitude literally extends from coast to coast, and one of the frustrations has been a temptation to rewrite portions of the story long ago completed when subsequent conversations with performers and musicians have opened up nuances too tantalizing to ignore. But as that great legend of popular song Ruth Etting told me in a long distance telephone conversation a matter of days before her death in Colorado, "There comes a point at which time stops." Certainly there comes a point at which any writer must stop, even though he knows there is more to tell and often wants desperately to go on.

I must first thank David D. Van Tassel of Case Western Reserve University, who initially suggested a broader topic as the logical successor to my previous books on opera in Chicago and opera in the American West. Van Tassel later admitted he had in mind a brief paperback survey of American music with emphasis on interpretation. Obviously I misunderstood and went my own direction, preferring to write a longer version with the undergraduate cultural history student and the curious layman in mind. A grant from the Graduate Council of Humanities at Southern Methodist University enabled me to begin my research in 1966, and I soon found gracious assistance in SMU's Fondren Library, especially from Dorothy Bosch, Margaret Hamzy, and Esther Smith. Much of the material needed was furnished through Inter-Library Loan, and there were many trips to the University of Texas at Austin, where a competent staff turned tedious work into an adventure. Most of the photographs in these three volumes came from the Hoblitzelle Theatre Arts Collection in Austin, and a special thanks goes to W. H. Crain and the dedicated personnel in the Humanities Research Center on the University of Texas campus.

Robert W. Richmond of the Kansas State Historical Society read the entire manuscript and offered constructive criticism at a formative stage of the writing, while my colleagues Luis Martin and R. Hal Williams provided encouragement when I needed it most. Richard B. Allen at the William Ransom Hogan Jazz Archive of Tulane University made useful notations on

XII

the jazz chapters and earlier opened a mass of invaluable material for my use. Lee Breeden read the introductory volume from a musician's viewpoint, as did Ann Burk some time later. Eleanor Solon typed and retyped the whole manuscript, read galley proofs, and labored over index cards above and beyond the call of duty. My appreciation to her is boundless. Mary Plunkett and JoAnn Brown also read galley proofs, volunteering fresh eyes when they were especially welcome.

Two sections of the work, "Sentimental Songs in Antebellum America" and "Early Jazz," have appeared in the *Southwest Review*, and as always Margaret Hartley proved a dream editor. Valcour Lavizzo edited the final copy, rescuing me from any number of foolish errors.

I owe a special debt to Clifford L. Snyder, who has aided my writing ventures repeatedly over the years and was instrumental in the completion of this one. Also I have been fortunate in having the cooperation of Robert E. Krieger and his production staff.

Personal gratitude must be expressed to Joe B. Frantz, Anne Russ, Bruce H. Beard, Robert R. Wade, Frank and Jane Moffit, and William and Elaine Sweet, all of whom gave supportive strokes between chapters.

R.L.D.

Illustrations

Contents

CHAPTER

I

The Rise of the Symphony

Orchestra

In 1864, as the Civil War still raged farther north, Michael Hahn was inaugurated governor of the restored Union state of Louisiana. To celebrate the occasion bandmaster Patrick S. Gilmore, who was with General Nathaniel Banks' forces, prepared an immense festival concert. Gilmore assembled a chorus of 5000 adults and school children, a band of 500 pieces, a huge fife and drum corps, and arranged for church bells and artillery to accent the climaxes. The spectacle took place in Lafayette Square on March 4; the program consisted mainly of patriotic music, concluding with "Hail Columbia." The anthem closed with the firing of thirty-six cannons, set off by electric buttons from the conductor's podium. The extravaganza was considered an enormous success, and Gilmore suddenly became a household word.

Yet New Orleans was but a beginning for Pat Gilmore as a national figure. Realizing the public's fascination for the "monster" concerts introduced to America earlier by Antoine Jullien and Louis Moreau Gottschalk—and adoring such displays himself—the famous bandmaster returned to Boston after the Civil War, determined to dazzle the country with even greater musical spectacle.

Born in Ireland on Christmas Day, 1829, Patrick Sarsfield Gilmore learned to love music as a boy from the British military bands stationed in the town of Athlone, where he worked. Eventually one of the bandmasters taught Pat to play the cornet and later found him a place in a regimental band. When the regiment was sent to Canada, Gilmore went along. At nineteen he obtained his release from the British army, migrated to Boston, took a job with Ordway's Music Store, and performed both with Ordway's band and minstrel troupe. For a time he was a member of the Salem Band and afterwards its leader. A handsome lad with a vigorous personality, Gilmore quickly became known for his skill as a bandmaster and cornet virtuoso. In 1859 he reorganized the Boston Brigade Band and the following year took the group to the Republican national convention in Chicago, where Lincoln was nominated for the Presidency. When the Civil War broke out, Gilmore's band paraded through the streets of Boston, attracting recruits for the Massachusetts Twenty-fourth Volunteer Regiment. Soon the band itself, including Gilmore, enlisted with the regiment as a body. Serving about a year in North Carolina, Gilmore's band was mustered out, although Pat himself was urged by General Banks to come to Louisiana and assume the directorship of music under his command.

Back in Boston after the success of his gargantuan festival in New Orleans, Gilmore formed a new band, took it on extensive tours, went into business manufacturing band instruments, and laid plans for his forthcoming National Peace Jubilee. Intended to commemorate the country's regained unity, the jubilee was held in Boston on June 15-17, 1869, following months of preparation. A coliseum seating 50,000 people was constructed in St. James Park, while a chorus of 10,000 voices and an orchestra of 1000 instruments were being readied. Singing societies from far and near accepted invitations to join in the celebration, and Julius Eichberg, director of the Boston Conservatory of Music, agreed to direct the massive chorus. The now legendary Ole Bull consented to serve as concert master of the great orchestra. An organ was built for the occasion and a giant bass drum, the head of which "may have been ten or twenty feet in diameter." All winter long choruses and musicians in countless New England towns and villages rehearsed the music they were to perform in Boston, while the genial Gilmore talked millionaire bankers, doctors. lawyers, and merchants—anyone of influence or means who would listen—into supporting the mammoth venture.

The National Peace Jubilee, hailed as "The Grandest Musical Festival Ever Known in the History of the World," attracted crowds from all parts of the country, even from as far west as California. Gilmore had arranged with railroad companies for half fare tickets for visitors coming into Boston, while newspapers advertised low-priced rooms and lodgings for the week of the celebration. President Ulysses S. Grant had promised to attend. as had Admiral Farragut, Admiral Thatcher, Commodore Winslow, the governor of the state, and a host of other dignitaries. When the venerable Edward Everett Hale lifted his voice in the opening prayer, the three and a half acre hall was filled to capacity, thousands upon thousands banked from floor to roof.

The tall, slender figure of Pat Gilmore appeared on stage and was enthusiastically greeted. He bowed, as every eye became fixed on the striking leader—immaculately groomed, his face framed by black sideburns and a distinguished goatee. Suddenly he raised his hands, a baton in the right. Then with a forceful swoop, orchestra, chorus, and organ all burst forth in "A Mighty Fortress Is Our God." At the conclusion of the hymn the audience went wild with cheers and applause, as Gilmore bowed again and hurried off the stage. His place was taken by Carl Zerrahn, Boston's top conductor, who moved the program to the overture from Wagner's *Tannhauser*.

Although neither the Handel and Haydn Society nor the conservative music critic John Sullivan Dwight (who purposely spent the week at his summer home at Nahant) would have any part of the Jubilee, much of the music offered was drawn from the classics. The "Gloria" from a Mozart mass was presented, the overture from Rossini's *William Tell*, Gounod's "Ave Maria" sung by the corpulent soprano Parepa-Rosa, selections by American composers John Knowles Paine and Dudley Buck, all the way to patriotic tunes and hymns like "Nearer, My God, to Thee." And yet the atmosphere in which these compositions were performed was almost circuslike. The violin obbligato for one of Mme. Parepa-Rosa's pieces, for instance, was played by two hundred instruments. "The Star-Spangled Banner" was rendered by full chorus and orchestra with cannons fired by a Boston artillery company. To keep the thousands of musicians synchronized Gilmore had ordered speaking tubes attached to the podium, through which the conductor could give cues to his several assistants scattered throughout the orchestra. But the sensation of the 1869 Jubilee was a rendition of Verdi's "Anvil Chorus" that employed not only complete choral and orchestral forces, but a hundred local firemen in regulation helmets and red flannel uniforms pounding real anvils as well.

At the end of this cacophony the mass of spectators, as Thomas Ryan recalls the scene, "rose to their feet, jumped up and down, and nearly dislocated their arms by waving handkerchiefs, fans, hats, parasols, even babies....Fifty thousand people in a wooden building can make some noise." The firemen marched out, carrying their long-handled hammers over their right shoulders like muskets. The applause continued. The firemen marched back in, entering in two files that separated as they reached the orchestra, framing the musicians on either side in red. With Gilmore at the podium, the performance was repeated! While critics and purists insisted the whole festival was nonsense, the public was not only titillated, but considered the tumult true culture in the most imposing sense. Gilmore's profits from the affair netted almost $40,000. Even more, he had become the musical idol of the American masses.

Pat immediately left for Europe to rest, but returned a short time later, announcing plans for an even grander World Peace Jubilee. His efforts were exactly doubled. This time he would assemble a chorus of 20,000, an orchestra of 2000, and construct a coliseum seating 100,000. To add to the international flavor military bands were invited from Europe—the Grenadier Guards from

London, a German infantry band from Berlin, the Garde Republicaine from Paris, the Royal Constabulary from Ireland, and others. And *coup* of *coups,* the great Johann Strauss was brought over from Vienna to conduct the army of singers and instrumentalists in his most popular compositions. Strauss himself remembered the event with horror:

> [T]here were twenty thousand singers; in front of them the members of the orchestra—and these were the people I was to conduct. A hundred assistant conductors had been placed at my disposal to control these gigantic masses, but I was only able to recognize those nearest to me, and although we had rehearsals there was no possibility of giving an artistic performance, a proper production. . . . Now just conceive of my position face to face with a public of four hundred thousand Americans. There I stood at the raised desk, high above all the others. How would the business start, how would it end? Suddenly a cannon-shot rang out, a gentle hint for us twenty thousand to begin playing *The Blue Danube.* I gave the signal, my hundred assistant conductors followed me as quickly and as well as they could and then there broke out an unholy row such as I shall never forget. As we had begun more or less simultaneously, I concentrated my whole attention on seeing that we should finish together too! Thank Heaven, I managed even that.

Like its predecessor, the World Peace Jubilee was held in Boston, in the summer of 1872, theoretically to celebrate the end of the Franco-Prussian War. It lasted three weeks, with a number of internationally famous soloists participating. Musical selections ranged from the sextet from *Lucia di Lammermoor,* sung by a "bouquet of artists," to "Pizzicato Polka," to the expected national airs. "The Anvil Chorus" was repeated, and the "Soldiers' Chorus" from *Faust* was given with simulated fire and all sorts of other effects. But the crowds did not come. On one occasion there were an estimated 22,000 performers on stage and a bare 7000 people in the audience. The festival was simply too much repetition and ended in financial disaster.

Yet architect Louis Sullivan, a student at the Massachusetts Institute of Technology at the time, later recalled the Jubilee with fondness, judging it "refreshing and gay, melodious above all." Sullivan remembered Johann Strauss mounting the conductor's stand "like a little he-wren," his violin in his hand, dancing as he led the great orchestra. The young architect thought Strauss "the biggest little man on earth." But for Louis Sullivan, as for hosts of other Americans, Gilmore's Peace Jubilees were an introduction to great music, and it was there that the architect experienced for the first time the power and perfection of the trained single voice, conveying the gamut of human emotions. "I believe," Thomas Ryan acknowledges in his *Recollections of an Old Musician* (1899), "the Jubilees are as worthy of being put on record as would be a first performance in America of the *Parsifal* by

Richard Wagner; though in comparison with the latter, the Jubilee music is like a boy compared with a man. But w·thout the first, the other could not be. *Parsifal* is the man fully grown..., while the Jubilees represent the boy—the tearing, rowdy young fellow, in his first stage of musical growth."

The untutored American public of Gilmore's day had progressed little beyond the level of musical appreciation exhibited during the tours of Ole Bull and Jenny Lind. The Jubilees were enjoyed primarily for their size and theatrics, whereas concerts by distinguished soloists, chamber musicians, and serious orchestras went largely unattended. Among the multitudes vastness was still equated with quality, display mistaken for art. Audiences continued to be attracted more by the personality of performers than by the music they presented. Child prodigies were well received by the curious, while mature artists either resorted to gimmicks or played to empty houses. Touring musicians found misunderstanding at every turn. When pianist Anton Rubinstein played a recital in Memphis, Tennessee, on his visit to the United States in 1872, he was advised by a friendly stagehand that he should hurry to blacken his face before the "show." When the Mendelssohn Quintet traveled across the country, they were frequently asked which of them was the famous Felix Mendelssohn. When a concert pianist informed a midwesterner that he had just played Beethoven's *Sonata No. 1, Opus 2,* the rustic exclaimed, "Oh, how wonderful! I just love opuses!" Even in New York artists who refused to indulge in exhibition played to scant audiences. One concert manager there resorted to hiring empty carriages to give the appearance of a crowd an hour or so before a piano recital was to begin, in the hope that the parade might stir the interest of passersby.

If things were limited for foreign artists, they were worse for native talent, particularly musicians without European trappings. Pianist Olga Samaroff (born Lucy Hickenlooper, in San Antonio, Texas) was told by a leading concert manager in the early 1900s, "If you played like Liszt and Rubinstein rolled into one, I could do nothing for you without European notices." Sometimes the efforts of serious musicians were received with a green enthusiasm that was hardly less startling than the public's ignorance. Violinist Efrem Zimbalist was touring as soloist with Walter Damrosch's orchestra one season and had arrived at the opera house in Fargo, North Dakota. The musician was sitting in the wings listening to the symphony's concert before he played his selections. Suddenly a young cowboy, anesthetized by spirits, appeared at his side, dressed in high boots, flannel shirt, and slouch hat. The cowboy sat enraptured, as the orchestra poured out sounds that were both strange and appealing to him. Each time the music swelled into a climax, he would grab Zimbalist's knee and convulse with delight: "God damn it, but I like that music!" Then he would sit in silence until the next crescendo, whereupon he would seize Zimbalist again and shout: "They can go to hell, but they know how to play!"

As late as 1908 the great Russian basso Feodor Chaliapin could justly write, "I pity Americans because they have no light, no song in their lives.

They are but children in everything pertaining to art." Certainly Americans in the late nineteenth century possessed slight understanding of the subtleties of great music, and it took an event of the proportions of Gilmore's festivals to dramatize the classics in terms an unsophisticated public could comprehend. Even that could be overdone, as the failure of the World Peace Jubilee in 1872 indicates. The indomitable Pat apparently realized this, for he staged only one more giant spectacle—in Chicago in 1873, to celebrate the rebuilding of the city after the great fire. Following that he concentrated on the band music that was a more natural part of the country's musical life, performing light compositions that would nevertheless provide an important background for the development of a taste for more serious instrumental works.

In the summer of 1873 Gilmore was invited by the officers of the Twenty-second Regiment of New York to become the director of their band. For the next twenty years he would devote himself to developing that band into the nation's finest. Having tired of showmanship, he now endeavored for musical excellence; yet he still appealed to the crowd. Band music had been popular in America since before the Revolution, but Gilmore carried it to new heights, training his players meticulously and taking them on tours of the United States, Canada, and eventually Europe. His programs were the most advanced of their day. Along with the predictable quadrilles, polkas, marches, patriotic medleys, cornet solos, and popular songs, Gilmore added good transcriptions of standard orchestral overtures and excerpts from the classics, including modified selections by Mozart, Beethoven, Verdi, and even Wagner. He attempted some composing himself, although he never ranked high in this regard; "When Johnny Comes Marching Home," written late in the Civil War, remained his best piece.

Yet Gilmore became the most cosmopolitan, best informed bandmaster of his age, setting standards for years to come. He enlarged his band to sixty-six members, supplemented on special occasions to almost one hundred. His concerts were planned on a businesslike basis, and for thirteen consecutive summers his musicians played at New York's popular Manhattan Beach resort. Gilmore and his band were featured attractions at the Centennial Exposition in Philadelphia in 1876 and performed at similar gatherings across the country. While playing at the St. Louis Exposition, September 24, 1892, Gilmore suddenly died.

World's Fairs were viewed by post-Civil War America as a golden opportunity for demonstrating the nation's growth in international stature, in art as well as in industry. It was at the Centennial Exposition in Philadelphia that Pat Gilmore achieved one of his greatest successes. But the celebration was far less a triumph for the musical director of the fair, Theodore Thomas, who had become the recognized bulwark of orchestral music in the country. Thomas had planned more than two hundred musical programs for the Centennial, scheduled concerts by symphony orchestras from Boston and New York, choral societies from two dozen American cities, and bands from Europe and the far reaches of the United States. A special hall

had been erected, and Richard Wagner had been commissioned to write a
"Grand Centennial Inaugural March." John Knowles Paine composed a
"Centennial Hymn" to words by John Greenleaf Whittier, while Dudley
Buck turned out a "Centennial Meditation" to a text by Sidney Lanier. Music
clubs from all over the country had agreed to participate. And for the opening
of the Women's Pavilion, Thomas arranged an entire program of music
composed by women.

All of this was to prove that in the hundred years since the signing of the
Declaration of Independence America had come a long way in the cultivation
of music as a serious art. But it became obvious soon after the inaugural
ceremonies that Thomas' ambitions were to be thwarted. To begin with,
Wagner had accepted $5000—raised by the Women's Centennial Committees
and paid to the composer in advance—for what was decidedly one of the more
inconsequential things he ever wrote. Even more disappointing, while the
band concerts at the exposition were generally well attended, the more serious
efforts were not and had to be cut back. People clearly came to the fair to see
rather than hear, and "Theodore Thomas' Unrivalled Summer Nights
Concerts" were no match for the mechanical horse, the statue of Moses
perched on a fountain with water pouring from between its toes, Swiss chalets
rising out of shrubbery, the first public exhibition of Alexander Graham
Bell's telephone, the Art Gallery's colossal figure of George Washington
rising heavenward on the back of an eagle, or the "Sleeping Iolanthe"
modeled in real Arkansas butter in less than an hour and fifteen minutes.
Although the fair itself took in gross receipts of over $3,500,000, the financial
losses on the music programs were alarming. Thomas himself, since he was a
partner in the series and therefore accountable for debts, was forced to the edge
of bankruptcy. At one point his music library, instruments, baton, even his
ink stand, were seized by the Philadelphia police and sold at auction.
Fortunately a generous friend bought the property and returned it to the
musician. All through the active months of the Centennial the Thomas
concerts were persistently advertised as "THE GREATEST MUSICAL
SUCCESS" that had ever taken place in Philadelphia. But the conductor knew
better; for him the exposition spelled financial ruin and heartbreak.

Thomas was not a man to accept defeat, however; he had worked too
hard, fought the battle for serious music in America too long for that. Born on
October 11, 1835, in the north German village of Esens, where his father was
the town musician, Theodore Thomas had been brought to New York as a
boy of ten. The family left Germany in the hope of finding improved
economic conditions, but supporting a large number of children on the
meager wages of a musician proved no easy task in antebellum America. Soon
young Theodore was forced to tuck his violin under his arm and look for
work. He played for dances, theaters, weddings, even in saloons where he
passed the hat. His formal training was slight, mainly coming from his
father, but his aptitude and artistic curiosity were great.

At fifteen Thomas made a concert tour—unaccompanied—through the

South, billing himself as "Master T.T.," the prodigy. He traveled from town
to town on horseback, giving performances in hotel dining rooms or public
halls for what money he could take in. He was his own manager, made his
own posters, was his own press agent, and collected tickets at the door before
hurrying backstage to dress for the concert. After announcing his
appearance in one town in Mississippi he was ordered by authorities to leave,
because townspeople believed the devil was in his fiddle! He returned to New
York determined to go to Europe for formal training, but discovered that
Europe, including scores of musicians, had come to the United States. He
began the study of harmony and counterpoint in New York and in 1853
occupied a post in Jullien's orchestra. Before he was twenty Thomas had
organized a series of chamber music concerts with William Mason.

Meanwhile he had become increasingly dedicated to the cause of good
music and grew determined to bring the best of the European musical
tradition, particularly the German, to American audiences. Music for
Thomas was no luxury, but one of life's essentials. He was appointed
concertmaster of the orchestra at the New York Academy of Music and in
December, 1860, made his debut as a conductor. Karl Anschutz, the regular
conductor at the Academy, was suddenly taken ill before a performance of *La
Juive*, and Thomas was asked to fill in, even though the score was unfamiliar
to him. When Anschutz later retired permanently, Thomas took his place. He
conducted a symphony concert for the first time in 1862 and found it the
richest experience of his life. At that point he laid aside his violin
professionally, vowing to devote his energies "to the cultivation of the public
taste for instrumental music."

Thomas was convinced that what America needed to raise its taste in
music was "a good orchestra, and plenty of concerts within reach of the
people." In 1864 he organized the Theodore Thomas Orchestra, which
presented its first concert at Irving Hall in New York on May 13, opening
with Wagner's overture to *The Flying Dutchman*. The orchestra gave a
number of performances during the next few years both in Irving and
Steinway Halls, coming into direct competition with the New York
Philharmonic. To supplement his season Thomas accepted summer
engagements for his orchestra in 1865 in Belvedere Lion Park, and during the
next two summers his musicians made a total of 187 appearances at Terrace
Gardens on Fifty-eighth Street. In the spring of 1868 Thomas moved his
orchestra to the newly completed Central Park Garden, where 1127
instrumental concerts were presented over the next eight summers in
essentially beer garden surroundings.

Thomas' programs contained a great many of the popular selections of
the day, although whenever possible the conductor would slip in a great
overture or a movement from a major symphony. A born teacher, Thomas
realized that an appreciation of the classics had to be built slowly and was
aware that to attract audiences in post-Civil War America light music and
an informal atmosphere were necessary. For his early programs at Central

Park Garden he relied heavily upon pieces of quality that were not too complex for the untrained ear—the waltzes of Johann Strauss, for example. To these standard favorites he might add Wagner's overture to *Rienzi*, Weber's overture to *Oberon*, or the Scherzo from Mendelssohn's "Reformation" Symphony. Gradually Thomas educated his New York audiences to accept complete symphonies, including those of Mozart and Beethoven, as well as compositions by Liszt, Berlioz, Schubert, Brahms, and Schumann. "At last the summer programs show a respectable character," the conductor wrote in his notebook; "we are rid of the cornet!"

While the Thomas orchestra could give well-attended nightly performances at Central Park Garden for almost six months, the hunger of the New York public for orchestral music seemed satiated during the winter months by the six annual concerts of the Philharmonic Soci .y plus the five customarily given by Thomas. The extensive summer season, therefore, provided the conductor with the opportunity to attract the country's best musicians; gathering them together, he perfected an ensemble that the meager, more formal winter engagements would never have permitted. There were almost daily rehearsals, for while Thomas was willing to lighten his programs, he stubbornly insisted on technical excellence. In the beginning the orchestra numbered around forty players, although this size was eventually expanded to nearly sixty.

Even with the garden concerts, however, Thomas was unable to offer his musicians fulltime employment. To keep the orchestra busy during the winter, it became necessary to travel. In 1869 the Theodore Thomas Orchestra took to the road for the first time, touring the breadth of America with such regularity over the next two decades that its itinerary became jokingly known as the "Thomas Highway." The orchestra traveled everywhere, promoting the cause of good music. No city was too small, and many of the towns had never heard a symphony before. Public response varied. A leading citizen of one hamlet congratulated Thomas on the amazing ability of his violinists to turn the pages of their music together. In another place the local press commented that "the concert last night was the greatest orchestral circus the city has ever seen." In a western town one yokel amused himself during an excerpt from Beethoven's *Fifth Symphony* by chewing tobacco and aiming the juice at the bass player's bald head. In another village the chairs were cleared away after the concert on the assumption that the orchestra would entertain with dance music as well.

But Thomas evidently possessed limitless patience. He pressed on year after year, arguing that musical discrimination in the hinterland would come in time. Exposure to serious music was the important thing; appreciation would follow. And so he conducted concerts in churches, town halls, and railroad stations from New England to the Pacific coast, performing reasonably advanced works in the larger cities, more popular pieces at first in the smaller towns. Each program contained at least one selection above the heads of most of the audience, although Thomas was careful to compensate by offering something tuneful. As the hinterland became more familiar with the classics, he insisted on greater discipline from audiences. On one occasion, while the orchestra was playing Liszt's "Mephisto Waltz," the house became so noisy that Thomas stopped the music, took a watch from his pocket, and sternly announced that he would give the disturbers exactly five minutes to leave the hall before he began again. The music resumed in tomblike silence. Another time Thomas stopped in the middle of a piece, just as a lady in the front row pierced the silence with, "And I find it tastes *so* much better fried in butter!"

Discouragement was endless. Financial problems constantly plagued the musicians, and the tours themselves were brutally exhausting. The orchestra arrived in Chicago in 1871 a few hours before a scheduled concert, only to find that the city, including the opera house where they were to play, was in flames. Thomas once confessed to his friend George P. Upton, "I have been swinging the baton for fifteen years, and I do not see that people are any further ahead than when I started, but"—and he banged his fist on the table—"I am going to keep on if it takes another fifteen years."

And he did. He recouped his economic losses after the disastrous Philadelphia Exposition by taking to the road again. When the American Opera Company, with which he later became involved, ended in bankruptcy, he did the same thing—succinctly dismissing the opera venture: "Good intentions, bad management, no money." In 1877 Thomas became conductor of his former rival, the New York Philharmonic Society, replacing Carl Bergmann. The following year he took over the newly formed Cincinnati College of Music, but resigned after a few months, when he discovered that the backers of the school had primarily commercial intentions. He returned to New York and the Philharmonic, remaining the Society's conductor until 1891. Thomas not only injected the orchestra with a new artistic vitality, but rescued the Philharmonic from financial insecurity as well.

New York audiences were at last ready, Thomas believed, for the best in serious music. Although much of Berlioz, Liszt, and Wagner had been introduced by Bergmann, Thomas conducted the Philharmonic in many of the unfamiliar modern classics, including works by Sibelius, Bruckner, and Richard Strauss. When he played music from Wagner's *Tristan und Isolde* for the first time in America to an apathetic audience, he characteristically vowed, "I will keep on playing it until they *do* like it!" Gradually he built the Philharmonic into a genuinely outstanding symphonic body, while continuing to tour the interior with his own orchestra. His faith in the American public remained unshakable. "I have gone without food," he asserted, "and I have walked when I could not afford to ride. I have played when my hands were cold. But I will succeed, for I shall never give up my belief that at last the people will come to me, and my concerts will be crowded."

Eventually Thomas' efforts began to show results. In 1878 Leopold Damrosch established the New York Symphony, which gave its first concert

in Steinway Hall on November 9. Damrosch, another German, immigrated to
the United States from Breslau in 1871, when he received an invitation to
conduct the Arion Society of New York. A mature musician and a friend of
Liszt and Wagner, Damrosch immediately became a force in planting serious
music in the United States, second only to Theodore Thomas. A soft-spoken,
affable man, he made powerful friends and with their financial assistance
founded the Oratorio Society of New York in 1874, recognized immediately as
one of the major musical organizations of the country. The competition
Damrosch's New York Symphony offered the Philharmonic under Thomas
stimulated both orchestras and whetted the city's appetite further for good
music. With the cooperation of the Oratorio Society, the one year-old New
York Symphony gave the first American performances of Berlioz's
Damnation of Faust in 1879, five performances hailed as little short of
sensational. In May, 1881, Damrosch presented New York with an impressive
music festival, during which the Berlioz *Requiem*, Handel's *Messiah*, and
Beethoven's Ninth Symphony were all heard. A chorus of 1200 was
assembled, and the week-long concert series was held in the Seventh
Regiment Armory, where an audience of 10,000 could be accommodated.
When Leopold Damrosch died in 1885, his son Walter took over both the
Oratorio Society and the New York Symphony.

Outside New York City the pulse of the nation's musical life was also
quickening. The St. Louis Symphony was founded in 1880, after sporadic
attempts over the previous two decades. A regular concert series had been
launched in 1860 by the St. Louis Philharmonic Society; it continued
through the Civil War, but the society disbanded in 1870. Theodore Thomas
made St. Louis a regular stop on his tours, paving the way for the more
determined effort by the city to establish a professional concert orchestra.

Even more significant was the creation in 1881 of the Boston Symphony
Orchestra, the nation's first really permanent orchestra. The early music
center of the United States, Boston had seen the first chair of music founded at
Harvard University in 1875, marking a general growth in the community's
musical culture. But the Boston Symphony soared to prominence largely
through the virtually unlmited philanthrophy of financier Henry L.
Higginson. In the spring of 1881 Major Higginson calmly announced that
he intended to hire an orchestra of sixty men and a conductor, paying the
musicians a weekly salary on a fulltime basis. He anticipated an annual
operating deficit of $50,000, for which $1,000,000 in principal would be
needed, and this he planned to supply. "To the more fortunate people of our
land," Higginson insisted, "belongs the privilege of providing the higher
branches of education and art." The musical director of the orchestra,
however, would have complete charge of artistic matters, while administration would concern itself with creating the circumstances necessary for
quality performances.

The Boston Symphony gave its initial concert on Saturday evening,
October 22, 1881, under the leadership of George Henschel. The orchestra

instantly won the support of Boston's elite and became the focus of the city's social life. Major Higginson's patronage made possible daily rehearsals by musicians who could devote themselves exclusively to the symphony's weekly concerts. Programs were rich and varied. When Henschel resigned after three years as conductor, Wilhelm Gericke took his place. A firm disciplinarian, Gericke experimented with the orchestra, made a number of replacements, and succeeded in perfecting the organization into one of technical brilliance, the unrivaled model of American orchestras. Theodore Thomas himself bowed before Boston's accomplishment, declaring that Higginson's contribution to art reached far beyond Boston itself. "His cultivated taste," Thomas wrote, "would not allow him to make concessions to the ignorant, as he knew perfectly well that a first-rank orchestra can be maintained only by preserving the highest standard, and that the public ultimately would accept it. Other cities soon had the benefit of his generosity, and the influence of his organization spread; for New York had now gone backward, and the musical standard of the East was set by the Boston Orchestra. He came at the right time to help every sincere conductor throughout the land, and he certainly saved the ship on which I was sailing."

Thomas' ship had sprung a leak during the hard times of the 1880s, forcing him to disband his itinerant orchestra in 1888. He remained conductor of the New York Philharmonic, but the society gave only six concerts a season. To add to his distress, Mrs. Thomas died in 1889. The musician suddenly found himself, at fifty-three, alone. It was the low point of his life; his career had dwindled to a shadow of its recent greatness. Then, unexpectedly, Thomas was asked by a group of Chicago businessmen, headed by Charles Norman Fay, if he would come west to found an orchestra in Chicago. It would be a permanent orchestra, sufficiently subsidized to assure artistic excellence. The invitation was the realization of a lifelong dream—no more scrimping on costs, no more months of travel. Thomas flashed his reply to Chicago: "I would go to hell if they would give me a permanent orchestra."

The Illinois city had reached that point in its development when it quested for the benefits of art and gentility. Having grown sensitive to its image as the meat-packing center of America, the great "Porkapolis" of the prairies, Chicago sought to soften its reputation with a veneer of sophistication. Civic leaders, therefore, worked feverishly to cultivate the trappings of civilization. The Art Institute was organized in 1882 with Mrs. Potter Palmer among its ardent supporters, a pioneer in the crusade for French Impressionism. In December, 1889, the Chicago Auditorium was completed, designed by Dankmar Adler and his young partner, Louis Sullivan, and ranking as one of the most acoustically perfect theaters in the world. The University of Chicago was established with Rockefeller money in 1891, and on October 17 of that year, Theodore Thomas led the Chicago Symphony Orchestra in its first concert. The program featured Beethoven's Fifth Symphony, while the orchestra consisted of thirty local musicians and sixty-nine recruited from elsewhere, many of them former members of the

Theodore Thomas Orchestra. The symphony had the backing of the McCormicks, the Armours, the Swifts, Marshall Field, and most of the city's leading entrepreneurs, who saw the orchestra as a mark of civic progress.

Thomas contended that good music entailed a soothing quality that an active business community sorely needed. "One reason why I came to Chicago," he later insisted, "was because I understood the excitement and nervous strain that every one, more or less, suffered who lived there, and realized the consequent need of establishing a permanent musical institution in such a community." But the conductor shortly learned that, although Chicago was a city of nearly two million people, the great majority of its inhabitants were employed in mills, factories, and stockyards and possessed neither the funds nor the background for enjoying classical music. The cultivated class, on the other hand, was relatively small and basically shallow in its musical taste. Consequently teaching opportunities to supplement the income of Thomas' musicians were limited, and attendance at the orchestra's concerts was unreliable, depending mainly on the draw of soloists. Nevertheless, Thomas felt that the days of pampering audiences were over, and he demanded progressive programs and the highest standards. At his second concert he offered major works by Bach, Gluck, Schumann, Tchaikovsky, and Wagner, shortly discovering that his public considered such programs too severe. The first season of the Chicago Symphony closed showing a deficit of $53,000, which the backers covered. While there was dissatisfaction and grumbling, Thomas was given the nod to go ahead. The next year the conductor compromised slightly, reducing the number of symphonies and substituting shorter pieces, but the deficit was another $50,000.

Then in 1893 Thomas agreed to serve as musical director of the World's Columbian Exposition, and the opposition that had been building surfaced viciously. The fair would be held in Chicago and was to be another of those grand demonstrations of American progress. As he had done for the Philadelphia Centennial, Thomas arranged an impressive schedule of musical events, assembled a chorus of 3500 and an orchestra that included six harps. Johannes Brahms was invited to participate, but he declined. Thomas, however, did secure the services of Camille Saint-Saens and Ignace Jan Paderewski. John Knowles Paine wrote a "Columbus March and Hymn" for the occasion, and George W. Chadwick composed a "Dedicatory Ode" to lyrics by Harriet Monroe. The latter was given a performance that required one hundred drummers. The Exposition's opening concert included selections by Haydn, Mendelssohn, Handel, and Beethoven.

The trouble began when Paderewski demanded to perform on a Steinway piano, even though that was not one of the products exhibited at the fair. Thomas supported him, much to the dismay of piano manufacturers who had paid for exhibit space and considered the free advertising that came from using their piano in the Exposition's concert hall part of the bargain. Thomas argued that art should not be impeded by the market place and saw to

it that Paderewski had his Steinway. Business representatives were made all
the more uneasy by the outbreak of the financial Panic of 1893, and Thomas
soon found his position as musical director of the Chicago World's Fair being
undermined. Funds for his concerts were severely cut back by Exposition
officials, while Thomas himself suffered all sorts of abuse. He had been
bribed by Steinway and Sons, his enemies charged, and was nothing but a
crook! Seeing no chance of carrying out his programs, Thomas resigned from
the fair's staff and went to his summer home in Maine to await his third
season with the Chicago Orchestra.

But the storm had broken. Hostile Chicago newspapers and patrons who
had grown unhappy with Thomas' advanced programs over the past two
seasons now attacked the conductor openly. "Mr. Thomas should have been
leader of a barrack band in a mountainous camp in North Germany," the
Chicago Herald fumed. "He is a small despot by nature; a dull and
self-opinionated man, who has had unbounded opportunity in the land of his
adoption and has disappointed, year after year, the sanguine friends who have
been sympathetically petitioned to hold him up." Only George P. Upton
defended him. "Mr. Thomas' experiences with expositions," the *Tribune*
critic later understated, "was unfortunate." Yet for several seasons after the
Chicago World's Fair the press in general demanded, "Why does Mr. Thomas
play the soggy tunes of Bach, Brahms, and Bruckner? Has he never heard of
Victor Herbert and Sousa?"

As it was, Thomas had heard more of John Philip Sousa than he would
have liked, for the Sousa band had been the musical sensation of the
Columbian Exposition, much as Pat Gilmore's had been the success of the
Philadelphia Centennial. The band had attracted thousands of listeners to
every concert, and Thomas clearly looked upon this success as competition
for his own programs. The conductor had spent his whole life attempting to
"help the public to get beyond certain so-called 'popular music'—which
represents nothing more then sweet sentimentalism and rhythm, on the level
of the dime novel," and Sousa's band represented a triumph of the very
dilution Thomas had worked against. "Light music," the conductor
maintained, "is the sensual side of the art and has more or less devil in it."

Not all serious musicians, however, were so critical of Sousa. Anton
Rubinstein found his band a distinct creation. "They have Thomas
orchestras in other countries," Rubinstein argued, "but America has the only
Sousa." The bandmaster himself looked to Theodore Thomas as the ideal
conductor, much as he viewed Wagner as the ideal composer. And in his own
way Sousa did much to build an interest in instrumental music in the United
States and, in a less direct way than Thomas, lay the groundwork for future
American orchestras. As Sousa himself put it, "Thomas had a highly
organized symphony orchestra...I a highly organized wind band....Each
of us was reaching an end, but through different methods. He gave Wagner,
Liszt, and Tchaikowsky, in the belief that he was educating his public; I gave
Wagner, Liszt, and Tchaikowsky with the hope that I was entertaining my

public."

Born in Washington, D.C. on November 6, 1854, Sousa, as a boy, had lived in the capital throughout the Civil War. In the spring of 1861 the city was turned into an armed camp, with military bands periodically parading through the streets. Sousa claimed that he fell in love with band music at that time and begged his parents to allow him to take music lessons. His father, Antonio Sousa, of Portuguese descent although born in Spain, arranged for the lad to study violin with an old Spanish friend. It was during Lincoln's funeral that young Sousa first realized how sad music could be, and years later he was haunted by the sounds of muffled drums and the solemn, minor strains of the bands marching in the cortege. The Grand Review of the Union armies in Washington on May 23-24, 1865, celebrating the end of the war, made a jubilant impression on the boy, as it did on the multitudes that lined the streets to watch. Hundreds of thousands of soldiers and countless bands marched down Pennsylvania Avenue in a procession that took two days to pass the White House. The youth was determined that someday he would lead a marching band himself and at thirteen organized a quadrille band in which he played first violin.

In 1868, primarily to dissuade his son from running away with a circus, Antonio Sousa enlisted John Philip as an apprentice in the Marine Band. He began by running errands, sorting music, and moving music racks, but later performed with the musicians. Meanwhile he continued with his music lessons, learned to play the trombone, and added to his income by performing in theater orchestras. He stayed with the Marine Corps for seven years, then went to Philadelphia, where he was a member of several theater orchestras and for about six months played first violin in the orchestra conducted by Jacques Offenbach at the Centennial Exposition. It was also during the 1876 World's Fair that Sousa first heard Pat Gilmore's band. Later he coached an amateur production of Gilbert and Sullivan's triumphant operetta *Pinafore*. The combined exposure to Offenbach and the work of Gilbert and Sullivan made Sousa anxious to try an operetta of his own, and he gradually became convinced that his talents and interests were best suited to commercial music for entertainment.

He returned to Washington, D.C. in 1880, and on October 1, was installed as director of the United States Marine Band, a post he held for twelve years. He built the formerly mediocre organization into the finest marching band in the country. He improved the band's library, modernized its instrumentation, added members, and generally raised the level of musicianship. The band remained primarily a marching unit, although during Sousa's last years as director its repertoire began to assume symphonic proportions. Upon Sousa's request Congress granted permission for the Marine Band to make a national concert tour, and the director particularly impressed audiences with his showmanship. At that time Sousa was in his early thirties and a man of distinctive appearance. He wore gold-rimmed glasses and immaculate uniforms, with a square-trimmed black beard and a sword hitched to his belt. Before each performance he insisted on donning a pair of clean white kid gloves, an unseen ritual that the public heard about and found enchanting.

Sousa left the Marine Band in July, 1892, to establish his own concert band. After intensive rehearsals in New York, the Sousa Band gave its first public concert at Stillman Music Hall in Plainfield, New Jersey, September 26, 1892, two days after the death of Pat Gilmore. Receiving a telegram the day before informing him of Pat's death, Sousa hurriedly arranged "The Voice of the Departed Soul," Gilmore's own composition, for the opening number. It was a fitting gesture, for Sousa was the undisputed heir to the Gilmore mantle. The first Sousa Band was composed of forty-nine members, in addition to two soloists—a vocalist and a violinist. Following the Plainfield concert, the organization embarked on a nine-week tour of the East and Midwest, a financial disaster. Sousa blamed the failure on his manager, maintaining that the wrong towns had been selected, towns not fully apprized of his earlier success with the Marine Band.

Within a year after Gilmore's death, Sousa had inherited nineteen of Gilmore's best players, including the great cornet soloist Herbert Lincoln Clarke. Then came the appearances at the Columbian Exposition in 1893, for which Gilmore had originally been engaged, and instant national acclaim. With that, a group of Chicagoans formed a corporation to send the Sousa Band on the road, and over the next three decades the band's concerts were an unqualified success. The tours were organized along strict business lines, and Sousa's personal income by 1900 was reputed to be in excess of $50,000 a year, counting royalties from his compositions. The band's size varied, on occasions enlarged to seventy-five members. While Sousa seldom worried about elevating his public, playing mainly waltzes, popular medleys, marches, and the lighter classics, he nevertheless introduced thousands of Americans to Rossini, Verdi, Wagner, and even Mozart and Beethoven, through transcriptions. His band made annual journeys across the United States and Canada, performing to capacity crowds. Sousa conducted "one-night stands" in skating rinks, greenhouses, Baptist Churches, garages, and theaters so small that half the band had to sit in the auditorium itself. The musicians traveled thousands—millions—of miles, mostly by train. They made four trips to Europe, beginning in 1900, and one thirteen-month tour around the world. The band played at the Cotton State's Exposition in Atlanta in 1896, the Paris Exposition in 1900, the Pan American Exposition in Buffalo, New York in 1901, the St. Louis World's Fair in 1904, and at scores of lesser celebrations. Between 1911 and 1914, the average weekly attendance for the band's yearly concerts in New York City was over sixty thousand. Meanwhile Sousa's name became as integral a part of the American scene as baseball, cowboys and Indians, Huckleberry Finn, chewing gum, and Fred Harvey restaurants.

Sousa made a point of following heavier numbers on his programs with lighter ones. He gave frequent encores, the most popular of which were his own marches, prompting a London journalist to bestow upon him the title of "March King." Sousa began composing in 1876, while among his most popular pieces are "Semper Fidelis" (1888), "Washington Post" (1889), "The Liberty Bell" (1893), and especially "The Stars and Stripes Forever" (1896). The latter came to Sousa on an ocean voyage from Naples to America and is estimated to have earned the composer over $300,000. At the turn of the century Sousa's marches ranked near the top of America's commercial music—in quality, as well as sheet music and record sales. These marches were generally well written, characterized by a jaunty melody, simple, yet wide-ranging harmony, and a strong, infectious rhythm. Several of them were composed for operettas and were originally sung. Sousa wrote ten operettas, the most successful of which was *El Capitan* (1896). He also wrote more than twenty suites, between forty and fifty songs, and a grandiose work for orchestra, choir, and organ. The European influences on his style were many—Offenbach, Johann Strauss, but particularly Wagner.

At the same time Sousa's marches contain an unadulterated Americanism that is unmistakable. Their popularity came at a time when the United States was entering an intensely nationalistic period, coinciding with the American defeat of Spain, the nation's emergence as a world power, and the country's involvement in World War I. Sousa's martial music became a symbol of the surging national strength, reinforcing America's group spirit in an age when diplomatic isolation was proving impossible. If Stephen Foster's music "is all heart," Mellers contends, Sousa's "is all body." Neither were especially cerebral, yet each captivated the public as no other American composer of his day; each reflected a shift in popular attitudes. Foster looked backward, to childhood and the womb; Sousa focused on an adolescent present, a moment of much physical activity. Whereas Foster was pessimistic about a coming industrial system, Sousa was vigorously optimistic.

But the heyday of Sousa's success also overlapped the revival of the two-step in social dance. A number of his marches were rearranged as dance music, and when the two-step was introduced to Europe, it was known for a time as "The Washington Post," since that was the tune most closely associated with it.

By World War I, Sousa had become as identified with the march as Strauss was with the waltz. During the war he gave up his band and large salary to join the Great Lakes Naval Reserve. Later, he reassembled his musicians and formed an even larger concert band. He continued touring until a sudden heart attack took his life on March 6, 1932, at Reading, Pennsylvania. By then scarcely a town in the United States had not had some opportunity to hear a Sousa performance.

Between 1890 and 1910 band concerts emerged as perhaps the country's most popular musical attraction. While Gilmore and Sousa were the most eminent reasons for the craze, there were scores of others. Liberati, Innes, Creatore, Brooke, Pryor, and Conway all became legends around the turn of the century, each shuttling with tireless regularity back and forth across the nation with his band, sometimes traveling the Chautauqua circuits. Each was something of a showman and knew how to milk applause. Liberati, a dapper cornetist and circus bandleader, occasionally directed from horseback. Creatore, the most popular of the Italian bandmasters, was said to have engaged in antics that made Jullien look "like a wooden soldier."

Besides the professional bands, by the early 1900s there were few hamlets in America without a village band. A band was as essential to community pride as a fire department. The town's merchants usually bore the cost of forming and supporting the band, since civic boosterism in whatever form was ultimately advertisement for them. Additional funds came through ice cream socials, amateur theatricals, or from paid engagements like fairs and political rallies. The band was under the direction of a "professor" and generally practiced one or two nights a week. On practice evenings the players scurried home from work, bolted down a quick meal, snatched up their instrument cases, and sped off to the firehouse or city hall, where they rehearsed in shirt sleeves. During the summer months the band normally played a free evening concert once a week for the community and afternoon concerts on holidays.

A wooden bandstand had been erected in the park or town square, usually circular or octagonal and big enough for the band's eight to twelve players. Naked electric light bulbs were strung around the bandstand's high-peaked roof, each attracting swarms of assorted bugs, which now and then got into the mouths of players or became trapped in the valves of instruments. The smell of hamburgers, hot dogs, mustard, popcorn, peanuts, and candy filled the air, while families sat in farm wagons and fringed carriages along the hitching racks, or spread blankets over the lawn. Boys met girls at the lemonade stand, babies cried, ladies gossiped, men exchanged yarns and a chew of tobacco; urchins chased each other and climbed up on the bandstand, dangling their feet over the sides and swatting bugs, while the band played on.

Stores stayed open on concert nights. Women shopped, while the men drifted off to discuss politics or get a horse shod. The blaring sounds of the band could be heard all over the downtown section, and the musicians played melodies that were as relaxed as the occasion. Variations on "Listen to the Mockingbird" was a favorite; the *Poet and Peasant* Overture would have been considered a bit heavy. Village bandmasters tended to take seriously John Philip Sousa's dictum that "a march should make a man with a wooden leg step out."

But there were also military bands, industrial bands, Salvation Army bands, circus bands, and school bands. In 1893 seventy-one different bands marched in the inaugural parade for Grover Cleveland, while 136 bands paraded in the Knights Templar conclave in Boston two years later. In 1896, when open bidding was announced for the contract to furnish music for the Nebraska state fair, 200 bands applied for the ten day engagement. The Third Regiment Band of Arapohoe, Nebraska, was selected. After 1910, however, the band frenzy was on the decline. The Chautauqua circuits were failing; village seclusion was breaking down; and the automobile, phonograph, radio, movies, and jazz all siphoned off audiences. The more famous bands— Sousa's and later Edwin Franko Goldman's—held out a while longer, in demand at amusement parks, fairs, and "gardens," but the concert band as a flourishing American institution had received the death knell.

When Theodore Thomas was asked what musical activities should be planned to attract large crowds for the 1904 World's Fair in St. Louis, the conductor superciliously advised, "Have plenty of band music, out of doors." Thomas apparently had forgotten that he had once performed al fresco concerts, where refreshments were served, and that he himself had once placed flutists in trees at Central Park Garden to titillate audiences. The Chicago Symphony director had perhaps lost sight of the fact that before 1890 there were only four major orchestras in the country; in 1910 there would be but eight. For the vast majority of the American people bands were the equivalent of a symphony orchestra—orchestras without fiddles that played music the public understood.

Yet by the 1890s Thomas had at last achieved his personal goal: a permanent orchestra. He was working hard to build that organization into a major symphonic force and was in no mood to compromise on standards. The time had come for quality, and Thomas was willing to ride roughshod over whoever stood in his way. He could be cold, aristocratic, imperious. When Adelina Patti sang a concert under his direction the two disagreed on interpretation. Patti reminded the conductor that *she* was the prima donna. Thomas corrected her: "Excuse me, madam. Here *I* am the prima donna."

Tenaciously he clung to his ideals. "The man who does not know Shakespeare is to be pitied," he once wrote; "and the man who does not understand Beethoven and has not been under his spell has not half lived his life. The master works of instrumental music are the language of the soul and express more than those of any other art." Although Beethoven and Wagner remained the pillars of his programs, his repertoire continued to be progressive. Slowly he enlarged his public's conception to embrace Dvorak, Tchaikovsky, and Richard Strauss; he resurrected Bach. Yet by the end of his sixth season in Chicago the annual deficit had been reduced to $27,000, as attendance gradually increased. The Chicago Symphony began making yearly tours of the Middle West and by 1900 was recognized as second only to Boston among American orchestras. When Richard Strauss came to Chicago in 1902 to conduct "Also Sprach Zarathustra," the composer was amazed at the orchestra's virtuosity and was satisfied with a single rehearsal.

Having drilled his orchestra into excellence and developed reasonably sophisticated audiences, Thomas had one last ambition: to build a hall suitable for his concerts. While the Chicago Auditorium was superb for opera and ballet, it was too vast for symphonic works, forcing the orchestra to play louder than was ideal. The members of the symphony board were persuaded that a new house was essential, gifts were requested from the wealthy, and a public subscription was launched. Some 8000 donors contributed $75,000, in sums ranging from ten cents to $25,000. Construction on the new house began on Michigan Avenue, up the lake front a short distance from the Auditorium. On December 14, 1904, Thomas conducted the opening concert in Orchestra Hall. Three weeks later he was dead. He had taken ill during rehearsals for the inaugural concert, contracted pneumonia shortly after, and died on January 4, 1905. His podium was taken by Frederick Stock, his young assistant conductor, who had come to the United States from Germany in 1895, first performing with the Chicago Orchestra as a viola player.

Without question, Theodore Thomas stands as the giant of nineteenth century American conductors, having done more for the development of orchestral music in the United States than any single individual. Sometimes the tyrant, often the arbiter of public taste, the dignified Thomas devoted more than four decades to building a symphonic tradition in a land that had little musical awareness, seldom yielding to discouragement, even when the frustrations appeared to be overpowering. To the end he remained poised, erect of carriage, resolute. "Throughout my life," he was finally able to say, "my aim has been to make good music popular, and it now appears that I have only done the public justice in believing, and acting constantly on the belief, that the people would enjoy and support the best in art when continually set before them in a clear and intelligent manner."

But Thomas' triumph was not easily duplicated. When the musician left the New York Philharmonic Society for Chicago in 1891, his place was taken by Anton Seidl, then principal conductor of the Metropolitan Opera and a dominant personality. Seidl led the Philharmonic through exciting and distinguished seasons, premiered Dvorak's *New World* Symphony on December 15, 1893, but died suddenly in 1898. For the next four years Emil Paur was the Society's conductor, followed by one year under Walter Damrosch. The next three seasons saw a parade of visiting directors, one of whom was Victor Herbert. Then came Wassily Safonoff (1906-1909), the great Gustav Mahler (1909-1911), and the fairly lethargic leadership of Josef Stransky (1911-1923).

Popular support of the Philharmonic concerts, evidenced in attendance, declined after 1898, prompting the orchestra to engage renowned conductors with commanding personalities in an effort to bolster the Society's image. Continued financial problems forced a total reorganization in 1909, when control of the orchestra passed from the musicians to a board of directors. Heretofore, under the arrangement operating since the Philharmonic's inception in 1842, the players had paid yearly dues, received a token fee for their services, and divided the profits at the close of each season. With the reorganization the board of directors assumed responsibility for the annual deficit and guaranteed each musician a stated salary. Upon his death in 1911, Joseph Pulitzer left the Philharmonic a gift of $900,000 with the request that his favorite composers receive special attention. Since the newspaper man's favorites were Beethoven, Wagner, and Liszt, the stipulation presented no particular obstacle to programming.

Meanwhile the competing New York Symphony under Walter Damrosch was facing financial troubles. The charming Damrosch, however, was always highly regarded by society leaders, would later marry the daughter of James G. Blaine, and by 1903 had secured for his orchestra the personal subsidy of Harry Harkness Flagler. For several seasons Flagler assumed full responsibility for the Symphony's operating deficits, freeing Damrosch to extend his series and prepare his concerts largely as he saw fit. In 1887 the young conductor was on board a steamer for Europe; during the voyage he met Andrew Carnegie, who was honeymooning with his young bride. Damrosch and Carnegie became good friends, and the musician persuaded the steel tycoon that New York needed a modern concert hall. Four years later, Carnegie Hall was completed on the corner of Seventh Avenue and Fifty-seventh Street.

Tchaikovsky himself came over to conduct the grand opening, May 5, 1891—the first major composer to visit the United States. New York made the most of the occasion. The noted Russian was taken on a sightseeing tour of the Wall Street area, where he found the buildings "ridiculously colossal." In the vault of the subtreasury building the musician was permitted to hold a bundle of bills valued at ten million dollars and was surprised to learn that "Americans prefer the soiled, disagreeable bank bills to metal." The inaugural concert and the new hall drew extremely good notices, but Tchaikovsky was the center of attention.

Beginning in 1892 both the New York Symphony and the New York Philharmonic played their seasons in Carnegie Hall. Distinguished guest artists also performed there at the turn of the century with one or the other of the orchestras, among the more illustrious Paderewski, Richard Strauss (who complained about New York's "badly paved streets"), Ruggiero Leoncavallo, Camille Saint-Saens (who insisted on playing the organ part of his Third Symphony), the young American pianist Olga Samaroff, and Sergei Rachmaninoff (who had composed his third piano concerto expressly for his United States debut). In 1900 Austrian-born Ernestine Schumann-Heink and the American Lillian Nordica sang a joint concert in the hall to symbolize the coming together of the musical traditions of the old and new worlds.

When Walter Damrosch resigned as director of the Oratorio Society of New York in 1898, his brother Frank was elected his successor. Between the two of them, Walter and Frank Damrosch assumed much of Theodore Thomas' role as music educator of the nation. Walter gave annual lectures in New York and later would have a radio program for young people. Frank launched a Young People's Symphony Series in 1898, in conjunction with his brother's orchestra. Walter initiated the practice of Sunday afternoon concerts and toured with his fifty musicians each spring, penetrating deep into the South and West. He encountered much the same lack of appreciation in the hinterland that Thomas had earlier. As late as 1904, a Damrosch concert in Oklahoma City was interrupted to announce that Stewart's Oyster Bar would be open after the program. On his way back to his hotel, following the same concert, the conductor overheard a crowd discussing his music. "Well, how was it, Jim?" an approaching friend inquired of one of the concert-goers. To which the disgruntled Jim muttered, "This show ain't worth thirty cents."

Urban critics, on the other hand, were showing signs of a new sophistication. The inflexible John Sullivan Dwight died in 1893 without ever accepting Wagner and the later romantics. But Henry T. Finck, who came into prominence before the turn of the century, not only accepted Wagner, he wrote a book explaining him, as well as a biography of Paderewski. The critic also explored philosophy, esthetics, the primitive love instinct, and the neglected sense of smell. W.J. Henderson found time, between writing reviews and program notes, to publish short stories, poems, and books on yachting and naval subjects. By the early twentieth century a more personalized style of criticism had emerged in the persons of Carl Van Vechten, Paul Rosenfeld, and most notably James G. Huneker. Huneker shook himself free from the genteel critics' conviction that art must reflect the ideal. He held no fixed attitude except that art is a significant impulse in man and should be encouraged; it brings both pleasure and understanding of the human condition. A force in the intellectual rebellion that preceded World War I, Huneker argued that taste was the greatest good, art the worthiest religion, and epicurean sophistication America's most urgent need.

Yet for most Americans, art—particularly music—still connoted effeminacy and consequently fell largely under the jurisdiction of women. As symphony orchestras came to be organized in the major cities of the United States, they were indulged primarily by the wives of the community's business leaders, who fashioned themselves the pillars of refinement and respectability for an aspiring leisure class. Orchestras received financial backing primarily out of the civic pride of businessmen, coupled with a vague feeling that it was *good* for the city to have a symphony, that somehow the odious aspects of the industrial world were offset by a pursuit of the arts. But having contributed their money, most business leaders were more than willing to delegate matters concerning art administration to their wives. Since art became a recognized avenue for social advancement, its patrons demanded a sure commodity, art sanctioned by tradition. Therefore while Huneker and a select group of American intellectuals were beginning to advocate liberation for the arts, those who paid the bills wanted the established mode. In symphonic music this meant adherence to the German school, more especially the German romantic school.

The number of American orchestras grew slowly in the two decades before World War I; they were manned by German musicians essentially, and often rehearsals were conducted in the German language. By 1920 symphonies had been established in Cincinnati, Minneapolis, Pittsburgh, San Francisco, Cleveland, Detroit, and Los Angeles. But the founding of the Philadelphia Orchestra in 1900 marked the most significant addition to organized orchestral societies in the United States at the turn of the century.

The orchestra's first concert was held at the Philadelphia Academy of Music on Friday night, November 16, 1900, under the direction of Fritz Scheel. Six years later the orchestra under Scheel introduced to Philadelphia and New York the sensational twenty year-old Russian pianist Arthur Rubinstein, who played the Saint-Saens G minor Concerto. Gradually the ensemble was improved, with Karl Pohlig assuming the conductorship in 1907. Many of the musicians were imported from abroad after the directors had traveled through different European countries to procure various specialists—Germany's brass players, Austria's violinists, Holland's cellists, and France and Belgium's woodwind players.

But the Philadelphia Orchestra did not enter its period of greatness until the arrival of Leopold Stokowski as conductor in 1912. Born in London in 1882, Stokowski came to the United States as a youth to become organist at St. Bartholomew's Church in New York. His reputation as an organ virtuoso spread, and in 1909 he was invited to accept the directorship of the reorganized Cincinnati Symphony. The young musician had virtually no experience as a conductor and at the first rehearsal in Cincinnati had to ask members of his orchestra how to proceed. Within a short time, however, Stokowski proved himself a dynamic leader and a sophisticated showman. He remained in Cincinnati three years before resigning from the orchestra in March, 1912. Three months later, while touring Europe, he announced his appointment as conductor of the Philadelphia Orchestra.

At the time Stokowski arrived in Philadelphia, the New York Philharmonic had fallen under the routine leadership of Stransky. Walter Damrosch, despite his vast enthusiasm and personal popularity, was never considered a first-rate conductor by critics, and the New York Symphony suffered accordingly. The Chicago Symphony continued to be a fine orchestra, but Frederick Stock had trouble establishing himself as a personality. Of American orchestras, the Boston Symphony alone held a reputation for unqualified excellence. But early on in his twenty-three year role as conductor, Stokowski turned the Philadelphia Orchestra into one of the most brilliant ensembles ever heard in this country, a marvel of shading, power, and precision. In addition, Stokowski established himself as the glamor boy of the baton, the first American conductor to become a matinee idol.

When Stokowski came to Philadelphia in October, 1912, he was just thirty years old, stood six feet tall, possessed a lithe, slender physique, blue eyes, a Grecian nose, and bountiful blond hair. He dressed in a wardrobe tailored to perfection. The musician was then married to the attractive, artistic Olga Samaroff. Both evidenced magnetic personalities and a social ease that endeared them to the city's fashionable set. The couple's home quickly became one of the social centers of Philadelphia. On the dias Stokowski delighted his public by conducting without a baton in a broad, sweeping, personalized manner that soon emerged as something of a national vogue.

Yet besides being eloquent to watch, Stokowski was a man of keen intellect and a musical genius. He made all sorts of experiments in seating to achieve the sound he wanted from the Philadelphia Orchestra and gradually broke away from the traditional German repertory, spicing his programs with modern novelties. Compositions by contemporary masters like Richard Strauss, Rachmaninoff, Sibelius, Debussy, Elgar, Gliere, and Enesco were introduced to Philadelphia; later he offered selections by Stravinsky and Schoenberg. The conductor secured undisputed national distinction for his orchestra in 1916 with the American premiere of Gustav Mahler's Eighth Symphony. Since the work required a huge chorus that would fill the stage, an apron on which the orchestra would assemble was extended out into the house. Critics from most of the leading newspapers of the nation were drawn to the premiere, causing civic pride to spiral. The day low-priced tickets went on sale a line began forming outside the Academy of Music at five o'clock in the morning—despite weather that was twelve degrees below zero. By mid-morning scalpers were getting $100 apiece for the better seats. The concert was immensely successful, and the boyish Stokowski suddenly discovered himself a national celebrity. By 1920 the Philadelphia Orchestra was probably the most talked-about orchestra in the country and one of the most financially secure.

Still, until 1918, the Boston Symphony Orchestra maintained the edge in pure artistic accomplishment. Henry L. Higginson's generosity had continued, both for the Boston Symphony and its offspring, the Kneisel Quartet. Symphony Hall, designed by the architectural firm of McKim, Mead, and White, had been built in 1900, and the orchestra's programs had stayed on a consistently high level. But Major Higginson, having acquired his interest in symphonic music in Vienna as a young man, had made a practice of engaging only German conductors, firmly believing that Germany alone could provide the Boston orchestra the leadership it required. Emil Paur had conducted the Boston Symphony before assuming the directorship of the New York Philharmonic, and Karl Muck was engaged to replace Paur in 1906. Muck remained until 1908; but after resigning from what proved to be a temporary post at the Berlin State Opera, he returned to the Boston Symphony Orchestra in 1912 with a five-year contract.

Although born in Darmstadt in 1859, Muck had grown up in Switzerland, where his father, fearing Prussian domination of his native Bavaria, had moved the family when Karl was about eight. As a youth Karl returned to Germany for both academic and musical training, earning a doctorate in classical philology at Heidelberg in 1879. He made his debut as a concert pianist the following year. Thereafter he devoted himself to music and within a decade emerged as one of the finest conductors of his time. He became especially noted as an exponent of Wagner, directed the *Ring* in Russia during the 1888-1889 season, winning the admiration of Rimsky-Korsakov, and led extensive Wagnerian performances at Covent Garden the next year. By 1900 Muck had distinguished himself as a regular conductor of the Vienna Philharmonic and had been invited to supervise *Parsifal* at Bayreuth.

Shortly after assuming the leadership of the Boston Symphony Orchestra Dr. Muck was praised nationally for having lifted the orchestra to new heights. As events leading to World War I erupted in Europe, Muck made no secret of his pro-German sympathies, but continued to win acclaim from American audiences even after the invasion of France. Critics admired his readings of the Beethoven and Brahms symphonies in particular, and his renditions of works by Strauss were judged to be full of intellectual concentration. Seeing obvious signs of trouble ahead, Muck asked to resign from the Boston Symphony after America's entry into the war in April, 1917, having fulfilled his initial five-year contract. Major Higginson refused the resignation, assuring the conductor that his position as an artist would be respected, even though the United States and Germany were now belligerents and the rancor of the American public had been sharply aroused by the German submarine activity of the preceding months.

Muck renewed his contract with the Boston Symphony Orchestra only to find that what had been subtle innuendo earlier had turned into a hate campaign against him, paralleling the general war hysteria. Considering the public sentiment, the orchestra's publicity office suggested playing "The Star-Spangled Banner" at the 1917-18 concerts, but manager C. A. Ellis vetoed the idea, arguing that a symphony concert was not an appropriate place for such gestures. The issue came up again early in the season, when the Boston Symphony Orchestra was scheduled for a concert in Providence, Rhode Island, October 30, 1917. Shortly before the performance manager Ellis received a telegram from a number of prominent women's organizations, asking that the orchestra render the national anthem to open the concert. Ellis evidently discussed the matter with Major Higginson, and the two decided to ignore the telegram and not to mention the matter to Dr. Muck. The Providence concert was given without incident. Muck was told of the request for "The Star-Spangled Banner" on the train ride back to Boston.

But the damage was done. The next morning the *Providence Journal* denounced the conductor bitterly, and resolutions were shortly adopted that condemned Muck for his insult. An agent of the Department of Justice in Providence recommended that the Boston Symphony Orchestra be barred from playing anywhere until Muck agreed to open his concerts with the national anthem. Major Higginson was infuriated, insisted that "The Star-Spangled Banner" had no place on a symphony program, and threatened to disband the orchestra and close Symphony Hall if the public frenzy did not stop. With characteristic honesty, Karl Muck bluntly explained, "Art is a thing by itself and not related to any particular nation or group. It would be a gross mistake, a violation of artistic taste and principles for such an organization as ours to play patriotic airs."

Public indignation continued to mount, while even the *New York Times* indicted artists of Muck's viewpoint as "rather more Germans than musicians." On November 2, during an afternoon concert in Boston, Muck led the Boston Symphony Orchestra in "The Star-Spangled Banner," and Major Higginson in a public statement took full responsibility for the anthem's not having been played earlier. Nevertheless, a scheduled performance by the Boston orchestra in Baltimore five days later had to be canceled when mob violence was threatened to prevent Karl Muck's appearance from insulting "the people of the birthplace of 'The Star-Spangled Banner.' " It was soon reported that when Muck conducted the anthem in Boston, he had done so with clenched teeth. On a tour of Public School 45 in New York, Theodore Roosevelt was taken into the music room as a group of youngsters were singing "America." The former president supposedly remarked, "Any man who refuses to play 'The Star-Spangled Banner' in this time of national crisis should be forced to pack up and return to the country he came from."

Although the concert in Baltimore had already been canceled, a mass meeting took place there, led by Edwin Warfield, president of the Fidelity Trust Company and ex-governor of Maryland. Warfield stirred the gathering by shouting that Muck should be imprisoned. After "The Star-Spangled Banner" was sung, the ex-governor emoted, "The day is coming when that anthem will be sung by every nation on the globe. Talk about your musical art—what does art amount to when it is in competition with patriotism?" Then raising his fist towards the gallery, Warfield cried out that no real American could be satisfied until Muck had been "mobbed" to death. At this point one gray-haired lady in the crowd lost her dignity for the moment and exclaimed at full voice, "Let's kill the bastard!" Before long the Dolly Madison Chapter of the Daughters of 1812 had joined the crusade against the Boston Symphony Orchestra conductor, and the Daughters of the American Revolution rallied with them.

In an age of unreason—when the German language was dropped from the curriculum of American schools and even sauerkraut became dubbed "Liberty Cabbage"—the venom against Muck grew into a psychotic rage. It was rumored that the Kaiser had sent the conductor to the United States as a paid agent, that Muck had a secret telephone hidden in the cellar of his Boston home, that he was plotting the kidnap of major American businessmen, that he had been overheard discussing a shipment of dynamite to be used in blowing up the Longfellow house and Faneuil Hall. During the summer of 1917 the Mucks had rented a cottage at Seal Harbor, Maine. The owner, an eccentric bachelor and amateur scientist, had once installed a small radio transmitter in the house, although the set no longer worked. It was reported nevertheless that the conductor had used the wireless to send messages to German submarines lurking off the coast and that beams of light had been seen coming from his window—more signals to U-boats. The musician suddenly found himself under close surveillance; his mail was censored and his home occasionally searched. His effigy was burned, and his concerts were boycotted. Ladies groups resolved that anyone entering Boston's Symphony

Hall should be branded a traitor.

It did not matter apparently that Muck was not a German citizen at all, but a naturalized Swiss. When he conducted the Boston Symphony Orchestra in concerts in New York and Brooklyn in late November, the police were there to observe. His rendering of "The Star-Spangled Banner" was judged listless. By the end of the month, under the terms of President Wilson's proclamation regarding enemy aliens, Muck and twenty-two other orchestra members were barred from performing in Washington, unless granted special permission by the President. Muck's Swiss citizenship was dismissed by Washington officials as a technicality. Popular opinion had become so clouded and unreasonable that a Detroit newspaper referred to Muck as "the world's worst conductor." By March, 1918, the furor had reached such outrageous proportions that even the stalwart Major Higginson was forced to bend. The announcement was made that Muck would relinquish his baton at the end the season. But a rabid public *still* demanded vengeance.

Dr. Muck maintained his dignity and honesty through the entire episode. He admitted that he felt the Belgian atrocities had been exaggerated, that he had once been a friend of the Kaiser, and that he believed the image of the German people was suffering abuse from Allied propaganda. But he was an artist not a politician, the conductor emphasized, and as an artist he could maintain strict neutrality. Muck continued his painstaking preparation of concerts and during the last weeks of March was working long hours rehearsing Bach's *St. Matthew Passion* for the Boston Symphony Orchestra's final concert of the season. Around nine o'clock in the evening on March 25, agents of the Department of Justice and Boston police officers appeared at the conductor's home and arrested him under provisions in Wilson's enemy alien proclamation. His papers and letters were seized. The musician was taken to the East Cambridge jail and questioned the next day in the Federal Building. The interrogation was later continued by the Federal Bureau of Investigation. The arrest was justified on the grounds that Muck's presence constituted a danger to the peace and safety of the country, and the conductor was turned over to military authorities. In April he became "Prisoner 1337" at Fort Oglethorpe, Georgia. He remained in prison for more than a year. On June 9, 1919, with the war over, it was announced that Dr. Muck would shortly be deported. On August 22, a representative of the Department of Justice escorted the conductor and his wife aboard the ocean liner *Frederick VIII*. The ship's captain was instructed to make certain that the musician did not leave the vessel until it was outside the three-mile limit. Muck never returned to the United States, although he later had good offers from orchestras, and insisted to the end that he had never refused to conduct "The Star-Spangled Banner." He resumed his European career an embittered man, assumed the directorship of the Hamburg Symphony Orchestra, and returned to Bayreuth, where his *Parsifal* in particular was universally acclaimed. He died in 1940 at the age of eighty.

While the case of Karl Muck was the most notorious, he was not the only

German musician to suffer in the United States during World War I. Frederick Stock voluntarily retired from the Chicago Symphony in August, 1918, for the duration of the war—to be welcomed back six months later. Violinist Fritz Kreisler was refused the right to perform in Pittsburgh, while Ernst Kumwald, the Austrian-born conductor of the Cincinnati Symphony, was arrested on espionage charges, interned at Fort Oglethorpe with Muck, and eventually deported. The exalted positions of Bach, Beethoven, and Brahms on the programs of the nation's leading orchestras was seriously challenged, while a number of subscribers to the Philadelphia Orchestra ostentatiously walked out during the playing of a Wagner selection. The New York Philharmonic agreed not to perform the music of living German composers, and the New York Symphony followed suit. The popular German-American Walter Damrosch was spared injury, but at no little cost to his personal integrity. The New York Symphony conductor clearly responded to the Muck affair with ingratiating overstatements that often seem astonishingly irresponsible. Damrosch, for example, referred to Muck as "a supercilious, arrogant Prussian of the worse Junker type" and "an abject coward and renegade." Regarding the deportation of the former Boston conductor, Damrosch commented, "I cannot see that he has cause for anything but gratitude toward this country and its lenient treatment of him."

But Damrosch had reason for insecurity; the war hysteria had degenerated into sheer hate. Several American cities—Pittsburgh among them—had banned *all* German music, and even the most respected German musicians had cause for alarm. A nation that musically had been a colony of Germany for nearly a century abruptly turned on its traditional paragon and banished it. After World War I German musicians and the works of the German masters were welcomed back, but the strong German influence was broken. The American concept of great symphonic music proliferated within a few years to include the modern French, Russian, and Scandinavian composers particularly. Leopold Stokowski and Walter Damrosch had moved in this direction before the war, but the trend was soon accepted by most of the major orchestras. The temporary shattering of the German ideal left a void in musical leadership that came to be filled largely by the French. But the French ascendancy was neither as rigid nor as lasting as the German influence had been. When Henry L. Higginson retired as an active patron of the Boston Symphony Orchestra in April, 1918, after thirty-seven years of support, deeply disillusioned by the Muck affair, the orchestra suffered an appreciable decline in reputation. Yet Muck's successors, Henri Rabaud (1918-1920) and Pierre Monteux (1920-1924), clearly reflect America's transfer of musical ideals from German to French.

The pluralization in music that followed World War I joined with the nativism that was currently sweeping the country to provide the flexibility and the justification for giving American compositions a greater hearing. Whereas American orchestras had been reluctant earlier to play works by native musicians, it became somewhat fashionable after the war to include

American pieces on symphonic programs and, what was even more desirable, to introduce domestic works that had never been publicly performed. The American composer remained more valued as a curiosity than for his genius, but the initial cracks in the foreign monopoly of the serious instrumental repertory were becoming vaguely discernible.

CHAPTER

II

Grand Opera and the

"Nouveau Riche"

An event that was characteristic of the holiday mood pervading the North at the close of the Civil War was the grand opening of Crosby's Opera House in Chicago, scheduled for April 17, 1865, eight days after Lee's surrender to Grant. Jacob Grau's Italian Opera Company from the New York Academy of Music had been brought to town for the occasion, and the city's *nouveau riche*, having purged local shops of opera glasses, fans, cloaks, crystal hair pins, ties, gloves, and handkerchiefs, were preparing for a social revel. Two days before the arranged opening, news came that President Lincoln had been shot. As a stunned nation went into mourning, the celebration in Chicago was postponed. Finally, on Thursday, April 20, the inauguration of Crosby's Opera House took place, despite a thunderstorm that had carriages lined up for blocks along Washington and Dearborn Streets. While the rain beat down and thunder pealed across the heavens, Jacob Grau's company presented an agreeable performance of *Il Trovatore*. The next evening American soprano Clara Louise Kellogg gave a "birdlike" performance of *Lucia di Lammermoor* and a few nights later received baskets of flowers for her singing of Marguerite in *Faust*.

On May 1 and 2, Chicago's new opera house was again dark, for Lincoln's body, on the way to Springfield for burial, lay in state at the Court

House. Thousands of people waited in line all night to pass before the funeral bier. The city was hushed; windows and doorways were bordered in black crepe; the people were paying their final respects to their dead leader. From her windows at the Sherman House, Clara Kellogg watched the crowd file into the Court House. "From sunset to sunrise," she wrote years later, "the grounds were packed with a silent multitude. The only sound to be heard was the shuffling echo of feet as one person after another went quietly into the Court House, shuffle, shuffle, shuffle—I can hear it yet. There was not a word uttered. There was no other sound than the sound of the passing feet."

Following the funeral in Springfield, Chicago's opera festival was resumed. According to Miss Kellogg, "the end of the war had made the nation a little drunk with excitement and our performances went with a whirl." After four weeks Grau's troupe left the city, but returned a month later for a ten-night engagement. On June 12, a gala performance of Donizetti's *The Daughter of the Regiment* was staged with Generals Grant and Sherman in attendance. The house was decorated with flowers and flags, while the singers played up the military aspects of Donizetti's opera as much as possible. Basso Susini, attired in soldier's uniform, saluted the distinguished guests from stage center, and Clara Kellogg, accompanying herself on a drum, directed the "Rataplan" first to one general's box and then to the other.

But once the holiday atmosphere of victory faded, the enthusiasm for opera at Crosby's, as elsewhere in the United States, grew far less exuberant. The Ghioni and Susini Grand Opera Company, under the direction of Maurice Strakosch, played there with fair success in the early summer of 1866, but Uranus Crosby was already discovering that the demand for opera was not what he had imagined. More and more he was forced to rent the house to acts like Professor Herrmann's Magic Show and the Buislay Family's Aerialist Exhibition to bolster the box office. By the end of the year Crosby bordered on bankruptcy. To pull himself out of the doldrums the crafty promoter decided to hold a lottery, offering the opera house as first prize. Crosby built the scheme carefully, stirring public sentiment to a fever pitch by the day of the drawing. The lucky ticket holder was announced to be one Abraham H. Lee, from a small farming community in southern Illinois, but Lee never materialized. He supposedly sold the opera house back to Crosby for a fee of $200,000, but it was evident that the lottery had been a swindle. Rather than face a hostile public, Crosby turned the house over to his uncle and retired to New England. The uncle shortly found operetta and burlesque more profitable than grand opera, and the prestige of the theater sank accordingly. In the summer of 1871 the place was redecorated with carpets and upholstery imported from France, and the Theodore Thomas Orchestra was engaged to reestablish the house's reputation as a center for art. In October, a few hours before the concert was to begin, virtually the entire city was in flames, from a fire originating over in the Irish section. Around five A. M. Crosby's Opera House was consumed in the holocaust. Critic George Upton was standing a few feet away when the theater burst into flames. "The beautiful structure seemed to melt away," he recalled. "It did not seem to catch fire at any particular point. It was as if a huge wave of fire swept over and devoured it."

In capsule form the brief history of Crosby's Opera House dramatizes much of the story of opera in late nineteenth-century America—the link with high society, the festive atmosphere, the select audience, the impermanent commitment, the vast financial problems, the need for showmanship, the dependence on featured prima donnas, the frequently disastrous demises of America's opera palaces. The fundamental difficulty was—and still is—that grand opera, even more than the symphony orchestra, remained a costly, imported commodity that only the wealthy, well-traveled, sophisticated, or recently immigrated were able to appreciate. Not only have the composers, interpreters, and works themselves been largely foreign, but the very essence of grand opera is at odds with the general American temperament. While Americans have traditionally argued that they might like opera if they could understand the language, it is quite probable that the passionate utterances of the operatic stage, the unqualified surrender to the emotions, and the frank admission of an erotic life have ultimately been more disturbing to American audiences than the language barrier. Surely these characteristics have been considered more suited to foreigners, which perhaps explains why successful American operas have been so few and in part why opera in English has enjoyed limited acceptance. The blatant emotionalism of opera simply runs contrary to the basic American ideal of self-control, the belief that lack of emotional reserve is somehow undignified, inefficient, and an indication of weakness. Since an unrestrained emotional outpouring is the core of grand opera, Americans have experienced the art with discomfort, often approached it with an intellectual rather than an emotional attitude, and have been inclined to explain their own confusion in literal terms.

Failing to understand the spirit of opera, finding librettos absurd when examined intellectually, Americans have tended to prize the art more for its spectacle, social prestige, and extraneous glamor than for its music. Among the country's new rich especially, the costly nature of opera has made it all the more desired, its exclusive appeal all the more useful, and its foreign disposition all the more precious. In post-Civil War America grand opera emerged more clearly than ever as a chaste symbol of refinement, wealth, and cultural supremacy, and the ascending rich vowed their patronage to the art, much as the European royalty had done earlier. The analogy itself was worth much to the captains of industry that so often had made their fortune off Civil War profiteering and smarted from a frail heritage. In a gilded age when art treasures, chapels, and palaces were either transported piece by piece to the United States or duplicated by American entrepreneurs, grand opera was imported from Europe bag and baggage, the special ornament of the few.

New Orleans continued as the important exception, manifesting a broader, more natural grasp of opera than anywhere else in the country. The French Opera House there was reopened after the Civil War by the three Alhaiza brothers, who brought in a touring company in 1865 with enough success that they decided to import a full troupe from Paris the following season. Two of the brothers sailed for France, where a company was recruited. On the eve of sailing for America, Marcelin Alhaiza died. His brother Charles, however, boarded the ship with his artists, arriving in New York in September, 1866. A few days later Charles Alhaiza and his troupe embarked on the steamer *Evening Star* for New Orleans. The destination was never reached. On October 3, the ship with some three hundred persons on board was caught in a storm and foundered at sea, off the coast of Georgia. Only a handful of passengers survived, and the entire opera company, including its manager, perished.

Paul Alhaiza, the brother who had remained in New Orleans, still had hopes of bringing opera to the French Opera House during the 1866-67 season. He engaged the Ghioni and Susini Italian Opera Company for six performances in November, during which director Maurice Strakosch's wife, Amelia Patti, Adelina's sister, made the biggest impression, singing contralto roles. Later that year Alhaiza negotiated for the Italian Company of the Grand Theatre of Mexico to give a few performances.

By the early seventies the French Opera House was back in full operation with a resident company. The management was careful to keep standards high, for the French Quarter's taste in opera remained exceedingly sophisticated. Productions were well rehearsed, sets often lavish, sometimes imported from France, and the singers were the best available. Ballet was featured in the French tradition and adeptly prepared. Touring companies periodically supplemented the offering of the local management. Adelina Patti, for instance, returned to the city early in 1885, heading Her Majesty's Opera Company under the direction of the great British impresario James Henry Mapleson. The troupe also included the American prima donna Emma Nevada, and the on-stage rivalry between the two divas provided much of the excitement.

American premieres, usually of French operas, occurred regularly at the French Opera House. Massenet's *Herodiade*, Lalo's *Le Roi d'Ys*, and Saint-Saens' *Samson and Delilah* all received their initial staging in this country in New Orleans during the 1890s. Spectacle dominated the United States premiere of Gounod's *La Reine de Saba*, presented in the Louisiana city on January 12, 1899. The plot centers around Adoniram, a famous sculptor and molder of bronze, who is asked by King Solomon to decorate the palace in honor of his bride, the Queen of Sheba. In the third act Adoniram's workshops are shown, complete with a burning furnace. As staged at the French Opera House, the fire effects were executed most realistically. The furnace smoked and rumbled, while a fire engine stood ready outside the stage entrance. When the signal was given, the door of the furnace opened. At once a stream of molten metal poured forth and slowly ran into a mold. Suddenly, with a roar the furnace burst, and the burning metal flowed out upon the floor. "The stage, which a moment before had been trodden by swarms of people, was gone," the *New Orleans Times-Democrat* reported, "and in its stead a billowy sea of crimson fire."

A decade later M. Escalais, a tenor widely acclaimed in Paris, thrilled an audience at the French Opera House by rendering five times in one evening *"Di quella pira"* from *Il Trovatore*, with its three high Cs. A Creole descendant later recalled his father bursting into the house after the performance, waking up the family as he climbed the stairs shouting, "Fifteen high Cs, I tell you—fifteen!" Reyer's *Salammbo* was produced for the first time in the United States in New Orleans on January 25, 1900, and Massenet's *Don Quichotte* received its American premiere there in 1912. Then with France's entry into World War I, the artistic lifeblood of the French Opera House was cut off. The theater, which had suffered financial reverses a few years earlier, was badly in need of repair, while production costs had grown prohibitive. Gradually New Orleans had evolved from a Latin city to a predominantly Anglo-American one, and the popular fervor for French and Italian opera had receded correspondingly. Right before the outbreak of the war in Europe, the management of the opera house underwent a tremendous expense in compliance with a city rat-proofing ordinance; at almost the same time the Mardi Gras organizations, which for years had served as a major source of income for the house, began demanding a reduction in the rentals charged them. On September 29, 1915, a storm wracked the city, leaving the French Opera House in a sad state. Soon the theater was closed, as the opera association passed into the hands of a receiver.

Apart from the French Opera House the major center for the production of grand opera in post-Civil War America was the New York Academy of Music. For years there was no resident company at the Academy and no overall planning. The impresarios who leased the house had absolute control over performances. While the companies that played there varied in quality, standards at the theater tended to be fairly slipshod. The managers were generally careless about scenery and properties, blithely mixing them up and using pieces from one opera in another without much regard for appropriateness. Productions were poorly rehearsed, while principals rarely rehearsed at all. Casts and opera were frequently changed, and patrons bought tickets with no real certainty that they would indeed hear what they had paid to hear. The Academy was frequently in financial trouble, occasionally forced to close because of the difficulties of the current management.

Still there were moments of greatness in the Academy of Music's history. Most of the popular nineteenth century Italian and French operas were heard in the house. The legendary Adelina Patti made her operatic debut there in 1859, at age seventeen, while nineteen year-old Clara Louise Kellogg, the first important American prima donna, was introduced in 1861, as Gilda in *Rigoletto*. Christine Nilsson and Italo Campanini were both heard at the Academy, and the American premiere of Verdi's *Aida* was given there on November 26, 1873, before it had been heard in either London or Paris. German impresarios periodically leased the house, giving whatever works they presented in the German language. Maurice Strakosch, for example, opened a season of "German opera" in 1864 with *Faust*—sung in German. Italian companies like Max Maretzek's, on the other hand, customarily gave *Lohengrin* and the more lyric German operas, but in Italian.

Damaged by fire in 1866, the New York Academy of Music reached its heyday in the 1870s under the relentless Colonel James Henry Mapleson. Mapleson, after long experience in London, took over the direction of the Academy in 1878, offering a company of 140 artists and Luigi Arditi as principal conductor. In his first New York season the Colonel introduced the phenomenal Etelka Gerster, as Amina in *La Sonnambula,* and presented the United States premiere of *Carmen*, in Italian, with the American singer Minnie Hauk in the title role. Mapleson was a firm believer in the star system, and Adelina Patti shortly became his major attraction. In fact the Colonel was said to be the only manager alive who could persuade Patti to sing *before* she had been paid in cash. The British impresario not only staged in New York two months of opera during the winter and another month in the spring, but also brief annual seasons in Boston, Chicago, Cincinnati, St. Louis, Philadelphia, Washington, and Baltimore. At the same time he continued his commitments in London.

By the time Mapleson assumed the management, the Academy of Music had become the established social center of New York and was dominated by the so-called "Knickerbocker aristocracy." The boxes there were controlled by the Beekmans, Lorillards, Van Rensselaers, Bayards, Goelets, Schuylers, and other old Manhattan families, some of whom went back to the days of New Amsterdam. Mrs. William B. Astor was another powerful supporter of the New York Academy, as was August Belmont. But by Mapleson's regime this select circle was being challenged by the post-Civil War rich, led by the Vanderbilts. When Cornelius Vanderbilt died in 1877, he left a fortune of $94,000,000, most of it made off the recent railroad boom. His principal heir, William H. Vanderbilt, had doubled this inheritance by the time of his death eight years later. In 1880 the Vanderbilts had asked for a box at the Academy of Music, but had been politely rejected. It was rumored that William K. Vanderbilt had bid as high as $30,000, but the entrenched wealth stood its ground. The best the Academy could do for the upstarts was to offer to add twenty-six new boxes to the thirty already existing. But the *nouveaux riches* had been offended and were unwilling to wait. They would build their own opera house.

On April 7, 1880, George Henry Warren, one of the Vanderbilt lawyers, announced to the *New York Times* that a group of sixty-five associates, calling themselves the Metropolitan Opera House Company, had contributed $800,000 for the construction of a new home for opera. Each member had subscribed a minimum of $10,000, and each in return would be guaranteed a box in the opera house once it was built. Besides the Vanderbilts, the list of associates included Cyrus Field, who after much difficulty had succeeded in laying the first transatlantic cable; Jay Gould, Commodore

Vanderbilt's chief rival in the Erie Railroad War; William C. Whitney, Cleveland's Secretary of the Navy; Darius Ogden Mills, who had made a fortune from mining; James Harriman, who had gained even greater wealth from railroads; and William Rockefeller, the oil tycoon. While the founders consisted primarily of new rich, there were also Roosevelts, Iselins, Goelets, and other representatives of established families, who for one reason or another wanted to move from the Academy of Music. J. P. Morgan and a number of his business associates were also included in the list of subscribers.

Four architectual firms were invited to submit designs for the new house. The one proposed by Josiah Cleaveland Cady was selected, although Cady had never been abroad and had seen none of the world's great opera houses. The architect immediately sailed for Europe, studied the details of La Scala, Covent Garden, and the other major European houses, and returned to New York ready to oversee the construction of his design. Meanwhile the lawyers of the Metropolitan Opera House Company had been forced to abandon the original site selected for the theater, purchasing instead the block bounded by West Thirty-ninth Street, Broadway, West Fortieth, and Seventh Avenue. Since Cady's design had been conceived for a rectangular plot, much cutting and fitting was necessary to wedge the plans into the irregular Broadway site. The foundation had scarcely been laid before it became obvious that additional funds would be necessary, particularly since building costs were rising sharply. The house was completed in the spring of 1883, at a total expense of $1,732,978.71.

In May a meeting of shareholders was called to draw lots for the boxes. As originally constructed, the Metropolitan Opera House contained four rows of boxes, one hundred-twenty-two in all. Only those in the two center tiers were allotted to members of the Metropolitan Opera House Company; the rest were rented for $12,000 a season. While the outside of the house was not particularly impressive—Colonel Mapleson referred to it as "the new yellow brewery on Broadway"—the interior reflected New York in its Augustan Age and was made all the more sumptuous by the modest entrance and narrow labyrinth that led to the theater itself. The ornately carved box fronts, the blazing gas chandelier, the waffle-grid ceiling decorated with paintings and gold leaf, and the crimson silk upholstery combined to mirror late nineteenth-century America's concept of elegance. The stage curtain was initially light blue plush, embroidered with a border showing a Greek chorus, while later the names of six pivotal operatic composers were carved across the top of the gold proscenium—Gluck, Mozart, Beethoven, Verdi, Wagner, and Gounod—by no means representative of the Metropolitan's standard repertoire.

A problem that was evident from the beginning was the house's lack of storage space for scenery and properties. To fit Cady's design into the irregular site chosen and at the same time provide the desired number of boxes, an auditorium of minimum size, and a stage in proportion, there was simply no place left for storage except the space beneath the stage. The acoustics, however, were immediately judged outstanding for a theater seating nearly four thousand. Seeing was another matter, especially for the occupants of the gallery. The Metropolitan, John Briggs observes, was essentially "a semicircle of boxes with an opera house built around them, a private club to which the general public was somewhat grudgingly admitted."

The management of the house was first taken over by the Henry Abbey Opera Company, which opened a season of Italian opera on October 22, 1883, with a production of *Faust*. Christine Nilsson and Italo Campanini headed the cast. The curtain was held for a half hour, awaiting the arrival of boxholders. When they finally came, they arrived in polished carriages with coachmen, footmen, and high-stepping horses. The men wore opera capes lined with red satin, top hats, and pearl shirt studs; the ladies were gowned in satin, their wraps were of sable and chinchilla, and they sparkled with diamonds and emeralds. "Although there was hardly a true music lover in the lot," Quaintance Eaton maintains, "the men who lined the Golden Horseshoe at the opening of the Metropolitan Opera in New York represented all the royalty America could hope for." Since *Faust* was given in those days in five acts, there were four intermissions that allowed opening night patrons to view the theater and visit each other's boxes. Newspapers had printed diagrams that day indicating whose accommodations were where. Champagne corks were said to have popped throughout the performance. After Nilsson's "Jewel Song" showers of bouquets fell from the boxes, and baskets of flowers were passed across the footlights. It was well past midnight before the last carriage pulled away from the gaslit marquee on Broadway, but the favored arena of the new, industrial rich had been christened in style.

Yet all of the social activity in New York City that evening did not occur at the Metropolitan. Colonel Mapleson had audaciously decided to open his season at the Academy of Music on the same night, offering Etelka Gerster in *La Sonnambula*. To complicate matters even more the socially obligatory National Horse Show was being held at the old Madison Square Garden. The gathering at the Academy did not quite measure up to its customary brilliance, although most of the "Knickerbocker aristocrats" were in attendance, along with New York's two most respected musicians, Theodore Thomas and Leopold Damrosch. The reigning Mrs. William Astor had not even come into town for the occasion, but her appendage Ward McAllister paid his respects to both opera openings. Other social leaders split their evening three ways by including the horse show as well.

Two nights later, with less social pomp, Abbey presented a more interesting musical event at the Metropolitan, a staging of *Lucia di Lammermoor* that introduced Marcella Sembrich to America. Altogether the manager staged nineteen operas during the opening season of the new house, all of them sung in Italian. Nine were German and French operas sung in Italian, including *Lohengrin, Carmen, Hamlet,* and three works by Meyerbeer, billed as *Gli Ugonotti, Il Profeta,* and *Roberto il Diavolo.* From the beginning the Metropolitan repertoire was notably conservative, for Abbey's choice of operas closely reflected the established taste. Ponchielli's *La Gioconda* was the only work given that year that had not been heard in New York before. It was Abbey's policy to pay lead singers high fees—Nilsson and Campanini each receiving $1000 a performance—rather than attempt to build a strong ensemble. The Metropolitan's sets were among the most lavish seen in nineteenth-century America, while the entire wardrobe was supplied by Worth of Paris.

Meanwhile Mapleson was giving the Metropolitan some worthy competition. He too staged *Faust*, introducing a young woman with a huge voice from Farmington, Maine, named Lillian Norton Gower. She had begun her career singing with Pat Gilmore's band, during a time when Innes was solo trombonist, and later would become internationally renowned as Lillian Nordica. Mapleson still had Patti in his stable of singers, while his repertoire was dominated by the same Rossini, Bellini, Donizetti, and Verdi favorites that made up Henry Abbey's. But Mapleson's stage effects were frequently shabby, and the Academy of Music clearly lacked the glamor of the new Metropolitan. Consequently attendance at the Academy fell off sharply, except for those evenings when Patti or Gerster sang. Mapleson's deficit at the end of the season was staggering. Still he held on doggedly. When Patti deserted him, the Colonel pathetically maintained that he was no longer concerned with stars but with polished ensembles. Gradually his audiences became thinner and thinner, as more of the Academy's boxholders were lured uptown to the "yellow brewery" on Broadway. In 1886 Mapleson gave up in defeat: "I cannot fight Wall Street," he insisted. Although performances of opera were staged periodically at the Academy of Music for another decade, its days of splendor were over.

But all was not well at the Metropolitan either. Abbey finished his 1883-84 season, after a fairly extensive spring tour, with an alarming deficit of $600,000, more than a third of what it had cost to build the house itself. The expense of staging so many operas from scratch explains part of the losses, and the money spent on sets and costumes could be considered a permanent investment, but the fact remained that New York's enthusiasm for grand opera was not sufficient to support two houses. It was true that Abbey had very little experience in producing opera, that before the Metropolitan opening he had been more noted as a theatrical producer and concert manager, and that the impresario was something of a spendthrift. But Abbey realized that his public was more impressed by the grandeur of the Golden Horseshoe and the elaborate sets and Worth gowns on stage than with anything approaching musical values.

The Metropolitan backers had posted a guarantee of $60,000 against possible losses. Under the agreement it was up to Abbey to cover the remaining $540,000. The manager suggested that he would produce the following season without fee if the boxholders would assume the current deficit. This arrangement was found to be unacceptable, and Abbey was dismissed. Throughout the summer Metropolitan directors searched for another general manager. Before Abbey was engaged, Covent Garden's Ernest Gye had been considered, and negotiations with him were resumed. Not until August was it apparent that Gye was unavailable. With time growing short, the shareholders began to panic; perhaps the season ahead should be cancelled. Frantically the list of possible managers was considered—Maurice Grau (the nephew of the man who had opened Crosby's Opera House in Chicago), Italo Campanini, maybe Colonel Mapleson. Even vaudeville manager Tony Pastor was suggested.

Then Leopold Damrosch offered to put on a season of German opera, using his own New York Symphony and a chorus drawn from his Oratorio Society. Damrosch pointed out that he planned to go to Central Europe for his principal singers, thus avoiding the expensive Italian and French star system. A German repertoire would also have the advantage of attracting the support of New York's large German population, then numbering around a quarter of a million persons. Besides that, the Wagnerian operas particularly would have novel appeal, since these heavy German works had long been neglected in America. Although it differed drastically from the previous season, Damrosch's proposal was shortly accepted by the desperate Metropolitan directors, and the conductor immediately sailed for Europe to recruit a company.

With time against him Damrosch contracted his singers and prepared his season. On November 17, 1884, he was ready to open; *Tannhauser* was the opera he had chosen, with Anton Schott in the title role. Italian and French works, sung in German, were included in Damrosch's repertoire, but the climax of the season came with a staging of Wagner's *Die Walkure*, featuring Amalia Materna as Brunnhilde and Marianne Brandt as Fricka. Sets and costumes were copies of those at Bayreuth. New York had seen a poor performance of *Die Walkure* in 1877 at the Academy of Music and had heard excerpts of the opera many times in concert halls, but it was not until Damrosch's production on January 30, 1885, that the full impact of Wagner's masterpiece was experienced.

Even before the success of *Walkure*, it was evident that Damrosch's policy was working. His repertoire, which included *Fidelio, Der Freischutz,* and *Don Giovanni,* was as fresh to New York audiences as Colonel Mapleson's string of *Lucia*'s and *Barber*'s was stale. Lowering his top admission price to $4.00, approximately half what Abbey had charged, Damrosch was able to bring in twice the box office receipts during his first two months as compared with the season before. And critics had been impressed with his integrated ensemble and effective staging. By mid-January Damrosch's contract had been renewed for another year, granting the conductor both a salary and a share in the profits. The deficit at the end of the season was a negligible $40,000, much of the receipts coming from single ticket sales.

Yet the season had not escaped tragedy. Leopold Damrosch had carried both the artistic and administrative burden of the productions and had conducted every performance. In early February he came home one afternoon from an exhausting rehearsal, and laid down in an unheated bedroom. Pneumonia resulted. On February 11, twenty-three year-old Walter Damrosch took his father's place in the pit, conducting a performance of *Tannhauser.* Four days later the elder Damrosch was dead; his funeral was held on the Metropolitan stage with Henry Ward Beecher as the principal speaker. The musician's son and chorus master John Lund conducted the remainder of the season.

Once again the Metropolitan directors were faced with the dilemma of securing a suitable manager. Walter Damrosch was clearly too inexperienced. Tenor Anton Schott contended that he should fill the post, but instead the stockholders sent young Damrosch to Germany to offer the position to the thirty-five year-old Hungarian Anton Seidl, a celebrated Wagnerian. The imperious Seidl accepted; Walter Damrosch became his assistant, and Edmund C. Stanton was appointed manager in charge of administrative details.

Seidl opened his first Metropolitan season on November 23, 1885, with a mounting of *Lohengrin,* immediately proving himself a stickler for careful, well-rehearsed performances. That winter he presented the first stagings in the United States of Wagner's *Die Meistersinger* and *Rienzi,* although the big commercial success of the season was Goldmark's *Die Konigin von Saba.* The new musical director introduced Max Alvary, a lyric tenor with a matinee idol appearance, and the incomparable Lilli Lehmann, who strangely enough made her debut as Carmen. Seidl's conducting was judged incomparable, and the dignity and musicianship he brought to the operatic stage was unlike anything seen in New York before. While Colonel Mapleson might scoff at Metropolitan performances as "sauerkraut opera," the management's losses during the 1885-86 season were reduced to $25,000.

The following year Seidl conducted the initial American production of *Tristan und Isolde,* featuring Lilli Lehmann. *Aida* was first heard in the house later that season, in German, with Theresa Herbert-Forster in the title role. The soprano's husband, Victor Herbert, was a cellist in the Metropolitan orchestra. In the 1887-88 season *Siegfried* and *Gotterdammerung* were introduced, while the first complete *Ring* in this country was given in March, 1889. French and Italian operas continued to make up much of the Metropolitan repertoire. *Faust,* in fact, was staged with such regularity during the early years that critic W. J. Henderson eventually dubbed the house *"Das Faustspielhaus."*

But the novelty of German opera was wearing off, and the boxholders had become especially bored by the long, complex Wagnerian plots. The Metropolitan backers were simply not prepared to appreciate the intrinsic values of Seidl's productions and had found the German repertoire of brief interest largely for its scenic effects. As the spectacle of magic fire, the God's crossing the rainbow bridge to Valhalla, and the illusion of swimming Rhine Maidens lost its appeal, the boxholders grew restless. Gradually the audience came to be predominantly German (the *Times* estimated seventy-five per cent German), patrons who had bought tickets out of devotion to music and the *Vaterland*. Increasingly the single ticket holders complained about annoying conversation from the boxes, while the stockholders grew just as indignant over the hisses and rebukes from the general audience. W. J. Henderson suggested that the shareholders simply bar ticket holders from future performances. "It will cost them only seven thousand dollars each," the critic wrote facetiously, "to enjoy their conversations without the interruption of hissing."

The story is often told of a society matron, particularly noted for her tendency to gossip through entire acts of an opera. The lady supposedly asked a casual friend if he would enjoy attending a performance of *Tristan* with her. "I should very much like to come," the acquaintance answered; "I have never heard you in *Tristan*." Meanwhile manager Edmond Stanton struggled to placate both factions. Signs were placed in the boxes asking patrons not to talk during performances, yet in a production of *Fidelio* stagehands were ordered not to lower the lights for the Dungeon Scene, because stockholders objected to the gloomy atmosphere. One socialite even asked if the third act of *Meistersinger* might not be given first, arguing that it was the only act of the opera with any real music and that most of the boxholders were gone by the time it came around.

The German vogue continued through 1890-91, seven seasons in all. More and more the boxholders yearned for a return to the melodious Italian arias and the glamor of featured tenors and prima donnas. In 1891 the Metropolitan directors asked Henry Abbey to resume the management of the house. The impresario agreed to stage a season of *bel canto* opera strictly at his own risk. Since that first year at the Metropolitan, Abbey had taken Maurice Grau and Edward Schoeffel as partners, and the company was now known as the Abbey-Schoeffel-Grau Opera Company. Once again the tables were turned; most productions were given in Italian, although a few were sung in French. *Die Meistersinger*, one of the two Wagnerian dramas retained in the repertoire, was even billed as *I Maestri Cantori*!

Abbey, Schoeffel, and Grau opened their season on December 14, 1891, offering the American debuts of Jean and Edouard de Reszke and the American soprano Emma Eames. The opera was Gounod's *Romeo and Juliet*, the first work given at the Metropolitan in French. It was the beginning of the star system's golden age. Later that year Jean de Reszke sang *Otello*, with Emma Albani as his Desdemona, and later *Lohengrin*. Lilli Lehmann, whose repertoire ranged from Norma to Brunnhilde, returned to the house for her first role in Italian, Leonora in *Il Trovatore*. Lillian Nordica appeared in *Les Huguenots* and *L'Africaine*, and Emma Eames sang Santuzza in the Metropolitan's first production of *Cavalleria Rusticana*. In early April the directors announced that the Abbey, Schoeffel, Grau management had been signed for another two years.

That summer, since the house was not in use, scenery was being painted on the Metropolitan stage, one of the few places in the theater open enough to stretch out large quantities of canvas. Beneath the stage were stored most of the company's sets. On the morning of August 27, 1892, a workman dropped a cigarette amid the allegedly inflammable canvas that littered the floor. By the time the horse-drawn fire engines arrived, the whole stage area was in flames. By noon the blaze had been brought under control, but the damage was estimated at $300,000. Since the house was supposedly fireproof, the directors had insured it for only $60,000. The disaster spelled the end of the Metropolitan Opera House Company. Fifty-one of the seventy stockholders withdrew. The remainder, joined by sixteen newcomers, formed the Metropolitan Opera and Real Estate Company and voted to rebuild the theater.

The restoration began in April, 1893. The number of boxes was reduced, with the thirty-five in the parterre making the great Diamond Horseshoe the focal point of the auditorium. Each of the stockholders owned a box in the parterre and in return was assessed up to $4500 a year to meet production costs. Space in the Grand Tier above was rented on a seasonal arrangement and connoted a distinctly lower social standing. Those in the Diamond Horseshoe fell into three main groups: (1) the Vanderbilts, (2) Morgan and his associates, and (3) the Astors and the "Knickerbocker aristocrats" who had moved uptown from the Academy of Music.

The house was reopened on November 27, 1893, again with *Faust*, this time featuring Eames and the De Reszke brothers. Since the theater had been closed for eighteen months, excitement ran high, and Abbey and Grau gave the new stockholders an imposing array of artists. On December 4, Nellie Melba made her Metropolitan debut as Lucia and was compared favorably with Patti. The Australian diva later sang Ophelia in *Hamlet*, Elisabeth in *Tannhauser*, Elsa in *Lohengrin*, Juliet to Jean de Reszke's Romeo, and Nedda in the Metropolitan's first *Pagliacci*. On December 20, Emma Calve brought the house down with her spectacular Carmen, setting the standard for years to come. Hers was a vivid, three-dimensional portrayal, full of lust and fury—a kind of performance that was new to American opera audiences. "She chucked tradition to the winds," James G. Huneker observed, "also her lingerie." The twelve *Carmen* performances that year broke boxoffice records.

For three more seasons Abbey and Grau headed the Metropolitan management, emphasizing all-star casts. On December 3, 1894, Francesco Tamagno was presented as Otello, a part the tenor had created at La Scala under Verdi's supervision. Eames was his Desdemona, Victor Maurel, Iago. Maurel was heard later that year in the American premiere of *Falstaff*, while a production of *Les Huguenots* on December 26 was offered with Melba, Nordica, both De Reszkes, Pol Plancon, Maurel, and Sofia Scalchi heading the cast. With Calve absent for a season, Abbey and Grau compensated by presenting *Carmen* featuring the De Reszkes, with Melba and Eames alternating in the relatively brief role of Micaela. The stars were paid lavishly.

After one performance Eames is supposed to have remarked, "You must be a very rich man, Mr. Grau, to pay me eight hundred dollars to sing Micaela." Yet admission prices were held to a five dollar top by cutting expenses elsewhere. Members of the orchestra received fifty dollars a week, choristers fifteen.

With Abbey and Grau stars were the thing, even when staging Wagner. *Tristan und Isolde* was given in German by the managers on November 27, 1895, with Jean de Reszke as Tristan, Nordica as Isolde, Edouard de Reszke as Marke, and Marie Brema as Brangane. Anton Seidl had been invited back to conduct. Nordica and the De Reszkes were largely responsible for making Wagner popular again at the Metropolitan, although German opera had been given in the house since the spring of 1894, following the death of Leopold Damrosch, under the direction of Walter Damrosch, his son. Since Abbey and Grau initially were not interested in producing opera in German, they agreed to rent the theater and the necessary costumes and scenery to Damrosch on reasonable terms. But it was not until Abbey and Grau linked the Wagnerian dramas to their star system that the works enjoyed the sustained interest of the public. On December 30, 1896, even Nelli Melba made an attempt at heavy Wagner, singing Brunnhilde in *Siegfried*, opposite Jean de Reszke. It was among the most notorious disasters in operatic history, for the soprano was barely able to finish the performance. "It was like asking a French rapier to do the work of a German battleaxe," John Hetherington, Melba's biographer, contends, Later, Melba admitted, "I have been a fool," as she was forced to retire for a year to rework her voice.

In October, 1896, while Grau was in Europe scouting for talent, Henry Abbey died. This meant a dissolution of the Abbey-Schoeffel-Grau Opera Company and a recouping of finances for Maurice Grau. Eventually Grau's lease on the Metropolitan was renewed for three years, on the understanding that he would be free to rent the house to other companies during the 1897-98 season. Five weeks of the season were taken up by the Walter Damrosch company, who utilized a number of the artists under contract to Grau. During the fall of 1898 Maurice Grau assumed the management of the Metropolitan alone, concentrating on heroic singing in the grand Italian manner. The bearded, urbane Grau was primarily a businessman, who "knew where to spend a dollar and where to save a nickel." Jean de Reszke once claimed, "Grau will give you a good cigar, but not the match to light it with." The impresario was perfectly willing to let public taste dictate his offering, and audiences clearly wanted stars and social glamor.

Under the Grau administration it made very little difference what opera was playing; the big concern was, "Who is singing?" Performances were generally slipshod, with minor roles poorly cast and physical productions virtually in shambles. It seemed relatively unimportant that thrones were rickety, that props under stage balconies fell, that the chorus and orchestra were ragged, and that the right feet of ballet members rarely knew what the left were doing. If Melba or Jean de Reszke was on stage, all was well. Singers opera remained something of a mystery to Grau.

Social leaders like Mrs. Astor customarily appeared at the opera house promptly at nine o'clock, regardless of what time the performance had started. During the intermission she would receive members of her set, particularly those accompanied by out-of-town or European visitors, but she rarely left her own box. Until World War I the Metropolitan was the focal point of the winter social season, the Ward McAllister's famous Four Hundred sought to be seen as near the Diamond Horseshoe as possible, especially on Monday nights, the most fashionable of all. Attending the opera was a duty for anyone with social aspirations, and the boxes at the Metropolitan were slow to change hands. Daughters were presented to society at the opera, and it was there that prominent young men interviewed candidates for marriage. Henry James, on a visit to his native America in 1907, was amazed by "the general extravagant insistence on the Opera, which plays its part as the great vessel of social salvation."

For the wealthy "going to the opera" at the turn of the century was an almost religious ritual, somewhere between being presented at Court and attending High Mass in a grand cathedral; and Metropolitan boxholders dressed accordingly. Gentlemen suffered in swallowtail coats and bat-wing shirts with collars so high they could barely turn their heads. Dowagers came girded in corsets and swathed in bolts of white satin or black watered silk. Their gowns were augmented by accessories like full-length kid gloves, dog collars, ostrich feathers, sequins, boas, and jewelry: clusters of diamond rings, brooches, and sunbursts. Faces were made up with rice powder and beauty marks; hair was "ratted" into mountainous coiffures held together with pins, combs, and tiaras. They carried an arsenal of mother-of-pearl opera glasses, lorgnettes, and gold mesh purses. Suffocating under layers of apparel, they sat in their boxes straight and regal, paralyzed by too-tight girdles and the sheer weight of their elaborate costumes.

Meanwhile Maurice Grau's stars "consented to sing" for the handsome fees they preferred to call "cachets." Having also become the director of Covent Garden in London, Grau was able to command the talents of the most illustrious singers of his day, and for five seasons following Abbey's death he offered Metropolitan audiences casts of unparalleled artistry. In its first season, 1898-99, the Maurice Grau Opera Company presented Ernestine Schumann-Heink in her American debut, as Ortrud in *Lohengrin*. Jean de Reszke sang the title role, Lillian Nordica the role of Elsa, and David Bispham the Telramund role. Marcella Sembrich returned to the Metropolitan that season after an absence of almost fifteen years, while Antonio Scotti made his debut on December 27, 1899, as Don Giovanni, launching a long career as one of the house's most polished singing actors. Jean de Reszke sang his last season at the Metropolitan in 1900-01, for an unprecedented fee of $2500 a performance. Walter Damrosch conducted a number of the Wagner operas that year, and Puccini's *La Boheme* was introduced into the repertoire, with Melba finding her greatest role in Mimi.

Grau also presented the house with its first *Magic Flute*, an uncut *Ring*, and its initial *Tosca*. All five of the impresario's seasons following the dissolution of the Abbey-Schoeffel-Grau partnership were financial successes. Even the 1900-01 season, during which an expensive production of Reyer's *Salammbo* and an unprofitable western tour almost caused disaster, the company netted a profit of $15,290.

But by 1903 Grau's health had grown bad, forcing the manager to retire. His place at the Metropolitan was taken by Heinrich Conried, an Austrian actor, who like Grau knew little about singing or opera. Although Conried was less devoted to the star system than his predecessor, he opened his first season on November 23, 1903, with his ace—a new Italian tenor originally contracted by Grau, Enrico Caruso. Caruso made his Metropolitan debut as the Duke in *Rigoletto*, with a cast that included Sembrich, Scotti, Louise Homer, and Marcel Journet. The tenor was extremely nervous on opening night, as he often was, and sang badly. He quickly recovered, and by the end of the season patrons were buying tickets for Caruso performances without bothering to ask what opera they were going to hear.

Aside from Caruso's debut the big excitement of Conried's first New York season accompanied the staging of Wagner's *Parsifal*. In contrast to Grau, Conried sought to produce integrated performances; rather than thrill his public with stars, he preferred to offer operatic novelties, new or unfamiliar operas that with the right publicity could be made enticing to a wide audience. His decision to produce *Parsifal* created an immediate furor, since the composer's will had stipulated that the opera was not to be performed outside Bayreuth for fifty years after his death. Cosima Wagner, the musician's widow, held firm, refusing Conried or anybody else the right to stage her husband's final work. When the Metropolitan manager persisted, Frau Wagner brought suit. Since no copyright agreement existed between the United States and Germany, the American courts threw out the case. Next Conried ran into trouble with the clergy. Since *Parsifal* centers around a religious subject, there were those who claimed that a stage representation of sacred matter was impious. To make the situation worse Conried had scheduled the first performance for Christmas Eve.

The commotion continued up to the day *Parsifal* was presented, and Conried saw to it that the newspapers covered the turmoil in full. Meanwhile ticket orders poured in for the production, even though the price of admission had essentially been doubled. A special *Parsifal* train was chartered to bring Chicago ticket holders to the performance. Since the opera began at five o'clock in the afternoon, newspapers were flooded with questions concerning the appropriate dress. Suddenly there were advertisements for "Parsifal" hats, "Parsifal" cough drops, and "Parsifal" cigars. There was a breakfast food named "Par-see-fall," an historical novel called *Parsifal, Jr.*, and a Signor Parsifal, who read minds and told fortunes.

The five scheduled performances of Wagner's opera sold out so quickly that Conried announced six more. The production, nearly five hours long, was conducted by Alfred Herz, the cast headed by Milka Ternina and Alois Burgstaller. Curtain time was announced by a group of trumpeters stationed at the Metropolitan entrance, in the Bayreuth tradition. Altogether the eleven *Parsifal* performances earned $186,306, about half of which was profit.

All in all Conried's production standards were high, striving to present a polished ensemble. The manager modernized the stage equipment at the Metropolitan, had the house refurbished, and ordered new scenery for several operas in the repertoire. He was far more concerned with the orchestra and chorus than Grau had been and attempted to acquire the best conductors available. Still, Conried closed his first two seasons with a substantial profit, even though the 1905-06 season was marred by disaster. The company, on its spring tour of the West, happened to be playing San Francisco at the time of the great earthquake. None of the artists were hurt, although Caruso and Scotti had fled the town in a hired wagon as buildings toppled around them. But trainloads of scenery and costumes were destroyed, and a number of musical instruments were damaged beyond repair. The remainder of the tour had to be cancelled.

But in February, 1906, events began to portend another peril to the Metropolitan's livelihood. Showman Oscar Hammerstein announced he would build the Manhattan Opera House on West Thirty-fourth Street and declared plans for staging a season of grand opera there during the coming fall. The former cigar maker had developed a lifelong passion for opera as a child; as a teenager he had attended performances at the New York Academy of Music whenever his funds would allow it. He had earned a great deal of money from a cigar-cutting machine and from a trade journal for the tobacco industry, but most of Hammerstein's fortune had been made off the Victoria Theater, a vaudeville house eventually managed by his son Willie. Aggressive but charming, the flamboyant Oscar had a talent for attracting the attention of the press, held news conferences with regularity, and was later said to have the only tongue quicker than Mary Garden's. All his life Hammerstein dreamed of producing opera—it became an obsession. "Opera," he once claimed, "is not a business but a disease."

Leaving his son Arthur to oversee the construction of the new opera house, Hammerstein departed for Europe in the spring of 1906 to recruit a company. He had no partners, no stockholders, no board of directors, and no advisers for the project at hand. The Manhattan was to be *his* opera house, and the company would be *his* company. In contrast with the Metropolitan, Hammerstein hoped that the opera he produced would appeal to the masses; he did not want another society-dominated institution. There was no reason, he believed, why opera could not become democratic.

The impresario returned from Europe having contracted the Italian maestro Cleofonte Campanini as his principal conductor. It was a wise choice, for Campanini was a gifted artist who knew opera well. The musician had just resigned from La Scala and had been an assistant conductor at the Metropolitan under Abbey; he was also the younger brother of tenor Italo Campanini. Then Hammerstein announced another coup: he had signed

Nelli Melba to sing at the Manhattan. The soprano, still in her prime, had initially refused Hammerstein's offer. Later she insisted that the showman was "the most American of Americans, and the only man who ever made me change my mind." But Hammerstein had also engaged tenor Alessandro Bonci, a worthy rival for Caruso; as well as Charles Dalmores, a young dramatic tenor whom Conried wanted, Mario Ancona, a New York favorite ten years before, Emma Calve, Maurice Renaud, and the Italian baritone Mario Sammarco.

Before long it became evident that Hammerstein was not just putting together an opera season. He was preparing for battle. His aim, brazenly enough, was to drive the imperious Metropolitan out of business. The ambitious Oscar rarely did things half way. He made no secret of the fact that he detested the artificiality of the Vanderbilt-Morgan-Astor controlled house, and he was only slightly more veiled in his personal dislike for Heinrich Conried. By fall war had been unofficially declared, and the Metropolitan fortified itself against the coming attack. It was the first serious competition the Metropolitan had faced since the decline of the Academy of Music and the only real threat in the house's entire history.

Hammerstein opened his Manhattan Opera House on December 3, 1906, with a staging of Bellini's almost forgotten *I Puritani*. The opera served as a vehicle for the American debut of Alessandro Bonci, who proved himself a *bel canto* specialist of the highest order. Campanini conducted. The house itself, designed and decorated in a French style, recalling the period of Louis XIV, was completed just hours before the curtain went up. In fact the press claimed that in several places the paint was still wet. Boxes were minimized at the Manhattan, and while Hammerstein's opening drew an excited, capacity house, high society was conspicuously absent. "It is society in the broad sense that I hope to attract and to please," Hammerstein insisted. "It is my belief in the great and growing taste for music in New York that has led me to give it another opera house." It was noted, however, that Otto Kahn, chairman of the Metropolitan's board of directors, was present at the Manhattan opening, but much of the audience came from the city's rapidly growing Italian population.

Yet Hammerstein possessed certain advantages over the Metropolitan. To begin with Oscar himself was idolized by the public and admired by the press. Americans have characteristically been partial to the underdog, and the idea of the vaudeville man daring to challenge the entrenched Metropolitan —alone and without financial backing—was so improbable and hazardous that he was almost automatically turned into something of a popular hero. Then too, the more relaxed atmosphere at the Manhattan was an appealing contrast to the staid Metropolitan. But above all, Hammerstein presented good opera. His productions, on the whole, were far better integrated that Conried's: well rehearsed, imaginitively directed, with fresh scenery and costumes for each. His chorus was a revelation—young, attractive, energetic, vocally exciting. Most of the choristers Hammerstein had hand-picked personally from New York voice studios; he employed just enough professionals from Italy to season the youthful group with experience. Then there was Maestro Campanini, a perfectionist, whose authority and musicianship made even the old-fashioned operas seem thrilling. It was Campanini's rule that there be no encores, whereas at the Metropolitan encores were the stars' prerogative, no matter what the expense to dramatic continuity.

Maurice Renaud, the idol of the Paris Opera, made his New York debut at the Manhattan on December 5, 1906, as Rigoletto, with Bonci as the Duke. *Faust* followed, introducing Charles Dalmores to America. Calve sang Carmen, opposite the handsome Dalmores' Don Jose. Then on January 2, 1907, Melba made her first appearance for Hammerstein, in *La Traviata*, adding new luster to the company and attracting society people to the house in goodly numbers for the first time. Melba's engagement not only brought prestige, but proved to be a considerable artistic victory as well, for the diva sang better than she had in some time. The soprano later offered Mimi in *Boheme*, with Bonci as Rodolfo, sprightly Emma Trentini as Musetta. The orchestral parts had been pirated since the Metropolitan claimed exclusive rights to the Puccini score.

Meanwhile tension within the Conried forces mounted. The Metropolitan had opened auspiciously with *Romeo and Juliet* on November 26, 1906, highlighted by the American debut of Geraldine Farrar. The Boston born soprano had recently achieved sensational triumphs in Berlin, and she immediately became a favorite in New York, as renowned for her beauty as for her talent. But as if the problems posed by Hammerstein were not enough, Caruso—by now Conried's prize attraction—had gotten into an embarrassing predicament a few days before the season began. The tenor had been arrested in the monkey house of the Central Park Zoo, when a young woman claimed he had pinched her. Caruso in faulty English had proclaimed innocence, but a policeman had ungraciously hauled him into the East Sixty-seventh Street police station. The singer was later fined ten dollars. What effect the incident would have on the Metropolitan box office was by no means the least of Conried's worries as he entered his 1906-07 season. Caruso was scheduled to appear first in *Boheme* two nights after the Farrar debut, and the company approached the moment with misgivings. The roar of applause that followed Rodolfo's narrative was a joyous sound both to the tenor and the Metropolitan management.

In keeping with his policy of offering novelties Conried presented the American premiere of Giordano's *Fedora* on December 5, 1906, featuring Caruso, Scotti, and the gorgeous Italian soprano Lina Cavalieri. Berlioz's *Damnation of Faust* was introduced two days later with Farrar as Marguerite, while on January 18, 1907, the first Metropolitan performance of *Manon Lescaut* was given, under Puccini's supervision, also with Caruso, Scotti, and Cavalieri. The following Sunday, January 20, Conried called a dress rehearsal for another new opera, Richard Strauss's *Salome*, inviting a select audience to view the production before its public opening. Conried had hopes that *Salome* would create a furor equal to the tempest *Parsifal* had caused four years earlier. It did, but unfortunately most of the excitement was negative. The depravity of the subject and the psychological depth of the Strauss drama left those who gathered for the rehearsal more than a little stunned. Since a number of the observers had just come from church, Salome's decadence stood out in abrupt contrast to the pious mood they had experienced a few hours before. The performance on January 22, 1907, just two years after the opera's Dresden premiere, set off an explosion unlike anything the genteel Metropolitan had ever known. Olive Fremstad sang the title role, although the soprano's Wagnerian form precluded her doing Salome's Dance of the Seven Veils. A *premiere danseuse* substituted in the dance, seriously damaging the opera's dramatic value. But the impact of the final scene alone, where Salome caresses and kisses the severed head of John the Baptist, was enough to leave the Metropolitan boxholders in no mild state of shock. Overnight the management faced a storm of protests. The attack swelled as an indignant press and outraged clergymen voiced their disapproval; letters branding *Salome* obscene from self-righteous citizens soon poured in through the mail. Art that was not ennobling, traditionalists—including many critics—continued to hold, was no art at all. Despite the fact that three additional performances of the opera were nearly sold out, at advanced prices, the Metropolitan board of directors felt it had no choice; *Salome* was withdrawn after the one performance.

Shortly there were whispers that Conried was on his way out. The manager's physical condition had deteriorated over the past few years, and the strain of the current season had brought him close to a nervous breakdown. Eventually he was forced to limit his activities at the opera house, giving Hammerstein still another advantage. But Conried was not through yet. In February he presented Puccini's *Madama Butterfly*. A cast including Farrar, Caruso, Scotti, and Louise Homer performed the opera with Puccini himself present. Similarly, when *Hansel and Gretel* was introduced, Humperdinck was brought over for the occasion. Ernestine Schumann-Heink even agreed to sing the part of the Witch.

The Metropolitan ended the season with a deficit of $84,039. While tales of mismanagement circulated, Conried pleaded that the cost of producing opera had increased tremendously. Hammerstein, on the other hand, closed his season showing a profit of $100,000. In March the Manhattan impresario announced that subscriptions for the following year already totaled $200,000. During the spring, both Conried and Hammerstein made efforts to steal the other's stars. Alessandro Bonci joined the roster of stars at the Metropolitan the next season, and Nordica and Schumann-Heink were signed to sing at the Manhattan.

Heinrich Conried was clearly a dejected man. Afflicted with neuritis that made walking difficult, he nevertheless left for Europe after the exhausting 1906-07 season, determined to bolster the Metropolitan artistic personnel. In

Berlin he met composer-conductor Gustav Mahler and with much difficulty convinced the musician to leave the Vienna Opera and take charge of a number of productions at the Metropolitan during the coming season. It was Conried's last great service for the New York house, for the conducting staff there had been weak. Arturo Vigna, who directed many of the performances, was certainly no match for Campanini. Mahler made his Metropolitan debut on New Year's Day, 1908, conducting *Tristan und Isolde*. Olive Fremstad was the Isolde. The maestro had rehearsed the Metropolitan musicians unmercifully, would tolerate none of the house's ordinary laxities, and insisted that even principals attend every session. But the sounds Mahler brought from the orchestra were unmatched in Metropolitan experience, an aura of beauty that combined authority and intellect with glistening richness. He went on to conduct *Don Giovanni, Fidelio, Die Walkure,* and *Siegfried,* all with unflagging brilliance.

Yet Mahler himself was a depressed man, periodically ill. Like Conried the musician could be stubborn and tactless. He rarely attended social functions, but when he did, he was prone to be morose and silent. There was little about Mahler to endear him to society leaders, and his musical ideals were frankly too lofty for the general public. Therefore, while the conductor added a perfectionist quality to Metropolitan performances, he contributed almost no personal traits that would enable Conried to capture the limelight from Hammerstein.

The Metropolitan opened its 1907-08 season with another novelty, Cilea's *Adriana Lecouvreur,* featuring Caruso and Cavalieri. Mascagni's *Iris* and Boito's *Mefistofele* were offered later; both productions were qualified successes. Feodor Chaliapin made his debut in the Boito opera, rudely shocking audiences with his naturalistic acting. The charming Geraldine Farrar was heard several times, including Margherita and Violetta among her new roles. But Conried's major thrust in the war against the Manhattan was the presentation of Bonci twenty-five times and Caruso fifty-one times. Between the two of them they appeared in more than half of the Metropolitan performances that season. Yet aside from Mahler and Chaliapin—both of whom, in very different ways, were beyond the grasp of the New York public —Conried's roster was not highly distinctive. Bonci after all had been standard fare at the Manhattan the year before. And the novelties staged by the Metropolitan that season met with modest acclaim at best.

By itself Conried's 1907-08 season might have been considered a rather distinguished one, but in comparison with the surprises Hammerstein had lined up, it seemed lacklustre. The Manhattan had opened with *La Gioconda*; Nordica and a brilliant young tenor named Giovanni Zenatello headed the cast. Offenbach's *The Tales of Hoffman,* the early novelty of the season, was a definite triumph. Then came the American debut of the incomparable singing actress Mary Garden, November 25, 1907, in the United States premiere of Massenet's *Thais.* With that a fresh dimension was introduced into New York's opera war—a new repertoire and a production technique that ultimately would affect the course of the nation's operatic development.

Garden was one of those performers, almost unknown on the operatic stage of her day, who could suggest practically any situation merely by walking across the stage, convey an entire idea with the simple movement of an arm, and heighten the drama by the intonation of a single word or phrase. Her characterizations were masterfully drawn, refined until they breathed with life, yet remained part of the ensemble. She knew how to costume and apply make-up with commanding effect and possessed a stage presence that bordered on sorcery. Her acting was universally praised; her singing proved more controversial. Garden used her voice to deepen her portrayal, rather than for its intrinsic beauty, and critics frequently misunderstood this. Still her top tones often left much to be desired. After her New York debut, one of the critics claimed that the soprano's high notes were "like the snakes of Ireland." Puzzled by this, Garden asked her father what was meant. "Mary," he gently explained, "there aren't any snakes in Ireland."

Like Hammerstein, Garden had a way of making everything she did seem exciting, on stage and off. Born in Scotland, the soprano had been raised in Chicago. At twenty she returned to Europe to study voice, financed initially by Mrs. David Mayer, wife of the Chicago department store owner. On a now legendary evening in 1900, the young singer was sitting in the audience at the Opera Comique, listening to a performance of Charpentier's *Louise*. During the intermission after the second act, she was called backstage. The soprano singing the title role had collapsed. Could she take over? Mary Garden, twenty-three years old, suddenly found herself on the stage of the great Paris opera house, in a role she had never rehearsed, with Louise's big aria, *"Depuis le jour,"* opening the third act. She finished the performance and found herself the toast of the city. Already modern French opera had become her specialty.

But Garden had the ability to make headlines with her private life, too, and she was always good for a statement on something. She was winsome, spirited, and above all brainy. While singing for Hammerstein, the attractive diva was invited to a dinner party, at which she was seated next to the New York politician Chauncey Depew. All during dinner Depew kept staring at the singer's low-cut gown, until finally she asked him what he found so entrancing. "I am wondering, Miss Garden," Depew confessed, "what keeps that gown up." Mary flashed him one of her famous smiles and replied, "Two things, Mr. Depew—your age and my discretion."

The *Thais* premiere at the Manhattan left critics in a quandry, confused both by Garden and the Massenet score. Reginald De Koven, writing for the *New York World*, clearly caught the significance of the moment: "Something new has come into opera." After an uncertain beginning *Thais* became one of Hammerstein's most popular productions. On January 3, Garden introduced American audiences to *Louise*, and her success this time was undisputed, despite the opera's theme of free love. In February she appeared in the first

American staging of Debussy's *Pelleas et Melisande*, a part Garden had created at the Opera Comique in 1902. Debussy himself had coached her. If the music of Massenet and Charpentier was strange to New York, Debussy's was a revolution, a masterpiece of impressionistic writing. Garden's Melisande was quiet, moody, almost still. Yet the public was enchanted by this fresh approach to opera. With *Thais, Louise,* and *Pelleas et Melisande,* Hammerstein scored three of his greatest successes, while Garden emerged as his unfailing magnet. Contemporary opera now became central in the Manhattan repertoire, with Campanini again proving himself a genius in the pit.

But Hammerstein had other surprises. Less than two weeks after the premiere of *Louise,* coloratura Luisa Tetrazzini (Campanini's sister-in-law) made her debut in *La Traviata.* Tetrazzini was a huge woman, who seemed to have gained weight every time she performed. She made practically no attempt at acting, but sang with a shimmering beauty. Her high notes particularly were matchless. Aside from Mary Garden, Tetrazzini was the rage of the Manhattan's second season, appearing also in *Lucia di Lammermoor* and *Rigoletto.*

Hammerstein was having such success with his new singers that the more established ones were almost forgotten. Nordica, for instance, had been contracted for thirty performances; she sang *Gioconda* four times, *Aida* once, then was released. Schumann-Heink sang at the Manhattan exactly one time, as Azucena in *Il Trovatore.* The indefatigable Oscar was enjoying the time of his life—offering a repertoire that differed markedly from the Metropolitan's, importing whole productions from Paris, staging them in a realistic manner, and exploding new stars in Heinrich Conried's face.

On February 20, 1908, the day after the American premiere of *Pelleas et Melisande,* the Metropolitan board of directors announced that Giulio Gatti-Casazza, formerly director of La Scala in Milan, would replace Conried as general manager at the end of the current season. Andreas Dippel would become administrative manager. It seems that about the time Conried had been negotiating with Gustav Mahler in Berlin, Otto Kahn, head of the Metropolitan board, had been talking privately with Gatti-Casazza in Paris. When Kahn informed his board that Gatti-Casazza was willing to entertain an offer, the J. P. Morgan faction voiced opposition, indicating that they preferred an American as manager. Not wanting to antagonize the Morgan group, Kahn suggested a codirectorship with Dippel sharing the management. Dippel had been a standby tenor with the Metropolitan since 1898, and while his singing had made little impression, he possessed a great deal of experience in the opera world and knew everyone. With the duo-directorship agreed upon, a permanent Metropolitan Opera Company was formed, which meant that the house would no longer be leased to the current manager. Instead a resident company and staff would be maintained and made available to the manager under contract.

At the close of the 1907-08 season Conried was presented with a silver cup and let go. His final deficit totaled almost $96,000. In mid-April Gatti-Casazza arrived in New York aboard what would soon become the torpedoed *Lusitania.* He was met at the pier by Andreas Dippel and was astonished to learn of the codirectorship arrangement. Dippel's name apparently had not been mentioned earlier, and there was friction from the beginning. But Gatti-Casazza was by far the stronger man, one of those rare individuals who could keep sight of the box office and artistic standards at the same time. "An opera house exists to be filled," Verdi had told Gatti when he became director of La Scala, and the impresario took the advice to heart. He shortly announced that Arturo Toscanini, with whom he had worked in Milan, would conduct at the Metropolitan during the coming season. When asked if he objected to sharing the podium with Mahler, Toscanini supposedly replied that he would rather serve in a house where there was excellence than one dominated by mediocrity.

Gatti-Casazza formally launched his twenty-seven-year reign at the Metropolitan on November 16, 1908, with a memorable *Aida.* Toscanini conducted a cast headed by the new Czech soprano Emmy Destinn, Caruso, Scotti, and Homer. Sets and costumes were borrowed from La Scala. The Italian conductor proved himself a firm disciplinarian and shortly demonstrated his rank as a Wagnerian by directing a *Gotterdammerung* of great breadth and intelligence. New operas that year included Puccini's one act opera *Le Villi,* Catalani's *La Wally,* a Toscanini favorite, d'Albert's *Tiefland,* and Smetana's *Verkaufte Braut,* a highly successful production which Mahler conducted. Mahler's triumph of the season, however, was *Marriage of Figaro,* performed after twenty orchestral rehearsals, with Eames, Sembrich, Farrar, Scotti, and Adamo Didur. Even more than Conried, Gatti-Casazza refused to deify the singer, preferring to attract the public's attention through works that were either new or rarely given. Yet Metropolitan boxholders continued to like the old favorites. Soprano Frances Alda, who was Gatti-Casazza's wife and sang in the house for several years, later wrote that the sentiment of boxholders in 1908 "seemed to be that what had been good enough for their fathers and for themselves back in 1883 was still good enough." But the Golden Age of singers was nearing an end. Sembrich and Eames would both retire in 1909, and the careers of Melba and Nordica were approaching a close.

At the Manhattan, Garden and Tetrazzini remained the featured attractions, although Melba returned for a few performances during the 1908-09 season; included in these was an appearance on Christmas Day as Desdemona. Maria Labia and Zenatello opened the season for Hammerstein in *Tosca,* and Garden scored a great success in the American premiere of Massenet's *Le Jongleur de Notre Dame* as the boy Jean, a role conceived for a tenor. But the sensation of the third Manhattan season was a staging of *Salome* with Mary Garden. Almost as if to mock Conried's earlier failure, Hammerstein presented the Strauss opera, scoring a major hit. With no board of directors to worry about, the shock element in *Salome* was not of real concern for the Manhattan impresario. Hammerstein could produce what he wanted without fear of offending social leaders and potential backers. Garden did not have the Wagnerian voice needed for the Strauss drama, but she looked the part and acted it superbly. She even performed the Dance of the Seven Veils herself, having spent some time the previous summer studying with the *premiere danseuse* of the Paris Opera.

By this time, however, the Manhattan was not Hammerstein's only operatic enterprise. Exhilarated by his success in New York, the impresario had recently built a larger theater in Philadelphia, initiating an opera season there on November 17, 1908, with Labia, Dalmores, and Renaud in *Carmen*. Three special trains were arranged out of New York for the Philadelphia Opera House opening. But the cost of running two concurrent seasons soon proved staggering and eventaully sealed Hammerstein's doom. While the Manhattan continued to fare quite well, the Philadelphia Opera House would hang like a giant albatross around Hammerstein's neck.

Inside the Metropolitan as well as the Manhattan companies there was strain during the 1908-09 season. Campanini and Hammerstein quarreled, resulting in the conductor's decision not to return the following year; consequently the artistic quality at the Manhattan suffered noticeably. At the Metroplitan Gatti-Casazza and Andreas Dippel feuded all season, although it became evident early that Gatti had won the support of the board of directors. Dippel was very much on the defensive. Financially, the Metropolitan closed its season showing losses of $205,201, the largest sum to date; the Manhattan reportedly made $229,000, although Hammerstein's overall situation was far less bright. The drain of the Philadelphia Opera House meant that the impresario was forced to use profits from his Victoria Theater to cover much of the increased opera costs.

To offset Hammerstein's expanded ventures and to strengthen his own position with the company, Dippel took the lead in getting the Metropolitan board to sanction the opening of the New Theater uptown (where the former tenor planned to stage drama and light opera); he made preparations for extensive out-of-town seasons in Philadelphia, Baltimore, and Brooklyn, and an exchange arrangement with the new Boston Opera Company. Hammerstein, on the other hand, was preparing a second season for Philadelphia, had announced forays into Baltimore, Washington, Brooklyn, Boston, Pittsburgh, and Cincinnati, and was talking about a new opera house in Chicago. On November 8, 1909, the Boston Opera House opened with a resident company managed by British impresario Henry Russell, son of the composer of "Woodman, Spare that Tree." The inaugural production was *La Gioconda* performed by a cast headed by Nordica. That same evening Hammerstein opened the Manhattan with Massenet's *Herodiade*, starring Cavalieri, Dalmores, and Renaud. He was frankly capitalizing on the Salome epidemic he had stirred up the season before. Still that same night the Metropolitan launched a season of twenty performances in Brooklyn with Farrar as Manon. Within a week the Metropolitan, under Dippel's command, had initiated seasons in Philadelphia, Baltimore, and at the New Theater in New York. The Metropolitan itself opened on November 15, with Toscanini conducting a *Gioconda* that featured Destinn and Caruso.

Suddenly there was more activity in the opera world than the country had ever known. The recent wave of immigration from Italy and southeastern Europe had produced a greater demand for opera in cities along the East Coast, but the war between Hammerstein and the Metropolitan served as the real reason for the increased attendance at the opera houses. Hammerstein had clearly gotten carried away with his own success and entertained fantasies he could never have sustained. The Metropolitan demonstrated confusion about Hammerstein's out-of-town attack, but was fearful enough to listen to Dippel's argument in favor of "fighting Hammerstein with fire." The Metropolitan therefore entered a period of aggressive imperialism—in part to preempt Hammerstein, but also to allow Dippel to focus on activities outside the house itself. The Metropolitan not only had the struggle with Hammerstein to deal with, but its own civil war as well. Each of the combatants had maneuvered themselves toward an extreme, and Hammerstein and the Metropolitan were both dangerously overextended financially. Yet there was no turning back. The fight would be to the death. Either Hammerstein would succeed in his dream of ruining the Metropolitan, or he himself would be crushed under the weight of his own empire.

The Manhattan's fourth season was conducted in an atmosphere of nervous excitement. Mary Garden repeated her success as Salome and participated in the American premiere of two works by Massenet, *Sapho* and *Griselidis*. Neither was particularly successful; *Sapho* was dropped after three performances. Tetrazzini returned on the second night of the season, plumper than ever, making her entrance as Violetta dressed in "an extraordinary gown of blue satin, gold meshes and diamonds" and blowing kisses to the audience all the while. Making his American debut as Alfredo that evening was the twenty-five year-old John McCormack, who looked even younger, but sang like a veteran. The major new opera that year was Strauss's *Elektra*, another American premiere, but sung in French. Hammerstein lavished much on the production, including months of preparation, extra rehearsals, and an augmented orchestra. Mariette Mazarin, the Elektra, proved especially powerful. But with Campanini's departure something had gone out of the company. "What had been brilliant and sparkling was now flat and routine," Garden remembered. Yet Hammerstein squandered money, putting together expensive mountings of operas like *Lakme* and *Andrea Chenier* that were presented only once. "No doubt his age and ego, as well as years of overwork, were determining factors during the final two seasons," John F. Cone, historian of the Manhattan Opera House, concludes of Hammerstein, paving the way for the impresario's self-destruction.

Gatti-Casazza's season meanwhile was highlighted by the debut of the burly Czech tenor Leo Slezak as Otello, a production of Gluck's *Orfeo* with

Homer, and a new staging of *Tristan*—all with Toscanini at the helm. Among the several novelties was Tchaikovsky's *Pique-Dame* under Mahler's direction. On March 21, 1910, Mahler conducted his last performance at the Metropolitan; he died in Vienna the following year.

The moment of defeat for Hammerstein had come. Even in the face of disaster, he recklessly continued to overstretch himself financially. Since he had made little effort to cultivate society and business leaders, even alienating the Clarence Mackays who had been sympathetic, he had few avenues of support in time of crisis. While the Metropolitan, to be sure, had suffered heavy losses during the past four seasons—heavier than Hammerstein's—the older house had the backing of the wealthy. Otto Kahn alone contributed an average of $100,000 a year to the company's operating expense, and Kahn, a Jewish financier, was not even among the Metropolitan's boxholders. With expenses at the Philadelphia Opera House again proving murderous, Hammerstein's surrender was inevitable. The vanquished Oscar's only hope was to frighten his opposition into as painless a settlement as possible.

On April 26, 1910, Arthur Hammerstein, representing his father, met with Metropolitan board members in the New York home of Otto Kahn. An agreement was eventually reached whereby Hammerstein sold his entire opera holdings, except for the Manhattan Opera House, to a delegate of the Metropolitan. Title to the Philadelphia Opera House and all scenery, stage properties, costumes, and scores in the Manhattan's repertoire would be transferred to the Metropolitan emissary. Hammerstein's exclusive rights to certain operas, together with his contracts with Garden, Tetrazzini, Dalmores, Renaud, and others, would be included in the transaction. The Metropolitan would be free to use these contracts and assets in whatever way its directors saw fit. Finally Hammerstein agreed that neither he nor his sons would attempt to produce grand opera in New York, Philadelphia, Boston, or Chicago for a period of ten years. In return he would receive a cash payment of $1,200,000.

The great opera war was over. To the end Hammerstein remained the darling of the press, much of the public, intellectuals, and progressive critics like James G. Huneker. But the Metropolitan had the funds, enough to buy the Manhattan impresario off once the cracks in his enterprise became obvious. Hammerstein used $900,000 of the money he received to pay his debts. The rest he shortly invested in an opera house in London, suggesting once again that for the impetuous Oscar opera was indeed "a disease." The venture went bankrupt two years later. The Metropolitan immediately began negotiating with a group from Chicago who were interested in forming an opera company there. Shortly the Chicago Grand Opera Company was organized with Metropolitan support much in evidence. Otto Kahn even served as the new company's vice-president and contributed $5000 to help launch the project. Andreas Dippel became the Chicago Grand Opera's general manager. Most of Hammerstein's scenery, costumes, rights, and contracts—for which the Metropolitan directors needed to find some use—

were sold to the Chicago company.

The Chicago Grand Opera Company began as a satellite of the Metropolitan, at first giving performances in the Philadelphia Opera House as well as in the Chicago Auditorium. The company's principal backers were Harold F. McCormick, head of the International Harvester Company, and financier Charles G. Dawes, later Vice President of the United States. Over the next ten years Harold and Edith Rockefeller McCormick came to dominate the company more and more, personally underwriting an increasing portion of the annual deficit and freeing the management to produce sumptuous opera without much regard for costs. Artistically the Chicago Opera inherited the Hammerstein legacy, modified slightly by Metropolitan influence. Modern French opera was initially the crux of the Chicago repertoire; Mary Garden remained a pivotal figure for twenty years; and Cleofonte Campanini even returned to become the company's artistic director.

The Chicago Grand Opera Company opened on November 3, 1910, with a production of *Aida*. Then came Garden and the cream of the Hammerstein repertoire: *Pelleas et Melisande, Louise, Thais*, and *Salome*. But whereas opera at the Manhattan had enjoyed Hammerstein's unique independence, in Chicago it was subject to the same social pressures that operated on the Metropolitan. And *Salome* was again banished. Leroy T. Steward, Chicago's police chief, who had been sent to check out the performance, reported that it was disgusting. "Miss Garden wallowed around like a cat in a bed of catnip," Steward snorted. "If the same show were produced on Halsted street the people would call it cheap, but over at the Auditorium they say it's art." Amid much controversy, the Opera's board of directors withdrew the work after two performances, fearing that the company's future might be jeopardized if charges of indecency were allowed to continue. Mary Garden's reaction was typical of the artists' point of view: "I always bow down to the ignorant and try to make them understand, but I ignore the illiterate." Charles Dalmores, the production's Herod, felt that Chicago would become the laughingstock. "Why, in Europe we talk about America as the land of the free. You are not," the tenor insisted. "Berlin and Vienna will laugh when they hear this. They will say: 'The great Chicago! What is it? Still a manufacturing city without the true love of art.'"

But with *Salome*'s withdrawal things returned to normal. Sammarco, McCormack, and Renaud—all Hammerstein veterans—sang with the new company. *The Tales of Hoffman*, one of the Manhattan's great successes, was staged, and Melba appeared as Mimi and Violetta. Farrar and Scotti teamed for *Tosca* and *Madama Butterfly*, representing the Metropolitan faction, while the season was closed by Caruso himself.

Andreas Dippel remained with the Chicago Opera for three years. After his resignation the company essentially became independent of New York; with its reorganization in 1915, even Otto Kahn was no longer on the board of directors. While the Chicago repertoire gradually became more Italianate, the

Hammerstein heritage was in evidence for decades. Luisa Tetrazzini first sang in Chicago in 1911, but gradually the company began to discover its own stars, notably baritone Titta Ruffo, tenor Lucien Muratore, dramatic soprano Rosa Raisa, mezzo soprano Cyrena Van Gordon, and coloratura Amelita Galli-Curci. Mary Garden's popularity was constant, and she added new operas to her repertoire almost every season: Massenet's *Cendrillion* and *Don Quichotte*, *Carmen*, *Tosca* (which she sang in French, except for *"Vissi d'arte"*), Fevrier's *Monna Vanna*, Montemezzi's *L'Amore dei Tre Re* (her only role in Italian), and Victor Herbert's *Natoma* (in which she played an Indian maiden). *Natoma* was given its world premiere by the company in Philadelphia early in its second year, in the hope of producing the first great American opera, but the work was dropped after two seasons. Far more success accompanied the American premiere of Wolf-Ferrari's *The Jewels of the Madonna*, presented by the Chicago Opera in 1912 with the composer in the pit. The opera continued as an interesting novelty for many years. Franchetti's *Cristoforo Colombo* received its first American staging by the Chicago forces in 1913, with Ruffo as Columbus and Raisa as Isabella of Aragon, and Leoncavallo conducted his *Zingari* two years later. Other American premieres included Saint-Saens' *Dejanire* in 1915, with Muratore singing the role of Hercules; Mascagni's *Isabeau* in 1917, based on the Lady Godiva legend and featuring Raisa; and Montemezzi's *La Nave* in 1919, conducted by the composer and staged by Norman Bel Geddes at a cost of $60,000.

Meanwhile Harold and Edith Rockefeller McCormick presided over the Chicago Opera like benevolent eighteenth-century monarchs, providing the social leadership and paying a lion's share of the bills. Mrs. McCormick (John D. Rockefeller's daughter) genuinely loved opera. At dinners in the McCormick home before performances the hostess reputedly sat at one end of the table with a clock beside her, insisting that the dinner progress according to a strict time schedule. She served no liquor, and if a guest dallied too long over his food, he might have his plate snatched out from under him, as Mrs. McCormick indicated that time for a particular course was up. The party not only arrived at the Auditorium on time, but in their box Edith McCormick sat straight in her chair, her eyes glued to the stage throughout the performance.

By the eve of World War I the Chicago Opera Association ranked second only to the Metropolitan among American opera companies. The New Theater in New York had never been a success, in part because of its location. The Boston Opera Company had lasted only five seasons, filing bankruptcy proceedings in 1915. Fortune Gallo had initiated a fairly durable touring company, the San Carlo Opera, in 1913, but traveling companies like the Boston Ideals, the Castle Square Opera Company, and those headed by Clara Louise Kellogg, Emma Juch, Emma Abbott, and Henry Savage had all vanished. The Tivoli Opera House in San Francisco, where Tetrazzini first sang in the United States, was destroyed in the 1906 earthquake. The French Opera House in New Orleans, reopened after the war, burned in the early morning of December 4, 1919, and was never rebuilt. Novelist Harnett Kane, then a boy of nine, recalled being taken to the ruins at Bourbon and Toulouse Streets: "I remember the steaming wreckage, and my surprise that the ladies with odd foreign accents were crying so hard. This one had been the company's Delilah, that one the Gilda. This singer had lost jewels in her dressing room, that one a complete wardrobe."

At the Metropolitan Gatti-Casazza breathed more easily with Hammerstein off the scene and his principal competition safely relocated on Lake Michigan. Toscanini remained his principal conductor until 1915, and during that time the house enjoyed both financial well-being and a period of remarkable artistic accomplishment. The first world premiere in Metropolitan history occurred on December 10, 1910, when Puccini's *La Fanciulla del West* was given amid much publicity. The libretto was an adaptation of the David Belasco play that had enjoyed enormous success on Broadway a few years before with Blanche Bates, and the public grew excited at the prospect of a grand opera with an American locale. Both Puccini and Belasco were present during final rehearsals. Toscanini conducted a cast headed by Destinn as Minnie, Caruso as Dick Johnson, and Pasquale Amato as Jack Rance. Less than three weeks later, Humperdinck's *Konigskinder*, another world premiere, provided Farrar, as the Goose-Girl, one of her most fetching roles, aided by a flock of live geese. Giordano's *Madame Sans-Gene* was heard in the house for the first time anywhere in 1915, with Farrar as the laundress, Amato as the Little Corporal, and Toscanini in the pit. Enrique Granados came the following season for the world premiere of his colorful *Goyescas*, a journey that ended tragically when his returning ship, the *Sussex*, was torpedoed by a German submarine in the English Channel. Neither Granados nor his wife survived.

Gatti-Casazza dreamed of discovering "some good American operas" which he could produce and maintain in the repertoire. In 1910 he mounted the first American opera performed at the Metropolitan, Frederick Converse's *The Pipes of Desire*. The work had been given a semi-professional staging in Boston four years before. The Metropolitan cast was headed by Pittsburgh born Louise Homer. The opera is a one act fantasy, full of mermaids, sylphs, salamanders, and gnomes, yet it was the first production sung in English at the Metropolitan during a regular season. Gatti's feeling that native compositions should be encouraged was strong enough that he convinced the Metropolitan's board of directors to offer a prize of $10,000 for the best original grand opera by an American. More than thirty scores were submitted. The jury eventually selected as the winner *Mona* by Horatio Parker, head of the Yale music department. A full-length work, *Mona* was staged by the Metropolitan on March 14, 1912, with Homer in the title role and a predominately American cast. The opera was almost a parody of Bellini's *Norma*. Like Norma, Mona is a British druid in love with a Roman soldier. Still the druid is determined to drive the Romans out of Britain. When her kinsmen are slaughtered in an attack, Mona kills her lover, thinking he has betrayed their plan. The score contains passages of considerable beauty, but the characters fail to come to life. The first performance was greeted with much enthusiasm, yet the house was half-empty for the second. "Parker was a learned musician," Gatti observed, "but not a man of the theatre."

In search of another American opera the manager next turned to a composer who definitely *was* of the theater, one who had virtually grown up in the Metropolitan itself. In 1913 Walter Damrosch's *Cyrano de Bergerac* was performed for the first time, with Frances Alda and Pasquale Amato. The libretto had been adapted from Edmond Rostand by critic W. J. Henderson. Damrosch's first opera, *The Scarlet Letter*, had been staged in Boston by the Damrosch Opera Company in 1896. Johanna Gadski, a great Isolde, had sung the role of Hester Prynne. Damrosch later admitted that the score "had been conceived under the overwhelming influence of Wagner." When Anton Seidl heard *The Scarlet Letter* in New York, he called it a "New England Nibelung Trilogy." The opera was shelved after six performances. *Cyrano de Bergerac* was musically more mature, but proved scarcely more stageworthy. It's sets and properties soon joined *Mona*'s in the Metropolitan warehouse.

Victor Herbert's one act *Madeleine* was produced by Gatti-Casazza in 1914 and lasted for six performances. Gatti called it "a mild success." After a lapse of three seasons the manager tried again, this time offering Reginald de Koven's *The Canterbury Pilgrims*. Edith Mason sang the role of the Prioress, but De Koven's efforts were judged inferior to Herbert's. It was during a performance of *The Canterbury Pilgrims*, however, that word came that President Wilson had asked Congress for a declaration of war on Germany. Artur Bodanzky, the conductor, immediately struck up "The Star-Spangled Banner."

The most successful of Gatti's American operas was Charles Wakefield Cadman's *Shanewis*, the only native work to remain at the Metropolitan longer than one season. Initially staged on March 23, 1918, *Shanewis* continued in the repertoire for another year. Cadman had spent much of his life studying Indian tribal lore and song and selected for his opera a subject with which he had some familiarity. The work opens with a costume party in the southern California home of the wealthy Mrs. J. Asher Everton. Present is Mrs. Everton's Indian protege, Shanewis, whose vocal studies are financed by the prominent clubwoman. Lionel, the fiance of Mrs. Everton's daughter, becomes fascinated with the Indian girl. When Shanewis returns home to a reservation in Oklahoma, Lionel follows. Aware that he is engaged to Mrs. Everton's daughter, the Indian girl refuses his advances. When Lionel persists, he is shot with a bow and arrow by Shanewis' Indian lover. Cadman's score flows smoothly and includes Indian dances and a great deal of local color, while the text is free of flagrant absurdities. At the Metropolitan premiere Sophie Braslau sang the title role, and the Cadman opera was combined with an American ballet, Henry F. Gilbert's *The Dance in Place Congo*. Of the 110 novelties Gatti-Casazza produced during his Metropolitan tenure, thirteen were premieres of American operas.

New singers were introduced by Gatti in the years before World War I, legends like Lucrezia Bori, Frieda Hempel (the Metropolitan's first Marschallin), Giovanni Martinelli, and Claudia Muzio. Besides the Italian repertoire Toscanini conducted a Gallic *Manon*, several of the Gluck operas, the house's first *Boris Godunov*, and extensive Wagner. Before Toscanini withdrew from the Metropolitan in a fit of temper in 1915, German opera had become well represented in the repertoire. During the 1915-16 and 1916-17 seasons complete *Ring* cycles were given under the direction of Artur Bodanzky.

In the spring of 1917 *Tristan, Die Meistersinger,* and a Good Friday presentation of *Parsifal* all went on as scheduled. Then in April, Johanna Gadski was urged to retire from the company, supposedly because of a deterioration in her voice and art. The singer's marriage to a reserve officer in the German army was well known, however, and it was said that her home had been the scene of a celebration after the sinking of the *Lusitania*. By fall Gatti-Casazza had announced that no German operas would be given during the coming season, nor any other work that "could cause the least offense to the most patriotic Americans." In October the New York Board of Education ruled that German operas were not to be discussed in the classroom, and almost simultaneously the Museum of Natural History forbade a lecture on *Parsifal*.

In 1915 the Chicago Opera Association had staged its first complete *Ring*, presented on successive Sunday afternoons. After a *Rheingold* performance the *Chicago Tribune* reported that the audience "sat rapt before the stately unfolding of this epic music drama. No such tribute to any performance here has been paid within our memory." The Wagnerian cycle was repeated the following year and was almost a total fiasco. Letters of protest poured into the management and press. One writer was shocked that anything so immoral as *Die Walkure*, with its incestuous relationship between Siegmund and Sieglinde, would be staged on the Sabbath. Wagner's music was condemned as barbaric, and attendance fell off sharply. Apparently even the city's German population, traditionally so reliable in their enthusiasm for Wagner, stayed away—perhaps because they had become absorbed into mainstream American life by this time, more probably because they feared being condemned as un-American. Maestro Campanini staged nine German operas that year, the most he ever gave in one season, and seemed little disturbed by their slight attendance. "When the day comes," he argued, "that art is so impersonal that it is not touched by nationality, then we shall have a thinner, more meager art; we shall have a purely technical art." But no German opera was given during the 1917-18 season.

During the war season in Chicago, some of the ladies actually knitted at performances, while intermissions found "four-minute men" giving speeches on the sacrifices necessary to "stop the Hun." During a performance of *Dinorah* with Galli-Curci, conductor Campanini suddenly heard a hissing sound behind him. Someone had placed a bomb under a vacant seat on the right hand-center aisle. Campanini quickly stopped the opera, struck up "The Star-Spangled Banner," and ordered Galli-Curci before the footlights. "Sing, madame," he commanded, and sing she did—an octave too high. Meanwhile a fireman sitting nearby rushed to the empty seat, wrapped the bomb in his coat, and carried it outside. It all happened so fast that the audience scarcely had time to panic, although one man is supposed to have jumped over the orchestra rail and hidden behind a cello. Fortunately the bomb was a crude, homemade affair that failed to go off. The person who planted it was later picked up by the police, but his name was not released. In an atmosphere of war hysteria, it was difficult to convince many people that the whole episode had not been a German plot.

German opera did not return to the Chicago repertoire until the 1920-21 season, when *Lohengrin* and *Die Walkure* were both given in English. The latter was even billed as *The Valkyrie*. Gatti-Casazza staged Weber's *Oberon* in translation in 1918 and a trimmed version of *Parsifal* the next year, with an English text prepared by critic Henry Krehbiel. Wagner in German was not restored at the Metropolitan until 1921.

Gatti's opening in 1918 took place on the very day that the Armistice was signed, November 11. At the end of the first act of *Samson and Delilah*, the entire company was massed on stage for the singing of the anthems of the Allied Nations. The highlight of the season came on December 14, with the world premiere of Puccini's three one act operas *Il Tabarro, Suor Angelica*, and *Gianni Schicchi*. Muzio sang Giorgetta in the grisly *Tabarro*; Farrar was the hapless Suor Angelica; but *Gianni Schicchi* scored the biggest hit, with Giuseppe de Luca as the roguish title character. A month earlier Verdi's *La Forza del Destino* was given in the house for the first time, with Caruso and an unknown American soprano by the name of Rosa Ponselle. It was Ponselle's introduction to the operatic stage. Six months before she and her sister Carmela were appearing in a New York vaudeville theater. Gatti-Casazza and Caruso heard them there, and Rosa was immediately signed to a Metropolitan contract. She learned Leonora, one of the most demanding roles in the Italian repertoire, over the summer. The *Forza* premiere on November 15 was an unnerving moment, but the girl from vaudeville proved a sensation. "It is vocal gold," Huneker said of her voice, "dark, rich, and ductile."

If Ponselle ushered in a new generation, another was coming to a close. On December 11, 1920, Enrico Caruso broke down during a performance of Donizetti's *L'Elisir d'Amore* on the stage of the Brooklyn Academy of Music. Refusing to take his indisposition seriously, the tenor sang three more times over Gatti-Casazza's protests. His final appearance was as Eleazar in *La Juive*, his last new role and his most penetrating character study. He collapsed again on Christmas Day with what was diagnosed as a painful case of pleurisy. He returned to Naples, where he died on August 2, 1921, at age forty-eight. In his eighteen seasons at the Metropolitan, Caruso had sung 607 times in thirty-seven different operas. During that time he had starred in sixteen opening night productions and came to command a salary of $2500 a performance.

The tenor's earnings at the Metropolitan totaled approximately a million and a half dollars, while the Victor phonograph company paid him another $1,825,000 in record royalties. Eight months after Caruso's death, Geraldine Farrar retired from the operatic stage at age forty, as she had always said she would. Her final appearance at the Metropolitan, April 22, 1922, was as the lovesick music hall singer in Leoncavallo's *Zaza*, her last great characterization. The opera had received its world premiere at the Metropolitan two seasons before, with David Belasco as stage director.

By 1920 the days when a select number of wealthy individuals alone could support grand opera were also drawing to an end. The economic reforms enacted during the recent Progressive Movement in politics, particularly the graduated income tax, had simply made exclusive patronage impossible. The financial base of the nation's opera companies had to be spread out, with the result that the control of the social elite weakened. While opera by no means became highly democratic, it did move toward a broader following. The coming of phonograph records, radio broadcasts, more dynamic music education programs, and a developing intellectual community contributed to the eventual creation of larger audiences. By World War I an ornate mahogany cabinet of a Victrola had become as much a part of the refined American parlor as the piano had been earlier. Thousands of families who would never set foot in an opera house nevertheless owned recordings of the *Lucia* sextet, Galli-Curci singing Lakme's "Bell Song," or Caruso laughing through tears in *"Vesti la giubba."* Yet unlike the symphony orchestra, opera failed to become an integral part of America's urban life. In 1920 the United States could claim only two resident opera companies, and of those the Metropolitan alone would prove permanent. While symphonic music had put down a number of firm roots and had made strides toward becoming an organic element in a few cities' cultural growth, grand opera remained far more tentative. With the conspicuous rich on the retreat opera's golden age was over; further expansion must now await the development of more sophisticated musical tastes and the evolution of a new method of financing.

CHAPTER

III

The Revolution in Dance

Despite the phenomenal success of Fanny Elssler in the early 1840s no sustained tradition of ballet developed in the United States during the nineteenth century. Foreign dancers with dynamic personalities or remarkable techniques were acclaimed from time to time, but there was no continuous succession. There were no native ballet companies and few schools where formal dance could be studied. Yet instruction in ballroom dancing was viewed by high society in the post-Civil War period as a desirable means for instilling their young with a sense of beauty, rhythm, and poise. For almost a hundred years, from 1835 to 1920, Allen Dodworth and his nephew George dictated the standards in social dance through their Dancing Academy in New York. By 1880 dancing masters had become recognized arbiters of social grace, while learning to dance was considered both recreational and healthy. Young ladies of proper background were frequently enrolled in ballet classes to correct poor posture, knock-knees, and flat feet. Still professional dancers were held in low esteem. Male ballet artists were barely tolerated, and ballerinas—no matter how pure their art—were supposed depraved by definition.

Dance performances in late nineteenth-century America tended toward the more robust genre, closely related to the popular theater. With the founding of the Metropolitan Opera in 1883 dancers were imported for a resident *corps de ballet*, and opera ballet took on some signs of permanence. The great Danish ballerina Adeline Genee won the plaudits of New York in 1908, but it was not until the arrival of Anna Pavlova two years later that the excitement created by Elssler was duplicated. Pavlova's American debut took place at the Metropolitan Opera House, February 28, 1910, on a double bill with the Massenet opera *Werther*. Her success was instantaneous. The Metropolitan manager, Gatti-Casazza, was none too sympathetic with dance in general, and the Russian danseuse had been engaged largely through the efforts of Otto Kahn. Since *Werther* alone was a full three acts, it was nearly 11:30 P.M. before the curtain rose on Delibes *Coppelia*, the vehicle selected for Pavlova's debut, but the response was sensational. The ballerina's partner, the athletic Mokhail Mordkin, was nearly as enthusiastically received as Pavlova herself. The nation's slumbering interest in ballet was suddenly revived, but for the next twenty-five years ballet to most Americans meant Pavlova.

Anna Pavlova was born in St. Petersburg in January, 1881, of peasant parents. Her father died when Anna was still quite young, and her mother worked as a laundress. The premature child was so frail that she was near death twice—once from scarlet fever, later from diphtheria. When she was about eight, Pavlova was taken to a performance of the Tchaikovsky ballet *The Sleeping Beauty*, whereupon she grew determined to study dance so that one day she might perform Princess Aurora. At ten the sickly girl entered the Imperial Ballet School, attached to the Mariinski Theater in St. Petersburg, gradually overcoming her ill health. In 1899 she made her debut at the Mariinski Theater, dancing Aurora in *The Sleeping Beauty*, and within seven years had become *prima ballerina*. Pavlova was a different kind of dancer, thrilling audiences with the fire of a magnetic personality. What she lacked in technical virtuosity, she compensated for in interpretation. A woman of radiant beauty, she possessed an unquenchable artistry, was light in her movements, unbounded in her style, and embodied on stage the Spirit of Classicism. She danced with simplicity, with a lambent sincerity, injecting vitality into the lyricism of classical ballet.

In 1912 Pavlova exiled herself from Russia and took up residence in London. She made numerous coast-to-coast tours of the United States, appearing in opera houses, auditoriums, schools, vaudeville houses, and movie theaters, stirring uncertain audiences with the spirit of her technique. On her first American tour she danced with Mordkin, supported by members of the Imperial Russian Ballet. Pavlova's perennial specialty was *The Dying Swan*, choreographed for her in 1905 by Michel Fokine, while Mordkin's was *The Bow and Arrow Dance*. Delighted with his virile appearance, American audiences persistently observed Mordkin's physique and endurance in terms of field and track experience. Indicating something of the level of appreciation in the country, the souvenir booklet for the tour stated that the dancers were "introducing an art new to America, the interpretation of the ponderous messages of the great composers through the most primitive and yet potent of mediums—motion!" Advertising declared: "Not a line is spoken, not a word sung." Mordkin later described the tour as "a nightmare." The company gave from eight to eleven performances a week, as opposed to the customary two at the Imperial Ballet. At the end of their second American season Pavlova and Mordkin separated. He promptly established himself in this country as a teacher, while she continued her grinding tours of the United States until 1925.

Year after year as the Pavlova legend solidified, *The Dying Swan* remained her symbol. Under her spell little girls all across the nation flocked to ballet schools, hoping to recreate before rehearsal hall mirrors the enchanted movements they had beheld in the theater. Pavlova was not merely the first great exponent of traditional Russian ballet to visit America, she was the performing artist *par excellence*. The flow of her movement was sublime, her balance phenomenal. While her repertory was huge, including examples of Oriental dances, the classic technique was always her forte. Consequently for most Americans ballet became synonymous with toe dancing.

But in 1916 the Metropolitan Opera hosted another Russian invasion in the form of Serge Diaghilev's Ballets Russes. In contrast with Pavlova, the Diaghilev company introduced a new form of dance, one incorporating the recent reforms of Michel Fokine. Diaghilev had formed his Ballets Russes in Paris in 1909, employing Fokine as his first choreographer. With the reforms evolved by Fokine ballet became, essentially, more natural, closer to ordinary human movement. The Ballets Russes was shortly recognized as an exciting avant-garde experience in dance, while Fokine emerged as the father of modern ballet. Breaking from the formal perfection and unalterable formula of the classical technique, Fokine's innovations revolved around five basic principles. The first insisted that dance steps correspond to the period represented and the character of the individuals portrayed. The second rule demanded that dancing and gestures serve to enhance the dramatic action. The third held that the entire body must be used as an expressive instrument. The fourth emphasized the importance of ensemble. The fifth rule stated the necessity of fusing dance with the other stage arts—scene design, drama, music—into an integrated expression.

Michel Fokine, born in St. Petersburg in 1880, had graduated from the Imperial School of Ballet. Although he had been a successful soloist with the company, he had grown dissatisfied with the rigid conventions of the Mariinski Theater, where the ballerina reigned supreme, settings and costumes were stylized decorations, and dramatic structure was almost irrelevant. He proposed his reforms first to the Imperial Ballet, but withdrew when his ideas were rejected. Among the masterworks created for the Ballets Russes, in which Fokine liberated permanently the art of dance, were *Scheherazade, Prince Igor, Petrouchka, Firebird, Les Sylphides, Carnaval, Le Spectre de la Rose*, and *Coq d'Or*. The choreographer left Diaghilev in 1913, but returned a year later for another season.

The first exposure American audiences had to Fokine's innovations came during the summer of 1911 in a pirated form brought by the Diaghilev dancer Theodore Kosloff, with a company imported by vaudeville star Gertrude Hoffman. Unauthorized versions of *Scheherazade, Cleopatra*, and *Les Sylphides* were staged from memory by Miss Hoffman and Kosloff at the

Winter Garden in New York, without credit to Fokine. Although the La Saison Russe, as the company was called, met with positive response in New York, the subsequent tour was less successful.

Five years later Diaghilev himself arrived in the United States. He had taken refuge in Switzerland in 1915—his company disbanded, his funds exhausted. He was invited to present his troupe at the Metropolitan Opera House the next year and to engage in an American tour under the Metropolitan's auspices. The arrangement was a bad one from the beginning. Diaghilev accepted the offer with bad grace, even though it saved his company during World War I. Gatti-Casazza was still indifferent to dance and downright hostile to Diaghilev. The Metropolitan had its own resident ballet company, and there was much fear of competition. As with Pavlova earlier, the Diaghilev troupe had been engaged primarily because Otto Kahn had insisted.

The venture was fraught with all sorts of personal friction and misunderstanding. Diaghilev was arrogant, irritating, often unreasonable. Fokine had left the company to return to the Mariinski Theater, and neither of Diaghilev's great stars, Karsavina and Nijinsky, were initially available for the American tour. Instead Adolph Bolm came to the United States with the Ballets Russes in the double capacity of choreographer and *premier danseur*. American audiences, on the other hand, were entirely too conservative for Diaghilev's pioneering efforts, while the Metropolitan auspices remained halfhearted at best.

The Fokine works were still fundamental to the Ballets Russes' repertoire, and Americans frequently did not know what to make of them. The voluptuous *Scheherazade* was considered shocking, and *Narcisse* was banned from the Metropolitan as a perversion. The management's explanation that *Narcisse* was from classical literature and represented the spirit of youth rather than overt homosexuality made little impression on a scandalized public. Toward the end of the Ballets Russes' first American season, Nijinsky was released from Hungary and joined the company in New York. His *L'Apres-midi d'un Faune* created quite a commotion, since the Faune is amorously inclined towards seven nymphs. Authorities were convinced that this could not be altogether wholesome, and at one performance the police arrived and carted the Diaghilev company off to jail.

More discriminating Americans, however, caught the excitement of the Ballets Russes performances. Unlike the Royal Ballet and the Bolshoi, the Diaghilev programs featured two or three short works instead of a single, full-length production. The dancing contained a vigor not previously associated with ballet, while scenic effects were used skillfully and dramatically. Under Nijinsky's influence the male dancer assumed more important recognition than ever before in this country, encroaching upon the prestige of the ballerina for the first time. Even with the opposition from prudish factions the Ballets Russes had enticed the United States with a stirring new theatrical experience and laid a groundwork for the development of modern dance.

Still the tour was not a financial success, and at the end of the first season Diaghilev departed in a rage. Nijinsky was appointed director of the company's second American tour, although he was temperamentally unsuited for an administrative position. Adolph Bolm continued with the company at Diaghilev's urging, to assist Nijinsky with managerial details. While visiting the United States Nijinsky created *Til Eulenspiegel*, set to Richard Strauss's music, in association with the dynamic young stage designer Robert Edmond Jones. Critical opinion was sharply divided, but the ballet was withdrawn from the repertory after a few performances in New York and Boston. This failure aborted another promising Nijinsky-Jones collaboration to the strains of Franz Liszt's *Mephisto Waltz*. For two years after his American appearances Nijinsky had to be confined to the surveillance of psychiatrists.

Fokine came to the United States in 1919 to stage the dances for the musical *Aphrodite*, based on Pierre Louys' book. The choreographer never regained his inventiveness after leaving Diaghilev and in 1921 founded a school of ballet in New York City. Later, with his wife, he organized a small company, the Fokine Ballet, composed largely of advanced students. The Metropolitan Opera commissioned Bolm to stage *Le Coq d'Or* and in 1919 restored *Petrouchka*. The choreography for both was patterned on Fokine, although the original creations gradually paled with constant revivals. Bolm prepared a work of his own for the Chicago Opera in 1919, *The Birthday of the Infanta*. The Russian choreographer collaborated on the production with a number of American artists—composer John Alden Carpenter, designer Robert Edmond Jones, and ballerina Ruth Page.

The innovations that had taken place in dance before World War I, radical as they were, were nevertheless part of a larger revolution. The times themselves were provocative, and the arts generally were rebelling toward modernism. Since the great scientific discoveries of Copernicus and Newton, western civilization had been in a metamorphic state, but the pulse had quickened with industrialization and the accompanying rise of the city. Then came Darwinian biology, Freudian psychology, and the nascent precepts of sociology and anthropology, rounding out man's image of himself. As a result of this scientific emphasis, the arts began to consider life more realistically, became freer and bolder in their interpretation of the human condition. Under the influence of Darwin artists stressed the primitive aspect of man and his capacity for survival, while after Freud the irrational, emotional facets of the human personality were probed; gradually the inner self came to be recognized in relation to the individual external personality, as well as collective society.

In France novelist Gustave Flaubert published *Madame Bovary* in 1857, a scrupulously truthful portrait of bourgeois life, paving the way for a greater realism in letters. Twenty years later Emile Zola was writing in a more naturalistic vein, viewing life as a struggle and man's fate as determined by social and natural forces over which the individual has no control. In Russia

Dostoevsky revealed a psychological imagination and a power of dramatic construction that would influence dozens of writers in the century ahead.

Similarly in painting Courbet had looked to nature for a greater realism, while Daumier emerged as a pioneer of naturalism, producing art that was powerfully direct. During his early career Cezanne sought to create purely imaginary compositions, expressing his own internal moods, yet his portraits breathed with psychological undertones. His fundamental concern was to exalt his own feelings rather than to represent phenomena of the visible world. Eventually he came to look upon nature with a more contemplative eye and became increasingly precise and methodical in his technique. Cezanne's philosophy of art evolved toward a belief in some underlying, permanent reality, consistent with the basic instincts of human nature. In his search for a formal unity he increasingly relied on geometry for harmony; he saw the world in planes, spheres, cubes, and cylinders. By the 1870s Renoir, Monet, and the Impressionists were freer, emphasizing mood over objective reality and feelings, haziness, and the fleeting over order. Reflecting their belief that life was more than what could be empirically observed, the Impressionists experimented much with technique, particularly with light and color, to achieve the desired effects. For Post-Impressionists like Gauguin and Van Gogh color was vital, and both were beguiled by nature, the primitive, and the commonplace. Van Gogh's work especially was intensely emotional in its display of the ordinary. In a less exact way Matisse and the Fauves were fascinated with the primitive and the expressiveness of color, while Picasso and the Cubists were more concerned with the three-dimensional, the irrational, the subconscious; they endeavored to reveal more than the eye could see. Altering the whole western concept of what the artist should do, the Abstractionists openly rejected objective reality in an effort to capture human emotion. In a variety of ways each of these painters was striving for a greater truth, often by broadening the concept of reality to include personal feelings, illusions, the intangible, and individual creativity.

In Norway Henrik Ibsen introduced realism and human psychology into the theater, beginning in the late 1870s, by stripping his dramas of artifice and melodrama. Ibsen was attempting to find in drama the same truth and naturalism that the modernists in dance sought to express. At the turn of the century the Russian theatrical producer Stanislavsky revolutionized acting by infusing the art with the idea of psychological motivation, sometimes at the expense of gentility and ethereal beauty. More immediately influential on modern dance was the earlier Delsartian method, which brought to the stage a humanistic style as opposed to a behavior that was larger than life. The expressions of everyday life replaced the stylized gestures of the stage. Delsarte was a French teacher of music who made a scientific analysis of gestures and emotional expressions, studying the movements of people under all sorts of stress. He even visited morgues and mines after an explosion to watch how the bereaved displayed their grief. He studied children at play from behind bushes in parks and noted the differences in behavior between attendants who loved children and those who did not. His theories on the expressional capacity of the body greatly influenced the graphic arts.

Yet the intellectual and artistic revolt that had crystallized in Europe during the late nineteenth century did not fulminate in the United States until just before World War I. Clearly there had been a serious conflict in American values since the Civil War, and the contest between rural and urban attitudes had grown increasingly heated as the nineteenth century progressed. But it was not until the years 1912 through 1917 that the "end of American innocence," prompted by obvious limitations in an ungainly material system and the complications of industrialized society, became apparent especially among intellectuals and the cultural elite. Henry May has argued convincingly that Americans on the eve of World War I were beginning to move away from their traditional optimism, denying the frontier canon that anything is possible, that no social or economic evil is too great to remedy. Likewise the nation's more sophisticated segment had broken with rural absolutes and were openly questioning materialism, conventional morality, inherited cultural standards, and even the democratic process.

As the first cracks began to appear in the wall of American traditionalism, real pessimism, occasionally blatant cynicism or nihilism, was evidenced from certain circles. Bohemian cults appeared in Chicago, New York, San Francisco, New Orleans, and elsewhere, largely rejecting free enterprise materialism, puritanical morality, and "rugged" individualism, substituting instead a less competitive value system and emphasizing the worth of art, beauty, and personal fulfillment. Expatriates like T. S. Eliot, Ezra Pound, and Gertrude Stein had grown so disgusted with puritanism and stifling commercialism in America, a country they considered to be an esthetic desert, that they fled to London, Paris, or Italy.

The rebellion in ideas was accompanied by significant changes in politics and radical innovations in art. Twenty-five years after Flaubert wrote *Madame Bovary*, William Dean Howells formulated a realism in American letters that took cognizance of urban society and industrial problems. Like the scientist, Howells gathered his data from observation, presented it factually and in as objective a manner as possible. His reality in large measure was achieved through detail, by heaping specific upon specific, somewhat as Chaucer had done. Henry James, another pioneer in American realism, also relied on massive detail, although his psychological depth was far greater than Howells'. By the turn of the century Theodore Dreiser emerged as a distinguished example of American naturalism, questioning his society's moral code, materialism, and rags-to-riches ideal. Like Zola in France, Dreiser saw existence as a struggle, where the weak perish and the most adaptable triumph. Similar to their European counterparts, American naturalists tended to focus on the primitive and sensual side of humanity, often dwelling on the sordid, unpleasant, bestial aspects of life; yet Stephen Crane more than any other recognized the importance of emotions, illusions, and the irrational in man's make-up. Early in the twentieth century Edgar

Lee Masters and Sherwood Anderson led the assault on the village in American literature, attacking small town bigotry, hypocrisy, social pressures, Victorian mores, and ignorance.

As art in the United States became more truthful, its dependence on European archetypes grew less rigid. With the shattering of old ideals, the premise that art, by definition, must be pretty began a long retreat. Realistic painters like Winslow Homer and Thomas Eakins not only demonstrated an interest in the American scene, but concerned themselves with an accurate representation of the ordinary, the less than perfect. Eakins lost his position at the Pennsylvania Academy for using a naked male model in classes where there were women students, while in his own works he dared to show a surgeon at the operating table with blood on his hands, the lowbrow sport of boxing, and physical blemishes in portraiture of the upper middle class. By the turn of the century the "Ash Can School" painted urban dwellers in everyday situations and humble workers at their toils—a sharp break from the earlier notion that art should be aristocratic, ennobling, and grand. At Alfred Stieglitz's gallery in New York and, more significantly, at the Armory Show in 1913 the American public received its first real look at modernism in art. Marcel Duchamp's cubistic *Nude Descending a Staircase* titillated many, although more enlightened viewers were dazzled by the variety of Post-Impressionist paintings on display at New York's 69th Regiment Armory. For most Americans this was the initial exposure to Picasso, Matisse, and the Abstractionists, and the Armory showing came as a cultural bombshell.

Paralleling the development of a more indigenous and individualistic painting, architecture in America evolved toward less ornate, more utilitarian, and in several regards more truthful forms. Henry H. Richardson in the late 1870s and 1880s had stripped his buildings of much of the extraneous decoration that had characterized construction in this country since the Gothic influx. Richardson's "American Romanesque" was a heavy, massive, unadorned style that its formulator considered in keeping with America's pragmatic ideals. More revolutionary was Louis Sullivan's functionalism, which revolved around the concept that the purpose of a building should determine its form. Embellishment to Sullivan should be used sparingly, must fit into the overall mood of a structure, and not be added for pretentious reasons. The skyscraper, the architect held, was ideal for the city, since space was at a premium and land expensive. The height of a skyscraper should be emphasized by accentuating the vertical lines, so that every inch became "a proud and soaring thing." Sullivan's protege, Frank Lloyd Wright, was even more determined that the physical surroundings of a building should influence its form. Basically anti-urban, Wright designed his "prairie homes" in the early twentieth century, in and around Chicago, stressing the horizontal lines to harmonize with the flatness of the Middle West. Strongly anticipating the frustration and alienation of modern man in an industrial complex, Wright sought to return his clients to the serenity and freedom of a "natural" shelter by exposing unpainted wood and local stone in the interior, providing a flow of space rather than boxlike rooms, taking full advantage of natural light through extensive use of glass, and centering the home around the fireplace, which became the symbol of the family hearthstone. A Wright home not only blended into its site, but was designed to serve the special needs and personality of the family that would live there. Ever fearful that urban society would stifle individualism, Wright worked to give his clients as personal a haven as possible, one that would offer maximum emotional comfort.

Conservatism in the American theater proved more entrenched, largely because of the hold of the syndicates and the strong profit motive. Still there were signs of progress. Minnie Maddern Fiske injected a greater subtlety into acting, a less melodramatic and more internalized method that stood her in good stead when she portrayed Nora in Ibsen's *A Doll's House* in 1894. Later, in *Salvation Nell*, she sat on the floor holding her drunken lover's head in her lap for a full ten minutes without saying a word, almost without moving. When Mary Garden saw the performance, she effused, "Ah, to be able to *do nothing* like that!" But the great revolution in drama came not from Broadway but in the experimental "little theater" movement before World War I. The first plays of Eugene O'Neill were presented by the Provincetown Players on Cape Cod in 1915. O'Neill rejected most of the old formulas and introduced a philosophical and psychological depth heretofore unknown in American drama. Another innovator, Robert Edmond Jones, designed the sets for a number of the early O'Neill plays, attracting much attention for the boldness of his conceptions and frequently employing expressionistic techniques.

The symphonic repertory in America, although still basically foreign, was broadening in the years before World War I to include the works of contemporary composers like Richard Strauss, Debussy, Ravel, Franck, Rachmaninoff, Gliere, and soon Stravinsky and Schoenberg. Grand opera after Verdi moved in a more realistic direction, as *verismo* opera came to supplant the earlier *bel canto* style. Puccini, Leoncavallo, Mascagni, Ponchielli, and Giordano all sought a closer look at life, concentrating more on representing raw human emotion than making beautiful sounds. The music dramas of Richard Strauss broached an even greater psychological element, as well as a more complex musical idiom. Consistent with the deepening emotional emphasis of later operatic composers, singing actors like Calve, Chaliapin, and Garden appeared around the turn of the century, using their voices more for dramatic intensity than as instruments of sheer beauty.

Gradually the arts came to mirror the conclusions of Darwin, Freud, and the behaviorists, tending toward a more rounded portrayal of life and giving increased attention to the range of human consciousness. The vanguard was clearly ahead of the general public and most of the critics, and clashes between contemporary artists and American society were unusually sharp at the beginning of the twentieth century. Copies of Dreiser's *Sister Carrie* (1900) were stored for years in the basement of Doubleday, Page, and Company, because Mrs. Frank Doubleday read the novel and was so shocked by its frank treatment of sex that she prohibited the book's sale. When the Armory Show was taken to Chicago in 1913, Matisse was burned in effigy by midwestern art students. Louis Sullivan lost a symbolic battle for modernism in architecture when the directors of the Columbian Exposition decided to turn Chicago's Jackson Park into something out of ancient Rome by constructing the fair's major buildings in a gleaming white classicism. The banning of *Salome* from the Metropolitan and the Chicago Opera is a notorious example of the conflict between new artistic concepts and the guardians of the genteel tradition. But conservative critics like Krehbiel even had reservations about veristic operas such as *Cavalleria Rusticana*, while the mayor of Boston in 1912 closed a production of *Tosca* with Mary Garden and Vanni-Marcoux because of the realism of the second act.

When police hauled the Diaghilev company off to jail over Nijinsky's controversial *L'Apres-midi d'un Faune*, the episode was more extreme than unique; still Fokine's dance innovations at the Ballet Russes remained much in keeping with advanced trends in art. The revolution in dance was of special importance for the United States, since it was carried forward by two American women, Isadora Duncan and Ruth St. Denis. As a result of their work, modern dance moved from the remote stages of upper class theatergoers and into the arena of everyday experience, ultimately into the very thoughts and feelings of ordinary people. With Isadora Duncan particularly dance left the world of dying swans and distraught butterflies and entered the realm of human emotions, was taken away from a select cult and presented in a form that everybody was urged to practice, and was decidedly freed from the stilted conventions of the past. Modern dance emerged from the general spasm of artistic creativity preceding World War I, reflected shifting values in western society, and proclaimed a new naturalness and self-expression that defied purely objective analysis.

Dora Angela Duncan was born the youngest of four children, on May 27, 1878, in San Francisco. Her father had gone to California from Philadelphia during the Gold Rush of 1849, but deserted his wife and children before Isadora was born. The mother, Mary Dora Gray, supported the family by giving piano lessons. Isadora grew up in San Francisco during a time when the city was enjoying an influx of theatrical companies and musicians of international renown. But Isadora largely taught herself to dance; nature was her mentor, and she later wrote that as a child she had danced by the sea, imitating the motion of the waves. She also watched the sway of flowers and the flight of birds, and as an adult concluded that "dance is the movements of the human body in harmony with the movements of the earth."

While still in her teens, Isadora went east with her mother, hoping to launch her career as a dancer. She made the rounds of the booking offices in Chicago, dancing Chopin's mazurkas and waltzes for managers. "You are a pretty girl," she was told time and again, "but in our business we need some peppery stuff, something with frills and kicks." Finally she was hired by Charles Fair, a vaudeville manager, for three weeks at the Masonic Roof Garden, where she was billed as "The California Faun." She soon met Augustin Daly, the great playwright-producer, who hired her for a show in New York. She worked for Daly two years before crossing the Atlantic on a cattle boat in the spring of 1897 to appear with his company in England. In London she studied ballet with Katti Lanner, a Viennese ballerina, who was then ballet mistress at the Empire Theater. Isadora later returned to New York briefly, where she took additional lessons. During the summer of 1900, she and her mother packed their few belongings and went to Paris, the city she would consider home for the rest of her life.

Although she had received training in formal ballet, Isadora rejected the classical technique early as both puerile and contrary to the laws of nature. "I am an enemy of the Ballet," she later insisted, "which I consider a false and preposterous art, in fact, outside the pale of all art." Dance, she believed, should spring from inner emotions rather than from strictly delineated movements. Instead of executing a prettified spectacle of pirouettes, which Isadora regarded as spiritually empty, the body should be free to move meaningfully, free to transmit man's most profound thoughts and feelings. The power of the music should release the dancer to express the passions locked within, while form should be left largely to instinct.

And yet Isadora did not improvise her dances on stage. Many of the overt aspects of her dance were colored by Greek art and sculpture. During her first years in Paris she spent hours studying the Greek vases in the Louvre, and she would eventually argue that "dance and sculpture are the two arts most closely united, and the foundation of both is nature. The sculptor and the dancer both have to seek in Nature the most beautiful forms, and the movements which inevitably express the spirit of those forms." The Greek ideal was the beginning point for Isadora, the external source of inspiration; her goal was "to start from its beauty and then go toward the future." Later, on a trip to Athens, she danced amid the ruins of the Theater of Dionysus. "I naturally fall into Greek positions," she wrote of her art, "for Greek positions are only earth positions." In her early dances she wore a transparent white or blue tunic and either sandals or no shoes at all, giving the appearance of a statue come to life, while maximizing bodily freedom.

Isadora believed that her destiny was to bring Beauty back into the world, through dance. She earnestly considered herself descended from the Greek gods and to be a mortal incarnation of Aphrodite, who had instructed her to dedicate herself to Dionysus. "I belong to the Gods," she maintained. "My life is ruled by signs and portents, which I follow to my set goals." A rebel in her personal life as well as her art, Isadora was an advocate of free love and opposed marriage on philosophical grounds. She fell in love with stage designer Gordon Craig, the son of English actress Ellen Terry, and in 1905 bore the first of her two illegitimate children. At Craig's request the child was named Deirdre, after the heroine of an Irish legend.

Through Craig, Isadora was introduced to a number of significant people in London and learned much concerning the theater, particularly about lighting. Several English art patrons became interested in her work, and she became the darling of a wealthy group calling themselves "the Hellenics," who were pledged to a Grecian Renaissance. She danced in a number of fashionable salons and won recognition in the theater. Isadora, statuesque and majestic, her hair hanging loose, her legs bare, was best when she held the stage alone. She danced to the music of Beethoven, Tchaikovsky, Gluck, Schubert, Chopin, and Wagner rather than to the usual ballet scores. A woman observing her around 1900 wrote, "Miss Isadora Duncan is the very latest in the way of plastic dancers. She does not undertake the terpsichorean art in the ordinary way, but illustrates poems or poetic ideals to music of what seems to be perfectly artless and natural dance movements."

She visited St. Petersburg in 1905, a year after Fokine had submitted his concepts for a new form of ballet to the directors of the Imperial Theater—ideas which the directors quickly rejected. Yet Isadora's visit to Russia was particularly successful, and she was soon celebrated there as something of a prophet. Compared to the sumptuous Russian ballet, the simplicity of her steps and her plain, flowing costume were surely startling. Instead of elaborate painted scenery, she danced with only blue draperies behind her. At first Isadora's performances were indeed "shocking to many who did not understand her art," an ex-Russian dancer affirmed. "But after her appearances in Russia perhaps a fourth of the dancers in the Imperial Ballet immediately were captured by her idea of dance expression and interpretation. After five or ten years everybody realized that hers was a real art, and went over to follow her." Isadora, however, was influenced by the Russians too, particularly Stanislavsky's belief that a performer should become completely identified with the character he is playing.

Having earned a growing reputation in Europe, Isadora returned to the United States in 1908. Americans had received only occasional reports of her European activities and were unprepared for her art. Consequently her initial appearances in the United States were disasters. Audiences not only failed to understand her efforts at free bodily expression, but her private life was much discussed and condemned. To most Americans she was simply a barefoot dancer who flounced around on stage nearly naked and had conceived a child out of wedlock. She was first presented in this country under the management of Charles Frohman, whose touring arrangements were far from ideal. Publicized as a virtual music hall attraction, Isadora was often forced to dance Gluck's *Iphigenia in Aulis* and Beethoven's Seventh Symphony to the accompaniment of small, inadequate orchestras and was received by audiences that were uncertain whether they should cheer or laugh. Frohman considered her art over the heads of the public, and his six-month contract with her was terminated before the tour was completed. Then Walter Damrosch invited Isadora to appear as a guest at the Metropolitan Opera House with his New York Symphony Orchestra. Presented under favorable circumstances and with the aid of Damrosch's personal popularity, the Metropolitan performance on November 16, 1908, was sold out and enthusiastically acclaimed. Included on Isadora's program were the Bacchanale from Wagner's *Tannhauser* and excerpts from the Flower Maiden's music from *Parsifal*. With this late success Isadora agreed to come back to the United States the following season.

She returned to Paris and enjoyed perhaps the greatest triumphs of her career, the same year that Diaghilev's Ballets Russes launched Fokine's reforms in ballet. Isadora's second American tour brought cautious admiration from a few, derogatory comments from the multitude. In Europe she had found a new lover, the handsome, cultured, wealthy Paris Singer, whom Isadora referred to as her Lohengrin. Most of the gentleman's fortune came from the American Singer Sewing Machine Company. In May, 1910, Isadora gave birth to Singer's son, Patrick, who, along with Deirdre, was to Isadora a precious source of pride and fulfillment. But in April, 1913, tragedy struck: Isadora's two children and their nurse were drowned when the car in which they were riding freakishly plunged into the Seine. Isadora never fully recovered, and from this point on her life became more and more erratic. She performed again in the United States in 1915, with dancers from her Paris school, the six "Isadorables," essentially duplicates of herself. She grew increasingly interested in the approaching Russian Revolution and initially saw the Communist movement in the most idealistic terms. On the day the Revolution was announced Isadora celebrated by dancing the *Marsellaise* wearing a red tunic, followed by her interpretation of *Marche Slave*, in which she pictured the downtrodden serf under the lash of the whip. "On the night of the Russian Revolution," she wrote in *My Life*, "I danced with a terrible fierce joy. My heart was bursting within me at the release of all those who had suffered, been tortured, died in the cause of Humanity."

Then came her wild, tempestuous, inebriated affair with Russian poet Serge Essenine, a man seventeen years her junior. In 1922 she married Essenine, primarily to enable him to accompany her to the United States. Her last American appearances were poorly received—partially because of the continued controversy over her art, even more now because of Isadora's acknowledged sympathy for the Russian Revolution, in part because of Essenine's capricious, sometimes demented behavior. Her liaison with the young poet led to great dissipation; Isadora grew heavy, and the tragedy of her life weighed in her face and body.

Her desire to found a permanent school of dance persisted. She had hoped for a state supported school from the Russians, but was disappointed. As early as 1904 she had demonstrated an interest in teaching her art to children, since children lacked the inhibitions of adults. Her first school was established near Berlin, and she would later teach in France and Russia. "Listen to the music with your soul," she repeatedly told students. "Now, while listening, do you not feel an inner self awakening deep within you?" In time imitators sprang up both in Europe and America, as barefoot little girls with wreaths on their hair and plump matrons in tunics and sandals were taught to pose dramatically to pretty music—much to Isadora's disgust. "Don't be merely graceful," she cautioned her students. "Nobody is interested in a lot of graceful young girls. Unless your dancing springs from an inner emotion and expresses an idea, it will be meaningless."

She broke with Essenine, whom she always considered a boy, only to learn in 1925, while dressing for a New Year's Eve party, that the poet had committed suicide. As the months wore on, she fell deeply into debt, grew more haggard in appearance, more desperate in her efforts to grasp the fruits of life. At Nice, September, 1927, she became interested in a Bugatti racing car and more especially in its handsome Italian driver. In a playful moment Isadora asked to be taken for a drive in the powerful vehicle. Since the car was open, she wrapped a red shawl with a long fringe around her neck. As the car leaped forward, the shawl caught in the spokes of a wheel. In an instant Isadora was dead, her neck broken. "I have killed the madonna," the handsome Italian sobbed.

For the highly sophisticated, Isadora Duncan was a fresh breeze blowing through the staid parlor that represented chaste American culture at the turn of the century. Yet for the mainstream, she was far ahead of her times. In an age when women's legs were modestly referred to as limbs, Isadora's bold contention that the "noblest art is the nude" was bound to provoke violent opposition, as was the candor of her personal life. Even S. Hurok, under whose management she danced during her last American tour, admitted, "Goddess that she was, Isadora's frailities too were on an Olympian scale. Moderation was a word without any meaning whatever to her. She had no conception of money, mine, yours, or her own; she was incapable equally of unkindness or tact; she breakfasted on port, dined on whisky and supped on champagne. Still I adored Isadora, and I adore her still."

Her rebellion was not merely directed against the ballet, for she sought to liberate women, mankind, and human emotions as well. Like many advanced thinkers of her generation, the arts to Isadora offered an avenue by which the urbane individual could preserve his identity in a society becoming increasingly regimented. "Art," she insisted, "gives form and harmony to what in life is chaos and discord." For Isadora dance was above all concerned with the nobility of the human spirit and the exploration of the passion of being.

At virtually the exact moment that Isadora Duncan was dancing beside the sea in San Francisco, Ruth St. Denis was growing up on a New Jersey farm. Born in 1880, St. Denis was far better grounded in classical dance than Isadora, although she too was much influenced by nature—the roll of the grass, the bending of flowers. Ruth Dennis began her stage career as a girl in vaudeville, giving eleven performances a day. She was later hired for Augustin Daly's show *The Runaway Girl* and for five years worked as an actress for David Belasco. In Belasco's *Zaza*, starring Mrs. Leslie Carter, Ruth Dennis was given the tiny role of the ballet girl. Belasco eventually changed her name to St. Denis.

She toured America and went to England with Belasco's company. In Buffalo, New York, she and a girl friend from the troupe stopped into a drug store for a soda. Behind the counter was an eighteen by twenty-four inch poster advertising a brand of cigarettes called "Egyptian Dieties." The poster depicted the goddess Isis sitting on a throne with her feet in the waters of the Nile, holding a lotus. The poster so fascinated young Ruth that she bought it from the clerk for a dollar. It was to alter her entire life.

What Aphrodite was to the ancient Greeks, Isis was to the ancient Egyptians, the symbol of feminine beauty and power. St. Denis envisioned herself dancing this role in the theater, and shortly after buying the cigarette poster, in 1904, she made herself a costume like the one in the picture. At a time when "Little Egypt" was causing a sensation with her scandalous "hootchy-kootchy," beginning with her debut at the St. Louis World's Fair, any Egyptian dance was likely to command attention, but St. Denis had in mind something more profound. Her research led her from major collections of Egyptian art to the midway at Coney Island, where the imitators of "Little Egypt" performed. What emerged were *Radha* (1906) and *Egypta* (1910), the first of her Oriental dances.

St. Denis' creations were both exotic and spiritual, about the God deep within. They grew out of her concept of the Orient, combined with attitudes rooted in her own conscience and colored by those of Mary Baker Eddy. St. Denis won her early success as a dancer in Europe between 1906 and late 1909; then she returned to America. She toured the United States from coast to coast, performing for the most part in vaudeville houses. But the American public was scarcely better prepared for St. Denis than they had been for Isadora Duncan the year before, and *Radha*, which its interpreter danced with her legs and midriff bare, caused much argument and confusion, yet stole headlines across the nation.

In 1914 St. Denis met, began dancing with, and shortly married Ted Shawn, who had dropped out of theology school at the University of Denver to become a dancer at a time when American males would have little to do with the likes of ballet. Shawn was born in Kansas City, Missouri, in 1891, but by age fifteen had moved to Colorado, when his father became the chief editorial writer for the *Rocky Mountain News*. As a young man Ted had worked in a sawmill, which added muscle to his frame, and when he met Ruth St. Denis, he stood over six feet tall and weighed around 185 pounds. As a college student, Shawn had contracted diphtheria; an overdose of antitoxin caused paralysis. He became interested in dance as a result of the exercises he performed in therapy. He later studied classical ballet and responded well to the training. Whereas St. Denis' approach to dance was feminine and intuitive, Shawn's was boldly masculine, direct and pragmatic.

Together they continued the religious themes of the East, flavoring their art with the lore of India, Arabia, Siam, Japan, Greece, and Egypt. Shawn also devised his own lusty dances, frequently using everyday subjects like the cowboy, laborers, and the American black. Although St. Denis was mercurial in temperament and rhythmic by instinct, as opposed to Shawn's more mathematical and scientific approach, the two were able to blend their personalities and divergent dance styles in romantic duets that exquisitely fused the powerful with the delicate.

While they eventually separated in private life, Ruth St. Denis and Ted Shawn continued to work together. From 1914 to 1932 they managed Denishawn, a school and company of modern dance, and trained a lion's share of the distinguished American dancers of the generation ahead. St. Denis herself enjoyed a long life and was still dancing at eighty-seven. She died on July 21, 1968. Shawn lived until 1971.

Both Isadora Duncan and Ruth St. Denis were intuitive dancers, independently resourceful rather than disciplined in the scientific sense. Neither were concerned with steps as such, but believed that the body, though trained, should be free to express beliefs and feelings. Both were romantics, emphasizing the idyllic spirit in dance. Both were mavericks, revolting against an art form they considered mechanical and soulless. Yet Isadora's dance was far more autonomous, for she idealized the dancer and was primarily moved by the beauty of the human body. Her art was born out of her personal rebellion. She disclosed to audiences "the most secret impulses" of her soul. "From the first," she wrote, "I have only danced my life." St. Denis, on the other hand, built her career on the mystery and seductiveness of the East, was motivated by religious impulses, both "pagan" and "sacred," and in her art idealized Woman. "All my life," she confessed late in years, "I've worshipped...the God in heaven, the god of art, and the god of physical love."

But while Isadora prepared her dances carefully and worked from a definite framework, St. Denis was much more a woman of the theater. For Isadora dance was the individual; for St. Denis it was a medium for projecting more universal concepts. Isadora expressed herself through dance, whereas St. Denis portrayed a character. Although St. Denis built her creations upon a personally evolved technique of movement and from genuine spiritual convictions, she nevertheless perceived her art as theater and was aided in the construction of her characterizations by her instinct for gesture, a dramatic use of her fluttering arms, and her talent for effective drapery. Living in an age when the female was militantly crying out for her rights, Isadora demanded the liberation of her sex without compromise. In her dance the male was virtually ignored. For Ruth St. Denis woman attained much of her feminity in relation to man, and this was especially reflected in her duets with Ted Shawn.

Isadora Duncan's legacy to art is largely her legend. Her influence in America was not strongly felt until long after her death. From Ruth St. Denis and Ted Shawn, however, sprang the hierarchy of American modern dance. Although the public was unready for any form of interpretative ballet at the turn of the century, Denishawn worked to build both understanding and a tradition of modern dance in the United States. Isadora, on the other hand, spent most of her mature years abroad, essentially turning her back on a native land that was incapable of separating its condemnation of the dancer's belief in free love from an untainted response to her ideas on free *dance*. Yet Isadora's emancipation significantly enriched the soil in which the work of St. Denis and Shawn took root and flourished.

Isadora Duncan in dance has been compared with Walt Whitman in poetry, and certainly her impact on ballet in the United States has been vital, if belated and indirect. Unlike St. Denis, Isadora in her search for freedom rejected her heritage so completely that she clouded her own identity and grew increasingly lost. Her quest for freedom in art and life was all consuming, but ultimately freedom became her prison. Although St. Denis revolted against the status quo in dance and drew much from primitive and exotic peoples, along the road to maturation she maintained a closer touch with her own cultural birthright. Isadora on the contrary remained so much the child of nature that maturity was impeded. Her tragedy, which her art reflected, was that in the act of rebellion she was unable to establish a personal creed that was ongoing once the bloom of youth was gone.

Despite a late exposure to ballet, the United States eventually contributed much to dance. The lack of a classical tradition is perhaps part of the explanation, since American artists were not shackled to established forms. Although both Isadora Duncan and Ruth St. Denis received their first accolades from Europe and won their early attention at home because of foreign acclaim, with experience Americans were far better equipped to appreciate the naturalness and fervor of modern dance than the stylized techniques of classical ballet. Duncan and St. Denis, heroines of the human spirit and fierce sensations, were controversial, yes, but somehow more comprehensible to Americans who were beginning to be stifled by their moralistic, unromantic attitudes; the emergence of modern dance gave a release that the ethereal and elitist ideals of classical ballet could not. Likewise, the virility of Ted Shawn's creations was considerably more acceptable to American audiences than the untempered and impenetrable grace of the traditional *danseur*.

As the industrial nation grew more preoccupied with physical fitness, middle class Americans through schools and urban recreation centers began to accept dance as a means of healthy exercise, especially for women and girls, as well as a route to social refinement. In the professional theater the revolution in dance continued, carried forward by American ballet companies and, even more, the Broadway musical stage. As the bond between serious ballet and the commercial theater strengthened, the impact of modern dance as a living art broadened, while a meaningful avenue for the expression of new dance ideas was permanently opened.

CHAPTER

IV

The Growth of Serious

Composition

The pleas of William Henry Fry and George F. Bristow for an American art music were but slightly answered in the years after the Civil War. Times had changed, but conditions for the serious composer had altered little. Bristow and Fry had sounded their protests against the supremacy of foreign music in the United States during the 1850s, a period of intense nativism, and had expressed their views largely in New York City, the center of anti-foreign sentiment. Following the 1846 potato famine in Ireland and the political disturbances of 1848 in Central Europe, the rate of Irish and German immigration soared to such proportions that many Americans had grown alarmed, then hostile. But during the Civil War immigrants often proved desirable, both in the battlefield and behind the lines. With the industrial boom after the war, labor of all types was in great demand, and aliens were frequently employed as workers on railroad construction, in steel mills, meat packing houses, and mines. While a nativistic strain continued, the panic over the European influx subsided, intensifying again late in the century with the mass migrations from southern and eastern Europe. With the tempo of urban life quickening, the call for an American culture voiced by Emerson in

1837 and much of the intellectual ferment of the 1840s were temporarily pushed aside, as the young nation concentrated on building its industrial strength, content once more to take its esthetic identity from Europe. A movement to exploit local color as an impetus of artistic expression prevailed, but urban sophisticates essentially looked abroad for guidelines in art. And in no other category was this more the case than in the composition of serious music.

With a few honorable exceptions, art music in the United States until after World War I was distinguished more by inspired adjectives than by inspired music. Americans frequently appeared sensitive to the dearth of native compositions, awarded prizes to American composers in an effort to induce works of quality, but the atmosphere surrounding serious musicians of the United States was anything but mature. Those who aspired to creativity had almost all satiated themselves with European precepts, and many viewed art and life through the haze of an academic atmosphere. The results were repeatedly artificial and sterile, for the gap between art and life was rarely bridged. Music for American composers remained an ideal, one that floated too far outside their own experience and beyond the cultural environment of their nation.

"Art is a coral reef," composer Daniel Gregory Mason wrote in 1928, regarding the dilemma of American music, "and the greatest artist is only one more insect, owing his virtue more to his attachments than to himself. Hence it is no small matter that there is in American music no main reef, but only a confusion of tendencies. With us even the most gifted individuals find it difficult to attach themselves anywhere; instead, they swim distractedly about, make head-on collisions, and generally get in one another's way." The realization of art music was so slight in the United States that composers had difficulty distinguishing between what was feasible and fantasy, what had substance and that which was merely pretty, what was vibrant and that which simply followed the rules.

Slowly a tradition built. Upon the isolated efforts of earlier generations an institutional scaffolding appeared which linked the creativity of individuals and permitted an exchange of ideas and skills. Conservatories of music were founded, among them the Oberlin Conservatory in Ohio (1865), the New England Conservatory in Boston, the Cincinnati Conservatory, and the Chicago Musical College (all 1867), the Peabody Institute in Baltimore (1868), and the National Conservatory in New York (1885). George Eastman, the Kodak manufacturer, purchased the Institute of Musical Art in Rochester in 1918 and created the Eastman School of Music, affiliated with Rochester University. The Juilliard Graduate School in New York and the Curtis Institute of Music in Philadelphia both came into existence in 1924. In 1915 Rudolph Schirmer began publishing *The Musical Quarterly*, a respected journal of musicology, with Oscar G. Sonneck as editor. The music education program pioneered by Lowell Mason continued, although often bogging down into the tedium of note reading, using dull, uninspired textbooks, and inane ditties. After the Civil War music courses expanded into the college curriculum. The first full professorship in music was established at Harvard in 1875, followed closely by the University of Pennsylvania and Yale.

Although New York clearly remained the performance center of serious music in the United States, the ideological center in the late nineteenth century was undoubtedly Boston. A group of New England composers, known variously as the Boston Classicists or the New England Academics, formed a venerable school that labored fervently from about 1880 to World War I. The oldest member of this school, John Knowles Paine, was also Harvard's first professor of music and exercised tremendous influence over the next generation of American composers. Like the later Boston Conservatives, Paine was much under the spell of the German romantics and thought little of venturing from accepted paths. He admired Beethoven, Schumann, Mendelssohn, and Brahms, but found Wagner destructive to established forms. His goal was to shed new light on the old; his weakness stemmed from a studied formality and a scholastic dullness that guaranteed neglect.

Paine was born in Portland, Maine, on January 9, 1839. His father, the son of an organ builder, opened a music store in Portland and directed the city's first band. An uncle became a music teacher in the town, while an older sister taught both piano and voice. Paine himself first studied music with Hermann Kotzschmar, a local teacher who had come to this country from Germany in 1848 with the Saxonia Band. The boy made his debut as an organist at eighteen and a year later went to Berlin to study organ, composition, and orchestration. He worked with Haupt, Wieprecht, and others, later toured Germany as an organist, and in 1867 conducted his Mass in D Minor at the Berlin Singakademie. He returned to the United States, became organist at West Church in Boston, and was shortly appointed organist and music director of Harvard University. His first recital after completing his studies abroad received much praise from *Dwight's Journal*: "He is a missionary of Bach, and Bach has no more enthusiastic a worshiper, nor so admirable an interpreter in the United States or Disunited States of America."

Paine volunteered to give, at no extra pay, a series of lectures on musical form at Harvard. A few students came to hear the talks, although they carried no credit toward a degree. When the innovative Charles W. Eliot became president of Harvard, Paine was permitted to teach a course in harmony and later one in counterpoint. His courses grew popular enough that degree credit for them was eventually granted. Paine was appointed to an instructorship in music in 1872, made assistant professor the following year, and in 1875 became a full professor. Harvard's Music School soon was the model for other universities, and Paine's role in pioneering college music courses corresponded with Lowell Mason's work in the public schools.

As a composer Paine was much attracted to the larger musical forms and was the first American to win serious consideration in Europe with orchestral works. Compared with his contemporaries, he was something of a giant. His Mass in D Minor was performed at the Boston Music Hall in the spring of 1868, and his *St. Peter* oratorio was heard in Portland on June 3, 1873, and in Boston a year later. Historian John Fiske claimed that his friend's *St. Peter* merited "the right to be judged by the same high standard" as Handel's *Messiah* and Mendelssohn's *Elijah*. Paine was particularly fond of program music and in 1877 wrote a symphonic poem based on Shakespeare's *The Tempest*. He composed an overture to *As You Like It*, a fantasy inspired by the legend of Poseidon and Aphrodite, and set Keats' *Realm of Fancy* and Milton's *Nativity* to music. He wrote a prelude and music for the choruses for Sophocles' *Oedipus Tyrannus*, used in a Greek performance at Harvard in 1881. He composed eight songs and several piano pieces, but smaller selections were never his forte.

Paine wrote two symphonies. The first, his Symphony in C Minor, was initially performed in 1876 by the Theodore Thomas Orchestra in the Boston Music Hall, but was not published until 1908 and then not in the United States but by Breitkopf and Haertel of Leipzig, Germany. The Second Symphony, issued by a Boston publisher, is an attempt at program music and is entitled *Spring*. The opening movement, called *Nature's Awakening*, deals with the conflict between Winter and the Awakening, with the inevitable succumbing of Winter to Spring. The second movement, *May Night Fantasy*, is a scherzo in which the bassoon contributes to the merriment, while the third movement, *The Promise of Spring*, is a Romance in rondo form. The final movement offers thanksgiving for *The Glory of Nature*. The Second Symphony was first performed in 1880 under Theodore Thomas in Boston and won praise from contemporary music critics. Louis Elson found the last movement comparable to the finale of Schumann's B-flat Symphony. The premier audience reportedly went wild over the work. Ladies waved handkerchiefs, men shouted approval, while the sedate John Sullivan Dwight is said to have stood on his seat, frantically opening and shutting his umbrella to express his uncontrollable enthusiasm.

Paine's three act opera, *Azara*, was based on the medieval legend of Aucassin and Nicolette. Written in 1900, with a libretto by the composer, *Azara* never reached a dramatic staging, although it was given a concert performance in 1903 with piano accompaniment and another in 1907 by Boston's Cecilia Society with orchestra, chorus, and soloists. The three Moorish dances from the score were played several times on orchestral programs.

Organ pieces, string quartets, and concert selections for violin and cello were included among Paine's compositions. Besides his *Centennial Hymn* for the Philadelphia Exposition of 1876 and the *Columbus March and Hymn* for the 1893 Columbian Exposition in Chicago, he wrote a *Hymn to the West* for the St. Louis World's Fair in 1904, which was performed the following year in Boston by the Handel and Haydn Society. His cantata *Song of Promise* was sung at the Cincinnati Festival of 1888.

Paine's workmanship can scarcely be faulted, and certainly his serious intentions cannot be denied. His problem was rather one of aspiring too high, attempting to achieve such profundity that he dared not relax. The composer's avowed purpose was to adhere to "the historical forms as developed by Bach, Handel, Mozart, and Beethoven." Even when treating American subjects such as the Isles of Shoals off the New Hampshire coast in his *Island Fantasy*, he followed European patterns. The *Island Fantasy* pictured the contrasting themes of the dangers and beauty of the sea, but, as Daniel Gregory Mason pointed out, "it was within easy sailing distance of Mendelssohn's *Hebrides*." Paine even took a light bit of Americana like "Over the Fence Is Out" and made it the subject of a fugue.

Pedant that he was, Paine was enshrined on a pedestal in his own day, becoming the recognized dean of American composers. By 1899 the Boston Symphony Orchestra had performed his works more than eighteen times, while his music for *Oedipus Tyrannus* won a gold medal at an international concert in Berlin in 1904. Yet in no real sense did Paine disclose American characteristics; his compositions shortly lost whatever freshness they may have had and eventually disappeared from the repertory.

His most lasting contribution ultimately was his teaching, for he inspired many. "It is due to him," John Fiske maintained, "that music has been put on the same level with philosophy, science, and classical philology." His students were by no means in agreement regarding the tenor of his classes. Some later spoke of "his sleepy lectures in musical history." Others remembered his rigid classroom standards, but thought back on Paine himself as a simple, unaffected man, genial and helpful. His puns were notorious, and a disciple recalled the musician's saying that one scene in *Azara* required four trumpets in the orchestra and four strumpets on stage. Conservative though he was, Paine was not so inflexible that his mind could not be changed. In his later life, for example, he did come to regard Wagner as a genius and even imitated him. Certainly Paine gave the American composer a professional dignity he heretofore had not enjoyed. He held the chair at Harvard for thirty years, retiring in 1905. He died in Cambridge a year later, April 25, 1906, while working to complete a symphonic poem based on the life of Abraham Lincoln.

Paine's mantle fell largely to George W. Chadwick, another of the Boston Conservatives. Like his Harvard predecessor, Chadwick struggled to write refined, proper music, but went a step further by adding a spark of inspiration, an emotional warmth, even a sense of humor. Although Chadwick, too, approached music from an academic standpoint and concerned himself much with form, his compositions possess a life that Paine never attained. With Chadwick there is a genuine vitality, which if seldom thrilling, is nonetheless an important step toward humanity.

Chadwick was born in Lowell, Massachusetts, November 13, 1854. His father, an old-fashioned Congregationalist, named his son after the famous Methodist revivalist George Whitefield. The mother, in her fortieth year when George was born, died in childbirth. Although Chadwick's father was initially a farmer and later worked in a machine shop, he gratified his love for music by teaching a neighborhood singing class, eventually forming a small chorus and orchestra. Until he was three, George was placed in the care of relatives in New Hampshire, but returned to Lowell when his father remarried. The family moved to Lawrence in 1860, where the father opened a life and fire insurance company. The business flourished, especially after the Boston fire of 1872.

Young George learned to play the piano and organ from an older brother, and together they practiced four-hand arrangements of Beethoven's symphonies. At fifteen George played the organ in a Lawrence church and after graduating from high school made regular trips by train into Boston for piano lessons. Until he was twenty-one, the youth worked in his father's insurance business, meanwhile taking organ lessons and studying harmony at the New England Conservatory.

In 1876 George became "head and rump" of the music department at Olivet College in Michigan. He arrived on campus looking more like a student than a professor, showing not the faintest sign of a beard, in an age when whiskers were looked upon as a mark of dignity. The president of the college was horrified, but had no time to look for a hairier teacher, since classes were about to start. Chadwick taught piano, organ, and harmony, led the choir and glee club, gave weekly organ recitals, and lectured on music history and esthetics. He saved his money, for he definitely had in mind for himself a trip abroad for advanced study. By letter his father warned him time after time about the dim future for a professional musician and urged his son to return to the insurance business.

Despite his father's objections, George sailed for Europe in the fall of 1877. He went to Berlin and for a time studied with Karl August Haupt, one of Paine's teachers. But Chadwick wanted instruction in orchestration, which Haupt could not give him, so he moved to Leipzig to work with Jadassohn. Under Jadassohn's direction he wrote the *Rip Van Winkle* Overture, two String Quartets, and learned much regarding counterpoint. After two years he went to Munich, where he studied with Rheinberger, from whom he acquired a greater sense of discipline. When he left Germany, his musical expression had become more orderly, and he was confirmed in his desire to compose in the larger forms.

Chadwick returned to the United States in 1880, settling in Boston. He rented a studio and began teaching. He conducted choral societies and for seventeen years was a church organist. In 1882 he became an instructor at the New England Conservatory and fifteen years later was made its director. He taught composition and orchestration and conducted the Conservatory orchestra. He also wrote a textbook on harmony that went through many editions. As a teacher he proved erudite, unflaggingly energetic, demanding strict discipline both in composition and performance. Although he could be abrupt, most students found Chadwick tactful and kind, and he clearly had a way of impressing those with imagination. He remained head of the New England Conservatory until his death, April 4, 1931.

Chadwick's reputation as a composer was built chiefly on two symphonies, several concert overtures, and six pieces of chamber music, including five string quartets played with some regularity during the Kneisel days. Eclectic and versatile in his work, the composer was happiest when writing for the orchestra. He possessed a distinctive instrumental imagination and was able to translate persons, moods, and actions into orchestral sounds of color, meaning, and beauty. He composed twenty major works for orchestra, although the concert overture offered him the most flexible means of expression. Not only is Chadwick's music less labored than Paine's, but there is often an intangible Yankee quality which Philip Hale described as "a certain jaunty irreverence, a snapping of the fingers at Fate and the Universe."

Of the overtures *Thalia* (1883), *Melpomene* (1891), and *Adonais* (1899) were probably the most played. Chadwick's carefree spirit was effectively projected in *A Vagrom Ballad* (part of his *Symphonic Sketches*, 1907) and his symphonic ballad *Tam O'Shanter* (1917). His Second Symphony, a movement of which was played by the Boston Symphony Orchestra in 1886, included hints of American black melodies, revealing an awareness of a national folk heritage not common among Chadwick's conservative peers. The composer's String Quartet in E minor (1895) is clearly idiomatic, although it reflects neither Indian nor black influence—the most conspicuous native subjects in nineteenth-century American culture. Chadwick could write naively, even rustically, but customarily sought vernacular guidelines from the hymns and ballads of his own New England experience.

The composer won less distinction for his choral works. Besides his setting of Harriet Monroe's *Ode* for the opening of the Chicago World's Fair of 1893, he wrote *Ecce Jam Noctis* for male voices, two cantatas for mixed chorus, and *Noel*, a Christmas pastoral, performed at the Norfolk Festival in 1908. He published well over a hundred songs, some of them inspired by the American folk tradition. One of his best is a setting of Sidney Lanier's "Ballad of Trees and the Master." Chadwick attempted stage works ranging from operetta to grand opera. *Tabasco*, a comic opera, first given professionally in Boston in 1894, contained marches, gallops, waltzes, jigs, hymn tunes, and a plantation ballad. *Judith* (1901) was far more somber, bathed in Saint-Saens-like lyricism and held together with Wagnerian leitmotifs. *The Padrone* (1912) ranks among the few examples of early twentieth-century American verism and deals with the exploitation of Italian immigrants in Boston by their landlords and guarantors, the *padroni*. In addition, there was an operetta, *Love's Sacrifice*, as well as incidental music to the morality play *Everywoman*.

At the turn of the century Chadwick was definitely regarded as one of America's foremost composers. While he basically followed continental models, he did not disdain simplicity and was free enough to draw on occasions from vernacular idioms within his own knowledge. In his later instrumental works particularly Chadwick seemed to lose the German conservatory style and move toward a more mature, personal musical language. Unlike Paine, Chadwick possessed a dramatic instinct and the ability to project into his music a feeling of the tragedy and comedy of life. There was at once a steadiness and a freshness in Chadwick's work that was almost unknown in American art music at the time. As Philip Hale wrote in 1894, "He has not only melody, rhythm, color, facility; he has a strong sense of humor, an appreciation of values, and that quality known as horse-sense." While Chadwick's music may today seem like thin perfume from a bygone era, his compositions were lifted above most contemporary efforts by their relatively honest vigor. If the sounds are more European than American, Chadwick's statement was singular enough that domestic elements crept into his music from time to time—often as shadings, sometimes as phrases, occasionally with greater substance.

When Chadwick returned to Boston from his European studies, one of his first students was Horatio W. Parker, whom Chadwick found an argumentative, stubborn scholar, but a delightful person. In later years Parker would stand near the top of the conservative New England composers, eventually becoming to Yale University what Paine had been earlier to Harvard and what Chadwick was to the New England Conservatory. As a creative musician, Parker ranked as America's leading composer of choral works. Although his writing was rarely dramatic, often pedantic, even austere, much of what today might be viewed as old-fashioned in Parker's music was considered in his own time correct and learned.

Parker was born on September 15, 1863, in Auburndale, Massachusetts. His father was an architect and his mother, the daughter of a Baptist minister, gave music lessons and was organist in the Auburndale village church. Although Isabella Parker instructed her son in the piano early, young Horatio preferred the neighboring woods and Charles River until he was fourteen. Suddenly the boy's interest in music deepened, and he soon revealed a special talent for harmony. At sixteen he not only became organist of a small Episcopal Church in Dedham, but began writing hymn tunes and anthems for the choir. He studied piano and harmony with several Boston teachers, and at eighteen developed an interest in orchestral composition, perhaps stimulated by the success of John Knowles Paine. It was at this time that he came to Chadwick. "He had already acquired remarkable facility in harmony and modulation," the older musician remembered, "to which was added a very fertile vein of lyric melody, and both his melodies and harmonies had a distinct and individual character of their own." Parker himself was already doing some teaching, but as he afterwards explained, "not enough to do any harm."

In 1882 Parker left for Munich, where he entered the Royal School of Music. He studied organ and composition with Chadwick's teacher, Josef Rheinberger. From Rheinberger he acquired a contrapuntal mastery that aided him greatly in his later choral writing. After three years abroad Parker returned to the United States and for the next seven years lived in New York. He was placed in charge of the music department of the Cathedral School in

Garden City and served as organist at St. Andrew's and later Holy Trinity Church. He was appointed instructor at the National Conservatory of Music during the time Antonin Dvorak was director. He returned to Boston in 1893, as organist and choir director of Trinity Church. The next year he was invited to become head of the music department at Yale, a position he held until his death on December 18, 1919.

Until almost the end of his life, Parker held a church position of some sort. He continued at Trinity Church for six years after becoming Professor of Music at Yale, traveling to Boston each week to direct the church's choir. He was later organist at St. Nicholas in New York and conducted choral societies in various other cities. Still he found time for recreation; he loved to play golf with friends and ride his bicycle. Immaculate in dress, worldly in conversation and appearance, Parker commanded a social standing seldom enjoyed by professional musicians at the time. His friends were artists, writers, and professional people—rarely musicians. His wife, Anna Plossl, the daughter of a Munich banker, had been a fellow music student in Germany.

Parker's brusque manner and quick temper often frightened students, and he was inclined to fluster members of his class, then ridicule them for their confusion. He only respected those who stood up to him. New Haven associates claimed it was almost a pleasure to be insulted by Parker, for he could apologize so graciously. His students were expected to compose from the beginning, since Parker believed that "the best way to appreciate music is to make it." He virtually created the Yale School of Music, became dean in 1904, conducted the New Haven Symphony Orchestra, and composed incessantly.

His most successful work was the cantata *Hora Novissima* for mixed chorus and orchestra, initially performed by the Church Choral Society of New York, May 2, 1893. It was given the following year in Boston by the Handel and Haydn Society and at the Cincinnati Festival under Theodore Thomas' direction. Parker was invited to England to conduct the cantata at the Three Choir Festival at Worcester, where it was well received. Written during a period of ill health, when Parker was mourning the death of a sister, *Hora Novissima* is a setting from a twelfth-century Latin poem by Barnard of Cluny, describing the glories of Heaven. The musical influences are many, although essentially it is a New England hymnody that has been inflated to German oratorio proportions. While much of the fugal writing leans toward the conventional, Parker demonstrates an instinct for massed effect, and several of the arias contain a soft and poignant sweetness. Much of Parker's instrumentation is colorful and varied, and his style is masculine, if at times unduly calculated. *Hora Novissima* clearly turns its back on the wilderness and the terrors of the lone individual, but Wilfrid Mellers finds in Parker's writing a hazy nostalgia for the American garden which has now become a dream. "The final chorus," Mellers contends, "with its wandering modulation over which soars the soprano solo, becomes a lament for the New

Eden that has been betrayed; one can see the piece as a swan song on the dream of Jeffersonian democracy. The hope that Europe might be reborn in the New World...had been undermined by the Civil War and the triumph of industrial commercialism—which exploded in the European War of 1914-18." Certainly for Parker, World War I did destroy much that he believed in, and shortly after its conclusion he was dead, a broken man.

A person of deep religious conviction, the musician always seemed most at home treating sacred themes. *The Legend of St. Christopher*, an oratorio, was written in 1897 to a text by the composer's mother. Somewhat Wagnerian in the largeness of its conception, the work was performed by the Oratorio Society of New York under Walter Damrosch in 1898 and later at the Norwich and Bristol Festivals in England. Again Mellers observes an underlying element of uneasiness in Parker's writing: "In the final chorus of *The Legend of St. Christopher*, Parker attains a truly epic or 'pioneer' grandeur in the broad period of the deeply resonant sonority, to which the rapidly shifting modulations give a hint of instability, if not of fear."

The deeper dramatic quality of *The Legend of St. Christopher* may have led Parker to try his hand at opera. Besides *Mona*, produced at the Metropolitan in 1912, he wrote *Fairyland*, which won a $10,000 prize offered by the National Federation of Music Clubs in 1913. Lighter than *Mona*, *Fairyland* was staged six times at the Federation Biennial in Los Angeles in 1915. Parker had little feel for the theater and frequently called opera "a beautiful mess." His efforts at writing for the stage were largely synthetic, inspired by prize money and little else. *Mona* was most effective in its choral passages and when establishing a sacrosanct atmosphere.

Parker showed a tremendous capacity for winning prizes (five in all) and commissions for his work. No other American composer of his day was so sought out. His Victorian cantata *The Dream King and His Love* won a National Conservatory contest in 1892, which the judges, including Dvorak, favored over *Hora Novissima*. He received a $1000 prize in 1901 for *A Star Song*, another cantata, and wrote the *Wanderer's Psalm* for the Hereford Festival in England. He was awarded the Doctor of Music degree by Cambridge University in 1902, his reputation having become nearly as distinguished in Great Britain as it was in the United States.

Some of Parker's choral selections are less grand, including a number of *a cappella* Latin motets. He wrote nine orchestral works, some chamber music, and several pieces for piano and organ. He performed his organ concerto with the Chicago Symphony Orchestra in 1903 and soon afterwards with the Boston Symphony Orchestra. His most important work for orchestra alone is probably the *Northern Ballad*, while his final composition was a setting of Brian Hooker's commemorative poem "A.D., 1919," known simply as *The Ode*. The piece was written for a service to honor the Yale men who had died in the war, and it also served as Parker's own requiem.

Paine, Chadwick, and Parker were but three of the New England composers who trained in Germany during the late nineteenth-century but lived most of their adult life in or around Boston. The other representatives of this school were likewise conservative in viewpoint, tended to choose grandiose subjects and musical forms, and generally were either academicians, church musicians, or both.

Dudley Buck, born in Hartford, Connecticut, the same year as Paine, pioneered in the larger forms of choral writing and taught many of the church composers of the next generation. Buck entered the conservatory in Leipzig at nineteen, but after four years in Europe he spent the rest of his life in Hartford as a church organist and teacher. Like Paine, his symphonic equivalent, Buck's music conspicuously exhibits conventional paraphernalia. The only member of the New England Conservatives not to study abroad was Arthur W. Foote. A student of John Knowles Paine, Foote graduated from Harvard, became organist of the First Unitarian Church in Boston, and taught in the Boston area for over sixty years. He wrote choral works, a symphonic prologue to *Francesca da Rimini,* piano pieces, thirty works for organ, chamber music, and about 150 songs, basically following German models. Although Arthur B. Whiting lived the last forty years of his life in New York City, he was born in Cambridge, Massachusetts, and studied with Chadwick at the New England Conservatory. He afterwards went to Munich for work with Rheinberger, then returned to Boston for another ten years.

Slightly younger was Amy Marcy Cheney—better known as Mrs. H. H. A. Beach—one of America's first outstanding women composers. Born in Henniker, New Hampshire, in 1867, she married a physician at age eighteen, and lived in Boston until her husband's death. At seventeen she had played the Mendelssohn D Minor Concerto with the Theodore Thomas Orchestra in Boston and later performed her own Piano Concerto with orchestras throughout Germany. Her *Gaelic Symphony,* written in 1896, was also heard abroad. Another student of Chadwick's was Henry K. Hadley, born in 1871 at Somerville, Massachusetts. After studying composition in Vienna, Hadley returned to the United States both to compose and conduct. His works, including five symphonies and a number of concert overtures, were widely performed in his own time. *Azora, Daughter of Montezuma* was mounted by the Chicago Opera Company in 1917, while *Cleopatra's Night* was staged at the Metropolitan in 1920. Frederick S. Converse, whose *The Pipe of Desire* was the first American opera produced by the Metropolitan, studied with both Paine and Chadwick, followed by work in Munich with Rheinberger. He returned to Boston in 1899 to teach harmony at the New England Conservatory. Like his colleagues, Converse's music reflected both his academic training and his conservative tastes.

By the turn of the century Boston had practically become a musical suburb of Munich. Although the New England Conservatives undoubtedly expressed stronger idealism than technique, and more technique than originality, they nevertheless contributed significantly to the development of American serious composition, laying a foundation on which greater talents could build and instilling a concern for precision from which more ingenious minds could resourcefully extricate themselves. American composers were rapidly increasing in number, even though the chances of their work's being performed or published were still relatively slight. The numbers of musicians going abroad to study composition as well as to perfect performance techniques clearly suggests the growth of a creative impulse. Yet with so little precedent, the guidelines for ingenuity were vague. Unsure of themselves and faced with a public intrigued with the prospect of an American art music, yet paradoxically indifferent to it, composers of late nineteenth-century America were often driven to musical overstatements. This penchant for hyperbole in part reflected a basic insecurity, in part was merely characteristic of an aggressive age that equated bigness with progress. The New England Conservatives not only clung to Germany, but to a romanticism that America had never intellectually experienced. Consequently their romantic efforts were frequently more form than substance. Their mood tended to be more wistful than cogent—nostalgic not only for Europe, but for the innocence of the American past and the vision of Old World ideals reborn.

A reaction against the German domination of American art music was inevitable. When the revolt came, it took two forms—much like the contemporary rebellion in American letters. Some composers sought to revitalize American music, and at the same time create a national school, by turning to native subjects and infusing their work with elements of folklore. Others responded enthusiastically to new methods of expression emerging out of France and Russia. Similarly in literature, the Chicago Renaissance writers drew much from the American heartland in their effort to invigorate an anemic American verse, finding inspiration in the plain life of the farms and villages of the Midwest. The literary expatriates, on the other hand, found fresh air for creativity abroad, contributing their talents to cosmopolitan currents that were drawn toward modernism.

In the autumn of 1892 the Bohemian composer Antonin Dvorak arrived in New York to assume the directorship of the National Conservatory; he had been lured to this country by the then tremendous salary of $15,000 a year. Dvorak himself was an ardent patriot and in his compositions had worked much with Bohemian themes. A trend toward musical nationalism had spread across the non-German countries of Europe since the 1860s, prompted by romantic interests in folk material, combined with the desire to liberate Western music from the German grasp. Moussorgsky, Borodin, and Rimsky-Korsakov in St. Petersburg, Tchaikovsky in Moscow, Smetana in Prague, and Grieg in Norway had all helped to bring the national movement in music to a peak in Europe before Dvorak came to the United States. The Bohemian composer was dismayed to learn that Americans had moved so little in this direction.

Dvorak soon became interested in Negro spirituals, at a time when they were only slightly known outside the South. He discussed black music with H. T. Burleigh, one of the Conservatory's black students, asked Burleigh to sing several spirituals for him, and was particularly impressed with "Swing Low, Sweet Chariot." Within a few weeks after his arrival in Manhattan,

Dvorak set to work on his *From the New World* Symphony, using snatches of melodies he had heard from Burleigh and attempting to elaborate their spirit into a major composition. He also encouraged American musicians to free themselves from the European yoke by making greater use of indigenous material, such as the songs of the Creoles, Indian tribal chants, the ditties of frontiersmen, but particularly black melodies. In an influential article for *Harper's Magazine*, February, 1895, Dvorak insisted that the various types of American folk tunes offered the foundation on which a national music could be built. "Undoubtedly the germs for the best of music lie hidden among all the races that are commingled in this great country," the Bohemian composer concluded.

Dvorak remained in the United States three years. His challenge to American composers came at a time when the nation's patriotic sentiments were clearly surfacing—coinciding with Sousa's early success, on the eve of the Spanish-American War and the emergence of the United States as a world power. Whereas Anton Heinrich's efforts to utilize American subjects more than a half century before had been heavy-handed and isolated, a school of nationalist composers followed in Dvorak's wake, determined to do for American music what Grieg, Moussorgsky, Smetana, and others had done in Europe.

This group was led by a midwesterner who had never heard a symphony orchestra before enrolling as a student in the Massachusetts Institute of Technology in Boston. Born in St. Paul, Minnesota, April 23, 1872, Arthur Farwell eventually became so interested in music that he gave up the notion of becoming an engineer and began studying composition. He went to Germany, where he worked with Humperdinck and Pfitzner, and later studied with Guilmant in Paris. He returned to the United States in 1899 and enjoyed a long teaching career, first at Cornell University, then at the University of California (both at Los Angeles and Berkeley), and ultimately at Michigan State College. For a time he was an editor for *Musical America* and Supervisor of Municipal Music for the City of New York.

Around 1900 Farwell became greatly interested in American Indian music and spent some time in the Southwest studying tribal melodies and dance rhythms. He later wrote a number of piano pieces based on Omaha Indian themes. *Dawn*, an orchestral selection, was first heard at the St. Louis Exposition in 1904. He gradually expanded his scope to include settings of black, cowboy, and prairie melodies. But even more significant, Farwell devised a plan for assisting native composers.

All around him the musician found widespread attention to American compositions, including his own works, obstructed because no publisher would accept them. In 1901 he founded the Wa-Wan Press in Newton Center, Massachusetts, with the aim of establishing the American composer by freeing him of commercial interests. Farwell expressly intended to accept "Dvorak's challenge to go after our folk music," and much of the music published by Wa-Wan looked to America for inspiration. Its founder did not mean to discard German models, which he respected, but sought an enlightened eclecticism. America's originality, he felt, would come from the interplay of manifold influences. The first step toward artistic individuality was a consideration of all styles and forms in the environment. While the maintenance of traditional standards was important, to slight "native and democratic developments" was in Farwell's view to impede progress. Wa-Wan was therefore especially hospitable to composers demonstrating an interest in folk material, particularly Indian and black themes, printing works that commercial publishers judged unacceptable. Through the press Farwell was able to launch the careers of thirty-seven of his colleagues in all, among them two of Dvorak's pupils, Harvey W. Loomis and Rubin Goldmark. In 1912 the Wa-Wan catalogue was sold to the firm of G. Schirmer.

Closely associated with Farwell was Henry F. Gilbert, whose training in music was completely American. Born in Somerville, Massachusetts, on September 26, 1868, Gilbert's parents were both musicians and encouraged their son along that path. The youth studied at the New England Conservatory, then became one of Edward MacDowell's first American pupils. During his student days Gilbert supported himself by playing the violin in theaters and for dances, becoming well-versed in current vernacular music. Bored by the routine of a performing musician, he roamed the country for ten years, trying several different ways to earn a living and acquiring a Whitman-like knowledge of his country in the process. For a time he worked in a music publishing house in Boston as an engraver and arranger and was successively a real estate agent, a foreman in a factory, a raiser of silkworms, a collector of butterflies, and eventually a bread and pie cutter at the Chicago World's Fair. Gilbert had long been interested in composers who used folk themes in their work, and at the exposition in Chicago he met a Russian prince who had been a friend of Rimsky-Korsakov and was able to tell him much about nationalist trends in contemporary Russian music. After 1895, when he acquired a small inheritance, Gilbert spent some time abroad, but returned to the United States. When he heard of the coming premiere of Charpentier's *Louise* in Paris, he became so enthusiastic, knowing that the opera used popular themes, that he worked his way to France on a cattle boat to hear the performance. He was so stirred by the work that he decided to devote the rest of his life to composition.

At thirty-three Gilbert came back to Somerville, found a job tending a horse and a cow to pay his board, moved a piano into the barn among the buggies, and began to compose on a breadboard atop a flour barrel. Despite his New England heritage, he was determined to break away from the conservative mold. German traditions had shaped the development of American art music so long, Gilbert argued, that "the true spirit of America is lost sight of, and that great potential spirit which is the birthright of the American composer..., has been thoughtlessly bartered away for a mess of clever European pottage." Gilbert's writing is often clumsy and amateurish, but it is stamped with the composer's own personality and at least a superficial nationalism. He found his inspiration in Anglo-American folklore, minstrel tunes, Indian chants, and all sorts of black music, all of which to Gilbert were close to the soul of the people and hence intimately related to the American character.

His greatest popular success came with the *Dance in Place Congo* (1906), based on five Creole songs and suggested by George W. Cable's description of the slave dances in Place Congo. Originally written as an orchestral tone poem, the composer later reworked the music into a ballet, performed at the Metropolitan Opera House in 1918. Gilbert captures the exotic atmosphere of the famous New Orleans' dances, coupling themes of tragedy and despair with lighter, wittier moments. *Americanesque*, a piece for orchestra written in 1903, was based on three minstrel tunes. His *Comedy Overture on Negro Themes* (1905), originally intended as the prelude for an operetta based on the Uncle Remus tales of Joel Chandler Harris, was first performed by the Boston Symphony Orchestra in April, 1911. *Negro Rhapsody* (1912) opens with a Negro "shout," then alternates a savage dance with a spiritual, and concludes with the spiritual's triumph. *Negro Dances* is a set of five quasi-ragtime piano numbers, which indicates that the composer could be quite effective in writing smaller, more relaxed selections.

Most of Gilbert's published work was written between 1902 and 1913, and much of it was issued through the Wa-Wan Press. Not all of his music was drawn from the black. A Prelude to Synge's *Riders to the Sea* made use of an old Irish melody, while his six *Indian Sketches* were based on American tribal chants. The composer's setting of Stevenson's "Pirate Song" ("Fifteen Men on a Dead Man's Chest") was made popular by opera singer David Bispham. Gilbert heard his *Dance in Place Congo* performed at the International Festival of Contemporary Music at Frankfurt in 1927 and died the following year in Cambridge, Massachusetts.

Dvorak's pupil Rubin Goldmark wrote a *Hiawatha Overture*, introduced by the Boston Symphony Orchestra in 1900, and another *Negro Rhapsody* (1923). Besides the opera *Shanewis*, produced at the Metropolitan in 1918, Charles Wakefield Cadman composed the *Thunderbird Suite* on Omaha themes. The piece, originally written for piano, was later orchestrated. Cadman achieved wide popularity with his song "The Land of the Sky Blue Water," in which he utilized American Indian material, although diluting it almost beyond recognition. Charles Sanford Skilton, born in Northampton, Massachusetts, became interested in American Indian music after graduating from Yale. From 1903 until his death in 1941, he headed the music department at the University of Kansas, near Haskell Institute, a school for Indians. Skilton's best known compositions were based on aboriginal material, most notably the *Suite Primeval*, which included the *Deer Dance*, the *War Dance*, the *Sunrise Song*, the *Gambling Song*, and the *Moccasin Game*. John Powell, a native of Richmond, Virginia, who studied composition in Vienna, used stylized Afro-American themes in his *Negro*

Rhapsody for piano and orchestra (1918) and *Sonata Virginianesque* for violin and piano (1919), but later turned to Anglo-American folk music for his overture *In Old Virginia* (1921) and *Five Virginia Folk Songs* for baritone and piano.

Even the fundamentally conservative Daniel Gregory Mason was sufficiently impressed by the search for a national art music that he puzzled over the problem philosophically and occasionally incorporated folk material into his own compositions. Unlike Farwell and the conscious nationalists, however, Mason denied using indigenous themes for the reasons Dvorak had suggested, maintaining that he was attracted to these simple tunes for their own worth alone. To Mason the "Anglo-Saxon element in our heterogeneous national character, however quantitatively in the minority nowadays, is qualitatively of crucial significance in determining what we call the American temper." Yet musically Mason was an eclectic. European oriented by preference, he nevertheless drew on the Appalachian ballads recently uncovered by Cecil Sharp and others for his Suite after English Folk Songs and made use of black material in his String Quartet on Negro Themes, centering the piece around the familiar "Deep River."

Mason was the son of piano manufacturer Henry Mason and the grandson of Lowell Mason. He was born in Brookline, Massachusetts, on November 20, 1873. He took courses with John Knowles Paine at Harvard, later studied with George W. Chadwick, and in 1901 went abroad to work with Vincent d'Indy in Paris. He returned to the United States as an active lecturer and teacher, joining the faculty of Columbia University in 1910. He was appointed MacDowell Professor of Music there in 1929, retired in 1942, and died in 1953. Although Mason had studied in France rather than Germany, he turned his back on the Impressionism of Debussy and Ravel, rejected Stravinsky's Primitivism, and remained under the spell of the later Romantics. The composer thought of himself as "a musical humanist" and held firmly to the classical ideal of balance and restraint.

Mason's first compositions are tentative and imitative; his early Violin Sonata, for example, is unmistakably Brahmsian in flavor. Gradually his work became more individualistic, even though the composer's basic principles did not change. Mason's chamber music has probably attracted most attention and provides the musician the best, and certainly the most personal, means of expression. His compositions are in the sanctioned molds, while his harmony is comfortably that of the romantic era. The first of Mason's three symphonies was begun while the composer was a student in France. His *Country Pictures* for piano is another early piece, as is *Elegy*, among his largest works for piano. The exuberant *Chanticleer*, an overture for orchestra, has been widely played, while Mason's thirty odd songs, including *Songs of the Countryside*, are in his usual, conservative style, at times, and his *Lincoln* Symphony (1937) is clearly a monument to patriotism.

While seldom as philosophical as Mason, most of the turn of the century nationalists in serious American music were conventional in style, adhering closely to approved European techniques. For the most part these composers simply embedded American subjects and paraphrases of native music in late Romantic forms, harmonies, and orchestration, rather than creating an authentic American idiom. What they produced was essentially a Romantic fabric shot through with richly colored strands from black spirituals, minstrel tunes, ragtime, Indian tribal melodies, and Anglo-American folk ballads. Their revolt was superficial, not substantive. Their American sketches resembled picture postcards rather than genuine art, all drawn from the stereotypes of the American garden. Since the musical nationalists passed over the mainstream of American civilization in favor of representations rapidly becoming exotic and exhibited a vision of their country more nostalgic than real, their accomplishments were transitory. By World War I the movement launched by Dvorak had crested and would shortly play itself out. New influences were on the horizon, influences that not only broke with European traditions but with the traditional altogether, influences that would greatly alter the course of art music in the United States and throughout the Western world.

The early decades of the twentieth-century found the proliferation of musical styles in Europe reaching a climax, as the several national schools flourished, then gave way to an even more particularized modernism. With the disintegration of the German influence, American serious composition likewise splintered into a confusion of styles, entering what Daniel Gregory Mason called a period of "indigestion." American composers in the decades encompassing World War I were attempting to absorb European modernism in music much as young American painters were struggling to assimilate the Post-Impressionist techniques displayed at the explosive Armory Show. While American art music continued to look to Europe for guidance, serious composition in the United States, as elsewhere, moved toward a more personalized expression.

Shortly after the turn of the century the French Impressionists made a definite mark on American music, as composers from the United States drifted to Paris for study and became attracted to the work of Debussy, Ravel, Faure, and others. Among the earliest "American" Impressionists was Charles Martin Loeffler, born at Mulhouse in Alsace, January 30, 1861. Alsace at that time belonged to France. Before the Franco-Prussian War the family moved to the village of Smjela in the Russian province of Kiev, where Loeffler's father worked for the government. At age eight young Martin began studying the violin with a German musician from the Imperial Orchestra in St. Petersburg. After several years in Hungary and Switzerland, Loeffler decided to become a professional violinist. He studied with Joachim in Berlin and later with Massart and Ernest Guiraud in Paris. While in Paris Loeffler became an intimate friend of Faure and read widely in French literature. He came to the United States in 1881, where he played first with

Damrosch's orchestra and occasionally with Theodore Thomas. In 1883 he was invited by Major Higginson to become a member of the Boston Symphony Orchestra, soon playing side by side with concertmaster Franz Kneisel. Loeffler resigned from the orchestra in 1903 to devote his entire time to composition. He lived the rest of his life (until May 20, 1935) on a farm outside Medfield, Massachusetts.

Loeffler was both a student of medieval thought and culture and a spiritual mystic. For him dreams and images constituted invincible realities, and from these he derived much of his music. His compositions were characteristically serene and subdued, often indefinite in thematic development. "He is a seeker after the realities of shadowy and dim illusions," Lawrence Gilman contended, "an artist in grays and greens and subtle golds." His sounds had little to do with the American environment, since they were drawn from a dreamworld that was Loeffler's own. Physically and spiritually isolated during his most active period of writing, Loeffler recorded in music his own perception of art and life. The results were frequently strange, often picturesque, sometimes exquisite. He demonstrated a strong bent for the ancient modes of the Roman Church, producing music that was austere—music that reflected the composer's longing for the quiet retreat of the medieval mystics. Although Loeffler may be comfortably considered an offshoot of the French Impressionist school, he molded his mature style into a personal message, delicately colored and at its best lustrous in its tonal sheen.

Loeffler's most frequently played composition is the *Pagan Poem*, based on an incident from Virgil in which a lovesick sorceress chants sensuous songs in an effort to lure her lover home. The music is dark and brooding, conjuring an imaginary odor of strange incense. The piece was initially written in 1901 as chamber music, but was later expanded into a work for piano and large orchestra. The revision was first performed by the Boston Symphony Orchestra in 1907 and probably represents the composer's pinnacle. The influence of the Gregorian chant is most evident in the Music for Four Stringed Instruments and in *Hora Mystica*, a symphony in one movement. The latter was written for the Norfolk Festival in 1916, inspired by a visit to the Benedictine monastery at Maria Laach. It exhibits a sublimely ecclesiastical mood and a deep spirit of devotion. The *Hymn to the Sun*, with its text by St. Francis of Assisi, was written for voice and small orchestra and again used medieval church modes. Loeffler composed two rhapsodies for oboe, viola, and piano, a suite for violin and orchestra, *Fantastic* Concerto for Cello and Orchestra, Divertimento for Violin and Orchestra, and the tone poem *Memories of My Childhood* ("Life in a Russian Village"). Much of the composer's orchestral music was introduced by the Boston Symphony Orchestra, while many of his chamber works were performed by the Kneisel Quartet. He also wrote several songs and an Iberian opera.

In terms of the American scene Loeffler was a pioneer, a creative artist who stood aloof from his surroundings—homesick for a sequestered past. Unique in his day, Loeffler was frequently viewed with reserve by contemporary critics. Paul Rosenfeld compared his music with the dead Queen Inez de Castro of Castile, whose embalmed body, dressed in full regalia, was set upon the throne in the great hall of the palace for all the vassals to honor. Likewise Loeffler's music, in Rosenfeld's judgment, "is swathed in diapered cloths and hung with gold and precious stones. It, too, is set above and apart from men in a sort of royal state, and surrounded by all the emblems of kingdom. And beneath its stiff and incrusted sheath there lies, as once there lay beneath the jeweled robes and diadem of the kings of Castile, not a living being, but a corpse."

While the charge of sterility has often been fixed on Loeffler's work, the composer's refined craftsmanship has rarely been denied. At his best Loeffler was a master of finesse, capable of moods ranging from an almost eerie delicacy to robust vigor. Although the composer clearly bore the mark of Debussy, Fauré, d'Indy, Franck, and others in his early work and remained preeminently Gallic in his artistic constitution, he later developed a style of vivid individuality. Subtle in thought, ecclectic in his knowledge of literature, sensitive by nature, Loeffler evolved a sublimated musical idiom that frequently resulted in sounds of poetic beauty and luscious atmosphere, rich with phrases touched with what Rosenfeld termed "a sort of narcissistic love."

Explorer that he was, Loeffler had little regard for experiments in the polytonal or atonal fields. His compositions reveal a search for nuances, a fascination with shades and impressions, and seldom ventured toward the dissonance of more advanced modernism.

Like Loeffler, Edward Burlingame Hill fell under the spell of Paris and contemporary French music. Born in Cambridge, Massachusetts, on September 9, 1872, Hill took courses with John Knowles Paine at Harvard and later studied with George Chadwick in Boston. In Paris he worked with Charles Marie Widor and became one of the first Americans to feel the lure of the Impressionists. He became a teacher at Harvard in 1908 and was chairman of the division of music from 1928 to 1939. His early compositions consist of a number of songs and piano pieces. In 1908 Hill was commissioned to write a ballet-pantomime for the Chicago Orchestra, for which he produced *Jack Frost in Midsummer*, his first orchestral music and clearly heralding his later style.

He wrote two *Stevensoniana Suites* for orchestra—the first in 1915, the second (inspired by *A Child's Garden of Verses*) in 1922. Two symphonic poems were produced during this same period, *The Parting of Lancelot and Guinevere* (1915) and *The Fall of the House of Usher* (1919). But it was with *Lilacs*, a tone poem based on a verse by Amy Lowell, that Hill found his individual voice. First performed in 1927, *Lilacs* is probably the composer's finest moment in the Impressionist idiom. The score is sensuous, full of strident color and without the vagueness often characteristic of Impressionistic writing. Nor has Hill turned his back on his native haunts, for he has composed persuasive music after Amy Lowell's lines:

Lilacs,
False blue.
White,
Purple,
Color of lilac,
Your great puffs of flowers
Are everywhere in this my New England.

Unlike Loeffler, Hill showed a recurrent tendency toward mild polytonality in his later work. He wrote three Symphonies, an *Ode* to celebrate the Boston Symphony Orchestra's fiftieth anniversary, a concertino for Piano and Orchestra, two sinfoniettas, a Concerto for Violin and Orchestra, and several chamber selections. By the mid-1920s some of his compositions exhibited traits derived from jazz. Much of his later music moved toward a simplification of style, was consistently vital, sometimes witty, with passages and movements of deep feeling and charm. While Mellers finds Hill's work "genuinely sensitive," he also depreciates it as "precious and parasitic." For the English musicologist the "sensory passivity" of the American Impressionists is a late refusal to face the wilderness, rather than a release from the frontier experience and a step toward sophistication.

Another of Paine's students who later came under the influence of the French Impressionists was John Alden Carpenter. Born on February 28, 1876, in Park Ridge, Illinois, Carpenter was descended from a family that traced its lineage to the *Mayflower*. The boy had his first piano lessons from his mother at the age of five and later studied with Theodore Thomas' sister-in-law. He entered Harvard at seventeen and graduated in 1897 with honors in music. Upon graduation he returned home to enter his father's fifty year-old business—George B. Carpenter and Company, a Chicago firm dealing in mill, railway, and ship supplies. He eventually became the company's vice-president. In Chicago he continued his musical training with Bernard Ziehn and on a trip abroad took lessons with the English composer Sir Edward Elgar. Although Carpenter remained with his father's business, music was always his primary interest.

When he began composing, his style was strongly Gallic in spirit. Carpenter's early songs exude a refined, aristocratic elegance and were drawn in tints rather than solid colors, bearing a striking kinship to Debussy. Yet "The Green River," one of his finest songs, with its whole-tone progressions, was composed in 1909, when Carpenter likely had heard none of Debussy's music. His first published songs, Eight Songs for a Medium Voice and Four Poems by Paul Verlaine, appeared in 1912, ushering in what William T. Upton called "a new era in American song literature." Carpenter's songs expressed a meditative disposition, the quieter aspects of nature, and nature's influence on the human experience. Few American song writers have been so sensitive to the moods of the great out-of-doors. His vocal music is steeped in an atmosphere of poetry, imbued with a poignancy and an emotional conviction not always present in his larger works. Carpenter set the six *Gitanjali* poems of Tagore to music in 1913 and two years later composed *Watercolors*, a cycle based on four Chinese verses, which soon gave him a taste of public acclaim. Some of his later songs were inspired by the American black and employ dialect.

The composer's sonata for piano and violin was performed in December, 1912, at Aeolian Hall in New York. He wrote several smaller piano pieces, including *Polonaise Americaine* and *Impromptu*, both published in 1915. *Little Indian* and *Little Dancer* followed the next year.

Carpenter's first important orchestral work, the widely performed suite *Adventures in a Perambulator*, was written in 1914. The piece is programmatic, describing the sensations of a baby being wheeled about a city park by his nurse. The results are delightful. The child first sees a policeman, who is "round like a ball—taller than my Father." The policeman and the nurse have a brief conversation, while the baby pretends not to listen. Then the baby hears a hurdy-gurdy, playing "such music—so gay!"—actually the "Miserere" from *Il Trovatore* ludicrously ground out by a xylophone, celesta, and piano. The baby thinks of dancing with his nurse and his perambulator. But the policeman comes and frightens the hurdy-gurdy away. Next the baby is fascinated by a lake and a white seagull in the air. He falls in love with the spot and calls it "My Lake." Suddenly the baby finds himself surrounded by dogs—big ones, little ones, brigand ones, kind ones, sad and happy ones. But when the excitement of the dogs has passed, the baby finds himself sleepy. To think more clearly, he closes his eyes. As he listens to the wheels of his perambulator, he muses, "How large the world is! How many things there are!" Carpenter's music is sparkling and whimsical as he depicts the sounds of the street organ and the barking dogs. It is not written in the grand manner, for infants do not think in grand terms. The composer accomplishes his purpose vividly and simply. *Adventures in a Perambulator* was introduced at Orchestra Hall, Chicago, in 1915 and was hailed with joy. Later audiences were enchanted with Carpenter's sense of humor and brilliant tonal coloring, while critics declared the work a little masterpiece.

With this success the composer began devoting more time to music, turning out several pieces quickly. In 1916 he wrote a Concertino for Piano and Orchestra, suggesting an intimate conversation between two friends— the piano and the orchestra. The Concertino is not only charming, but shows Carpenter with a firmer grasp on his art. He composed a symphony for the Norfolk Festival the next year. His first ballet score, *The Birthday of the Infanta*, was performed by the Chicago Opera Company on December 23, 1919. This work, based on Oscar Wilde's story, contains a Spanish flavor, with graphic music for the Infanta's birthday guests, jugglers, gypsy dancers, a mock bull fight, the dance of the dwarf Pedro, and the latter's horror at observing the reflection of his deformed body in a mirror. Only in the last scene—depicting Pedro's despair and death—did Carpenter miss his mark, appearing uneasy amid the tragic intensity he was trying to achieve. Appropriately enough Leopold Stokowski invited John Alden Carpenter to compose "A Pilgrim Vision" for a concert given by the Philadelphia Orchestra in connection with the Mayflower Tercentenary celebration in 1920.

Still maintaining his business activities, Carpenter next turned to the newspapers, more specifically to George Herriman's cartoon *Krazy Kat*, for musical inspiration. Reverting to the humor that had made *Adventures in a Perambulator* so charming, the composer wrote a ballet to a scenario by Herriman, whose Krazy Kat and Ignatz Mouse characterizations were familiar to comic strip readers across the nation. The score is remarkably subtle, and for the first time Carpenter used a jazz idiom. Although pure slapstick on the surface, the work is intensely human, for Krazy Kat's weaknesses and vanity are common in man, while the savage derision of Ignatz Mouse is life pulling us to earth from our lofty dreams. Carpenter was again able to fit grotesque and comical situations with close equivalents in sound and summon bizarre hues from the orchestral palette. Dance rhythms are combined with lilting tunes, and moments like the "Kat-nip Blues" are sheer delight. *Krazy Kat* was first played by the Chicago Symphony Orchestra on December 23, 1921, and given as a "jazz-pantomime" at Town Hall, New York, a month later. Adolph Bolm staged the work and danced the title role.

When word of *Krazy Kat*'s success reached Serge Diaghilev in Paris, the Russian director asked Carpenter to write a ballet that would incorporate the noise and bustle of American urban life. The composer responded with *Skyscrapers*, representing his most advanced phase. The work employs dissonance, polyphony, unconventional harmonic combinations, and other modernistic features to describe the cacophony of the city streets, but also relies on elements from the native vernacular—Afro-American music, strains of Stephen Foster, and especially ragtime and jazz motifs. There is no definite story, simply an attempt to portray the violent movements of work and play in the contemporary industrial complex. Carpenter captures well the vitality of American life, its feverish activity, boundless energy, nervous merriment, and somewhat underdeveloped emotions. Diaghilev made preparations to produce the ballet at Monte Carlo in 1925, but plans fell through. The work was performed at the Metropolitan Opera House the next year, with Robert Edmond Jones assisting in the staging. It was given later in Munich with good response.

Carpenter finished a String Quartet in 1927 and returned to the jazz idiom in *Patterns*, a piece in one movement for piano and orchestra, first performed in 1932 by the Boston Symphony. A year later he produced *Sea Drift*, inspired by the sea poems of Walt Whitman. *Danza*, performed by the Chicago Symphony in 1935, again suggests a Spanish influence, while *Song of Freedom*, for chorus and orchestra, was written in 1941. Carpenter's Second Symphony was introduced by the New York Philharmonic-Symphony under Bruno Walter, October 22, 1942. *The Anxious Bugler* appeared in 1943, followed by *The Seven Ages* (1945) and *Carmel* Concerto (1948). The composer died in 1951.

Since Carpenter derived his livelihood from the family business, he was free to compose as he wished; there was little need for compromise. The musician possessed the intelligence to develop his material. Rather than crowding his ideas one upon the other, Carpenter's works grant enough room to show the precise contours of the composer's genius. He was marvelously adept at coordinating his resources and bathed his music in the many hues of existence and dreams. Although his Impressionism comes through clearest in his early songs and piano pieces, Gallic tendencies continue in much of Carpenter's later work. He eventually emerged as a conservative modernist— several paces behind the European avant-garde, but downright radical when compared with Paine, Chadwick, or Parker. Eclectic in his tastes, Carpenter commanded the ability to absorb a variety of influences into his own style. He meditated musical philosophy, was sensitive to the moods of nature, and had the capacity to probe human experience with subtlety. It was his deeper vision of life that gave Carpenter's music its distinction. Gifted musician that he was, it was the composer's passion for truth and genuine humanity that set his work apart. Carpenter approached his music with such perception and such incorrigible sincerity that warmth and beauty came comfortably within range. His compositions are streaked with life, for Carpenter brought to his work a personal integrity that demanded he be himself.

But of the several American composers who flirted with French Impressionism probably the most sophisticated in that technique was Charles T. Griffes. Younger than Carpenter, Griffes died in 1920, before more advanced modernism burst upon the American scene. Born in Elmira, New York, September 17, 1884, Griffes was the son of a businessman. Both his father and mother had developed literary tastes and were fond of music. All five children in the family learned to play musical instruments, and Charles had his first piano lessons from an older sister. As a boy he was an avid reader and became particularly fascinated with the Orient and the poetry of Edgar Allan Poe. He was quite adept at drawing and painting with watercolors. He showed an unusual awareness of color and was often consulted on the family's artistic problems—matching pieces of quilting, proper flower arrangement, appropriate combinations of clothing, and the like. Young Griffes occasionally participated in neighborhood plays, was interested in photography, and showed his first real genius in music at age eleven, after falling ill with typhoid fever. At fifteen he began studying piano with Mary Selena Broughton, an English woman who taught at Elmira College.

In August, 1903, Charles set off for Berlin with the intention of becoming a concert pianist. Young Americans aspiring to be musicians were still pouring into Germany, where they studied, attended concerts and operas, visited the graves of the great masters, effected German accents, and frequently exasperated music teachers. Besides piano Griffes studied musical theory and composition; Engelbert Humperdinck was one of his teachers. At twenty he gave a public performance in Berlin of a piano sonata he had written. Upon returning to the United States in the summer of 1907, he obtained a position as music instructor at Hackley School for boys in Tarrytown, New York, about an hour away from New York City. He remained at the school for the rest of his life.

It was while Griffes was in Germany that he shifted his goal from concert pianist to composer. He wisely came to realize that his own playing was not exceptional enough for a distinguished career, yet knew he would be unable to support himself by writing. Family obligations necessitated that he teach, and he preferred the security of an academic post over private tutoring. His teaching, however, was irksome and a serious drain on his study and composition. Hackley was essentially a preparatory school for Harvard, Princeton, and Yale, patronized chiefly by wealthy families. His students were mostly mediocre and indifferent, and instructing them soon became a drudge. In addition to giving piano lessons, Griffes trained the choir, played the organ for Sunday chapel, played hymns on the piano during morning assembly, and occasionally gave recitals. He lived at the school in a small but comfortable apartment, spending holidays and summers in New York City, working on his compositions in a rented studio on West 46th Street. He often composed on the train ride between Tarrytown and New York City. He haunted Manhattan bookshops, built up a large and varied library, and accumulated a vast collection of scores. He visited Germany in the summer of 1908 and again in 1910. Although he was fascinated by metropolitan life, Griffes remained essentially the boy from Elmira, flabbergasted by the commotion of the big city.

In stature he was a small man—five feet, five and a half inches tall—with thin brown hair, a straight nose, high forehead, and of medium dark complexion. He possessed an extraordinary sense of humor and gave his life to a realistic struggle toward self-knowledge. His thoughts were in part molded by a personal atheism, not unusual among American intellectuals after the Darwinian revolution. He was an avowed homosexual, reading widely on the subject and keeping painfully honest notes on his psychological development. He devoted much effort to not being overcome by dreams and longings and sought to reconcile his impulses with dignity.

Griffes grew preoccupied with the relationship between color and music and came to sense a tonality of color. He began to associate certain keys in music with certain colors. The key of C major was for him an incandescent white, the most brilliant key of all and his favorite; E-flat was yellow or golden. Later he grew fond of scraping and mixing these colors. Yet the composer's early pieces reflect his German training, and his initial encounters with French Impressionism were less than enthusiastic. Gradually he assimilated French and Russian influences into his work, of these only the elements that were personal to him. The Impressionism he evolved was not fundamentally imitative, for Griffes' own nature was highly sensitive, his own outlook basically impressionistic.

His first published work, Five German Poems for solo voice and piano accompaniment, appeared in 1909. Many of the songs from the composer's Berlin days have not survived, but those salvaged from manuscripts after Griffes' death show the strong influence of Brahms, Wolf, and Strauss. As he moved away from this period of German control, Griffes found far greater difficulty in getting his works published. A number of his best liked piano pieces, however, date from his early years at Hackley School. Three Tone-Pictures, published in 1915, brought the composer to the attention of the musical world, followed shortly by Fantasy Pieces. Already his work evoked definite impressionistic moods. Three Tone-Pictures includes "The Lake at Evening" (1910), "The Night Winds" (1911), and "The Vale of Dreams" (1912), the latter a colorful and chromatic reflection of Poe's lines:

> At midnight, in the month of June,
> I stand beneath the mystic moon.
> An opiate vapor, dewy, dim,
> Exhales from out her golden rim,
>   And, softly dripping, drop by drop,
>   Upon the quiet mountain-top,
>   Steals drowsily and musically
>   Into the universal valley.

Fantasy Pieces contains "Barcarolle" (1912) and "Scherzo" (1913).

Griffes' long-standing interest in the Orient came forth in the tone poem *The Pleasure Dome of Kubla Khan*, his most important symphonic work. Based on Coleridge's poem and initially written as a piano piece sometime in 1912, the composition was revised and orchestrated four years later. It was introduced by the Boston Symphony Orchestra under the direction of Pierre Monteux on Friday afternoon, November 28, 1919. Carefully prepared, the work was a smash hit. The Chicago Symphony under Frederick Stock performed it the following January. Griffes once said, "I get much more inspiration from reading Oriental folk tales than I do from looking at a tree!" The truth of this statement seems evident in much of the composer's later work—certainly in Five Poems of Ancient China and Japan, a group of songs, and the ballet *Sho-Jo*, based on a legendary Japanese dance.

The influence of the French Impressionists over Griffes, both in harmony and melodic line, is well demonstrated in the four *Roman Sketches*, the best known of which is "The White Peacock," written for piano in 1915 and orchestrated just before the composer's death. The idea for this sketch came as Griffes was idly watching a sunset from a train between Tarrytown and New York City; he apparently associated the sunset with the image of a peacock. After 1915 the composer became increasingly disappointed with Debussy and the French modernists and began to free himself of their sway. His music now came to reflect in greater measure Griffes' personal struggle to achieve integrity and balance in his emotional life.

His Poem for Flute and Orchestra was completed in 1918, an exceptionally rich year for Griffes. Introduced by the New York Symphony on November 16, 1919, the Poem is among the composer's most mature works, ranging in color from the opening grey tones to the Oriental excitement of the dance section. His Sonata for Piano dates from the same year and shows a marked departure from Griffes' earlier impressionist style. Definitely one of the composer's most abstract works, the Sonata was written in an austere idiom, employing an original and arbitrary scale as its melodic and polyphonic basis. Edward Maisel, Griffes' biographer, finds the piece "exceptionally pure, absolute, uncompromisingly unemotional music, with not a cheap bar in it. The sound and the rhythm are the only rules here; no imagery could be associated with the composition." An exceedingly difficult piece, the Sonata is nonetheless powerful. For Mellers the work is "astonishing and frightening," demonstrating what can happen to the isolated individual in the industrial wilderness. The Englishman sees Griffes as disturbed, a man of extreme nervous sensitivity, who wore himself out in his youth. In his Sonata the composer is uttering a cry of anguish, for although he lives in the industrial society, he is opposed to it. He has become imprisoned in his own senses and has retreated into his art. The Sonata's Orientalism, Mellers argues, "is not an escape into dream but a consequence of desperation such as could have occurred only in a spiritually barbarous world. Debussy's revolution was balanced by his artistic conscience and by centuries of French civilization....Griffes' Sonata shows us how an American composer, given strong enough nerves, could experience Debussy's revolution 'raw.' "

Griffes was momentarily attracted to Indian themes in his Two Pieces for String Quartet, part of which was based on a Chippewa song of farewell. Less striking than the composer's better piano and orchestral works, his Indian sketches were first performed in 1918 by the Flonzaley Quartet and published by G. Schirmer four years later. The musician also turned out a *Notturno* for orchestra in 1918, as well as some of his best songs. Three Poems, set to texts by Fiona MacLeod, consists of "Thy Dark Eyes to Mine," "The Rose of the Night," and the shattering "Lament of Ian the Proud." All three reveal a free rhythmic development and a general mastery of the art of song. "Thy Dark Eyes to Mine" and "The Lament of Ian the Proud" delineate with unusual effectiveness moments of great emotional stress.

Despite the productivity of Griffes' last years, the composer labored against formidable obstacles, including poor health, a burdensome teaching assignment, and personal unhappiness. He died in Tarrytown on April 8, 1920, from an attack of influenza coupled with severe exhaustion. At the time of his death Griffes was a few months short of his thirty-sixth birthday and showed promise of evolving into a major talent. His last works contain a vigor that at times almost becomes violent, even vehement—in Mellers' view, the trapped genius beating himself against the cage into which he has fled. Although he worked in several styles, Griffes essentially progressed from the

German influence to the later French and Russian schools and eventually to a personalized modernism that mirrored his particular human dilemma. In this regard Griffes' development was not unlike the course of American composition generally around the turn of the century. Yet Griffes approached a mature stylistic synthesis, in which he himself was immersed, that most American composers before 1920 simply failed to achieve.

Whereas Paine, Chadwick, and Parker laid a foundation for composition that was instrumental in freeing later American musicians to search for an individual expression, their own writing is less important as art than as cultural history. The New England Conservatives failed in their attempt to transplant the bloom of the German tradition to American soil largely because their efforts appeared faded and lifeless in the dynamic atmosphere of a young, industrializing nation. Farwell and Gilbert, on the other hand, were hardly more successful in creating a national music from native themes or from stereotyped images of the American garden grafted onto an essentially conservative European style. While the local color of Indian suites and black rhapsodies might be pleasant nostalgia, neither the superficial use of native material nor the lingering symbols of the pastoral ideal were substantial representations of American life in an age of industrial turmoil.

As Germany became recognized musically as something of a dying swan in the years before World War I, increasing numbers of young Americans began going to France for study. While earlier students had come home orchestrating out of Wagner, the new breed learned their lessons out of Berlioz and later the French moderns. From their French contacts, however, American composers first tasted liberation. During the opening decades of the twentieth century a few of the most daring were beginning to cut themselves loose, independently searching for meaning amid a multiplicity of musical traditions that to the less venturesome spelled chaos. Then came the philosophical ramifications of World War I, ending both traditionalism and the dream of the American garden. A cluster of doubts, problems, outdated ideals, and loose ends suddenly fused into one giant explosion, leaving creative artists to reconstruct a new world for themselves. The search for values that had begun earlier suddenly became more frenzied, in music as in other areas of Western culture. Although many modern compositions were merely clever imitations of one experimental idiom or another, a distinguished few embraced real meaning, reflected sincere emotions, and occasionally captured the excitement of discovery. The paths ahead for American composers were far more confused than the well traveled thoroughfares left behind, but they were potentially fruitful ones, made all the more interesting by the artist's freedom to chart his own route and, in the case of genius, step to a different drummer.

CHAPTER

V

MacDowell and Ives

Had most Americans been asked in 1900 to name the greatest composer the
United States had produced to date, their answer most likely would have been
Edward MacDowell. MacDowell was the first American musician since
Gottschalk to win wide acclaim in Europe and the general respect of his own
countrymen. Trained in Germany and writing in a distinctly romantic vein,
the pianist-composer symbolized the American ideal in art music at the turn
of the century. Fifty years later MacDowell's reputation had tarnished a good
deal, and increasing numbers of sophisticates and critics were coming to
speak of Charles Ives as the nation's genius in serious music. Practically
unknown during his productive years, Ives was on the verge of being
canonized a decade after his death. "We have suddenly discovered," Leonard
Bernstein announced in 1959, "our musical Mark Twain, Emerson, and
Lincoln all rolled into one." Although the work of one was roughly
contemporary of the other, the distance between MacDowell and Ives in
temperament was vast. MacDowell in large measure was a summary of the
past, a gifted reflection of a fading era. Not only did he epitomize America's
version of German Romanticism, but his success signaled the decline of the
genteel tradition that had dominated serious music in the United States since
the days of Francis Hopkinson and James Hewitt. Ives, on the other hand,
was detached from the musical establishment, his work was more
experimental; and without intending to he looked far into the future.

MacDowell was the older of the two by thirteen years. Born in New York

City on December 18, 1861, Edward was the third son of Thomas and Frances Knapp MacDowell. His father was of Scotch ancestry, while his mother was Irish. The family had a Quaker background and enjoyed an upper middle class social status. Edward grew up a child of the city, experiencing little more of nature than what might be observed on family picnics in Central Park and on visits to his grandfather's farm. The boy was fond of sports, particularly baseball; he won a prize for his marksmanship. He attended public school and later a private French academy. Although Thomas MacDowell was a businessman, he harbored deep artistic interests and at one point had wanted to be a painter. When Edward showed an interest in music, his father was sympathetic, while his mother soon dreamed of her son becoming a concert pianist. The lad's first music lessons were taken at age eight from Juan Buitrago, a family acquaintance from South America. Edward proved no prodigy, but played the piano well enough that Buitrago's friend Teresa Carreño gave him a few lessons during one of her visits to New York.

The youth also enjoyed making drawings in a sketchbook and reading. He became fascinated with the legends of old Ireland and poured over tales of elves and fairies. At twelve Edward was taken to Europe by his mother, and the two of them spent a summer traveling through England, Ireland, Scotland, France, Germany, and Switzerland. The boy sketched many of the sights he saw and, like his father earlier, entertained the notion of becoming a professional painter. Upon returning to New York, young MacDowell spent another year at the French school and thereafter concentrated on music.

In April, 1876, when Edward was fifteen, he again went abroad with his mother, this time for study. He went first to France, where he entered the Paris Conservatory, studying piano with Marmontel and music theory with Savard. Within a year he was awarded a full scholarship. One of his fellow students was Claude Debussy. Edward's original teacher, Buitrago, had accompanied the MacDowells to Paris, and after the boy's mother returned to America, the two musicians shared a Paris apartment for a time.

After two years in Paris, MacDowell grew to dislike the French and became dissatisfied with the progress he was making at the Conservatory. Upon hearing Nicholas Rubinstein play the Tchaikovsky Piano Concerto in B-flat Minor, he wrote home that he could never learn to play like that if he remained in Paris. He moved to Germany and for a brief period studied at the Stuttgart Conservatory. Still unhappy with his training, MacDowell next tried Frankfort, where he studied piano under Carl Heymann and composition with Joachim Raff. Not only was his progress in the Frankfort Conservatory eminently satisfactory, but it was largely through the influence of Raff that the American decided to shift his emphasis to composition.

By 1880 MacDowell was a polished pianist and a carefully trained musician. When illness forced Heymann to retire from the Conservatory that year, he recommended the eighteen year-old pianist as his successor—a recommendation which Raff seconded. His youth and faculty politics kept MacDowell from getting the appointment. He continued to study with

Heymann privately and soon began taking pupils of his own. He also composed his first pieces. Raff had grown tired of mechanical exercises in composition and challenged his student to try something real. In response MacDowell wrote his First Modern Suite for piano. A Second Modern Suite followed shortly, written on train rides between visits to pupils.

With Raff's support the young musician secured a teaching position in 1881 at the Darmstadt Conservatory, where he taught mostly children of German aristocrats. The next year Raff sent his American protege to Weimar to show his work to Franz Liszt, whom MacDowell especially admired. The youth sat in the great man's garden for almost an hour, clutching his manuscripts, too petrified to approach the house. When he was finally observed and called inside, Liszt had other guests, but was cordial. MacDowell had brought along his freshly composed First Piano Concerto, which he played, with the composer Eugene d'Albert filling in the orchestral part at a second piano. Liszt praised both MacDowell's music and his slashing keyboard brilliance. "You had best bestir yourself," the master supposedly told d'Albert, "if you do not wish to be outdone by our young American."

MacDowell played for Liszt on other occasions before the composer's death in 1886, and it was through Liszt's intervention that Breitkopf & Haertel published the Modern Suites in 1883. Raff died in 1882, a real blow to MacDowell, for the old man had been almost a father to him. Professionally the teacher had made a lasting impression, and MacDowell's later work often bore the mark of Raff's own compositions.

Among his German friends MacDowell had become known as the "handsome American," for he possessed a fine physique, fair skin, blue eyes, and jet black hair. One of his first private pupils was Marian Nevins, an American girl who had studied briefly with Clara Schumann and then Raff. Feeling that the girl would do better with a teacher who knew her language, Raff sent her to MacDowell. Miss Nevins saw little point in traveling all the way to Germany to study with an American, but finally consented to work with MacDowell for a year. Her new teacher's response was initially reserved: "I really think you have a good deal of talent," he said after hearing her play, "but you play the piano very badly." For the first six months MacDowell gave the girl nothing but grueling exercises, then let her tackle a Liszt arrangement of a Bach prelude and fugue. Marian Nevins took at least two lessons a week with MacDowell for three years. And then they fell in love. The couple returned to the United States for a short vacation and were married in the Nevins family home in Waterford, Connecticut, July 21, 1884.

After a short honeymoon in London, the MacDowells took up residence in Frankfurt. Edward's decision to make a career of composing offered them little security. "Really from one month to the other we know nothing of our movements for the future," Marian wrote her sisters in 1885, "and it seems a question whether we will be able to settle down for any length of time anywhere." The next year they moved to Wiesbaden, renting an apartment of their own. "Our life in Frankfurt and Wiesbaden was very quiet," Marian remembered years later, "Edward working terribly hard and I doing the practical thing, making a very modest but real home for him." The couple eventually bought a small cottage near the edge of a forest.

Before his marriage MacDowell had composed five songs and a number of shorter piano pieces. A two-part symphonic poem, *Hamlet and Ophelia*, his first purely orchestral work, was written in Frankfurt soon after the London honeymoon. In Wiesbaden the composer completed *Lancelot and Elaine*, another symphonic poem; worked on *The Saracens* and *The Lovely Alda*, two orchestral paraphrases of fragments from the *Song of Roland*; began *Lamia*, after Keats; and was well into his Second Piano Concerto. His accomplished technique demonstrated the rigid discipline of the Paris Conservatory, although his style strongly mirrored the Romanticism of his German training. While MacDowell revered Liszt, Mendelssohn, and Schumann, his early compositions in particular sound strikingly like Grieg. Passages of the American's Second Concerto are virtually echoes of the Norwegian's great Piano Concerto in A.

The MacDowells had returned to Europe after their wedding determined that Edward should have four years free from teaching, four years during which he could devote himself exclusively to composing. Marian had an independent income which they planned to use, and Edward accepted infrequent concert engagements. The couple prepared to live simply, spending vacations on walking tours through Switzerland. They agreed that when they had only a few hundred dollars left, they would return to America. During these years Marian suffered intermittent poor health, became pregnant in 1887, but miscarried. Edward's mother was constantly urging the couple to come home, even offering to pay their way. B. J. Lang, a noted Boston musician, visited them and urged the composer not to become an "American foreigner, of which there were too many already."

Despite having spent almost half of his life in Europe, MacDowell was at heart an American, nurtured something of Whitman's faith in democracy, and perhaps felt a need to prove that there was room for the artist in his native country. Responding in part to Lang's impelling plea, the MacDowells left Germany in the fall of 1888, arranging for the sale of their Weisbaden cottage through a friend. They sailed for Boston, where they planned to live, with the intention that Edward would continue composing, but move more actively into the concert field. MacDowell's work was not unknown to America, for Teresa Carreño, the Venezuelan pianist who had given Edward a few lessons, had been performing his pieces since 1883. The last two movements of his First Piano Concerto had been heard in New York under Frank van der Stucken in March, 1885, and by 1887 both parts of *Hamlet and Ophelia* had been played in Chickering Hall, although at different times. The public was eager to hear MacDowell himself, particularly playing his own compositions.

MacDowell was now twenty-seven years old. His sense of humor, intelligence, good-natured personality, and attractive appearance soon won him a place in the Boston social circle. In October, 1888, B. J. Lang gave a party for the newcomers at his home, introducing the MacDowells to representatives of the city's professional and cultural life. Among those present was T. P. Currier, later a MacDowell pupil, who recalled meeting the musician:

> MacDowell...was a picture of robust manliness. His finely shaped head, carried a little to one side, was well set on slightly drooping shoulders. His very dark hair was close-cut, for he had no liking for the "artistic pose." There was about him no trace of the "professional artist," save perhaps in the stray lock prematurely streaked with grey that would persistently fall on his broad forehead, and in the Kaiser-like curl of his light sandy mustache, which at that time was balanced by a fairly large goatee.

During his last years in Germany MacDowell had spent so much time composing that his playing had suffered. He hated to practice and would gladly have forsaken the concert platform altogether. But he needed the money and realized that the only way to get his music solidly before the public was to perform it himself, capitalizing on the composer-pianist image Americans had adored in Gottschalk. The musician set about improving his technique, and his playing soon became virtuosic, although marked with original qualities. He detested scales and arpeggios for their own sake and sought to produce tone-pictures and atmospheric effects. He came off better when performing with an orchestra than he did in recitals, and he invariably made a deeper impression with his own works than when interpreting others. His playing of Beethoven, for instance, was often erratic and out of proportion. To have perfected his skill as a pianist, however, would have meant sacrificing hours for composition, and this MacDowell was unwilling to do.

His American debut as a pianist took place on November 19, 1888, in New York's Chickering Hall at a Kneisel String Quartet concert. He performed part of his First Modern Suite for piano and assisted in Karl Goldmark's Piano Quintet. He played more of his music for the Apollo Club on December 10, and was asked by Wilhelm Gericke to appear as soloist with the Boston Symphony Orchestra. He performed the world premiere of his Second Piano Concerto with the New York Philharmonic under Theodore Thomas on March 5, 1889, and repeated the work with the Boston Symphony a month later. The concerto was enthusiastically received on both occasions. H. E. Krehbiel wrote in the *New York Tribune* that it was "a splendid composition, so full of poetry, so full of vigor, as to tempt the assertion that it must be placed at the head of all works of its kind produced by either a native or adopted citizen of America." When James G. Huneker cornered Theodore Thomas a few days after the premiere, conversation turned to the MacDowell concerto. Huneker remarked that the piece "was very good for an American." "Yes," Thomas indignantly snapped back, "or for a German either!"

The Second Piano Concerto was presented the following summer on an all-American concert at the Paris Exposition, with MacDowell as soloist, under the direction of Frank van der Stucken. The work remained a favorite of MacDowell's and the one with which he received his greatest concert successes. He always played it "with magnificent verve, power and abandon"—his brilliant technique fairly glittering. When the concerto was published in 1890, after much revision, it was fittingly dedicated to the composer's friend and admirer Teresa Carreño.

MacDowell's eight years in Boston were essentially happy ones. He found the city's musical life pleasantly active, and after feeling like a stranger for more than a decade, he took pleasure in the sense of belonging he experienced in America. He became imbued with the desire to do everything possible to advance his country's musical development, pursuing his own career goals at the same time. He continued concertizing, making frequent trips into the Middle West. He tried to limit these tours to three weeks, since he found traveling exhausting and disliked being away from home. He played mainly his own compositions, but flavored his programs with "old chestnuts" like *Moonlight* Sonata.

He resumed teaching and by his third season in Boston was literally besieged with would-be piano students. Pupils were consistently charmed by his cordial personality and often attested to the magic of his pedagogy. His methods were unorthodox to be sure, sometimes quite impressionistic. "Make that run as if it were a sweep of color!" he would urge. He dreamed of teaching composition like Raff, but was dismayed to discover so few students in the United States with creative talent. To live in financial ease he was forced to give piano lessons, although this was much less distasteful to him than the periodic appearances as a concert artist.

His greatest satisfaction still came from composition, and the Boston years were the most productive of his life. His style remained unashamedly romantic and for some time in the German mold. Since Boston's loyalty to the Germanic tradition was at its height, MacDowell was comfortably at home. The composer's early growth is evident from a comparison of his First and Second Piano Concertos, yet his creative powers deepened even more after his return to the United States. The musician's own personality was singularly romantic and idealistic; he loved beauty and grandeur and viewed nature as a symbol of sanctity. Although his larger works avoided originality, they did embody much of the composer's own spirit and were written with extraordinary craftsmanship. MacDowell considered himself a tone-poet, and his pictorial sense—a carryover perhaps from his enthusiasm for painting—was repeatedly evident in his compositions and their titles. Late nineteenth-century America looked upon MacDowell's music as truly progressive, untinged as it was by classical restraint. His skill with melody and richly colored harmony were championed *because* of their blatant romanticism, and the composer soon became identified as the epitome of the cherished vogue. Only gradually did MacDowell begin to establish a glimmering of individuality, slowly becoming more intimate in his approach, less bold in his romantic statement.

His "Six Love Songs" were written shortly after the composer's return from Europe and published in 1890. As MacDowell began to acquaint himself with contemporary trends in American letters, he grew enthusiastic about the work of William Dean Howells and the literary realists and was inspired by their efforts to break away from European influence. Three of the composer's "Eight Songs" for voice were settings of Howells' poems. He wrote a number of smaller piano pieces and a Raff-like orchestral suite, introduced by Carl Zerrahn at a Worcester Festival in 1891.

The first of his four piano sonatas—the *Tragica*—was completed in 1893 and played by MacDowell at a Kneisel concert in Boston. The piece clearly demonstrates the composer's poetic nature, while his themes of pathos are developed without sinking into sentimentality. MacDowell said he sought to express tragic details in the first three movements and a generalization in the last—heightening "the darkness of tragedy by making it follow closely on the heels of triumph." The second sonata—the *Eroica*, finished in 1895—was based on the King Arthur legend. MacDowell never lost his childhood fascination for mythical literature and developed a deep love for medieval history, both of which crept into his music from time to time. The *Eroica* opens with the coming of Arthur, described in ferocious, warlike themes. The second movement suggests a knight in the forest surrounded by elves, while Arthur's supernatural qualities are indicated through a flibbertigibbet virtuosity and the magic of color. The grief of Arthur's farewell to Guinevere is pictured in the third movement, and the death of Arthur is the subject of the last.

MacDowell's Second Orchestral Suite—the *Indian* Suite—was his best and last symphonic work, loosely based on Indian material. The composer had grown increasingly interested in local color realism in American literature and had especially come to admire the regionalism of Hamlin Garland. This, rather than Dvorak's famous plea for American composers to make greater use of native themes, brought MacDowell to select an aboriginal subject. In fact the composer scornfully rejected Dvorak's premise (offered in 1895, while the Bohemian composer was director of the National Conservatory in New York) of a national music based on folk idioms. "Masquerading in the so-called nationalism of Negro clothes cut in Bohemia will not help us," MacDowell insisted. And to Hamlin Garland he wrote, "I do not believe in 'lifting' a Navajo theme and furbishing it into some kind of a musical composition and calling it American music. Our problem is not so simple as all that." For MacDowell nationalism had no part in art; music particularly was a universal language by which one soul speaks to another. "If a composer is sincerely American at heart," he said, "his music will be American." The *Indian* Suite was therefore conceived in MacDowell's customary romantic style with no intention of writing distinctly American music. The Indian melodies are not quoted directly, but refined and grafted onto broadly romantic contours. The work is scored with considerable skill and was first performed by the Boston Symphony Orchestra under Emil Paur in New York City, January 23, 1896.

With the completion of the *Indian* Suite, MacDowell gave up orchestral writing, which had never been his best medium, and concentrated on composing for the piano. "It's one thing to write works for orchestra, and another to get them performed," he told a friend. "There isn't much satisfaction in having a thing played once in two or three years." By writing for the piano the composer could play his pieces himself whenever he liked. But MacDowell had also reached the point where he wanted to express himself more personally in his music, and he could do this best in piano selections. After the *Indian* Suite—and again strongly influenced by the literary realists—MacDowell, the composer, became far more his own master, moving toward a more singular style.

The musician had become a distinguished figure in Boston. His life was busy but pleasureful. He enjoyed quiet strolls in the late afternoon after the grind of teaching, and he adored sports. He found great comfort in his Chestnut Street home, where evenings were spent reading, practicing, or writing. The MacDowells entertained frequently, for although the composer was awkward and shy around people he did not know, he delighted in a select circle of friends. When at ease he was a brilliant conversationalist and invariably enchanted guests with his winning sense of humor. The couple acquired two dogs, a collie named Charlemagne and a terrier named Charlie. The latter was MacDowell's constant companion, particularly during summer vacations in rural New Hampshire. The composer taught the terrier to bark happily when he heard the music of Wagner and to howl in anguish when he heard Brahms—much to the joy of special friends. Rollo Brown in his *Lonely Americans* portrays the musician as a sensitive, charming aristocrat, calling him "the handsomest thoroughbred that ever stepped up to address a golf ball."

But the contentment MacDowell had come to know in Boston was shattered in 1896, when the trustees of Columbia University asked the composer to head the new music department there. Frances MacDowell, the musician's mother, had been maneuvering for years to entice her "children" back to New York City and rarely missed a chance to mention these designs to Marian, her daughter-in-law. When Columbia received a sizeable sum of money in the fall of 1895 for the endowment of a chair of music, the composer's mother seized upon the opportunity and aggressively pushed her son's candidacy for the position. She eventually went to the renowned John William Burgess, Dean of the Columbia School of Law and a member of the selection committee for the music post, and requested that Edward be considered for the new professorship. Burgess informed Mrs. MacDowell that her son had already been recommended and in fact ranked high on the list of potential candidates. She had written her daughter-in-law earlier that since "Eddie" would not "raise a finger to get that or any position," she had decided she would! "Prof. Burgess is an old fogy and will do all he promises in the most substantial and dogged manner," she confided to Marian. "Nor shall I stop at this. I shall do all I can. I shall leave no stone unturned." None of this, of course, must be mentioned to Edward, Frances cautioned Marian, for "not even papa knows what I am trying to do."

MacDowell had played his Second Piano Concerto with the New York Philharmonic under Anton Seidl in December, 1894, and had covered himself with glory. Dean Burgess later wrote that he came away "from that concert pretty well convinced that MacDowell was our man." When Burgess asked the noted pianist William Mason whom he considered America's greatest living composer, the musician without hesitation named MacDowell. The *Eroica* Sonata, published a week earlier, had coincidentally been dedicated to Mason. Polish pianist Ignace Jan Paderewski wrote MacDowell a strong recommendation, stating without reservations that the composer was the best man for the position. The appointment was offered to MacDowell in March, 1896—despite a promise to the university of a $100,000 gift from a lady donor if a candidate named by her were selected. Columbia's president Seth Low assured MacDowell an annual salary of $5000 and "our fullest confidence and our complete support." Edward was flattered, and although his wife objected to the move, eventually decided the opportunity was simply too good to turn down. When his acceptance was announced to the press the next month, New York critics greeted the news with hearty enthusiasm.

The decision proved a fatal mistake. The post had appealed to MacDowell not only for the prestige and financial security it offered, but because he felt it would provide a framework through which he could demonstrate on a large scale his views on teaching and contribute something significant to the cause of American music. The eight months following his acceptance were feverish ones. Organizational details for the department of music had to be worked out, and there was the planning of his own courses. The MacDowells moved to New York City in July, and for the next year the composer enjoyed practically no time of his own. He gave his best to his teaching and worked well with students. He lectured on the history and esthetics of music and taught courses in harmony and composition. He corrected exercises with meticulous care, consulted regularly with pupils, and for a season conducted New York's Mendelssohn Glee Club. But from the beginning he was bored by administrative routine and felt hampered by academic procedure.

New York City had changed a great deal since MacDowell had left. The house where he had spent his boyhood was gone, and in its place stood an ugly tenement. The musician disliked visiting his parents too often, as his mother was prone to have strangers on hand to meet him. Marian finessed the problem by having the elder MacDowells to dinner once a week, making it something of an occasion by having a woman come in to cook an excellent meal and always serving good wine. "They loved it and he loved it," the composer's wife admitted later, "and neither of them realized that it was sort of a trick on my part."

Most of MacDowell's writing was now done during summers on his farm outside Peterboro, New Hampshire. The couple adored the place and each year with the close of the spring semester anxiously left the city. The musician would "fuss around" the farm until he was rested and then begin the season's composition. In the early morning he would slip off through the woods to a little cabin, where he could work in absolute quiet. Late in the day, particularly if he had finished something, he carried the manuscript back to the house with him. During the evening he would sit down at the piano and try the piece on Marian, whose opinion meant much to him.

His music was deepening. Not only was it becoming freer in form, but there was a more personal expression of the artist himself. His *Norse* Sonata—his third sonata for piano—was published in 1900 and dedicated to Edvard Grieg, the composer with whom the American was most sympathetic. Henry Gilbert, who had studied with MacDowell in Boston, recalled hearing his teacher say that he "almost felt as if he were Grieg's brother." In the *Norse* Sonata MacDowell achieved an epic breadth, as he depicted the barbaric feeling of the Norse sagas—widening his chord formations and extending the scope of his phrases. The work again reflects the musician's love of medieval history and interest in mythical literature. The composer obtains an atmosphere of mystery and heroic grandeur in the Sonata, suggesting battles, loves, and deaths in ancient castles. Huneker called the piece "an epic of rainbow and thunder," while Henry T. Finck said: "It is MacDowellish—more MacDowellish than anything he has yet written. It is the work of a musical thinker."

More satisfying to the composer was his fourth sonata, the *Keltic*, completed a year later and also dedicated to Grieg. MacDowell considered it the best constructed of all his larger works. Inspired by the mythology of the musician's own ancestry, the *Keltic* Sonata is epic in conception and rich in poetic charm.

But MacDowell was best as a miniaturist and ended as a composer of concise genre pieces. His songs make up about a third of his total output, and even in Germany the composer's lyric efforts had been distinguished by a melodic opulence and a tenderness of expression. Later he wrote a number of his own words and projected them clearly through music precisely fashioned. Before leaving Boston, MacDowell had written the *Woodland* Sketches, including "To a Wild Rose," "In Autumn," "To a Water Lily," "A Deserted Farm," and "By a Meadow Brook." The pieces are musical reveries, tenderly felt and exquisitely accomplished. They are impressionistic tone-poems, painted in delicate shades by an artist in awe of the natural world.

Two years later the *Sea* Pieces appeared. MacDowell's style is again terse, even though the subject matter is grandiose. The composer was fascinated by the sea, both loved it and was terrified by its power. Of his smaller selections the *Sea* Pieces were MacDowell's favorite, and they may indeed represent the composer's finest achievement. Contained in the set are "To the Sea," "In Mid-Ocean," "A Wandering Iceberg," and "A.D. 1620" (about the

Mayflower). The music's fundamental simplicity makes its impact all the greater; it is lyric, yet dramatic. The pieces are sensuous, wistful, personal. From time to time there are glimmers of darkness, for MacDowell was often plagued by doubts about life and man's fate in general. "In Mid-Ocean" not only conveys the motion of the waves, but something of the mighty natural laws governing them. There is a sense of determinism running through the selection that suggests the influence of the literary naturalists. The piece evokes the feeling of man's insignificance, his dependence on implacable forces, reminiscent of Stephen Crane's "The Open Boat."

Later the composer wrote *Fireside Tales*, including "Of Br'er Rabbit," and *New England Idyls*, among them "From a Log Cabin" and "From Puritan Days." Again the pieces are small in length only. Both sets are big in ideas and full of atmospheric effects. MacDowell has become comfortable in his impressionistic view of nature and feels free to express his innermost feelings. "To an Old White Pine," inspired by an enormous tree on the musician's farm, vividly pictures the swaying branches of the venerable tree. The listener hears the wind and audibly experiences motion. Many of these pieces are frankly nostalgic, and there is often an honest innocence. In Meller's judgment the composer's best work represents "a boy's view of the American past, looked back to from a premature middle age; and they are most successful when most unequivocally boyish."

Summers at Peterboro were also times of relaxation, and MacDowell delighted in tramping over the New Hampshire hills, riding in a sulky, gardening, doing occasional carpentry work, and pursuing his hobby of photography. He spent hours chatting with the farmer who tended his property and respected the freshness of the man's philosophy. And there was time for reading. The composer reveled in the world of books. He regretted his lack of formal education, but was determined to taste the great ideas. He fed on variety—Sophocles, Machiavelli, Schiller, Emerson, Malory, Cervantes, Tolstoy, Fiona MacLeod, Conrad, the early writings of Woodrow Wilson— and admired the vitality of their thoughts. For MacDowell the whole business of existence, uncertain as it may be, was exciting, and he explored the dimension of life with uncommon energy.

The farm increasingly became MacDowell's retreat, the haven that gave him serenity and time for thought. Once an unexpected visitor intruded and critically inquired why he had planted a field of corn so near the house. The musician answered bluntly, "Madam, that is so I may always be able to hide easily when I don't want to meet people who are coming to see me." Fortunately Marian found pleasure in solitude, too, and possessed an active mind. The couple enjoyed hours of lively conversation. MacDowell often tagged along with his wife in the garden or as she went about kitchen chores, while they discussed books they had read, ideas they had encountered. At Peterboro it was not unusual for the two to sit in the light of the fireplace until practically dawn musing over art and life.

But back in New York City the pace quickened. Constant demands were made on the musician's time; there was the strain of teaching, the treadmill of administration, the rehearsing of pupils for recitals. Each winter between semesters he took a brief leave from the university for a concert tour. He still disliked performing in public, resented the time required for practice, yet was tormented when he felt he had played poorly. He remained an enthusiastic teacher, resolved not to let the learning process sink into drudgery. In the classroom he was constantly at the piano, illustrating his points from the range of music literature. His teaching was at times over the heads of students who were not well grounded, but John Erskine, who studied with MacDowell at Columbia, found him "one of the most stimulating geniuses I ever met."

The composer rarely attended concerts. "You must not hear much if you are to write much," he told Henry Gilbert. His interest in sports, however, continued, and he once missed a faculty meeting to see a prize fight. Arriving at the ringside feeling guilty, he was amused to discover "about a third" of his university colleagues seated around him.

Yet friends noted that MacDowell looked tired. He appeared older; his mind seemed troubled, weighted down with the load he was carrying. He was forever hurrying from one engagement to another, as each year his schedule grew heavier. He interrupted a visit with a Boston acquaintance to keep an appointment, softly saying to his friend as he dashed off, "Things are very different here in New York."

MacDowell had consistently approached his academic duties as an artist and an idealist. He dreamed of building a center for music education that would bring music nearer the American public. He was vitally concerned about the relationship between music and the other arts and eventually proposed a freer program of instruction, embracing literature, architecture, painting, and sculpture. University officials saw this as impractical. Seth Low, who had sympathized with the composer's vision, was elected mayor of greater New York in 1902 and was succeeded as president of Columbia by Nicholas Murray Butler. It was soon evident that Butler had opposing ideas on how the division of fine arts should be organized. When MacDowell went on sabbatical the next fall, Butler took the opportunity to initiate his own plan. The composer returned to his academic duties a year later, highly nervous and discouraged by the changes that had taken place during his absence. He spent the Christmas holidays at Peterboro, and after much discussion with his wife, decided to resign from teaching. He informed President Butler of this decision privately in early January, 1904.

News of the resignation leaked out. MacDowell was clearly hurt by his recent differences with the administration, and when two student reporters interviewed him and chided him for being a quitter, the musician exploded with customary candor. The explosion was covered in the New York newspapers within a matter of hours. The *Times* quoted MacDowell as saying college graduates were "barbarians" and that in his eight years at Columbia he had had only three students with whom he was truly satisfied. Over the next few weeks a heated exchange occurred between Butler and

MacDowell in the syndicated press. There was the strong implication that the composer had neglected his teaching duties and permitted his assistant to cover most of his classes. This infuriated MacDowell more than anything else and hurt him deeply. The trustees meanwhile accepted the musician's resignation, but reprimanded him for making his grievances public. His action was considered in the official report "an offense against propriety, a discourtesy to the Board, and a breach of that confidence which the Board always seeks to repose in every officer of the University."

With commencement exercises in June, MacDowell left Columbia, a depressed and disillusioned man. His assistant, Leonard McWhood, remembered the composer's returning to his room on the ground floor of South Hall when commencement ceremonies were over. His personal belongings were already gone. MacDowell took off his academic gown and was ready to leave. He held the gown in his arm; his face was sad—tragic. The memory haunted McWhood:

> Several times he tried to cross the threshold into my room, and some force held him back. I was speechless, transfixed by the vision. His tears flowed freely. It seemed that all his hopes and joys, all his fears and sorrows were centered, after eight years, in one supreme moment. Finally, he stretched forth his hand, as though he would enter the room; but no, he could not. Then speech came to him—two words! Trembling, gulping in his throat, speaking with great effort and in a voice of infinite pathos, he said, with a pause between the words: "Well—good-bye!" Then, suddenly, he was gone.

The composer brooded and brooded. He lay awake nights, unable to clear his mind of restless thoughts. He had always had trouble communicating his ideas on music to others and had a history of brutal honesty. But he felt severely wronged, betrayed by those he had trusted, and was uncertain as to why this had happened.

A few weeks before, MacDowell's parents had paid their weekly call on Edward and Marian, who by then were living in the Westminster Hotel. The weather was bad, the streets slippery. After dinner the MacDowells decided to walk the elderly couple to a streetcar. At the corner of Broadway and Twentieth Street, the composer stepped into the street to help his parents board a trolley. As he stepped back a hansom cab swung around the corner and threw him to the icy pavement, its wheels going across his spine. From the sidewalk Marian watched in horror. "Something kept the horses from stepping on him; otherwise he would have been killed," she wrote later. "He was bruised and miserable for days and complained constantly of his back." Gradually the aches and pains receded, and the incident was forgotten.

That summer in Peterboro the musician was tense and irritable. He could not get the Columbia business out of his mind, and he talked of it repeatedly. Weeks went by, and still he was able to think of little else.

Composing was out of the question. In the fall the couple returned to New York City. With the coming of winter Edward's mood grew more sullen. As he was strolling with Marian in the park one day, he suddenly felt unable to move. After a few minutes he recovered, and the two walked back to their apartment in the Westminster Hotel. A short time later they had dinner with their friend Hamlin Garland. "The dinner started gayly," Garland remembered, "but as it went on something in MacDowell's look and action disturbed me, and this disturbed feeling rapidly deepened into alarm. He looked ill—seriously ill. His mind wandered and his hands were nerveless. Worst of all, his face took on that empty look which I had observed once or twice before, an expression so unlike his brilliant usual self."

Within a matter of weeks the truth was obvious. MacDowell was losing his mind. At forty-three his once handsome body was suddenly that of an old man. His hair had whitened. His face more and more assumed a blank expression. He sat for hours in an easy chair by the window and gazed into space. He looked at pictures in books of fairy tales, as Marian turned the pages, as if his childhood images were the only thing still with him. He fondled with tenderness a loving cup his students at Columbia had given him. Old friends dropped by occasionally for a visit; MacDowell appeared startled. Sometimes he rallied to a faint effort at mental activity; sometimes he could offer no more than a vacant stare. Early in the spring Mrs. MacDowell wrote a friend, "Edward has broken down completely, and we are crushed....O! If we had never left Boston!"

The couple spent another summer in Peterboro. For a time MacDowell seemed improved. When Hamlin Garland saw him the following November, he was encouraged. "I was instantly relieved," the writer noted in his diary. "He greeted me with a cheery word and his familiar shy smile, and began at once to ask after my wife and my little daughter." By December the illusion of recovery was gone. MacDowell no longer was able to walk. The empty weeks stretched into months as the composer drifted into absolute helplessness. In his better moments he played dominoes or read slowly, rereading the same page many times. In bad spells he sat alone in dead grey silence.

Meanwhile letters poured in from across the nation, expressing concern and affection. A devoted student made transcriptions of some of the composer's more popular selections and sent the royalties to Mrs. MacDowell. Seth Low went to the musician's wife and told her: "I am partly responsible for this. Here is a check for five thousand dollars."

But the deterioration continued—with awful slowness. In November, 1907, there was one more tenuous turn for the better; then it was rapidly downhill. MacDowell had often said he did not feel destined for a long life. He died quietly on January 23, 1908, in the Westminster Hotel. Funeral services were held in New York, followed by interment at Peterboro. Although it was winter and the ground was covered with snow, the day was almost like autumn. The temperature was warm, the sky a deep blue. Exhausted by months of watching her husband's agony, Marian MacDowell was too worn to take in much of the funeral. But "I do remember so distinctly," she wrote forty years later, "a little bird which came and perched on the very edge of the coffin and sang a soft little song. Then the coffin was lowered into the bed of green boughs and everybody quietly left—a very beautiful end to a beautiful friendship."

MacDowell remains a classic example of the sensitive, creative mind crushed by institutional bureaucracy. Henry Finck remarked at the time of the Columbia affair that it is never wise to harness Pegasus. Yet the composer's particular tragedy was heightened by issues that at best seemed ill-defined. After her husband's death Mrs. MacDowell undertook concert tours of her own, playing Edward's music. Although she considered her talents meager, the widow agreed to perform to raise funds for an artist's colony at Peterboro, thereby fulfilling one of her husband's great wishes. Columbia University eventually established the Edward MacDowell Chair of Music.

The composer's exalted acclaim in his own day may in part have assured the eclipse of his reputation later. Gradually the original superlatives came to be replaced by condescension and then insular favor. While he was no Beethoven, MacDowell's music did achieve considerable heights and can scarcely be dismissed as sentimental falderal. He was surely the best trained musician America had yet produced. Although he was strongly romantic, his romanticism was forged from his own nature, training, and experience. He loved Europe, but he knew Europe intimately. The America he knew was a limited, urbane, sophisticated one, oriented more toward established civilization than toward vernacular roots. He was a dreamer, inspired by ancient castles, enchanted forests, and medieval lore, as well as vestiges of the American garden. But his dreams sprang from the heart of an idyllist. He essentially assimilated European motives into his own cultural orbit. Even in his more personal phase, the European romantics continued to haunt him, as his music bridged the gap between the composer's dreams and his reality.

While MacDowell's larger works are filled with Lisztian sweep and Tchaikovskian fervor, they often seem inflated and self-consciously grand. His smaller impressionistic pieces, however, contain a more convincing vigor and a more durable freshness. The composer was best as a tone-poet speaking in fragile terms about familiar images. His mood invariably is genteel, full of noble pathos, youthful tenderness, and adolescent bravura, for this was MacDowell. He was a quixotic Celt living in a land of vanishing Indians, industrializing Yankees, and rising organizational entrepreneurs—none of which he particularly understood. But he was confident that to live in the present one had to come to terms with a complex past. And so he read and thought and was receptive, in the hope of working it all out. But the life around him raced on, and there was no time.

Whereas Edward MacDowell searched for a soft beauty and tempered dreams with reality, Charles Ives looked much more squarely at the industrial complex dominating their age and sought a rugged masculinity in his music. Ives listened less to the winds for inspiration and more to the sounds of humanity around him. Almost a personification of John Dewey's "new individualism," Charles Ives rose to success in a commercial society by accepting the industrial system for what it was and earned a comfortable leisure for himself by capitalistic methods. During private hours, however, he pursued what was personally meaningful to him—works that expressed his singular life and personality, highly original music that he found both esthetic and fun.

Ives was born in Danbury, Connecticut, on October 20, 1874, and came from an ancestry that reached far back in New England history. His mother sang in the church choir, but it was from his father, George Ives, that the composer acquired most of his early ideas on music. George had been a bandmaster during the Civil War and had headed the Connecticut Heavy Artillery First Brigade Band during the siege of Richmond. At the time Charles was growing up, his father was a music teacher and leader of the Danbury brass band. The senior Ives had a sound musical training, but possessed an unusual interest in experimenting with acoustics. He worked with a quarter-tone instrument and investigated variations in harmony. He once arranged his band in three or four groups around the town square for a holiday celebration. The main group sat in the bandstand and played the principal themes, while the others were stationed on neighboring roofs and verandas and played the variations and refrains. Charles grew up convinced by his father that only a fraction of the means of musical expression was known.

George Ives took his son's musical education in hand when the boy was five. He was taught to play band instruments, and later was instructed in harmony and counterpoint; he was imbued with a love of Bach, Handel, and Beethoven. From the village barber, a member of George's band, Charles learned the rudiments of snare drumming, which the child adored. But the atmosphere in which the young Ives lived was saturated with church and camp meeting hymns, barn dance fiddling, minstrel show tunes, military marches, and sentimental ballads. Charles came to know them all, as he absorbed his father's enthusiasm, musical broadmindedness, and curious progressivism.

Perhaps more than anything else, George Ives taught his son to use his ears and mind and be less dependent on the customs and habits of the past. The composer could remember his father saying that man as a rule does not use the faculties God has given him hard enough. "I could not have been over ten years old when he would occasionally have us sing a tune like 'Swanee River' in E-flat while he accompanied in the key of C. This was to stretch our ears and strengthen our musical minds." By the time he was a teenager Charles was the snare drummer in his father's band, had learned to play the cornet, piano, and violin, was making arrangements of the classics for his father's instrumentalists, and was a church organist. But through it all ran George Ives' admonition to find new ways. "It's alright to do that, Charlie," he would tell his son, "if you know what you're doing."

Although grounded in the cultivated tradition, Ives grew to young manhood without hearing a symphonic concert. Danbury in the post-Civil War years was a medium size New England market town unable to support more than the seeds of high culture. What was there was generally of a homespun variety. At the camp meetings Charles attended, the worshipers sang gospel hymns essentially in the old lining-out method, unknowingly contributing quarter-tones and monotonous basses that did not appear on paper. In church the congregation sang ecstatically in nebulous pitch, adding its own accents, while the unmusical singers droned along behind, usually a bit flat. Young Ives noted that the members of the village band did not exactly play together. Someone was frequently a fraction ahead or a little behind. Others were a bit sharp or a tad flat. Sometimes the bass tuba assumed an indistinguishable pitch, almost a percussion sound. Occasionally the cornet player would break loose and play independently before finding his way back into the group. At barn dances the fiddle was often out of tune, by design rather than accident, producing slips and slides and slightly off pitch tones which the villagers relished. All of these idiosyncracies made an impression on Ives and were later absorbed into his music.

At an early age the composer envisioned a music in which he could express himself, and the musical structure he built was indeed his own. He pondered the questions of tone divisions, association of keys, and multiple rhythms, often breaking with the scale, harmony, and rhythm systems of the European tradition. Without discarding established musical values, Ives was never so tied to them that he could not incorporate himself and the American folk idiom. "From the rock-bottom of American soil, and with breadth of concept," composer Henry Cowell insisted, "he proceeded to write, each work going further than the last; and through feeling rather than a mechanically thought out plan at last created an individual style. His music finally travels far from its folk origins toward symphonic works of length and complexity. . . . Ives took the apparently slight thread of American folk music, and, by sympathetic cultivation, wove a new musical beauty."

The composer left Danbury to attend Hopkins Grammar School in New Haven and in 1894 entered Yale University, where he majored in music. A month after Charles enrolled in the university, his father died suddenly of a stroke at the age of forty-nine. The loss was a great one, for Ives always claimed that his father's "personality, character and open-mindedness, and his remarkable understanding of the ways of a boy's heart and mind" had influenced him more than anything else. At Yale the youth studied composition and theory with Horatio Parker, one of the distinguished Boston Classicists, most noted for his choral works, especially the recently completed cantata *Hora Novissima*. Ives had qualified "respect and admiration" for Parker, feeling that the academician's choral selections possessed "dignity and depth," but that he was dominated by the "German rule" and "perfectly willing to be limited" by what he had been taught abroad. Charles clearly mystified Parker, who after three weeks told the renegade student to concentrate on the work regularly assigned to the class and to quit bothering him with his own experiments. Ives basically accepted this, although he continued to clash with his professor from time to time. When the youth showed Parker some fugues with the theme in four different keys, the older musician was exasperated: "Ives, must you hog all the keys!"

But from Parker, Ives learned much about writing "correct" music. He also studied organ with Dudley Buck while at Yale, and for four years subordinated his independence to the conventions of fugues, rondos, sonatas, concertos, and symphonies. Privately, however, he persisted in experimenting with exotic scales, unusual chord structures, and what would later be known as polytonality and atonality. He occasionally tested these unorthodox ideas with the Hyperion Theatre orchestra in New Haven. He wrote music for shows put on by the various fraternities and tried his hand at ragtime.

To finance his way through college Ives took a job as organist at New Haven's Center Church. Fortunately the choirmaster, Dr. John Griggs, an old friend of Charles' father, was sympathetic to the music student's creative turn. When Ives occasionally let his imagination run free at the keyboard, Griggs was disposed to pat him on the back and say, "Never you mind what the ladies' committee says. My opinion is that God must get awfully tired of hearing the same thing over and over again, and in His all-embracing wisdom He would certainly embrace a dissonance—might even positively enjoy one now and then."

While at Yale the musician was active in sports, in part to offset the effeminacy so strongly linked with the pursuit of art music in the minds of his peers. Ives had been captain of the football team in high school and at Hopkins Grammar School had pitched for a team that beat the Yale freshmen. In college he distinguished himself as a member of coach Walter Camp's varsity football squad. He was elected to a senior society and, despite his interest in serious music—something he was always partially ashamed of—Ives was considered much the all-American boy.

Ives had done some composing even before coming to Yale. At seventeen he had written a set of variations on "America" for the organ, containing interludes in two keys and a great deal of boyish horseplay. He wrote his First Symphony as an undergraduate project for Parker. Modeled largely on the symphonic successes of Mendelssohn, Tchaikovsky, and Raff, the finished work is basically conventional, with almost no modern touches, although an earlier version had disturbed Parker no end. In the final draft the First Symphony is formally correct, while its melodies are pleasing, often echoing Beethoven and the European masters. Its orchestration shows brilliance and doubtlessly made the composer's academic taskmaster extremely proud. The piece is uneven, but contains a fetching, naive quality that is part of its charm.

Despite his thorough training as a musician, upon graduation Ives decided against a career in music. Most of his relatives were successful businessmen, and Charles was painfully aware that his father had been considered something of the family renegade, even dismissed as a crank by some of his neighbors. Young Ives knew that a musician, no matter how practical, faced great difficulties earning a living, and he was just as aware that his own music was far from practical. He remembered that his father, during the last few years of his life, had been forced to take a position in a Danbury bank because the music profession did not provide his family enough security. Rather than sacrifice his principles or let his future wife and children "starve on his dissonances," Charles resolved to enter business. By not making his living at it, the composer felt he would be free to write the kind of music he believed in. He would also avoid a profession he was conditioned to feel was somewhat contaminated.

After finishing at Yale, Ives went to New York City and secured a job as a clerk with Mutual Life Insurance Company, earning an initial salary of five dollars a week. He shared a huge apartment on West Fifty-eighth Street with a group of young bachelors about the same age, all former Yale cronies. Charles was known for his lively, bright personality and was much sought after by friends. Evenings were sometimes spent playing ragtime piano in a beer garden or walking with his roommates in Central Park. Often the group returned to what they affectionately called "Poverty Flat" and chatted until daybreak. Meanwhile Ives was serving as organist and choir director at First Presbyterian Church in Bloomfield, New Jersey, and later at Central Presbyterian Church in New York City. He occasionally went to concerts, although there was not much money for such pleasures. Despite all this he composed a vast amount of music, working mainly in the small hours of the morning.

He approached his business and his art with similar enthusiasm. "My work in music helped my business and my work in business helped my music," Ives once said. "You cannot set an art off in the corner and hope for it to have vitality, reality and substance." His was no split personality, but simply a creative energy applied to two areas. "My business experience revealed life to me in many aspects that I might otherwise have missed," he told an interviewer. "In it one sees tragedy, nobility, meanness, high aims, low aims, brave hopes, faint hopes, great ideals, no ideals, and one is able to watch these work inevitable destiny. . . . It is my impression that there is more open-mindedness and willingness to examine carefully the premises underlying a new or unfamiliar thing, before condemning it, in the world of business than in the world of music."

Ives allowed himself the luxury of composing slowly and carefully. He felt no pressure to publish and was willing to let ideas come to him leisurely. He gave himself time to mature, yet exercised an exacting self-criticism. The pioneering that was evident even before he left Parker's classroom found solid ground in the years ahead. His setting of the "Sixty-fourth Psalm," for instance, written the year Ives graduated from Yale, has the sopranos and altos singing in the key of C major, while the tenors and basses sing in G minor. When he did periodically show his early works to publishers or musicians, they consistently blanched at their difficulty and strangeness. Some smilingly pronounced them unplayable. Others argued that Ives was clearly ignorant of the fundamentals of music. Gradually the composer preferred to keep his manuscripts to himself. In later years, after some of his pieces had been performed, his advice to young musicians was still, "If you wish to write, get a job and don't depend on your writing for a living."

Ives worked on his Second Symphony off and on from 1897 until 1902; he was twenty-seven when it was finished. The piece contains little of the dissonance later characteristic of the composer and becomes something of a personal memoir. In it Ives records the sound images of *his* world, as he engagingly combines elements of the local music he had grown up with and representations of the great German tradition. There are references to Wagner, Brahms, Bruckner, Bach, and Dvorak. The opening notes of Beethoven's Fifth Symphony are quoted, but in Ives' hands they are hushed and mystic, not at all like Beethoven's bold statement. A fragment of Brahms' First Symphony is brazenly joined onto a phrase from "America the Beautiful." There are snatches of "Camptown Races," "Turkey in the Straw," hymn tunes like "Bringing in the Sheaves" and "When I Survey the Wondrous Cross," and college songs like "Where, Oh Where Are the Verdant Freshmen?" There are hints of Stephen Foster, a touch of "Long, Long Ago," a wild reference to "Reveille," and the triumphant emergence of "Columbia, the Gem of the Ocean" at the end. Yet this symphony is no hodgepodge, for it adds up to a cohesive entity, all transformed into Ives' personal commentary. "It has all the freshness of a naive American wandering in the grand palaces of Europe," Leonard Bernstein observes, "like some of Henry James' Americans abroad, or, perhaps more like Mark Twain's Innocents." The work is original, full of charm, eccentric. And through it runs Ives' developing style, where rules are blithely broken. "There are gauche endings," Bernstein continues, "unfinished phrases, wrong voice-leadings, inexplicable orchestration. There are those strange personal jokes of his—burlesques, takeoffs, deliberate infringements of conventionality, deliberately intended to shock—like the very last chord of the whole piece, full of wrong notes, incongruous as a Marx Brothers gag."

The Second Symphony is structured in five movements, the last of which is most "Ivesian." While the composer often seems to be jesting in the earlier sections, the final movement becomes more nostalgic and homespun. As Bernard Herrmann saw it, "The symphony orchestra has been swept aside to make way for country fiddlers and the firemen's band, for a Fourth of July jubilation, the shouting of children a politician's speech, and Old Glory." But the closing chord returns to humor, as the symphony ends in a magnificent squawk containing all twelve tones.

With the completion of the Second Symphony Ives gave up his position as church organist, thereby breaking completely with the professional musical world. He was already into the Third Symphony, although the work was not finished until 1904. This would prove the most fully realized and ultimately the most successful of the composer's four symphonies. Written in three movements, the Third Symphony was inspired by the camp meetings Ives had experienced so often as a child. Several of its melodies were drawn from old hymn tunes, particularly "Just as I Am," "O for a Thousand Tongues," and "What a Friend We Have in Jesus." The middle section describes the games children played at camp meetings while their elders listened to the preaching. In it the composer creates a kind of running, clapping effect, while the mood of the rest of the composition is far more meditative. Ives was growing increasingly unorthodox, for the Third Symphony is filled with cross-rhythms, unusual progressions, and free polyphony. Yet the spirit of the piece is pure New England, and it is clearly a work of deep sincerity, closing with the sound of distant church bells. When Gustav Mahler saw the score in 1911, he was so impressed that he took a copy back to Austria, planning to have the piece performed. But Mahler died that year, without hearing the Ives symphony.

There were shorter selections like *The Circus Band*, written while Ives was at Yale, *From the Steeples and the Mountains* (1901), the *Three-Page* Sonata for piano (1905), and *The Pond* (1906). The orchestral tone poem *Central Park in the Dark* (1907) contrasts the quiet of individual meditation broken through by the raucous noises of the city and the sound of a ragtime piano. *The Unanswered Question* (1908) finds a solo trumpet asking the perennial question of existence, while four flutes heroically attempt satisfactory answers. A muted string ensemble represents eternity and the unknowable mysteries. As the trumpet persists in asking man's question, the answers get increasingly agitated, become chaotic and polytonal as the flutes cannot agree, and end by mocking the trumpet's phrase. Finally the flutes remain silent, as the trumpet, undaunted, asks its question yet again.

Meanwhile Ives had become convinced that the life insurance business offered unlimited possibilities for a man of enterprise and foresight. In 1907 the composer launched his own agency, in partnership with fellow clerk Julian Myrick. After a slow start Ives & Myrick wrote nearly two million dollars' worth of insurance in a single year. Within two decades the firm had become the largest agency of its kind in the country. In a booklet called *The Amount to Carry: Measuring the Prospect*, Ives formulated principles of "Estate Planning" that made him famous in the insurance world. His business practices were often radical and daring, but based on hardheaded common sense. Many of his downtown associates knew nothing of his interest in music.

In 1908 Ives married a Hartford girl with the improbable name of Harmony Twichell, the sister of one of his roommates. The couple settled in the New York suburb of Hartsdale and six years later adopted a baby girl, Edith. To the outside world Ives was the conventional businessman—respected, pragmatic, invincible. To his wife and a close circle of friends, he was a man dedicated to art—in Virgil Thomson's terms "wildly experimental, ambitious, unchanneled, undisciplined, and unafraid."

Interestingly enough, it was during Ives' most active period in business that he did almost all of his composing. He wrote in the evenings, on weekends, holidays, and vacations, sometimes staying up until two or three in the morning. He worked in seclusion and rarely attended concerts. Occasionally, when he felt the need to hear how a work sounded, he would hire a few musicians to run through the piece. But most of his music Ives heard only in his imagination. Gradually he grew in confidence and composed more rapidly. Sometimes he went over and over a score, carefully correcting it; sometimes he threw hastily scrawled pages over his shoulder without looking at them again. With his head bursting with ideas, there was little time to keep manuscripts orderly. He simply stacked them on the floor; as they piled up, he stored some of them in a barn near Danbury, where they lay neglected for years. Parts of works were lost, and possibly entire compositions were either lost or destroyed. When friends suggested that Ives write pieces that the public might like, he could only retort, "I can't do it—I hear something else!"

Composing in isolation Ives produced modernistic sounds well ahead of his European contemporaries Stravinsky and Schoenberg. When reminded later that many of his ideas anticipated those European innovators, Ives replied, "It's not my fault." He knew nothing of Schoenberg, and the only thing he heard by Stravinsky was part of *The Firebird* shortly after World War I, a piece he judged "morbid and monotonous." It is highly probable that the American knew of no European composer later than Debussy during his creative period. Ives was not striving for dissonance; he was simply attempting to convey the truth of ordinary, virile sounds—old instruments out of tune, the cacophony of two bands passing one another playing different melodies, a group of singers croaking slightly different versions of the same song. But whatever his intentions, Ives did indeed use polychordal and polytonal harmonic textures, free dissonant counterpoint, multiple metrics, tone-clusters and chord-clusters, and stereophonic orchestral effects requiring several conductors. Much of his music is extremely difficult, yet the composer had no sense of its being unpleasant or in any way ugly. He could remember his father's saying of a local stonemason known for bellowing off-key at camp meetings, "Old John is a supreme musician. Look into his face and hear the music of the ages. Don't pay too much attention to the sounds. If you do, you may miss the music." To Ives music was more than traditional prettiness; it was the sounds of life.

The *Holidays* Symphony, completed in 1913, is an interesting example, recollecting as it does Ives' boyhood holidays in Danbury. The work consists of four parts: "Washington's Birthday," "Decoration Day," "Fourth of July," and "Thanksgiving Day." In the "Fourth of July" section several marching bands are depicted playing at once. At its climax three patriotic tunes ("Columbia, the Gem of the Ocean," "The Battle Hymn of the Republic," and "Yankee Doodle") can be heard simultaneously—all set against rhythm-clusters and tone-clusters sliding up and down in the strings.

When Ives gave the selection to his copyist, he warned: "Mr. Price: Please don't try to make things nice! All the wrong notes are *right*. Just copy as I have—I want it that way....Mr. Price: Band stuff—they didn't always play right and together and it was as good either way." In "Washington's Birthday" the orchestra changes from an allegro to a slow section. But the viola, still in an allegro mood, continues to play a modified version of it against the rest of the orchestra's adagio.

Polyrhythms and polytonality abound in *Three Places in New England* (1914). The opening movement, "The 'St. Gaudens' in Boston Common," suggests brooding, ghostly sentiments attached to the Civil War. In the second part, "Putnam's Camp, Redding, Connecticut," the scene is a Fourth of July picnic held on the grounds where General Israel Putnam's soldiers had their winter quarters during the Revolution. A child wanders into the woods and dreams of the old soldiers, of their hardships and desire to abandon the cause. Then the child runs down to join in the games and dances and listen to the band. Ives portrays two bands that stridently overlap; in a dissonant closing passage two march rhythms clash, four bars of one equaling three of the other. The last section of the piece, "The Housatonic at Stockbridge," describes an early morning walk along the river near Stockbridge and begins misty and impressionistic. The tranquility of nature is conveyed, as well as Ives' love for his wife, who is walking with him. Gradually the sounds of nature grow into a sonorous cataract that engulfs the love theme. Then the tumult abruptly ceases, leaving the love motif suspended. For Ives human love is central.

When the Boston Symphony Orchestra played *Three Places in New England* in New York City in 1931, conductor Nicolas Slonimsky apologized to the composer for a ragged performance. Ives supposedly reassured him: "Just like a town meeting—every man for himself. Wonderful how it came out!"

Although Ives came by his innovations intuitively, he nevertheless built his bold ideas on the knowledge of musical laws he had acquired from Parker. The composer was adamant that the release of fresh energy was only important after tradition had been mastered. Ives' experimenting, however, was unique, since it was independent of the systematic investigations of polytonality, polyharmony, and polyrhythm going on in Europe. In addition Ives occasionally incorporated ragtime and jazz effects into his work, for these were becoming an exciting part of the musical vernacular of urban America. Free as he was of accepted artistic standards, the composer rarely hesitated to break with the canons of good taste. Yet while his aspirations to experiment were great, Ives' orientation remained rooted in the church, parlor, stage, and dance music of small-town America and secondarily tied to the cultivated tradition.

The composer believed that the old and the new, the vernacular and the genteel were ultimately parts of the same substance. "The fabric of existence weaves itself whole," Ives insisted. To him Yankee folk music, German romanticism, and complex pioneering techniques belonged to a continuous spectrum. New worlds, he felt, could only grow out of old ones. While Ives' music on the surface seems infinitely complicated, confused, and dissociated, the composer was constantly seeking the universal and the spiritual, and he was convinced that the key to both lay in the world of nature. The artist's creation, therefore, should be analogous to the creativity in nature.

True to his heritage, Ives was deeply impressed with the New England Transcendentalists. He read and reread Emerson and Thoreau and devoured books and essays about the Concord thinkers. Transcendentalism remained the philosophical bedrock for Ives' search for unity and order, and like Thoreau he looked for Truth in his own vision of life. A man of deep religious convictions and an idealist, the composer nevertheless sought reality in common, everyday experiences. His music is marked by an unprecedented breadth and drive and contains an overwhelming sense of the fullness of life. Spiritually and artistically there is a strong bond between Ives and Walt Whitman. Like Whitman, Ives was devoted to the right of the American artist to be himself. The art of both men demonstrated a profound feeling for the common man, a rugged masculinity, and heroic pioneer virtues. Ives was the composer Emerson longed for when he wrote: "He finds that he is the complement of his hearers; that they drink his words because he fulfills for them their own nature. . . . The better part of every man feels: This is my music, this is myself." Ives identified completely with his cultural environment, succeeded in being local without becoming provincial, yet always saw this environment through his own personality. Add to this the composer's self-reliance, his belief in the strength of nature, and his view that music both permeates and is permeated by the rest of the universe, and it becomes clear why Ives considered himself blood brother to the Concord bards. Certainly the composer achieved in music, over a half century later, what Emerson and Thoreau had accomplished in literature and thought.

Ives' most developed exploration of Transcendentalism came with his Second Piano Sonata, the famous *Concord* Sonata, written between 1908 and 1915. In it the composer attempts impressionist sketches of Emerson, Hawthorne, the Alcotts, and Thoreau. Tightly organized, the sonata may well represent the summation of Ives' musical thought and is surely one of the most solid piano compositions in American music. The Emerson movement explores the fight of the ego with destiny; the Hawthorne movement deals with dreams and the fantastic; the Alcotts portrait is homespun and simple; while the Thoreau movement concentrates on the individual spirit alone with nature. Emerson emerges as the hero of American strife, Hawthorne of conscience, Thoreau of contemplation, while the Alcotts symbolize the domestic pieties. The work marks, even for Ives, a new richness of harmony, an advance in the freedom of rhythm, and continued experimentalism. In the Hawthorne movement, for instance, a ruler is used by the pianist to play an expansive two octave cluster.

The composer's First Piano Sonata, written almost a decade earlier, is scarcely less impressive. The work is bursting with energy and full of the spirit of rustic New England. There are experiments in complex rhythm, an astonishing use of ragtime, and striking examples of Ives' quotation technique. In the second movement, written in the form of verse and chorus, the verse is a travesty on "How Dry I Am," while the chorus is subtly built on "Oh, Susannah." One of the most hilarious moments in the sonata is a raucous setting of "Bringing in the Sheaves" in the fourth movement. Ives explained that the work is mostly about the outdoor life in Connecticut villages during the 1880s and 1890s. A ball game is remembered, in which one boy's father got so excited when his son hit a home run that he shouted. There are reflections of Aunt Sarah humming, of two boys leaving home to take a job in another town, of winter barn dances, and of summer revival meetings.

Much of Ives' work contains no quoted material whatever. The *Browning* Overture (1911), among his most daring works, is an example. In the manuscript Ives wrote under some harmonically difficult measures: "Browning was too big a man to rest in one nice little key . . . he walked on the mountains not down a nice proper little aisle." The composer's instructions are often delightful. In *Hallowe'en*, for strings and piano, also written in 1911, the musicians are told to play the music four times with slight variations. Ives suggests: "In any case the playing gets faster and louder each time, keeping up with the bonfire." Then he adds: "It has been observed by friends that three times around is quite enough, while others stood for the four—but as this piece was written for a Hallowe'en party and not for a *nice* concert, the decision must be made by the players regardless of the feelings of the audience."

Ives also wrote *Lincoln, the Great Commoner* for chorus and orchestra, *Three Harvest Home Chorales* for chorus, brass, string bass, and organ, five violin sonatas, a great deal of chamber music, several choral works, and over a hundred songs. The songs date from all periods. Some are simple, others extremely difficult and complex. Some are lyrical, others dramatic; some are written in a folk style. Ives selected texts from Keats, Browning, and Stevenson, as well as from contemporary poets. Some of the verses he wrote himself; others are by his wife. The moods range from Emersonian uplift to Sunday school sanctimoniousness to regional robustness to broad music hall humor. There are songs bristling with dissonances, including tone-clusters and chords produced by the elbow rather than the fingers, back to back with songs of harmonic simplicity. While several of his songs from the 1890s almost resemble MacDowell's in their rich harmony and conventional rhythm, one of his earliest, "Song for the Harvest Season" (1894), shows startling polytonal combinations. The piece is set for voice, trombone, cornet and organ, and each part is written in a different key.

The first songs of significance date from around 1900. With "The Children's Hour" (1901), based on Longfellow, Ives achieves a charming flow and proves himself a real creator. "In the Cage" (1906) is a sharper break from the traditional song style. The piece evokes the pacing of a wild beast, a recollection from the musician's childhood, when he watched a leopard in a cage and wondered if life was "anything at all like that." The animal's pacing is conveyed through a vocal line so unstably chromatic as to be atonal. There are constant rhythm changes, although bar lines are omitted. In the cowboy ballad "Charlie Rutlage" (1915) the composer turns to unpitched rhythmic declamation for climactic measures, while "Two Little Flowers" (1921) on the surface seems almost like a sentimental nineteenth-century parlor song. Set to a text by Ives' wife, the latter is about the couple's adopted daughter and her playmate. The piece begins in a sweet, uncomplicated lieder style, but suddenly there are unexpected dislocations of rhythm on certain phrases and a downward vaulting of an octave and a third in the melodic climax (although Ives has supplied a simpler alternative for singers who cannot make the plunge).

One of the composer's longest and most powerful songs is "General William Booth Enters into Heaven" (1914), after portions of Vachel Lindsay's poem. The selection is both dramatic and narrative, employing dissonance and musical quotation. Its military atmosphere celebrates the fanatic revivalism of the founder of the Salvation Army. Ives begins the song with the drum beat of a marching band, projected in dissonant clusters. Rather than quoting the Salvation Army hymn "Are You Washed in the Blood of the Lamb?" (as Lindsay's poem does parenthetically), Ives uses the revival hymn "Cleansing Fountain" ("There Is a Fountain Filled with Blood"). He presents the parenthetical in a key far removed from the tonal sphere of the main text. The gospel melody is developed in different ways through the course of the song. The verse mentions a banjo, at which point Ives quotes the introduction to James Bland's minstrel tune "O Dem Golden Slippers." There are trumpet calls and more marching sounds. The conclusion returns to a haunting, off-key statement of "Cleansing Fountain"; then the drum beats fade in the distance—"as a band marching away," Ives wrote in the manuscript. The work includes the yawp of instruments that are out of tune, while a singer, enraptured by enthusiasm, bellows off-key. But the chaos is part of the music, building to a superb climax of religious frenzy.

Ives wanted his music to retain a spontaneity and hoped that performances of his works would transmit a sense of involvement. In several of his scores the composer offers options to the performer. A passage in the Second Sonata for violin and piano, he instructs, may be repeated two or three times. Often his instrumentation is extremely flexible, while he allows soloists great freedom, even letting them fill in notes occasionally. But his music does evoke an astonishing immediacy. In the "General Putnam's Camp" section of Three Places in New England, the listener can virtually feel the movement and excitement of the crowd, just as "General William Booth Enters into Heaven" pulls the listener into the music and involves him emotionally.

The composer's mightiest work was among his last—the Fourth

Symphony, written between 1910 and 1916. Conceived for an immense orchestra, chorus, organ, two pianos, and special percussion, the symphony requires three conductors. The program revolves around the searching questions of "What?" and "Why?"—questions which man constantly asks of life. The mood is majestically set forth in the prelude. The movement is scored for two distinct groups—the main orchestra and a distant, ethereal chamber ensemble. It opens with the basses of the orchestra playing loudly and heavily against a soft background by the chamber group. Then the chorus enters with a setting of the hymn "Watchman, Tell Us of the Night," a particular favorite of Ives'. The movement includes quotations from "Nearer, My God, to Thee" and "In the Sweet Bye and Bye," growing more turbulent as it depicts the strife of existence. A "comedy" movement follows, in which an easy and worldly progress through life is compared with the trials of Pilgrims journeying through swamps and untamed wilderness. The Pilgrims' slow hymns are constantly being overshadowed by sounds of excitement—strident marches, rags, and patriotic ditties. The dream is at last ended by reality—the Fourth of July in Concord. The movement is of utmost complexity, superimposing incredibly difficult rhythms and quoting dozens of tunes. The third movement is a fugue on the hymns "From Greenland's Icy Mountains" and "All Hail the Power" and seems especially serene after the commotion of the previous section. An organ is brought in to reinforce the orchestra, as the simple, communal life is pictured. But Ives cannot resist a humorous touch; he ends the fugue with a lone trombone singing out a phrase from "Joy to the World." The final movement is built upon "Nearer, My God, to Thee" and in the opening bars recalls the prelude. Eventually there are three independent instrumental groups—the main orchestra, the distant ensemble, and the percussion. The instruments pursue their own paths in ever-changing rhythms, breaking into their own themes, while the chorus sings a wordless vocalism. The climax seeks a transcendental synthesis by combining these elements simultaneously. The effect is a great *sound* that swells and recedes. The finale gradually fades away, leaving a faint percussion with the last word.

Ives projected and made sketches for a fifth symphony on an even grander scale. The *Universe* Symphony was to be performed outdoors, with five or six orchestras, bands, and a chorus of hundreds. But in October, 1918, at the age of forty-four, the composer suffered a physical breakdown that left his heart damaged. World War I had come to him as a "shock of the first magnitude," shattering his vision of a world democracy. The impact of the war and the weakening of his once robust health accorded Ives little inclination to write music. "It seemed impossible to do any work in the evening as I used to," he wrote. He never gave up composing completely, writing a few songs in later years, making arrangements, and periodically adding notes to his unfinished *Universe* Symphony. But the verve was gone. He was disillusioned by the failure of Wilson's plan to involve the United States in the League of Nations and spent considerable energy during the 1920s advocating a Constitutional amendment that would take power from politicians and return it to the people. Ives dreamed of a direct democracy, based on a fully informed electorate, and ultimately of what he called a People's World Union.

He began to show an interest in getting his music before the public and in 1919 at his own expense had the *Concord* Sonata published. He had recently written pages upon pages of prose, which he published separately in a volume called *Essays Before a Sonata*. His *Essays* are witty, charmingly written, and explain a number of the composer's musical ideas. Copies of both the Sonata and *Essays* were sent free of charge to libraries, critics, a select group of professional musicians, and eventually anybody who asked for them. In 1922 Ives had his *114 Songs* printed, frankly explaining that some of "the songs in this book...cannot be sung." He explained his purpose in publishing the collection: "Various authors have various reasons for bringing out a book...some have written a book for money; I have not. Some for fame; I have not. Some for love; I have not. Some for kindlings; I have not. I have not written a book for any of these reasons or for all of them together. In fact, gentle borrower, I have not written a book at all—I have merely cleaned house. All that is left is out on the clothesline."

The musician continued working at his insurance business until 1930, when failing health forced him to retire. The year before Ives & Myrick had done nearly 50 million dollars worth of business. Ives now lived in virtual seclusion, blissfully unaware of what was going on in the musical world, rarely attending concerts, and keeping aloof from everyday happenings in the world at large. He would not read newspapers and on a trip to Europe during the fall of 1932 accidentally learned of Franklin Roosevelt's election from a French innkeeper. His wife protected him from excitement, shielded him from strangers, took care of his mail, and administered his daily shots of insulin. Although he was not interested in the development of modern music as such, he did occasionally stoke the embers of the cause. On one of his rare trips to the concert hall, a piece by Carl Ruggles was booed. "Don't be such a damn sissy," Ives shouted in rage. "When you hear strong music like this, get up and try to use your ears like a man."

For the first ten years after the publication of the *Concord* Sonata and the *114 Songs* neither received much comment. In 1927 the first two movements of Ives' Fourth Symphony were performed at Town Hall in New York under the direction of Eugene Goosens, and during the next few years something of an Ives cult developed among the avant-garde. Then in January, 1939, the American pianist John Kirkpatrick played the Second Sonata at a Town Hall recital. While most of the audience found the piece appallingly difficult, Lawrence Gilman of the *New York Herald Tribune* claimed, "This sonata is exceptionally great music—it is, indeed, the greatest music composed by an American, and the most deeply and essentially American in impulse and implication." Kirkpatrick repeated the selection several weeks later and soon recorded it. In April, 1946, Lou Harrison conducted the New York Little Symphony Orchestra in a performance of Ives' Third Symphony. It was given again the next month on an all-Ives program in New York and was acclaimed by the critics. In 1947, forty-three years after it was written, the Third Symphony received both a special citation from the New York Music Critics Circle and the Pulitzer Prize in music. When Ives was told of the Pulitzer award, he observed, "Prizes are for boys, I'm grown up," and promptly donated the $500 honorarium to charity. Four years later the New York Philharmonic under Leonard Bernstein gave several performances of the composer's Second Symphony. Although Ives had never heard the work played, he attended neither the rehearsals nor the performances, but did listen to the radio broadcast.

At seventy-three years of age Ives suddenly found himself the grand old man of American music. He spent his last years living with his wife in a gracious but simple house high on a Connecticut hill. He received infrequent visitors, and his failing heart made extended conversations impossible. He had come to look like a Yankee patriarch. Gaunt and wiry, his gray, scraggly beard giving a roundness to his face, the composer stood straight, with only the faintest suggestion of stooping shoulders, despite having to walk with a cane. When he removed his dark glasses, his eyes were still bright and alert. He wore rough, rustic clothes—usually blue denim trousers, a faded blue shirt, an old, darned sweater, and a gray tweed jacket. He would occasionally point his cane toward the window and say, "That's Danbury on the other side of that mountain. That's where I was born and grew up and learned a little about music." To the end he claimed that his father taught him most of what he knew. He remembered his father with tears in his eyes and, after a pause, would often murmur, "He was a real musician." Then, turning to his wife, he once told a guest, "We never went anywhere, and she didn't mind."

Ives died in New York City on May 19, 1954. He left a bulky legacy of manuscripts and pencil sketches, badly in need of sorting, editing, and deciphering. Many had lain untouched for years in the composer's barn. Mrs. Ives decided to present the manuscripts to the Yale School of Music, and they were transported to New Haven in the fall of 1955. On February 22, 1956, the Ives Collection was formally inaugurated.

Charles Ives accomplished two musical revolutions. One was to break radically with the European-derived style of his American contemporaries. The other was his unique revolt against conventionalism in serious composition, as startling as Isadora Duncan's innovations in dance. While the musicians in Boston were poring over Brahms and Wagner, Ives was absorbing the musical expressions of a New England village. Not since Billings had an American composer so fearlessly proclaimed himself his "own Carver." For Ives there was no "right" way of creating art; music was almost a living organism in his mind, growing out of the personal impressions and individuality of the composer and modified by the performer. Unlike the superficial nationalism inspired by Dvorak's visit, Ives created a vibrant American music by unreservedly committing himself to the vernacular, making it the grammar of symphonic speech. He incorporated, with intrinsic honesty, the warmth and humanity of small town New England into sounds flavored with his own humor, ecstasy, intellectual depth, and commonness. He combined the sacred and the secular, the colloquial and the cultivated, and lifted the mundane to the sublime. He turned ugliness into beauty, while the real became transcendental.

Ives himself stressed the experimental nature of his art and always saw the sound of music as less significant than the spirit in which it was produced. Still his work was rarely abstract, never haphazard. There was always a definite concept involved. While he sought to express all facets of life in his heterogeneous style, his creative genius was there to give his compositions unity. There are crudities and rough spots, as there are in Dreiser's prose and Whitman's verse, but there is always vitality in his work and—above all—life.

And yet, curiously enough, it may well have been Ives' deep-seated personal conservatism that was the source of his radical experiments. The composer, after all, had grown up in the tight conventionality of Danbury and Yale. Provincial America in the late nineteenth century tended to view music as a trifle, mere entertainment, while the whole cultivated tradition was seen as pretentious, aristocratic, and effeminate. Ives grew to manhood shaped by these popular notions, basically at odds with his own instincts. Renegade though he often seems, the composer remained old-fashioned in most of his attitudes, in love with a provincial America that was rapidly vanishing, embarrassed by many of the very things he held dearest. To pursue conventional art music openly was to be a "sissy," to be undemocratic, almost to be un-American. Vernacular music, on the other hand, he found more acceptable, more down to earth, speaking to men in terms of their everyday lives; whereas musical dissonance connoted a bold masculinity.

Frank Rossiter at least feels that Ives' decision to work in artistic isolation was motivated by his overriding desire to conform to the sociosexual mores of his day, from his determination to avoid the Bohemian life he considered beneath the dignity of a Yale man. Rossiter sees Ives as "a virtual prisoner of his culture," going his independent way a lonely, anguished man, personally devastated by his isolation, accepting himself as an artist only with the greatest difficulty. Like the Horatio Alger hero, Ives left home determined to seek his fortune, perhaps even feeling a bit guilty that he had been lured to the great city, but determined to hang onto the fundamental principles of his ancestors. Thus he joined his pioneering technical experiments with a nostalgia for the past, while inside himself the war between his emotional needs and an intellectual acceptance continued to rage.

Ives believed in an ultimate union of the spiritual and the material, while his musical reminiscenses became a kind of stream of consciousness device. The composer taught no pupils and founded no school, yet his manuscripts prophetically opened a whole new world for American music. Like the New England Transcendentalists before him, the musician's esthetic views encompassed mystical visions of an ideal democracy at one with God and nature. "The instinctive and progressive interest of every man in art," Ives was confident,

> will go on and on, ever fulfilling hopes, ever building new ones, ever
> opening new horizons, until the day will come when every man
> while digging his potatoes will breathe his own epics, his own
> symphonies (operas, if he likes it); and as he sits of an evening in his
> backyard and shirt sleeves smoking his pipe and watching his brave
> children in *their* fun of building *their* themes for *their* sonatas of
> *their* life, he will look up over the mountains and see his visions in
> their reality, will hear the transcendental strains of the day's
> symphony resounding in their many choirs, and in all their
> perfection, through the west wind and the tree tops!

Whereas MacDowell grew up in the city and became a spiritual
expatriate from Europe, Ives was raised in rustic tranquility and remained
loyal to his heritage. Unlike MacDowell, who sought pastoral refuge from a
collective society, Ives rose to the top of a corporate world and found his
uneasy peace in a Transcendental calm and spiritual isolation. MacDowell
early tasted the accolades of a society whose institutions ultimately crushed
him. Ives passed his creative years unheralded, yet lived to see himself
acclaimed America's greatest composer. Both were men of talent and genius;
both had intelligence and emotional maturity. But MacDowell's concept of
life and beauty were rooted in a romanticism at odds with a materialistic,
utilitarian, industrial complex that in its pursuit of progress placed little
value on the sensitive artist. Ives triumphed in that society, masked his true
identity, then demanded the privacy to pursue art on his own terms.
MacDowell became trapped in his own success; Ives became trapped in
himself, yet found freedom for his art by experiencing success elsewhere.

1. "The Origin of Jazz" from an old woodcut (Courtesy of Albert Davis Collection, Hoblitzelle Theatre Arts Library, University of Texas at Austin)

2. John Philip Sousa (Courtesy of Albert Davis
Collection, Hoblitzelle Theatre Arts Library)

3. Marine Corps Band at the St. Louis World's Fair, 1903 (Courtesy of Hoblitzelle
Theatre Arts Library)

4. Enrico Caruso and Frieda Hempel onstage in *L'Elisir d'Amore* (Courtesy of Hoblitzelle Theatre Arts Library)

5. French Opera House in New Orleans (Courtesy of Hoblitzelle Theatre Arts Library)

6. Interior of the Chicago Auditorium (Engraving, Courtesy of Chicago Historical Society)

7. Adelina Patti (Courtesy of Hoblitzelle
Theatre Arts Library)

8. Isadora Duncan (Courtesy of Albert Davis
Collection, Hoblitzelle Theatre Arts Library)

9. Harrigan and Hart, January 9, 1893 (Courtesy of Albert Davis Collection, Hoblitzelle Theatre Arts Library)

10. The Four Cohans, July 1878 (Courtesy of Albert Davis Collection, Hoblitzelle
    Theatre Arts Library)

11. Famous American Songwriters. Oscar Hammerstein at Piano; Standing: Jerome D. Kern, Louis Hirsch, A. Baldwin Sloane, Rudolph Friml, Alfred Robyn, Gustav Kerker, Hugo Felix, John Philip Sousa, Leslie Stuart, Raymond Hubbell, John L. Golden, Sylvio Hein, Irving Berlin. (1916) (Courtesy of Hoblitzelle Theatre Arts Library)

12. Lillian Russell (Courtesy of Albert Davis Collection, Hoblitzelle Theatre Arts Library)

13. Original Sheet Music Cover of Scott Joplin's "The Entertainer" (Courtesy of Hoblitzelle Theatre Arts Library)

14. Carl Van Vechten Portrait of Bessie Smith (Courtesy of Van Vechten Estate and Albert Davis Collection, Hoblitzelle Theatre Arts Library)

15. King Oliver (Courtesy of William Ransom Hogan Jazz Archive, Tulane University)

16. Peerless Orchestra from New Orleans. Seated, left-right: John Vigne, dr;
Charles McCordy, cl; Armond Piron, vl; Coochie Martin, g. Standing: Vic
Gaspard, tb; Andrew Kimball, tp; Octave Gaspard, b. (Courtesy of William
Ransom Hogan Jazz Archive)

17. Buddy Bolden's Band. Standing, left-right: Frank Lewis, Willy Cornish,
Buddy Bolden, Jimmie Johnson. Seated: Willie Warner, Brock Mumford.
[Before 1895]. (Courtesy of William Ransom Hogan Jazz Archive)

CHAPTER

VI

The Musical Theater

On the evening of September 12, 1866, *The Black Crook,* customarily considered America's first musical comedy, opened at Niblo's Garden in New York. The show was an extravaganza with music, loosely joining German melodrama and French ballet. This curious union had come about by accident. Henry C. Jarrett, an aspiring young theatrical manager, and Harry Palmer, a Wall Street broker, had brought over a French ballet troupe with the idea of presenting the recent Parisian success *La Biche aux Bois* at the Academy of Music. Shortly before the production was to open, the Academy burned down, leaving Jarrett and Palmer with an expensive ballet company and no theater in which to present it. Meanwhile, William Wheatley, the manager of Niblo's Garden, had signed an agreement with Charles M. Barras, an unknown author, for the production of his play *The Black Crook,* inspired by a performance of Weber's *Der Freischutz* given by a touring English opera company. With the melodrama in preparation Wheatley grew to doubt the merits of the script he had hastily purchased from Barras. When Jarrett and Palmer suggested combining forces, adding the French ballet to spice up *The Black Crook,* the manager of Niblo's saw a chance to avoid failure. Barras objected that the French dancers would ruin his "beautiful play," but the starving writer was quieted with a payment of $1500 and a royalty contract.

The result was the most lavish spectacle New York had seen. Barras' complicated plot revolved around a pact between Hertzog, the Black Crook, and the Devil, in which the former promised to win for Satan one human soul for each year of life granted him. It involved a mishmash of magic spells and enchantments, gnomes and demons, and peasant maidens enticingly attired. There was a grand ballet of gems, a hurricane through the Harz Mountains of Germany, a ritual by demons, fairies ascending and descending on silver couches, angels transported in gilded chariots, girls cascading down wild glens, and a breathtaking transformation scene for a finale—none of which made much sense. Yet Barras' Gothic hokum provided ample room for elaborate scenic effects and fabulous production numbers. Manager Wheatley well realized the value of novelty and pageantry and spared little expense on scenery, costumes, and properties. The stage at Niblo's Garden was completely made over, so that any portion of it could be pushed down or slid away in grooves. Trap doors could be created anywhere. The cellar beneath the stage was deep enough that entire scenes could be sunk out of sight with relatively simple machinery. Newspapers estimated the cost of the aggregate production at between $35,000 and $55,000, far more than any previous undertaking in American theater history.

The opening night performance lasted from 7:45 P.M. until 1:15 A.M. and was an unequivocal success. *The Black Crook* ran for sixteen months at Niblo's Garden and grossed more than a million dollars. The show was revived eight times in New York during the nineteenth century and was being presented somewhere on the road almost constantly for over thirty years. The blend of music with drama, visual extravagance with a hundred female dancers clad in silk tights, and pretensions at art with an element of suggestiveness proved irresistible to post-Civil War audiences who wanted to relax and enjoy themselves. The show attracted the carriage trade that normally frequented grand opera and serious drama, as well as devotees of the fleshly diversions characteristic of the lower class Bowery haunts.

The emphasis on feminine beauty, particularly the display of dozens of buxom forms diaphanously garbed in flesh-colored tights, brought shrieks of protest from outraged clergymen and reform-minded journalists—serving to swell the public titillation all the more. Aside from being great spectacle, *The Black Crook* was heralded as the most sensational leg show of its day— meaning not that the girls bared their limbs (which in the 1860s would have closed any theater), but that they simply wore no skirts. Certainly the production introduced that marriage of raciness and sophistication on which later musical comedy was to thrive.

The show's musical numbers, mostly by Niblo's conductor, Giuseppe Operti, were loosely strung together on Barras' transparent plot. The big show stopper, a sardonic comedy number called "You Naughty, Naughty Men," had nothing to do with the drama, but served merely to amuse the audience while the scenery was being changed. Milly Cavendish, who originally performed the song, simply stepped before the footlights, sang in a highpitched, baby voice, wagged a provocative finger at the men in the audience, and created a commotion in an age when women were supposed to react to any intimation of sex with blushing modesty. Most of the show's music was fairly uninspired, including "The Black Crook Waltz," a "March of the Amazons," and much piano-tremolo incidental music.

The Black Crook was essentially a highflown variety show with esthetic overtones. Yet its unwieldy format provided the foundation out of which much of America's musical theater would evolve. There were anticipations of burlesque, vaudeville, travesty, pantomime, operetta, and the musical revue. Although based on a German melodrama and featuring French ballet, vernacular ingredients were interpolated, increasingly so as the show's run continued. Despite persistent charges of indecency by conservative spokesmen, urban America for the most part found the artistic measure provided by the ballet and the ornateness of the production sufficient to justify attending *The Black Crook* in the name of Fashion.

The spectacle's success encouraged a melange of imitators which contributed significantly to the development of American stagecraft, if little to the growth of American music. Impresarios struggled to outdo one another in sumptuous, gargantuan offerings. Novel scenic devices, unusual lighting, rich costumes, lavish production numbers, and winsome chorus girls became the order of the day in the larger cities—clearly paling the unassuming minstrel show. A product of an urban rather than rural environment, *The Black Crook* and its descendants had more in common with the eighteenth-century ballad opera than with the more rustic forms of American entertainment, although there remained occasional nods to a bucolic heritage.

Musical comedy in the United States actually developed from two directions. On the one hand it evolved out of the minstrel tradition, the variety halls, vaudeville, burlesque, and the revue. On the other it devolved from European grand opera, opera buffa, operetta, and ballet. The modern form of American musical comedy steers a middle ground between opera and the variety show, conscious art and simple diversion. While the embryo was more formless in the late nineteenth century, already sophisticated audiences were demanding entertainment as extravagant, gaudy, and spirited as the conspicuous lifestyle of a people rapidly ascending to power, consistent with an age of rapidly amassed fortunes.

Eleven years after the opening of *The Black Crook*, a critic for *Galaxy*, commenting on the rash of leg shows since the Civil War, argued "as far as the display of feminine anatomy is concerned, the 'Black Crook' was a paragon of prudery compared with many of its followers." To be sure the scandalous aspects of the show had been diminished by the fall of 1868, when Lydia Thompson and her British Blondes arrived in New York from the London music halls. Preceded by extensive publicity, the beefy Blondes were introduced at Wood's Museum in the burlesque *Ixion, or The Man at the Wheel*, sharing the theater with exhibitions of a live baby hippopotamus. In the guise of mythological satire the girls offered a variety of suggestive songs, topical gags, puns, parody, snippets of ballet, specialty numbers, and much display of ruffled drawers. Lydia herself specialized in male roles, although the wearing of men's pants was considered particularly daring at the time. Pauline Markham was the Venus of the troupe, later creating a stir by becoming the mistress of a southern governor. The English Blondes won audiences by their unfettered romping and delicate double-entendre and produced a tempest of criticism, gossip, and imitation at the same time. One writer summed up the situation by saying, "The propriety of visiting the Blondes is a question which each individual must decide for himself. The number of individuals who have decided this question, by the way, is something astonishing." The girls toured the country in 1869-70, causing controversy wherever they appeared. When they played Crosby's Opera House in Chicago, the press was indignant: "Bawds at the Opera House! Where's the police?" The Blondes returned to the city early the next year, only to find themselves savagely denounced by Wilbur F. Story, editor of the Chicago *Times*. Story, Miss Thompson, insisted, was a "liar and coward," and she finally took out her animosity on the editor by thrashing him with a buggy whip.

Before the British Blondes there had been variety halls, especially in the West, where the entertainment was notoriously uninhibited and where girls alternately sang and danced and enticed male patrons into buying them drinks. But Lydia Thompson's troupe is usually considered the beginning of the road that ultimately led to the runway at Minsky's. The honky-tonks of the Barbary Coast and the Bowery continued to feature exotic dancers very similar to what would emerge in burlesque, although the more legitimate entertainers disclaimed any connection. The financial panic of 1873 lent considerable impetus to the development of burlesque, since prettier girls were available at low wages and indigent males sought less expensive forms of entertainment. The early eighties found little order to the burlesque business. Independent companies arranged engagements where they could and formed friendly alliances. Burlesque performers and vaudeville entertainers were often interchangeable. Around 1893 hootchy-kootchy dancers became a special feature of burlesque, following the phenomenal success of "Little Egypt" at the Chicago World's Fair. By the turn of the century belly dancers billed as Fatima, Coocheeta, and the Girl in Red were wiggling their torsos on established circuits, often adding distinction to their routine by throwing garters into the audience, tickling men with feather dusters, or tossing out fishing lines with candy attached.

The format of burlesque owed much to the minstrel show, and its olio section particularly was quite similar to vaudeville. While burlesque was an excellent school for comedians, it did little for the makers of music. Since the audience paid little attention to the music, managers were not inclined to waste either time or money on it. Ballads were frequently sung in burlesque, and song publishers and composers were anxious to place their tunes there. The preparations of these numbers, however, were normally slight, and the better singers moved on as quickly as possible to better jobs. Nevertheless,

Weber and Fields, May Howard, Al Jolson, Fanny Brice, and Eddie Cantor all took a turn at burlesque in their early years.

For the most part burlesque audiences were made up of workingmen, salesmen, traveling men, and nonintellectuals who could scarcely be bothered with anything serious. Admission was cheap, and audiences were eager to laugh, shed a surreptitious tear as the ballad singer wailed tunes like "What Is Home Without a Mother," quaff beer, spit tobacco juice on the floor, and roll empty beer bottles down the aisles. But mostly they came for the girls, anticipating the moment when voluptuous curves would transform barren boards into Walpurgis Night or Mohammed's Paradise. Despite its original identification with travesty and comedy, it was the bumps-and-grinds aspect that kept burlesque going, giving the urban male the luxuriant sense of misbehaving, of indulging in a he-man's amusement.

Bawdiness was also characteristic of early vaudeville, evolving as it did from the variety halls, as well as the minstrel show and the circus. Humor in vaudeville was rough, lusty, robust, mainly physical. Audiences initially consisted primarily of men, prostitutes, and slummers. Drunkenness was common. Programs were unsophisticated, brassy, eclectic. But from the beginning music was extremely important. The better song-and-dance men customarily wrote their own tunes and created their own dance steps, much as comedians wrote their own material.

Vaudeville's great turning point came with Tony Pastor, a native New Yorker and a graduate of both minstrelsy and the circus. In 1866 Pastor took over Volk's Garden, fixed it up, and renamed it Pastor's Opera House. For ten years he presented variety performances there, attempting to attract women and children to his theater by discouraging drinking and smoking and by staging clean entertainment. When the ladies proved reluctant, Pastor began offering door prizes of dress patterns, sewing machines, kitchen utensils, hams, bonbons, and half-barrels of flour. Tony's own specialty was the topical song, and he tried to introduce one or two new numbers each week, dealing with recent tragedies or the latest happenings in politics, fashion, technology, or business. By 1876, when Pastor moved further uptown to a new and larger theater on Broadway, the women were beginning to come. Fridays were set aside as Ladies' Night, when husbands could bring their wives and young men their sweethearts, free of charge. When he opened his Fourteenth Street Theater on October 24, 1881, in the Tammany Hall Building, the devout Pastor was assuring women that his offering was as wholesome as a prayer meeting, and vaudeville was on its way to becoming what Fred Stone later called the type of entertainment to which a child could take his parents.

Certainly the seasoned performers preferred the refined audiences to the old stag crowds, who were noisy and sometimes belligerent. Not only were the customers in the better theaters more attentive, but dressing rooms were more comfortable, scenery was brighter, props were available, and nobody had to work in afterpieces, since these were abolished. Stars of considerable magnitude were introduced at Tony Pastor's, including the now legendary Lillian Russell, before she moved on to musical comedy. But it was Tony himself who remained the most beloved figure on the vaudeville stage. Nightly, as his name was slid into the gilded shadow boxes on either side of the stage, the house roared with applause. Pastor appeared, immaculate in white tie and tails, a short, round man with an enormous paunch. In his hand was a collapsible silk opera hat, which he snapped open as the house noises died down. Cocking the hat on one side of his head, he would execute a few nimble dance steps before breaking into the first of his half dozen vocal numbers for the evening. He wrote most of his own songs, in a style that was simplicity itself—but one that seldom failed to please. Once in 1886, during the campaign of Abraham S. Hewitt, the millionaire merchant, for mayor of New York City, Pastor improvised a song, "What's the Matter with Hewitt?", to which the audience lustily responded, "He's All Right." Spontaneity of this sort was the stuff on which vaudeville flourished, for it aimed at enjoyment, pure and simple.

Much of the humor in early vaudeville was ethnic, making heavy-handed gibes at the recently arrived urban minorities. Irish acts were rife in the 1880s, and there were many Jewish songs and even more "Dutch" (German) dialect numbers, describing the antics of Hans *und* Fritz *und* Gus. Some of these were critical and by no means in good humor. Blackface tunes continued to be popular, and there were many lyrics referring to the problems of labor. Love ballads, however, constituted the largest single category of songs, and vaudeville quickly became a major vehicle in the diffusion of commercial music.

By the late eighties vaudeville halls were appearing all across the country. Barns, shooting galleries, churches, warehouses, livery stables, and other abandoned buildings were converted into makeshift theaters whose management bid for the acts listed in the trade journals. Provincial variety halls generally had an advertising drop which was let down between acts, usually depicting a small landscape in the center with the rest of the space taken up with notices for oyster houses, pool parlors, liver pills, beer bargains, rupture appliances, and funeral homes. Orchestras in such establishments varied in size from one piece—usually a piano, but sometimes a banjo—to seven or eight pieces. Most theaters used three pieces—piano, cornet, and drums. Performers rarely carried their own orchestration, except for a specialty, and accompaniment was left largely to the ingenuity of the local musicians.

B. F. Keith probably did more than anyone else to make vaudeville a national institution, introducing continuous performances and aggressively continuing Tony Pastor's campaign to make variety family entertainment. Performers were not only warned against uttering anything sacrilegious or suggestive, but were told not to use terms like "slob," "son-of-a-gun," and "hully gee" in their acts. Keith's eventual partner, Edward F. Albee, was largely responsible for dressing up vaudeville. Albee built opulent theaters with beautiful lobbies, dressing rooms, and baths, rich in marble, crimson and gold draperies, expensive rugs, oil paintings, gilded curlicues, and roseate cherubim. His larger theaters were virtual cathedrals, and performers were expected to costume accordingly. Early in the twentieth century the Keith-Albee Circuit dominated vaudeville in the East, while the Orpheum Circuit controlled most bookings from Chicago to the Pacific Coast. Oscar Hammerstein's Victoria Theater remained an independent thorn in the side of the Keith Circuit from 1904 until 1915, and there was other competition periodically from Klaw and Erlanger and the Shuberts. The most prestigious vaudeville theater in America, the Palace in New York, was built by Martin Beck, head of the Orpheum Circuit, with the hope of invading the lucrative Keith-Albee territory. By the time the house opened, March 24, 1913, Beck's opponents had seized control, leaving Orpheum only a twenty-five per cent interest.

Vaudeville reached its maturity around 1915, but had dominated popular amusements in the urban centers since the turn of the century. Programs over the years pretty much covered the entertainment spectrum, although skits, songs, dances, comic monologues, minstrel show humor, acrobats and animal acts (obvious holdovers from the circus) were the main components. Headliners emerged insisting on salaries commensurate with their pull at the box office. Whereas Lillian Russell had worked for Pastor in the Eighties for $35 a week, around 1910 Eva Tanguay commanded $3000 a week.

The tempestuous Tanguay was one of the most dazzling of the vaudeville stars. She had come up the hard way, was a master at publicity, and probably spent more money on costumes and material than anyone else in the business. A singing, dancing comedienne, she roared on stage with all the inhibitions of an assault and battery and flaunted Keith's puritanical dictum by injecting sex into her act right under manager Albee's nose. In a maudlin age when the vaudeville public was used to listening to such confections as "You'll Be Sorry Just Too Late," Tanguay jolted audiences by screaming "It's All Been Done Before but Not the Way I Do It," "Go as Far as You Like," and "I Want Some One to Go Wild with Me." Although she was often in trouble with the management and local authorities, Tanguay continued to shake her torso and wriggle her thighs, brazenly shrieking "I Don't Care" and "I Love to Be Crazy." Among her more controversial routines was a Salome dance put on in 1908, right after the big commotion in New York over the Richard Strauss opera. Tanguay won fame largely through the force of her personality and the brassiness of her delivery.

Nora Bayes, another great vaudeville headliner, was the mistress of poise, facial expression, the effortless gesture, flawless enunciation. Everything Bayes did was marked with style, and her ability to dramatize a song was without rival. With her husband, Jack Norworth, she wrote "Shine on Harvest Moon" and a number of other songs that have proven lasting pieces of Americana. Other vaudeville luminaries included Elsie Janis, Bert

Williams, Irene Franklin, Weber and Fields, the Dolly Sisters, Sophie Tucker, Eddie Foy, Fanny Brice, Gallagher and Sheean, Will Rogers, Texas Guinan, Ted Lewis, and W. C. Fields.

The circuits occasionally engaged foreign celebrities for status. Italo Campanini, Ernestine Schumann-Heink, and Sarah Bernhardt are but three of the several serious artists who performed for a time in variety. Fritzi Scheff, who had captivated New York a few years earlier in Victor Herbert's *Mlle. Modiste*, played the Palace in 1913, disappointing audiences by wearing the same gown throughout her act. A year later the young American actress Ethel Barrymore held the Palace stage with better results, but the song-and-dance acts remained vaudeville's life blood.

Audiences after 1900 became all-inclusive, drawing the patrician and the commoner alike. Matinee idols were adored equally by the little cleaning woman in the gallery and the debutante in the box. While vaudeville aimed at sheer entertainment, it became both a significant social institution and a mythic enactment of the aspirations of the American people. Albert F. McLean, Jr. argues in *American Vaudeville as Ritual* that variety served as a means by which the substrata of American thought came to grips with the development of a national identity and the trauma of urbanization. The disruptive experience of migration, both for European immigrants and rural Americans, was objectified and accepted on the vaudeville stage, helping to prepare the recent arrivals psychologically for life in the city. Vaudeville indoctrinated the migrants into accepted standards of speech, dress, manners, and social goals. It reflected the energy and pace of the Industrial Age, the comfort and luxury made possible by technology, and the diversity of contemporary American culture. It reinforced the belief in progress, glorified materialism, and restated the American dream of success. "Within the walls of these palaces," McLean insists, "gathered the hardworking and respectable members of society as well, caught up in the tinsel and gibberish, largely unaware that their world was being reshaped and revalued before their very eyes."

Not only did vaudeville suggest tangible images through which the new arrivals in the city could bring their spiritual and physical environments under control, but it also provided an avenue by which a plural society in the midst of urban flux could voice criticism and deal with ambivalence. Through humor, prejudices could be exposed, economic conflicts aired, and anxieties brought to the surface. The Puritan work ethic could be confirmed while enjoying an increased leisure. Fantasies of better things to come could be maintained, as an eclectic dream world invited escape from a confused, often weary present. Vaudeville, in McLean's analysis, was both an emotional safety valve and a means of self-recognition.

As variety grew in size and opulence, it gave rise to the revue—part vaudeville, part burlesque, part comic opera, mounted with the magnificence of an extravaganza. Unlike vaudeville, the revue was loosely held together by a central theme, but like the minstrel show, the middle section gave each member of the company a chance to perform his specialty. The concept of the revue derived from George W. Lederer, who became convinced that variety in an extended form and fancy dress could attract a select audience willing to pay a considerably higher admission price than that charged by Tony Pastor and his colleagues. In 1894 Lederer produced *The Passing Show* at the Casino Theater with sufficient success that the show was widely imitated. By the close of the century the revue had become a popular Broadway institution, reaching its classic form in 1907 with the first edition of the Ziegfeld *Follies*.

Florenz Ziegfeld was from Chicago, the son of an old-school German musician who became president of the Chicago Musical College. He entered show business in 1896 with a production of *A Parlor Match* starring the diminutive French singer Anna Held, whom he married the following year. The ravishing Anna was an enormous success in the musical, capturing men's hearts by rolling her black eyes and singing in a delightful accent, "Won't You Come and Play with Me?" For the next several years most of Ziegfeld's productions were built around Anna Held's personality. One of the best was *A Parisian Model* in 1906, during which Anna wore six different gowns in a single scene and again caused hearts to palpitate, singing "I Just Can't Make My Eyes Behave." Ziegfeld seized upon the idea of the *Follies* during a trip to Paris in 1906. His intention was to give the United States a revue discreetly patterned after the fabled *Folies Bergere*—one that would offer beautiful girls without the lascivious features of its French counterpart. His initial *Follies* opened on July 8, 1907, on the roof of the New York Theater, which Ziegfeld renamed the Jardin de Paris. The *Follies of 1907* cost a mere $13,000, contained another of the Salome dances then in vogue, and featured Nora Bayes. There was little of the luxury that came later, but Ziegfeld's instinct for glorifying the American girl was already in evidence.

The *Follies* remained an annual event until 1931, becoming the very symbol of show business grandeur. The new edition as a rule opened in New York in June, ran through the summer, then went on tour. While Ziegfeld's appeal was mainly to the eye, the ear was not altogether forgotten. Some of the most important names in American popular music provided songs for the various *Follies*, among them Victor Herbert, Rudolf Friml, Jerome Kern, and Irving Berlin. And there were stars! Nora Bayes returned in 1908, followed the next year by Eva Tanguay. Lillian Lorraine, the *Follies'* first great beauty, thrilled audiences in 1909 by appearing in a sea of soap bubbles and later singing "Up, Up, Up in My Aeroplane," as she circled over patrons in a miniature flying machine. Fanny Brice entered the Ziegfeld galaxy in 1910 with an Irving Berlin number called "Goodbye, Becky Cohen" and continued as a *Follies* regular for more than a decade, adding to her reputation with specialties like "Second Hand Rose" and "My Man." The Dolly Sisters, Hungarian twins who had grown up on New York's lower East Side, were lured away from vaudeville to dance in the 1911 edition, while Ann Pennington, the "shimmy" queen, was a sensation two seasons later. The list of luminaries goes on and on—Leon Erroll, Ed Wynn, Mae Murray, Eddie

Cantor, Will Rogers, W. C. Fields, Sophie Tucker, Marilyn Miller, Ruth Etting. Production costs had soared by 1918 to $110,000, as casts grew larger and production numbers more sumptuous. In the early twenties, Ziegfeld was spending more than $20,000 a week on salaries alone, but was commanding the cream of the carriage trade.

By the time the Ziegfeld *Follies* reached their height, in the years right after World War I, there were a number of serious competitors in the field. The Shubert brothers revived *The Passing Show* at the Winter Garden in 1912, attempting to surpass Ziegfeld by employing younger, slimmer girls for the chorus and using a runway so that audiences could get a better look. By 1914 legs were bare, and the midriff was a recent discovery. *The Passing Show of 1918*, introducing Fred and Adele Astaire in their first starring appearance on Broadway, focused on the War and included sketches about Saving Stamps and a burlesque picturing Salome with the head of the Kaiser. Although Sigmund Romberg wrote the score, the show's best remembered songs— "Smiles" and "I'm Forever Blowing Bubbles"—were interpolated, both obviously escapist in theme.

When *The Passing Show* went on tour, the Shuberts staged yearly extravaganzas at the Winter Garden, several of the more successful featuring Al Jolson. In *Robinson Crusoe, Jr.* (1916) an American millionaire dreams he is Robinson Crusoe, while his chauffeur—Jolson—becomes his man Friday. The two are transported to a Spanish castle, to a pirate ship, and to a forest where the trees turn into beautiful girls. In *Sinbad* (1919) Jolson played a porter taken back to ancient Bagdad to mingle with characters out of *The Arabian Nights* and interpolated four of his all-time hits—"Swanee," "Rock-a-Bye Your Baby with a Dixie Melody," "Chloe," and "Mammy"—into what was otherwise a Romberg score. In each instance Jolson demonstrated the continuing appeal of blackface, about the time the minstrel show itself was experiencing its final decline.

The Shuberts eventually took over the Hippodrome, opened in 1905, where on an enormous stage mechanical devices, electrical effects, and hundreds of supernumeraries carried the fetish for spectacle to circus proportions. The Hippodrome went in for dancing waters, scented perfume sprayed out over the house, elephants, horses, clowns, and girls. One year the whole chorus disappeared into a lake on stage and never came out! The girls simply marched down the steps of a large tank until their heads were beneath the water, swam underwater to a submerged shelf behind the orchestra pit, pulled themselves along with their noses barely sticking out, and climbed out of the tank when they reached the wings.

Raymond Hitchcock's *Hitchy Koo* revues began in 1917, followed two years later by George White's *Scandals*. A rash of off-Broadway theaters appeared in the Greenwich Village area before World War I, and in 1919 the *Greenwich Village Follies* opened, with emphasis on simplicity and taste. In the *Greenwich Village* series girls occupied a secondary position to smart sketches by literate writers, avant-garde costumes and scenery, and serious dances by Martha Graham. A little later came the *Music Box Revue*, the Earl Carroll *Vanities*, and the *Grand Street Follies*. While each of these shows introduced new and important theater music, of the bigger revues George White's *Scandals* was most innovative. None of them, however, quite matched Ziegfeld's flare or popularity. By 1930 most of the competition was gone, and Ziegfeld himself was in the throes of financial disaster. Refusing to compromise his standards, the great showman went deeper and deeper into debt. At the time of his death he was virtually penniless.

Since the mid-1920s vaudeville, too, had been in trouble, faced with competition from radio, the phonograph, the movies, and musical comedy. The Palace closed in 1932, signaling the end of big time variety. Much of vaudeville's original vitality had been lost in the move toward glamor, and the public had grown tired of the same old gags and song-and-dance acts. Urban audiences by the 1920s desired more sophisticated entertainment, while the multitude preferred the versatility, excitement, and gaudiness of motion pictures. Vaudeville had served its purpose, offered pleasure to townspeople confused by conflicting sets of values, yet was clearly out of touch with a less gullible population. Whereas the *Follies* became too expensive, vaudeville remained too homespun—at least for the multimillion dollar circuits.

The death knell for variety sounded about the time musical comedy was reaching maturity; this was no mere coincidence. While the revue had made pretenses at a connecting theme, there was no plot—no book, as in musical comedy. Essentially musical comedy took variety and unified it, giving audiences a story, but also a rounded evening of dancing, comedy, singing, and pretty girls. More directly than either burlesque or vaudeville, the book musical owed much to the success of *The Black Crook*, for it evolved from that prototype, although gradually sharpening its focus along the way.

Two years after the appearance of *The Black Crook*, George L. Fox produced *Humpty-Dumpty*, another extravaganza and one that shamelessly imitated the transformation scene, spells, and rituals of its predecessor. The show had little to do with Mother Goose, but had a longer initial New York run than *The Black Crook* and enjoyed many revivals. In 1874 Edward E. Rice's *Evangeline* opened in Niblo's Garden, the first attempt at an "American extravaganza" with native charcters. Rice, a Boston shipping clerk, structured his burlesque of Longfellow's poem after French opera bouffe and pre-Gilbert and Sullivan English comic opera. But *Evangeline* included homespun humor and for the first time an entire score created for a specific production. The show toured the country for nearly thirty years and returned to New York for frequent revivals. The composer's format was permissive rather than restrictive, so that his travesty took on new colorations in later performances. Rice, while no professional musician, remained a popular figure in musical comedy until the end of the century, always playing the piano by ear and setting his tunes down in a private musical shorthand for others to transcribe.

After four years on the road *The Brook* arrived in New York in 1879, a pioneer effort to achieve unity among plot, dialogue, and characters. With book and lyrics by Nate Salsbury, its music consisting of adaptations, *The Brook* was an attempt to bring naturalness and spontaneity to the American musical stage, dealing simply with the mishaps attending a picnic in the country. It employed the topical materials of variety, yet arranged these on the framework of a story. The show was informal, its songs and dances comfortably within the vernacular genre, and utilized none of the spectacular machinery, pantomime stylizations, hefty women in tights, or red-nosed comics currently in vogue. Like *Evangeline, The Brook* was family entertainment. It was also the first American musical presented in London.

Extravaganza continued, however, carried forward by the Kiralfy brothers, who in the 1880s became leaders in the field. Their great marvel, *Around the World in Eighty Days,* was more notable for its dazzling effects than for its melodies, while *Excelsior,* staged in 1883 under the personal supervision of Thomas A. Edison, was the initial production featuring electric lighting. Within another ten years spectacles revolving around nymphs and fairies had become old-fashioned, and critics were having a field day pointing out the absurdities and musical deficiencies of such works. Reviewing a show called *Kajanka* in 1890, the *New York Times* reported, "The good fairy was very thin and persisted in a hopeless attempt to sing. The bad fairy was very fat and persisted in an equally hopeless attempt to dance....The thirteen poorly costumed girls constituting the chorus bumped into each other as they marched, and each struck a different key when they sang." Yet musical fantasies endured well into the next century; *The Wizard of Oz* in 1903 went a long way toward pulling Broadway out of its recent doldrums.

Even so, a sense of realism had been injected into the musical theater as early as the 1870s—most conspicuously by Edward Harrigan and Tony Hart, in a series of comedies dealing with the *hoi polloi* of urban America. Their burlesques grew out of the parodies of the early 1880s, particularly the travesty portion of the minstrel show. But Harrigan and Hart created a world all their own, drawn from a broad caricature of life among the Irish, Germans, and blacks in contemporary New York. Their humor came in part from the blundering way in which their characters went about solving everyday problems, in part from the individual speech, distinctive behavior patterns, and personal mannerisms of their minority stereotypes. Harrigan wrote the plays; he and Hart starred in them; while the music was composed by their English-born conductor, David Braham.

Ned Harrigan had grown up among the people he would later write about—policemen, politicians, peddlers, bartenders, newsboys, sailors, Bowery toughs, pawnbrokers, storekeepers, servant girls, washerwomen— simple, ordinary people who made up life in the big city. While his attitude toward them was basically sympathetic, his portrayals also demonstrated a sharp command of satire. Harrigan had no formal education beyond grammar school, yet he came to be called the "Dickens of America," a title conferred upon him by William Dean Howells. "Polite society, wealth, and culture," Harrigan once said, "possess little or no color or picturesqueness." And it was primarily the habitues of the slums to which his attention gravitated. Harrigan was a stocky, serene man, with practically no interests outside the theater. He was a prolific writer, the author of thirty-five full-length plays (nearly all of them topical farces), an actor, singer, producer, director, and theater manager. He even wrote his own program notes.

Tony Hart was a Roman Catholic of pure Irish descent, twelve years Ned Harrigan's junior. He had entered show business at age ten, after running away from a reform school outside Worcester, Massachusetts. He had a round, clean-shaven face that Harrigan once said looked like an angel on a Valentine. The two complemented each other beautifully. "Hart could play all the parts seven Harrigans could write," the Boston *Traveller* maintained, "and Harrigan could write what seven Harts could play." While Tony Hart filled a wide range of male roles, he specialized in women's parts. In one play he impersonated six characters—three men and three women. In another he played both a mother and her son. His imitation of feminine movements and facial expressions was so believable that William Pinkerton, the detective, refused to accept that Hart was a man. Taken backstage and allowed to observe the performer's costume and make-up at close range, Pinkerton still remained unconvinced, until Hart pulled off his wig and let fly a few manly oaths.

Harrigan and Hart had become vaudeville partners by the summer of 1871. Two years later, during an engagement in Chicago, they performed David Braham's song "The Mulligan Guard" in a sketch built around Harrigan's character Dan Mulligan. Mulligan was Irish through and through, mixed his groceries with liquor, and seasoned both with politics. The characterization grew into a full evening's entertainment and eventually into a series of nine plays. In 1876 Harrigan and Hart leased a lower Broadway theater and staged the first of their "Mulligan" farces, called simply *The Mulligan Guard*. Then came *The Mulligan Guard Picnic, The Mulligan Guard Ball, The Mulligan Guard Surprise, The Mulligan Guard Christmas, The Mulligan Guard Chowder, The Mulligan Guard Nominee*, and The *Mulligan Guard Silver Wedding*. Harrigan often said that *haste* and *strife* were the two words that best summarized the New York of his time, and the "Mulligan" series had haste and strife aplenty. One scene in *The Mulligan Guard Ball* (1879) found Dan Mulligan in a barber shop talking with Simpson Primrose, a black barber, about a prizefight in which an Irishman had beaten a German. The second act closed in a dance hall inadvertently rented by its absent-minded German proprietor to both an Irish social club and a black social club for the same night. To avoid mayhem the proprietor persuaded the blacks to take a room upstairs, directly over the Irish. After much spirited dancing on both levels, the floor above gave way, and the scene ended with the ceiling caving in on the Irish and black bodies tumbling down upon the stage.

The Irish generally came off best in Harrigan's plays, but the writer was not beyond having Rebecca Allup, his sharp-tongued black housekeeper, suggest that if the Irish in America felt home rule was such a good thing, they could all jolly well go back to Ireland and rule there. Politicians and dishonest elections repeatedly came under attack. When Dan Mulligan beat out his German opponent for the job of alderman in *The Mulligan Guards Nominee* (insisting that he henceforth be called "Tiger"), ballot boxes were stuffed with practically everything on stage. As Harrigan insisted in one of his lyrics:

> *It's money, my boys, makes troubles and joys*
> *In politics, church, or the law!*

But always there was tumult galore. During a scene aboard the Albany night boat, half the members of the cast threw the other half overboard, before the boat itself exploded.

Harrigan had a great eye for detail. He would often station himself on a park bench in some inelegant section of town, notebook in hand, observing the people and conversations around him. Many of his plays contained sixty or seventy roles, requiring more than a hundred costumes. Before an opening he and Tony Hart used to search the second-hand stores and back alleys of New York for authentic garments and were even known to greet shiploads of immigrants at the dock. Some of the clothing they brought back to the theater was so verminous that they had to be boiled before performers would wear them. *Squatter Sovereignty* (1882) pictured slum dwellers living in huts and shanties on the barren, rocky flanks of Central Park, with goats, geese, dogs, and children running wild.

Harrigan's songs were realistic in much the same crude way. Two numbers from *Squatter Sovereignty* were "The Widow Nolan's Goat" and "Paddy Duffy's Cart," a nostalgic recital of lowly lives, some of which rose to eminence. A song entitled "McNally's Row of Flats" from *McSorley's Inflation* (also 1882) contained the chorus:

> *It's Ireland and Italy, Jerusalem and Germany,*
> *Oh, Chinamen and nagers, and a paradise for rats,*
> *All jubled togayther in the snow or rainy weather,*
> *They represent the tenants in McNally's row of flats.*

Two years later, the outstanding tune in *Cordelia's Aspirations* was "My Dad's Dinner Pail." Altogether Harrigan and David Braham collaborated on over 200 songs, including "Maggie Murphy's Home," "The Babies on Our Block," and "Dolly, My Crumpled-Horn Cow."

Composer Braham was hardly a highbrow. He had come to this country as a violinist, but by 1865 was leading the band at Tony Pastor's. Braham conducted all of the "Mulligan" shows and eventually became Ned Harrigan's father-in-law. His tunes for Harrigan's plain-speaking, witty lyrics were written in good British music hall style, but lacked the vitality that preserved the contemporary work of Gilbert and Sullivan, with whom Harrigan and Braham have sometimes been compared.

While the songs from the "Mulligan" shows would seem old-fashioned to later generations, they were much a part of their own day and highly popular. In New York during the late seventies, "The Mulligan Guard" could be heard everywhere. Newsboys, policemen, hot corn venders on street corners, and oyster sellers whistled the tune as they went about their chores, and it was cranked out by hundreds of organ grinders and played on thousands of pianos. Harrigan's farces were adored by the public, critics, and intellectuals alike. "A visit to New York would be as incomplete to the countryman if he did not see Harrigan and Hart," one New England guide book claimed in the eighties, "as if he had by some strange mistake missed going to Central Park."

The boisterous antics of the "Mulligan Guard" closely resembled the comedy of the minstrel show, while the timely songs and sketches of Harrigan and Hart gradually bridged the gap between vaudeville and musical comedy. By the time the team broke up in 1885, they had moved from the Bowery uptown as far as Thirty-fifth Street, assembled a more or less permanent company of supporting players, and added a quasi-realistic local color to the American musical stage that contrasted sharply with the mythical themes that dominated operetta and the extravaganza. Harrigan and Braham continued to write successful shows through the 1890s, but by the turn of the century a new audience had arisen, too sophisticated for Harrigan's rowdy humor and unpretentious songs.

The influence of Harrigan and Hart lingered, however, in the work of Weber and Fields and was strongly evident in the plays of Charles Hoyt. Hoyt's most popular production, *A Trip to Chinatown* (1891), realistically portrayed ordinary American life, interspersed with song. The plot dealt with two married couples strolling through San Francisco's Chinatown trying not to run into each other. Like Ned Harrigan, Hoyt depicted recognizable American types, but also poked fun at such contemporary issues as the temperance crusade, Woman's suffrage, and small town politics. Amid the satire were hit songs like "The Bowery," "Reuben, Reuben," and "Push Dem Clouds Away"—all written by Percy Gaunt, who had worked for a time with Harrigan and Hart. Charles K. Harris' waltz "After the Ball" was interpolated later. While Hoyt emphasized plot more than Harrigan had, there was still little integration of music and drama. *A Trip to Chinatown*'s songs were stuck into the plot arbitrarily, with almost no regard for character or situation. But the show did offer an American story, with American tunes and an American speech pattern. It ran for 656 performances, smashing box office records, while its producers were among the first to realize the potential from the publication and sale of sheet music.

Although a vernacular realism was sprouting in the American musical theater during the late nineteenth century, a parallel strain, more consciously esthetic, emanated from Europe. The trend began right after the Civil War with the success of Jacques Offenbach's *opera bouffes*. The composer's *La Grand Duchesse* received its New York premiere on September 24, 1867, starring the vivacious French singer Lucille Tostee, and was an immediate triumph. For more than two decades the country was flooded with the Frenchman's delightful works, particularly *La Belle Helene, La Vie Parisienne*, and *La Perichole*. Marie Aimee was the most popular of the comic opera divas in the 1870s, but the competition was keen. Companies toured from coast to coast, seriously cutting into grand opera audiences in New York, Chicago, San Francisco, and New Orleans alike. Offenbach himself visited the United States in 1876, lured over for the Philadelphia Centennial at a fee of $1000 a performance for thirty concerts. The rage continued into the 1890s, when Lillian Russell, wanting a break from the grind of musical comedy, was featured in revivals of *The Grand Duchesse, La Belle Helene*, and *La Perichole*.

But the French *opera bouffe* craze was nothing compared with the mania for Gilbert and Sullivan that swept the country following the American premiere of *H.M.S. Pinafore* at the Boston Museum on November 25, 1878. Presented in New York the next February, *Pinafore* was soon being given by some ninety companies across the United States, five of them running simultaneously in New York City. As the *"Pinafore"* fever spread, pirated versions of the Gilbert and Sullivan comic opera were being staged by church groups, schools, ladies' clubs, amateur theatrical organizations, and charities. There was a Yiddish *Pinafore* and parodies too numerous to mention. Gilbert and Sullivan came to the United States late in 1879 with the D'Oyly Carte Opera Company from the Savoy Theatre in London, causing the enthusiasm to soar all the higher. Sir Arthur Sullivan conducted a performance of *H.M.S. Pinafore* at the Fifth Avenue Theater in New York on December 1, with W. S. Gilbert appearing on stage as a sailor. Women began to flock to the theater like never before, as the Gilbert and Sullivan comic operas became socially smart and morally acceptable.

The frenzy lasted through the mid-eighties. *The Pirates of Penzance* had its premiere in New York on New Year's Eve, 1879, staged by the D'Oyly Carte Company. Then in rapid succession came the other popular Gilbert and Sullivan comic operas: *Iolanthe, Princess Ida, Trial by Jury*, and *Patience*. By 1884 the fever was beginning to subside, but returned with the appearance of *The Mikado* the next year. On a single evening in 1886, 170 separate performances of *The Mikado* are said to have taken place in the United States.

Austrian and German operetta had enjoyed success in English translation since the 1870s, particularly the works of Johann Strauss, Jr., Franz von Suppe, and Karl Millocker. The Casino Theater, which was the home of comic opera in America for a full decade, opened on October 22, 1882, with Strauss' *The Queen's Lace Handkerchief*. Millocker's *The Beggar*

Student was heard at the Casino a season later, while the composer's *Arme Jonathan*, adapted as *Poor Jonathan*, opened there with Lillian Russell in October, 1890. A scene in the original version, showing cotton picking along New York's Battery, was judiciously altered.

But public interest in Viennese operetta had declined by the turn of the century to so low an ebb that impresario Henry W. Savage watched the success of Franz Lehar's *The Merry Widow* in Vienna and Berlin for two years before risking an American production. When Savage did take a chance on the Lehar work, it proved an absolute sensation, giving Central European operetta a totally new lease on life. *The Merry Widow* swirled into New York on October 21, 1907, at the New Amsterdam Theater, inaugurating the greatest influx of European-inspired operettas in Broadway history. The production was lavishly staged and costumed and was duplicated almost immediately in Chicago and elsewhere on the road. The demand for sheet music, piano scores, and arrangements for small and large orchestras was unprecedented, as was the sale of gramophone records. Suddenly women's fashions reflected *The Merry Widow*'s impact, as the wasp-waisted gown and huge ostrich-feather hat came into vogue. The market was inundated with Merry Widow fans, Merry Widow shoes, Merry Widow gloves, and Merry Widow undergarments. Influenced by the "Merry Widow Waltz," ballroom dancing became warm, personal, a symbol of romantic love. Waltz contests were held across the nation, as Americans fell deeper and deeper under the spell of Lehar's colorful Slavonic music.

Dozens of foreign operettas followed in the wake of *The Merry Widow*. Leo Fall's *The Dollar Princess* was a tremendous success; so were Oskar Straus' *A Waltz Dream* and *The Chocolate Soldier*, both full of melody and style. "My Hero" from *The Chocolate Soldier* (1909) did much to keep the enthusiasm for the Viennese waltz alive, while Johann Strauss' *Die Fledermaus* was revived with far better results than had been the case almost thirty years earlier. The Shuberts presented an adaptation of the Strauss classic in 1912, featuring the Dolly Sisters, without securing rights and were roundly sued by the composer's widow. The show, given under the title *The Merry Countess*, proved to be a hit nonetheless. Henry Savage produced *Sari* by the Hungarian composer Emmerich Kalman in 1914, but the vogue for Central European operetta was coming to an end. With the approach of World War I, anti-German sentiment kept even the favored Franz Lehar off the American stage. In 1917 the Shuberts made the mistake of presenting Lehar's *The Star Gazer*. Although the score was a good one, the production was forced to close at the end of one week. No more Austro-German operetta was heard in the United States until well after the war.

Yet American imitations continued. Comic operas by native and naturalized composers had enjoyed intermittent popularity since the outbreak of *"Pinafore* fever" in 1878. Willard Spencer's *The Little Tycoon* had played 500 performances in Philadelphia before it opened in New York in 1887. More interesting for its topical humor than for its music, *The Little*

Tycoon was clearly patterned after *The Mikado* and contained any number of Gilbert and Sullivan touches. *Wang* by German-trained Woolson Morse was another work owing much to *The Mikado*, although this one took place in Siam. Other early American operettas meeting with success were William Wallace Furst's *The Isle of Champagne* (1892); *The Belle of New York* (1897) by German-born, Louisville-reared Gustave Kerker; Ludwig Englander's *The Strollers* (1901); *The Burgomaster* (1900) and *The Prince of Pilsen* (1903) by Gustav Luders, another German immigrant who helped establish an American school of comic opera in the Viennese tradition; and *Madame Sherry* by Karl Hoschna, a native of Bohemia who had received training at the Vienna Conservatory.

But America's most distinguished light opera composer before the turn of the century was Reginald De Koven. Born in Middletown, Connecticut, De Koven was taken to England as a boy and graduated from Oxford University at the age of twenty. He studied composition in Stuttgart, Frankfort, Vienna with Genee, and Paris with Delibes, before turning to comic opera. His first two efforts, *The Begum* and *Don Quixote*, were dismal failures. Then shifting to operetta, he wrote *Robin Hood*, his greatest success, during the winter of 1888-89. The work, containing the perennial favorite "Oh, Promise Me," opened in Chicago in 1890 and was staged in New York and Boston the next season. An aloof man, formal in dress and patrician in attitude, the composer was a bit staid for popular tastes and never again captured the public's imagination. De Koven wrote sixteen more light operas after *Robin Hood*, but was unable to equal his earlier success. In later years he resumed his career as a critic, which he had launched shortly after returning from Europe. He was the music editor of the New York *Herald* for a number of years and from 1902 to 1905 conducted the Philharmonic Orchestra in Washington, which he had organized.

By 1900 the Broadway musical stage had solidified into two distinct poles. One leaned toward the vernacular and included the extravaganza, musical farces, and the revue. The other favored European comic opera and operetta. The first was less formal, aiming at pure amusement and eye appeal; the latter was more cultivated. Somewhere in between were native musical comedies and British imports like *The Geisha* (1896), *Florodora* (1900), and *The Pink Lady* (1911). While the demarcation between one genre and another was not always clear, the terminals were fairly discernible. Preferences seemed to be about evenly divided between the "serious" and "popular" divisions.

The new century found two contrasting figures dominating the American musical theater—Victor Herbert and George M. Cohan. Herbert was a trained musician who longed to write grand opera and serious orchestral works. Cohan had graduated from vaudeville into the ranks of farce and the book musical. Herbert was drawn to operetta because it offered him the financial rewards serious music could not. Cohan was attracted to musical comedy because he considered it a step up from variety. One symbolized a popularization of traditional art, the other a refinement of vernacular entertainment.

Victor Herbert was born in Dublin, Ireland, on February 1, 1859, the same year as Reginald De Koven. Since his father died when Victor was three, the boy and his mother went to live with his maternal grandfather, Samuel Lover, a writer and dilettante musician. Young Herbert spent his formative years outside London, but when it came time for him to go to school, Lover insisted his daughter take the boy to Germany, where he felt they could find a better education cheaper. In Germany Mrs. Herbert married a physician, and the family made their home in Stuttgart. At fifteen Victor began studying the cello, largely because his mother thought a gentleman should know some musical instrument. It had pretty well been decided that the youth would follow his stepfather's profession. But Herbert's progress on the cello was so rapid that he soon gave up thoughts of medicine, dropped out of school, and eventually entered the Stuttgart Conservatory. He wandered over the Continent for several years playing with orchestras, sometimes as a solo artist and often as first cellist. He spent a year in Vienna, performing light music under the direction of Eduard Strauss, the brother of the Viennese waltz king. He served under such guest conductors as Liszt, Brahms, Rubinstein, Saint-Saens, and Delibes, before becoming a member of the Stuttgart Opera orchestra. A colleague in Dresden had told Herbert he should compose, and he now began studying harmony, counterpoint, and orchestration with Max Seyffrytz. Within a year the young musician had completed a Concerto for Cello that was performed by the Stuttgart Royal Orchestra.

Meanwhile, Herbert was acquiring quite a reputation as a dandy and a man-about-town. Tall, gregarious, and courtly, he enjoyed the good things of life, which for Herbert included not only art and music, but gourmet meals, vintage wines, and the company of beautiful women as well. Women adored him, and one in particular—Theresa Foerster, a handsome, statuesque soprano with the Stuttgart Opera—attracted his attention. The two were married in Vienna on August 14, 1886. A short time before, Walter Damrosch had come to Stuttgart looking for fresh German voices for the Metropolitan Opera. He offered Fraulein Foerster a contract, but the singer refused until her fiance was hired as first cellist of the Metropolitan orchestra. Two months after their marriage, the couple sailed for New York.

Herbert came to America much in his wife's shadow. She successfully opened the Metropolitan season on November 8, 1886, in Karl Goldmark's *The Queen of Sheba*, and won acclaim in three other roles. But Mme. Herbert-Foerster sang with the Metropolitan only one full season and soon gave up her career altogether. Her husband quickly gained the limelight. In January, 1887, Herbert was soloist with the New York Symphony in a performance of his Concerto for Cello and later played under the direction of both Theodore Thomas and Anton Seidl. He taught for a time at the National Conservatory, achieved notice with a cantata written for the Worcester Music Festival of 1891, and composed a second cello concerto for the New York Philharmonic three years later. In 1893 he became director of Pat Gilmore's

Twenty-second Regiment Band and was delighted when his men were selected to play for President McKinley's inaugural ball. Herbert was appointed principal conductor of the Pittsburgh Symphony in 1898, a post which he held with distinction for six years.

Already he had entered the operetta field. Herbert's first music for the stage was written during the Chicago World's Fair, when he was commissioned to put together some numbers for a pageant. The pageant was never produced, and Herbert's tunes were never performed. About the same time Lillian Russell encouraged him to write an operetta for her. The result was a piece called *La Vivandiere*, which was never staged, because the star with the hourglass figure had second thoughts about appearing in an operetta by an unknown composer. Then the director of the Bostonians, a light opera company, encouraged by the recent success of De Koven's *Robin Hood*, asked Herbert to write the music for *Prince Ananias*. The work, set in sixteenth-century France, opened in New York on November 20, 1894, but was a minor success at best. The Bostonians toured with the show and kept it in the repertory for two seasons.

The next Herbert operetta, *The Wizard of the Nile*, was not long in coming. After several out-of-town tryouts, the show opened at the Casino Theater on November 4, 1895, with comedian Frank Daniels as the fake Persian magician. It lasted for thirteen weeks, then considered a respectable Broadway run. But *The Fortune Teller* three years later was Herbert's first important operetta, its "Gypsy Love Song" his first great hit. Set in Hungary, the show called for music that was full of verve and passion, and the Herbert score was clearly painted from the same pallette as Hungarian composer Franz Lehar's. Yet "Romany Life" and "The Hussars' Chorus" unveiled the composer's ability at lilting melody, and demonstrated musical soundness and a craftsmanship uncommon on the American musical stage of that day.

Tunes poured from Victor Herbert's head, and he customarily worked with lightning speed. His style was eclectic, at times sounding French, frequently German, most often Viennese. Although he loved America and flourished in the zestful New World atmosphere, an American identity never really emerged out of the composer's songwriting. Still he brought to the American musical theater a freedom of expression, a grandeur of choral climax, a skill at orchestration, and a gift of lyricism that were to have an immense influence. He was a vain man, who loved magnificence and thrived on the glamor and excitement of the theater. He still wanted to compose serious music, but reconciled himself with the notion that he would write comic opera until he had enough money to compose whatever he wished. While he was conductor of the Pittsburgh Symphony, he wrote operettas in his spare time. Although he was criticized for wasting himself on light music, his reputation for versatility pleased him. He was exhilarated by his associates on Broadway, proud of his contact with great figures like Kreisler and Richard Strauss. Among the musician's early admirers was Andrew Carnegie, who used to say of the Pittsburgh Orchestra, "My idea of heaven would be to hear Victor Herbert and his men play for me twice every day."

When Herbert left Pittsburgh and returned to New York, he formed his own orchestra, giving indoor concerts during the winter and playing seasonal engagements at summer parks like Saratoga Springs. By this time he was turning out a comic opera on an average of every five months. And there was a stream of successes. *Babes in Toyland*, produced in 1903, was an extravaganza frankly attempting to capitalize on the current popularity of *The Wizard of Oz*. The show captured the child's world of fantasy and imagination through production numbers and ballets that were feasts for the eye. Herbert's music was simple, direct, infectious—especially "I Can't Do the Sum," "Toyland," and "Never Mind, Bo-Peep," all reminiscent of childhood ditties. The best moment musically was "The March of the Toys," an instrumental number which indicated that the composer was happiest when writing for the orchestra.

Mlle. Modiste, one of Herbert's greatest triumphs, opened at the Knickerbocker Theater on Christmas night, 1905. It featured the waltz "Kiss Me Again" and starred Fritzi Scheff, who had been lured away from the Metropolitan Opera for an earlier Victor Herbert work, the second-rate *Babette*. *Mlle. Modiste* is set in Paris, where the fetching Fifi is employed in a hat shop. She falls in love with Captain Etienne de Bouvray, but Etienne cannot marry outside his own aristocratic circle. Heartbroken, Fifi pursues her ambition of becoming a great singer. With financial help from a wealthy American, she develops into a famous prima donna under the assumed name of Mme. Bellini. When she is invited to perform at the estate of Etienne's uncle, she wins the old Count completely with her singing. The proud de Bouvray's can resist no longer and happily sanctions Fifi's marriage to Etienne. This is the sort of banal, Old World plot around which most of Herbert's operettas were woven. Yet the composer's flow of melody gave the production sparkle and charm; and for singer Scheff *Mlle. Modiste* more than compensated for a prior lacklustre association with a Herbert score.

When Herbert introduced American characters, he usually did so in foreign or exotic settings. *It Happened in Nordland* (1904) found an American ambassadress sent to a mythical kingdom. *The Red Mill*, written in 1906 for comedians Fred Stone and David Montgomery, dealt with two footloose Americans, Con Kidder and Kid Conner, stranded in a small Dutch town without funds. In the course of several disguises and much madcap goings-on, they promote and bring to a happy resolution the obstacle-strewn romance of Gretchen and Captain Doris van Damm. In one scene the visitors rescue the heroine from an abduction plot, hanging precariously from the arms of a big red windmill as they spirit her through a window. Along the way Herbert's tunes—most notably "Moonbeams," "The Isle of Our Dreams," and "Because You're You"—are sung with no particular regard for the plot. "Every Day Is Ladies' Day" revealed the composer's natural sense of humor, while "The Streets of New York" demonstrated his flair for big production numbers.

Other Herbert operettas were set in Hungary, Austria, Palermo, India, Afghanistan, Persia, Algeria, and Zergovia—wherever *that* may be, certainly nowhere near America. These provided atmospheres the composer could fill with sentimental ballads, swirling waltzes, and spirited marches. Herbert's vehicles thrived on the fancy and remote, the stilted and overelegant; characters were unfamiliar and gleefully improbable.

Even *Naughty Marietta*, set in eighteenth-century New Orleans, boasted a strong Creole flavor, with Italian seasoning. Marietta is a highborn Neapolitan, who has come to Louisiana to escape from an undesirable marriage. She falls under the protection of Captain Dick Warrington, a stalwart Kentuckian in pursuit of a dangerous pirate. The girl vows she will give her heart only to the man who can complete a fragment of a melody she has heard in a dream. Etienne, actually the pirate, courts Marietta and almost wins her. But Captain Dick intervenes just in time and completes the dream melody. The show opened in New York on November 7, 1910, and represents the height of Victor Herbert's career. It contains five of his finest and most durable songs: "Ah! Sweet Mystery of Life," "Italian Street Song," "I'm Falling in Love with Someone," "'Neath the Southern Moon," and "Tramp! Tramp! Tramp!" *Naughty Marietta* was produced by Oscar Hammerstein, right after the demise of his venture with grand opera, and starred vivacious Emma Trentini and rotund Orville Harold, both of whom had sung for Hammerstein at the Manhattan Opera House. In addition the impresario's former opera company supplied the show with other singers, most of the chorus, part of the orchestra, and its regular conductor. It was no typical Broadway company by any means, and critics praised both the vocal capacity of the cast and the rich sounds from the orchestra.

Herbert was now a major figure on Broadway, one to whom even the lions of the show business world deferred. When the composer entered a New York theater for rehearsals, he was announced—"Mr. Herbert, everybody!"—and people stood and applauded. He was recognized as more than a one-fingered melodist; he was an imposing Broadway musician and a man who knew his business. He clothed himself in the best garments money could buy and usually dressed formally even in the afternoon. He adored flattery, was careless with money, and frequented only the finest restaurants. He loved to stop into a favorite Broadway haunt, pull out a wad of bills, and signal a general treat, "All right, boys!"

The same year that *Naughty Marietta* opened, his opera *Natoma* was staged in Philadelphia and Chicago, originally intended for Oscar Hammerstein. Herbert piled assignment upon assignment and frequently turned out a complete score, including orchestration, within a month's time. "He would come in and work out a scene in my office," Florenz Ziegfeld later recalled, "and the next morning appear with the full orchestration." He sometimes worked on two shows at the same time, shifting from one to the other as melodies flowed from his mind. Yet Herbert lacked real substance and came to accept his limitations. He once told his friend James G. Huneker,

"You can keep to your ideals, Jim. I want to make money." And yet he knew his strengths, too. When *The Madcap Duchess* was poorly received by critics, the composer simply commented, "It was too good for the bastards."

Herbert's marriage became something of a disappointment, and Mrs. Herbert gradually receded into the background. While her husband delighted in metropolitan camaraderie and fun, she was content with her home and children. He was the dapper man-of-the-world, while she became more and more the sluggish *hausfrau*. The years were unkind to her. Shortly after marriage she grew stout, then heavy. Although her husband devoted most of his life to the American theater, Mrs. Herbert struggled to master even a working knowledge of English. The couple spoke German exclusively at home. Eventually the composer grew indifferent to his wife, finding companionship elsewhere.

As the years went by, Herbert, too, added weight. He loved to eat as he loved to laugh. He was appreciative of both cabbage and caviar and could wax eloquently about a keg of Pilsener. If he were going to be working at a theater for several days, he customarily had an ice box installed in his dressing room for beer and refreshments. In his studio he kept a small washtub filled with ice and wines. Music publisher Isidor Witmark remembered how he would keep Rhine wine and Moselle for the Germans, Claret and Burgundy for the French, and Chianti for the Italians.

Sweethearts, three years after *Naughty Marietta*, was Herbert's last box office success. The story takes place in ancient Bruges; the lovers are a prince from the mythical land of Zilania and a girl of seemingly humble station, raised by a laundress. The romance ends happily, however, when it is discovered that the girl is actually the crown princess of Zilania, who had been abducted during her childhood. The score is among the composer's best, but his reign as king of American operetta was coming to a close. *Eileen*, set on the coast of Ireland, opened in 1917. The show was a labor of love, contained the song "Thine Alone," yet was a failure. After the war Herbert's work kept coming, but was fast becoming an anachronism. He wrote a few numbers for the Ziegfeld *Follies* and some music for the silent movies. To a friend he remarked, "My day is over. They are forgetting poor old Herbert." He died in New York City, May 27, 1924.

The composer left a legacy of captivating melodies, many of which outlived their librettos. While Herbert's style was old, he injected standards into the American theater that were new. His composition and orchestration stood out in their day as models of excellence, bridging the gap between lighter and heavier forms. Herbert was part old world, part new, but he was happy to conform to the conventions of Viennese operetta he had loved as a young man and adhere to the musical values he had learned in Germany. As the placid, sentimental era in which the composer had risen to fame gave way to a more frenetic age, the tastes of the American middle class shifted to ragtime and jazz. Victor Herbert's romantic world of counts and princesses, wizards and enchantresses, brigands and viceroys seemed insipid and trite once the Broadway stage had moved toward a more modern format.

Yet the operetta tradition lingered as a minor theme well into the 1920s and was continued by Hollywood much later. The Herbert mantle fell principally to two Austro-Hungarian musicians, Rudolf Friml and Sigmund Romberg. Friml, born in Prague on December 27, 1881, was the son of a humble, music-loving baker. He had trained as a concert pianist at the Prague Conservatory and had studied composition with Dvorak. After performing all over Europe, Friml came to the United States late in 1901 for a concert tour with the noted violinist Jan Kubelik. He made his American debut at Carnegie Hall with Walter Damrosch and the New York Symphony, playing his own Concerto in B major. After the tour he decided to remain in the United States permanently.

In 1911 Victor Herbert was planning a new show for Emma Trentini, hoping to duplicate their recent success with *Naughty Marietta*. But the composer and his star had a serious falling out, which eventually meant they were no longer on speaking terms. When Herbert withdrew from the show, the unknown Friml was brought in. The young composer finished the score in about a month. The production, called *The Firefly*, opened in 1912 and was a huge success. The show centers around a street singer who becomes a prima donna, winning the millionaire playboy she had fallen in love with as a girl in the process. Friml's music—including "Giannina Mia" and "Sympathy"—was of the familiar operetta variety, full of ear-carressing melody. Not even Herbert could write so gracefully for the voice.

Over the next two decades Friml wrote more than twenty operettas, following the *Merry Widow* formula closely. "When I write for the theater," the composer once said, "I like books with charm to them, and charm suggests old things, the finest things that were done long ago. I like a full-blooded libretto with a luscious melody, rousing choruses, and romantic passion." His biggest hit came in 1924 with *Rose Marie*—fairly advanced in theme for its time, since murder plays an important part in the plot. The production takes place in the Canadian Rockies and contains such memorable tunes as the title song, "Indian Love Call," and "Totem Tom Tom." *The Vagabond King*, set in fifteenth-century France, appeared a year later, while the swashbuckling *The Three Musketeers*, Friml's last Broadway success, was sumptuously mounted by Florenz Ziegfeld in 1928. The composer continued to write for the stage until 1934, then was swallowed up by Hollywood.

Sigmund Romberg was born on July 29, 1887, in the small Hungarian border town of Nagykanizsa. His father was a businessman and amateur musician, who saw to it that his son had training in both engineering and music. As a student in Vienna, Sigmund came to love the operettas of Johann Strauss, Franz Lehar, and Oskar Straus. He arrived in the United States in 1909 and within five years was composing music for the Broadway stage. *The Blue Paradise* (1915), for which Romberg wrote his first score, was actually an adaptation of a Viennese work. The show introduced both "Auf

Wiedersehen," the composer's first song hit, and a new musical comedy star, Vivienne Segal.

Although Romberg's *Maytime* (1917) was set in New York, its flavor was distinctly Old World, based this time on a German operetta. Produced by the Shuberts, the show contained the song "Will You Remember?" and was such a sensation that a second Broadway company was opened. *Blossom Time* (1921) was loosely patterned on the life of Franz Schubert and employed adaptations of several of the musician's more popular melodies. *The Student Prince* (1924) proved one of Romberg's biggest successes and for a few years revitalized the vogue for operetta. Its music is clearly in the old manner, but is definitely some of the composer's finest. *The Desert Song* appeared in 1926, *Rosalie* in 1927, and *The New Moon* in 1928—the latter including four of Romberg's most durable tunes: "Softly, as in a Morning Sunrise," "Stouthearted Men," "One Kiss," and "Lover Come Back to Me."

After *The New Moon* the American musical stage would belong primarily to musical comedy and musical drama, yet Sigmund Romberg enjoyed one of his longest runs as late as 1945 with *Up in Central Park*. The book is set in the 1870s during the regime of the infamous Tweed Ring. While its music was highly romantic, *Up in Central Park* does represent a somewhat streamlined Romberg. His last show, *The Girl in the Pink Tights* (1954), was produced three years after the composer's death. Altogether he had contributed music to over seventy shows. To the end he lived basically in the past, writing for the past. "I'm two wars away from my time," he told his wife shortly before his death. "My time was pre-World War I. I've got to get away from Vienna. That's all passé. I've got myself stranded in Europe, and I've got to get out of it. I think I'll refuse anything from now on without an American background." But his roots were in Europe. Not until Romberg's death did the dynasty founded by Herbert come to a close.

Unlike the perpetuators of operetta, George M. Cohan was a child of vaudeville, a boisterous native son who never saw Europe until he had become an established theatrical figure. Born in Providence, Rhode Island, on July 3, 1878—not July 4, as he liked to say—Cohan in his youth aspired to emulate the success of Harrigan and Hart, then the idols of lower Broadway. George's father had been a minstrel performer, his mother a girl from Providence with no previous stage experience. Shortly after their marriage the Cohans put together a vaudeville act billed as "Mr. and Mrs. Jerry Cohan"; Mr. Cohan wrote the material. Helen Cohan became pregnant twice; each time the troupers returned to her home long enough to give birth, then resumed their travels along the vaudeville circuit. The Cohan children grew up in cold hotels, shabby boardinghouses, dirty dressing rooms, and noisy trains. As soon as they were old enough, they became part of the act.

George received a smattering of schooling in Providence and also took a few violin lessons, both of which he hated. He was a precocious child—moody, quick tempered, restless, often uncommunicative. He made his stage debut as an infant; by the time he was nine he was performing in a sketch called "The Two Barneys," billed as "Master Georgie." Meanwhile his sister Josephine, two years older, was doing skirt dances. George expanded his talents to include buck-and-wing dances, recitations, and singing; by 1888 the act was officially known as the Four Cohans. Within a year George was writing some of the material, his first sketch entitled "Four of a Kind."

Young Cohan enjoyed trouping as much as he detested school. He loved the smell of the theater, the constant movement, and the bizarre world of ventriloquists, trapeze artists, contortionists, magicians, acrobats, stilt-walkers, clowns, comedians, singers, and dancers. "Some troupe!" George remembered the Four Cohans of the late eighties. "Four in the cast, eight in the orchestra. The street parade was the big feature. I was the drum major and led the band of eleven pieces—eight musicians besides the manager, prop man and dad. The last three played the snare drum, bass drum, and cymbals. Mother and Josie followed the band in an open victoria draped with American flags." Money was scarce for the Cohans in those days, competition keen. They played cities, towns, and whistlestops, sometimes doing six shows a day. The family finally made a mark in New York City in 1893, playing Keith's Union Square Theater. Times had improved for them; the act was now in demand and would soon earn top billing.

By this time the jaunty George was specializing in Irish reels, waltz clogs, recitations, and a lively bootblack routine. He had already written several songs for the act and was considered the brains of the outfit. But it was Josie who was the favorite with the public and drew the best notices. The turn of the century found the Cohans out of the crumbling theaters, touring mostly the larger cities, and spending much of their time in New York. They were commanding the unprecedented sum of $1000 a week, with George dictating terms. The brassy youth was everywhere—ball games, fights, bars, meeting people and making contacts. His jerky walk and bobbing head, straw hat and bamboo cane became familiar up and down Broadway, as George set out to show the world that he was the smartest little guy and most regular fellow in town. He called everybody "Kid," thumped people on the chest with the back of his hand or jabbed them in the ribs to emphasize a point. He knew baseball players, fight promoters, jockeys, newsboys, ticket scalpers, bootblacks, bellboys, musicians, and gangsters. He frequented the polo grounds, the Friar's Club, Reisenweber's, Delmonico's, Rector's, and the Astor. Before long he was known as the man who owned Broadway.

Within a three-year period Cohan wrote over 150 monologues and sketches and several dozen tunes. His first popular song hit, "I Guess I'll Have to Telegraph My Baby," was introduced in vaudeville during 1898 by Ethel Levey, a former star of Weber and Fields extravaganzas. George married her the next year; she became the fifth member of the Cohans' act, billed as a singing comedienne. A few months later the family left vaudeville, supposedly over a dispute with B. F. Keith. Legend has it that the hotheaded George told Keith, "No member of the Cohan family will ever play for you again as long as we live."

They now turned to musical farces. *The Governor's Son*, which arrived on Broadway on February 25, 1901, was Cohan's first full-length show, an expansion of one of his vaudeville sketches. The production featured the five Cohans, with George directing. New York rejected the production after thirty-two performances, but it played on the road for over two years. When *The Governor's Son* returned to New York, it more than doubled its initial run there. Much the same fate awaited *Running for Office* (1903), an enlargement of another sketch. In 1904 Cohan formed a producing partnership with his brother-in-law Sam H. Harris that lasted until 1920.

But when *Little Johnny Jones* opened in New York on November 7, 1904, the five Cohans were back to four, Josephine having decided to go on her own. Johnny Jones, played by George, announces himself as a "Yankee Doodle dandy." He is an American jockey who has come to London to ride in the English Derby. Johnny is falsely accused of being in league with big time gamblers and of having thrown the race, while a detective, posing as a drunkard, works to clear him. Johnny learns of evidence proving his innocence at Southampton, where he has come to bid farewell to some American friends sailing for home. "Give My Regards to Broadway," he sings to them as the ship is about to depart. A signal of fireworks has been arranged to inform Johnny if the detective on board has gathered the evidence necessary to clear him. As the boat reaches the horizon, shooting flames leap skyward. Johnny can now propose to Goldie Gates, the girl from San Francisco he has fallen in love with. *Little Johnny Jones* was Cohan's first real musical comedy and—after revision and much work on the road—his first big success. "When I got through with the manuscript of *Little Johnny Jones*," the showman wrote, "I had an old-fashioned comedy melodrama 'all dressed up' in songs and dances."

Cohan often went into rehearsals with only a notion of what his shows were going to be about. He wrote and tightened them as he went along. *Little Johnny Jones* was sufficiently impressive, however, that the great Abraham Erlanger became convinced George was worth a gamble. Erlanger was looking for a musical play for Fay Templeton, and he asked Cohan to write one. For a year or so George had had ideas for a show with a prosperous suburb like New Rochelle as the locale. *Forty-Five Minutes from Broadway* was the result, and it was a solid success. The production opened at the New Amsterdam Theatre on January 1, 1906, and besides the title song contained "Mary's a Grand Old Name" and "So Long, Mary." Its plot had to do with a lost will, eventually found in an old suit. When the will is read, Mary Jane, a lovable housemaid, finds herself wealthy. But Mary Jane's romantic interest, played by Victor Moore, is both an inveterate gambler and an honorable man where Mary Jane is concerned. He refuses to marry a girl with money. Since love is more important to Mary Jane than riches, she destroys the will.

The original version of *Forty-Five Minutes from Broadway* did not include a part for Cohan, but he wrote another show that same year as a starring vehicle for himself. *George Washington, Jr.*, which opened in New

York a month after the Fay Templeton success, had Cohan playing a superpatriot who takes the name of his country's first President to defy his Anglophile father. The highlight found the performer prancing up and down the stage, draped in an American flag, singing "You're a Grand Old Flag." Cohan had initially called the song "You're a Grand Old Rag," the words suggested by a G.A.R. veteran, but protests from several patriotic organizations caused him to make the change.

From 1906 until the end of World War I hardly a season passed without at least one Cohan show on Broadway. *The Talk of New York* appeared in 1907, with "When a Fellow's on the Level with a Girl Who's on the Square" and "When We Are M-a-double-r-i-e-d" as its big song hits. *Fifty Miles from Boston* in 1908 contained one of Cohan's most celebrated Irish numbers, "Harrigan." Then came *The Yankee Prince* (1908), *The Little Millionaire* (1911), *Broadway Jones* (1912), *Hello Broadway!* (1914), and *The Voice of McConnell* (1918). Ultimately there would be a total of eighty plays and over five hundred songs.

The careers of George M. Cohan and Victor Herbert at their height ran parallel, and they reached their fame almost simultaneously. They dominated two aspects of the same world. While Cohan's shows were as naive and sentimental as Herbert's, his music and drama scarcely better integrated, they were as American as Herbert's operettas were European. Cohan's productions represented something fresh, up-to-date, personal. They possessed familiar characters, as a rule native settings, and breezy, colloquial dialogue. His shows were crude and noisy, compared with the more refined operettas, but they captured much of the vigor of a country just emerging to world leadership. At a time when Sousa was stirring the nation's pulse with *American* marches, Ziegfeld was glorifying the *American* girl, Gilbert was struggling to compose *American* music, and William Vaughan Moody was attempting to write *American* plays (like *The Great Divide*), Cohan made the Eagle scream on the musical stage. In personality Cohan bore a striking resemblance to Theodore Roosevelt, in the White House during the time "Yankee Doodle Boy" and "It's a Grand Old Flag" were introduced on Broadway. The performer not only caught the country's muscular nationalism, but also its jangling optimism, boundless energy, and the accelerated pace resulting from the automobile. As stage director, Cohan would bark at actors, "Speed! Let's have speed! Lots of it. Let's have perpetual motion!"

Before the footlights the entertainer was much like the nation itself—dressed in his slick, well-tailored suits, buttoned shoes tipped with gray cloth, and heels built up to give him stature. He sang out of the corner of his mouth in a whining nasal voice and strutted about the stage supremely sure of what he was doing, a man at one with his environment. "Here," Oscar Hammerstein II said, "was the kind of American we all hoped to be when we grew a few years older." Cohan cast his musical comedies with his own bulging ego and gave them an informality, a vigor, and a modernity that

Herbert's more sophisticated productions lacked. One reviewer claimed that a Cohan show gave "the impression of a great machine shooting out characters, choruses, songs, dances, with rapid-fire quickness and precision." And Finley Peter Dunne might well have had the indomitable George in mind when he had Mr. Dooley say, "When we Americans get through with the English language, it will look as if it had been run over by a musical comedy."

Whereas the mustachioed Herbert symbolized Victorian dignity and Old World refinement, Cohan was an untutored song-and-dance man who created most of his melodies from four chords he could play on the black keys of a piano. And yet the Cohan tunes sprang from their composer's heart and became part of the nation's bloodstream. "Over There," Cohan's most famous song, virtually became the leitmotif of World War I. The musician was at his home in Great Neck, Long Island, on April 7, 1917, when he read in the morning newspaper that Congress had declared war. "I read those war headlines and I got to thinking and humming to myself," he told an interviewer, "and for a minute I thought I was going into my dance." In less than half an hour he had the chorus written:

Over there, over there,
Send the word, send the word over there,
That the Yanks are coming, the Yanks are coming,
The drum rum-tumming everywhere.

First sung professionally by Nora Bayes, "Over There" had swept the country within a month after its publication.

Yet like Herbert, Cohan outlived his time. At thirty-five he was one of the wealthiest and most powerful figures on Broadway, boasting six shows running at one time in 1911. But his productions were becoming rehashes. His wife, Ethel, walked out on *George Washington, Jr.* and their marriage at the same time during a matinee performance in Cleveland in December, 1906. The couple were divorced the following February. Four months later Cohan married Agnes Nolan, a young actress who had played minor roles in several of his productions. Sister Josephine made a brief return to the fold for *The Yankee Prince*, but died in 1916. The mother and father made their last stage appearance in 1912 in *Broadway Jones*. Cohan attempted several serious plays, yet had little success. The actors' strike in 1919 disturbed him, and he joined the producers and managers in a bitter fight against the Actors Equity Association. Involving friends, he took these quarrelsome negotiations personally, and Equity's victory seriously altered his outlook on life. Gradually he began to lose his zest for the theater, and by the mid-1920s the Cohan name was losing its magic. "I guess people don't understand me any more and I don't understand them," he told a friend. "It's got so that an evening's entertainment just won't do. Give an audience an evening of what they call realism, and you've got a hit. It's getting too much for me, Kid."

He retired from time to time, had a disastrous experience with Hollywood, but returned to Broadway in January, 1933, in *Pigeons and People*, another of his own plays. Later that year he appeared as a serious actor in Eugene O'Neill's comedy *Ah, Wilderness!* He played President Franklin D. Roosevelt in the Rodgers and Hart musical satire on Washington politics, *I'd Rather Be Right*, which opened at the Alvin Theater on November 2, 1937, with an advance ticket sale of $247,000. While Cohan won honors for both of these last engagements, neither was satisfying to him. He talked mostly of the old days. He gave his final performance in *I'd Rather Be Right*, completely worn out, in late February, 1939. He underwent an abdominal operation in October, 1941, and spent the following year quietly in his Fifth Avenue apartment. Then he began to grow weaker. Convinced he would not live much longer, he asked his nurse to take him by taxi to the Hollywood Theater on Broadway to watch a few scenes from *Yankee Doodle Dandy*, his film biography. He died a few days later, November 5, 1942.

Although Cohan's style was an outgrowth of vaudeville and full of nostalgia, the performer injected a brashness into American musical comedy that was new. Yet even before World War I, the familiar Cohanesque touches—"My mother thanks you, my father thanks you, my sister thanks you, and I thank you"—were becoming anomalies, much as Victor Herbert's operettas were. Both had frozen into a standard formula that often made little sense. For a musical comedy to be a success, George Jean Nathan, coeditor of *Smart Set*, argued in 1915, "the words must read as well and as intelligibly backwards as forwards." Dance patterns seldom varied, and if the chorus line rocked, Nathan insisted, "its rock must be as unchanging as the rock of Gibraltar." The fetish for the ostentatious and gargantuan continued, while songs remained incidental to the overall text. Solos, love duets, choruses and dances were superimposed upon a vague plot line, frequently with the star's specialty interpolated.

Already there were signs of change, emerging out of the "little theater" movement that preceded American entry into the war. With a series of shows for the Princess Theatre, a small off-Broadway house seating less than 300 people, three young men set the American musical stage on a radically new course. The innovators were Jerome Kern, Guy Bolton, and P. G. Wodehouse. The shows they wrote for the Princess Theatre, beginning in 1915, were based on modern stories and dealt with people caught in humorous but believable situations. The casts were limited to around thirty members, while the orchestra consisted of eleven pieces. Massive choruses, stars, and spectacular scenery were eliminated; each production would have only two sets. But songs were integrated logically and meaningfully into the plot. "It is my opinion," Kern said, "that the musical numbers should carry the action of the play and should be representative of the personalities of the characters who sing them. Songs must be suited to the action and the mood of the play."

The Princess Theatre Shows represented musical comedy on a miniature scale—intimate in format, sophisticated in style and content. As Guy Bolton explained, the shows were "straight, consistent comedy with the addition of music. Every song and lyric contributed to the action. The humor was based on the situation, not interjected by comedians. . . . Realism and Americanism were other distinguishing traits. . . . Americans laugh more naturally at a funny hotel clerk or janitor than at a crudely drawn cannibal princess." The aim at the Princess Theatre was well-balanced casts, fresh ideas, tight construction, and an appeal to intelligent adults. The impact was decisive and permanent.

Jerome Kern, who composed the music for the shows, was born in New York City in 1885 and raised amid comfortable circumstances. He saw his first book musical at age ten, Victor Herbert's *The Wizard of the Nile*. The boy studied music, later attended Normal College in New York, and in 1903 made a trip to Europe, where he met P. G. Wodehouse. Wodehouse was twenty-four at the time, but had already published several stories and verses. The two collaborated on a song for one of Charles Frohman's London productions. When Kern came back to the United States in 1904, he went to work as a song plugger for the firm of Shapiro-Remick and helped turn the English musical comedy *Mr. Wix of Wickham* into a Broadway show, adding four tunes of his own. He went to work for Harms, one of the major Tin Pan Alley publishing houses, plugging sheet music in New York department stores and composing songs. He achieved his initial fame in 1905 with a number called "How'd You Like to Spoon With Me?" He later became a rehearsal pianist, which gave Kern the chance to interpolate much of his own work into other composers' shows. He wrote his first complete score for *The Red Petticoat* in 1912, a distinct failure. His first success, *The Girl from Utah*, another English adaptation, opened at the Knickerbocker Theater in 1914 and contained eight Kern songs, including the classic "They Didn't Believe Me."

The young composer was well aware that something was wrong with the American musical theater and grew determined to rid the stage of patchwork scores and artificial extravaganzas. He got his chance early in 1915, when Elizabeth Marbury, owner of the Princess Theatre, asked him to compose a different sort of score for *Nobody Home*. The show was adapted from an English musical comedy by Guy Bolton, who had started out to be an architect, then shifted to writing plays and librettos. *Nobody Home* was smart, witty, relying more on textual and musical materials than upon costumes, chorus girls, and scenery. Kern's score was tuneful, its high point a number called "The Magic Melody." Even the distinguished musicologist Carl Engel was impressed with this song, declaring that it marked "a change, a new regime in American popular music. . . . it was a relief, a liberation."

Nobody Home ran for only a few months and brought in a modest profit, but it was enough to convince Elizabeth Marbury to try again. *Very Good, Eddie*, with a book by Bolton and music by Kern, opened later in 1915. It was a solid box office success, playing at the Princess Theatre for over a year and realizing a profit of more than $100,000. The plot traced the escapades of two honeymooning couples who get scrambled on an excursion up the Hudson River. The emphasis was on broad comedy, sparkling dialogue, and characterization. Kern's score at one point parodied a waltz from Richard Strauss' opera *Der Rosenkavalier* (whose world premiere had taken place in Germany just three years before) and was full of rich lyricism.

Bolton and Kern were joined for *Oh, Boy!* in 1917 by lyricist P. G. Wodehouse. The show had an American college setting and was even more successful than *Very Good, Eddie*, running for 463 performances. Wodehouse's charming turns of phrases and graceful figures of speech blended masterfully with Kern's melodies. Among the score's best moments was the ballad "Till the Clouds Roll By." *Oh, Lady! Lady!* in 1918 ended the Bolton, Wodehouse, Kern collaboration. After that Kern returned full-time to the big, commercial theater. There was one more Princess Theatre musical, *Oh, My Dear!* later in 1918, with a score by Louis Kirsch. The novelty of the intimate little shows was wearing off, but their influence would become apparent on the Broadway stage during the 1920s.

The innovations unveiled at the Princess Theatre were to the elevation of musical comedy roughly what Isadora Duncan's rebelliousness was to dance, what Charles Ives' native instincts were to serious American composition. Within a limited capacity, they also became box office attractions. "The Princess?" Abe Erlanger exploded, when he heard of the success there. "That broken-down little cheesebox under the Sixth Avenue E.?" Yet by the end of three years, even the Broadway lions were forced to take the Princess' accomplishments seriously. The simplicity of these productions, their everyday settings and believable characters, their natural use of the vernacular, and their integration of music and drama constituted the most significant advance in the American musical theater since the Civil War. They made the fairylands of operetta appear foolish and the Cohan bravado technique seem obvious and crude. The doldrums into which the show business world had sunk during 1913 and 1914 were shaken with the wartime excitement and the postwar prosperity. As the entertainment industry entered a fifteen-year period of highflying, the old gap between the carriage trade and the mass audience grew less defined. But the new generation that flocked to the theater wanted modern approaches. For the musical stage the progressivism of the Princess Theatre Shows provided a solid point of departure.

Theater music was also undergoing development, and Jerome Kern led the way. Kern was as romantic as Friml and Romberg, yet possessed a tender tunefulness, a sharpness of rhythm, and a chromatic freshness that his foreign-born colleagues did not. With Kern each turn of phrase, each inflection became part of the overall structure, although extensive revision made his style seem deceptively simple and direct. His melodies were marked by a poignant beauty and an infectious lightness of touch. A meticulous craftsman, Kern was able to achieve originality without restricting his natural flow. He possessed a skill at characterization and a flair for humor, but concerned himself more with the score as a whole than with the individual song. Above all, he had the ability to twist the conventional into something extraordinary. "As the composer of ... the Princess Theatre Shows," Richard Rodgers later noted, Kern "was typical of what was and still is good in our general maturity in this country in that he had his musical roots in the fertile middle-European and English school of operetta writing and amalgamated it with everything that was fresh in the American scene to give us something wonderfully new and clear....Actually, he was a giant with one foot in Europe and the other in America."

World War I not only interrupted further importation from abroad, but also heightened America's confidence in her own culture. After the war the American theater became substantially more independent. What developed on the musical stage possessed, in its mature forms, both the technical proficiency inherited from European opera and operetta and the informality and pure entertainment values acquired from the vernacular theater. As musical comedy evolved toward musical drama, it was the integrity of the Princess Theatre Shows that served as the parent model, while Jerome Kern became the ideal for Richard Rodgers, George Gershwin, and others.

CHAPTER

VII

Tin Pan Alley

The growth that took place in the commercial music business during the Civil War increased after the conflict ended. Like heavy industry the music publishing business adjusted itself to peacetime demands and found a plentiful market in the spiraling cities. Despite the exuberance of the period, a general expansion in wealth, and abundant support for the country's traditional belief in progress, the macabre, sullen themes and the mood of self-pity so pronounced in the popular songs of the antebellum years persisted through the Gilded Age. Wistfully nostalgic tunes like "A Little Faded Rosebud in Our Bible" joined with doleful ones like "See That My Grave's Kept Green" to refurbish the old sentimental hues. "Mother" songs ran the gamut: "Always Take Mother's Advice," "A Boy's Best Friend Is His Mother," "A Lock of My Mother's Hair," "A Flower from Mother's Grave," "Why Did They Dig Ma's Grave So Deep?" Love ballads were still distinguished by a naive, ethereal quality and delicately suggested the kiss as the consummation of passion.

> *Over the garden wall, the sweetest girl of all . . .*
> *And you may bet, I'll never forget*
> *The night our lips in kisses met,*
> *Over the garden wall.*

Along with memories of girls' names and innocent rendezvous at mills, lanes, and gates, the popular music of post-Civil War America doted on plaintive thoughts of home and lost youth. "When You and I Were Young, Maggie" was a sensation in 1866, while "When You Were Sweet Sixteen" became no less the rage more than three decades later. Moralizing remained in vogue. "Papa Don't Drink Any More" appeared during the 1870s, followed in the next decade by "The Old Man's Drunk Again." A more realistic plea for temperance was made in "But Oh! What a Difference in the Morning," the tale of a young man who overindulges at the bar with bad aftereffects. Folk maxims frequently found their way into music: "You Never Miss the Water Till the Well Runs Dry" (1874) stayed a favorite for the rest of the century.

Topical songs continued to sing of current events. "Andy Veto" dealt harshly with the unpopular stands taken by President Andrew Johnson, as did "The Veto Galop." "Get Out of Mexico" (1866), inspired by the Maximilian episode, urged the exercise of the Monroe Doctrine. "We'll Show You When We Come to Vote" (1869) talked of women's rights, while the "Inflation Galop" enjoyed popularity during the Grant regime. The career of one of the period's most ruthless entrepreneurs was piously recounted in "Jim Fisk, or He Never Went Back on the Poor," without reference to his dishonest exploits. Other tunes denounced corruption in both business and politics. Each presidential election produced a number of songs: "Hurrah for Hayes and Honest Ways" in 1876, "Harrison and Protection" in 1888, and "Gold Is the Standard to Win" in 1896. Grover Cleveland's supposed illegitimate child gave rise to the ballad "Ma, Ma, Where's My Pa? Up in the White House, Dear," whereas "The Silver Knight of the West" sang the praises of William Jennings Bryan. The Homestead Strike was the consideration in "A Fight for Home and Honor," and the last of the Indian wars prompted "The Sioux Waltz" and "General Custer's Last March."

Disasters remained titillating song material. "Lost on the Steamer 'Stonewall,' or O Mamma! Why Don't Papa Come Home?" referred to the sinking of a Mississippi River boat in 1869, with 275 persons aboard. The great Boston fire of 1872 was bemoaned in "Homeless To-night!"—a song that ran through several editions. In 1874 a blonde, curly headed four year-old named Charley Ross was kidnapped and never restored. The crime probably stirred the nation more deeply than any event since the Civil War and resulted in the song "Bring Back Our Darling." The assassination of President Garfield by a disappointed office-seeker, Charles Guiteau, was another shock, giving rise to the vehement "Guiteau's March to Hades." And the Johnstown flood in 1889 was recorded in the dirge-like "The Torrents Came Upon Them."

The Darwinian controversy was too much in the public eye to be overlooked by American song writers. A satirical ballad entitled "Too Thin, or Darwin's Little Joke," appeared in 1874, with music by a composer calling himself "O'Rangoutang." Sports of all kinds were sweeping the country, but baseball was emerging as the nation's favorite pastime. "Tally One for Me" became popular in 1877, followed by the "Home Run Polka," "Slide, Kelly, Slide," and the more famous "Take Me Out to the Ball Game." "That Game of Poker" was another tune from 1877, while the roller skating mania of the 1880s brought about "Gliding in the Rink." The furor caused by Lydia Thompson and her girls resulted in a number of American women changing their hair color and songs like "The Blonde That Never Dyes" and "O Let Me Be a Blonde, Mother." In the 1890s "She Chews Gum" announced a change in status of an old custom, whereas the "Streets of Cairo" mocked the rhythm of Little Egypt's dance at the Chicago World's Fair.

Progress was heralded often in popular songs. All sorts of transportation numbers were sung in the 1870s, and the dedication of the Brooklyn Bridge in 1883 produced "The Highway in the Air, or A Ballad of the Brooklyn Bridge" and "The Brooklyn Bridge Grand March." The wicked city, on the other hand, was repeatedly denounced. "Don't You Go Tommy," published in Detroit in 1867, warned against the evil ways of urban living and brought the country lad face to face with the city slicker. The song became so popular that a sequel followed five years later, "Tommy Is Dead." The moral of Tommy's tragic end was all too clear:

> Shun all bad places, of gamblers beware,
> Don't trust yourself in the folds of their snare,
> They'll lead you to ruin, and then by and by,
> They'll leave you like Tommy, a drunkard to die.

One of Tony Pastor's numbers told of a young rustic who came to New York as a hired girl. When the mistress sent the servants off to church, where they "put in a good hour's sleep," the newcomer failed to return. A search found her inside a saloon, for "The Poor Girl Didn't Know."

American popular music after the Civil War became more distinctive and showed faint signs of inching its way toward naturalness. Maidenly blushes were fewer, lyrics slightly less artificial, and the sentiment a bit more genuine. By the 1880s even the most tearful narratives were often based on actual occurrences. "Somebody's Grandpa," for example, resulted from an incident reported by the New York *Tribune*. An old man found drunk on a doorstep was being mocked by a group of unkind children. One of the little girls went over to the man and wiped his face with her apron. Then looking up at the rest of the children, she begged "Oh, don't hurt him! He's somebody's grandpa!" In 1888 Joseph J. Sullivan, a vaudeville comedian and acrobatic dancer, was searching his attic for possible costumes when he came across an old hat, too small for his head and too tall for his short, stocky frame. Wearing it into the streets, Sullivan was jeered at by a group of boys, who yelled, "Where did you get that hat?" The phrase gave the performer the title for his most celebrated song. Another comedian, James Thornton, returned home from a drinking bout to find his wife Bonnie in tears. When she cast doubt on his love and fidelity, James supposedly reassured her, "My sweetheart's the man in the moon." Bonnie Thornton may or may not have been convinced by the explanation, but she did sing her husband's song of that name at Tony

Pastor's Fourteenth Street Theater with great success.

Among the prominent figures in the commercial music of the 1880s was Monroe H. Rosenfeld, who turned out words and music for scores of sentimental ballads. In 1885, as a stunned financial world was attempting to recover, Rosenfeld composed a clever song called "I've Just Been Down to the Bank." He wrote "With All Her Faults I Love Her Still," one of his greatest hits, three years later. "And Her Golden Hair Was Hanging Down Her Back," another Rosenfeld favorite, related the cynical story of a maid, simple and demure, who left her village for a visit to New York and came home quite changed. No longer was she shy—"But alas and alack! With a naughty little twinkle in her eye."

But the pivotal career in the early development of Tin Pan Alley was that of Charles K. Harris, whose "After the Ball" is customarily regarded as the first popular song to sell well over a million copies. Harris had spent his boyhood as a bellhop and free lance banjo player in the area around Lake Michigan. He began writing songs early, one of which was published by the Witmark brothers while Harris was still in his teens. His first royalty check amounted to eighty-five cents! Harris was so disgusted with the way the Witmarks had distributed the song that he decided to go into business for himself. About 1885 he convinced two of his friends to invest $500 each and join him in a firm that would mainly publish his own songs. Harris rented a one-room office at 207 Grand Avenue in Milwaukee and put out a sign reading:

Charles K. Harris
Banjoist and Song Writer
Songs Written to Order

Rent on the office was $7.50 a month; monthly overhead came to another $2.50. Yet at the end of the first year the company cleared a $3000 profit. Harris was clearly in the business of song writing to make money, and by advertising the fact he became a rightful precursor to the commercial music industry soon to center in New York.

Before 1880 the important song publishers were scattered throughout the country—in New York, Pittsburgh, Chicago, Detroit, Milwaukee, and San Francisco especially. A song's success in those days was largely a hit-or-miss proposition. There was little awareness of effective huckstering. Chance more than design determined the sale, and even the biggest song hits met with comparatively modest returns. Harris' vision was broader. He felt that the public was tired of the old minstrel tunes and the unvaried fare in popular music. He realized that it was primarily women who played the family piano and selected the sheet music purchased. He also knew that women liked love and tears and heavy sentiment. A publisher had told the young Harris that what the public wanted were songs about "birds, stars, rippling streams, the perfume of the flowers, and thee-and-thou songs." But the composer also understood the commercial value of lyrics that unfolded a story, particularly one taken from life and including a moral. "Kiss and Let's Make Up," an early Harris song, contained a simple plot, wherein a little girl and boy are at play upon the sand. The girl had built a small sand pile, which the boy has mischievously kicked over, causing his playmate to cry. Feeling sorry, he seeks to make amends:

> Kiss and let's make up, my darling.
> Dry your tears, don't cry in vain,
> For you know I love you, darling.
> Yes, I know I was to blame.

Interestingly enough, the words are not far removed from the tone ascribed to adult romances in the popular song literature of the period.

Harris shortly bought out his partners, moved into larger quarters, and opened a branch office in Chicago and eventually New York. In 1892 he composed and published his biggest hit, "After the Ball," inspired by an incident Harris had witnessed at a dance in Chicago. The narrative opens with a little girl climbing upon her uncle's knee and asking the old man why he never married. The uncle flashes back to the time when he took his fiancee to a ball. Leaving her for a moment, he returns to find her in the arms of a stranger. Convinced she is unfaithful, the young man leaves the ball without listening to her explanation. He never saw the girl again. Only years later did he discover that the man holding his sweetheart was her longlost brother. "Many a heart is aching after the ball," the old man sadly concludes to his niece, as explanation for why he never married.

The song was widely sung in vaudeville and performed by May Irwin. Then during the Chicago World's Fair, John Philip Sousa played a band arrangement of it that became so popular he had to include the tune on virtually every program. Sales began to soar. Later, the song was interpolated into Charles Hoyt's *A Trip to Chinatown*, and the success surpassed everything known in commercial music.

Yet Harris had other hits. Aware of the public's fixation for small children, he wrote a number of "baby" songs, the most popular of which was probably "Hello, Central, Give Me Heaven." The telephone had just recently come into domestic use, and the song stands as both an exaltation of technology and a digest of late nineteenth-century sentiment. A little girl, sad and lonely, notices that her father has not smiled either. Picking up the telephone, she sobs:

> Hello, Central, give me heaven,
>   For my mamma's there.
> You can find her with the angels
>   On the golden stair:
> She'll be glad it's me who's speaking.

Call her, won't you, please?
For I want to surely tell her
We're so lonely here.

Another little girl whose mother had died was less fortunate still. Her father had remarried, and the new mamma was "very cross" and scolded the child daily for being "Always in the Way."

Always in the way,
So they always say.
I wonder why they don't kiss me,
Just the same as sister May.
Always in the way,
I can never play;
My own mamma would never say
I'm always in the way.

Nostalgia for the old and the past filled Harris' lyrics. "Better Than Gold, or Three Wishes" pictures three drummers sitting in a Pullman smoker. To pass the time, they are each to tell three wishes. Bob, the oldest of the group, begins:

"Just to be a child again at mother's knee;
Just to hear her sing the same old melody;
Just hear her speak in loving sympathy;
Just to kiss her lips again;
Just to have her fondle me with tender care;
Just to feel her dear soft fingers through my hair.
There is no wish in this world that can compare,
Just to be a child at mother's knee."

"'Mid the Green Fields of Virginia," depicts a successful businessman, reared in Virginia, who had come North to seek his fortune. He gained wealth, but forgot his mother, home, and sweetheart. One day a small girl enters his office to sell him flowers. Their smell reminds the prosperous executive of his old home and loved ones in Virginia, and he decides to return. "For Old Time's Sake" tells of a "simple country lad," whose sweetheart ran off with a traveling salesman. Years later, on a trip to Chicago, he meets the girl on the street, looking worn and dejected. The salesman had quickly deserted her, and she has lived alone in misery. "For old time's sake, I told her that I loved her," the narrator sings, and for old time's sake he asked her to marry him. But no, a doctor has told the girl she can live only a few months more. "And I buried her," the narrator ends, "for old time's sake."

Harris' "Break the News to Mother" was revamped about the time of the *Maine* explosion and became a big seller during the Spanish-American War.

In Milwaukee the composer knew of an old minister who had presided over his congregation for years. The younger members of the church wanted him replaced with someone whose sermons would not put them to sleep. Moved by the pathetic situation. Harris wrote "Just Behind the Times," which closed:

> *And so at last the sermon ended*
> *And the old man slowly rose.*
> *"Just let me say a few words ere you go."*
> *Then slowly up the aisle he staggered*
> *To his pulpit as of yore,*
> *With trembling limbs and face as white as snow.*
> *"I've buried all your loved ones,*
> *I've wept beside their graves,*
> *I've shared your joys and sorrows many times."*
> *Just then he gave a start, for his poor heart*
> *Had broken from its pain.*
> *His last words were: "I am behind the times."*

Saccharine though they may seem to modern tastes, the contemporary public found Harris' woeful tales touching enough to buy his songs in remarkable quantities. One evening, after a performance of the Metropolitan Opera Company at the Chicago Auditorium, meat packer Philip D. Armour was returning to Milwaukee. A reporter happened upon the magnate and asked him how he liked the opera. Armour's reply, widely circulated by the press, was that Charlie Harris was good enough for him.

But Charlie Harris was not one to rely on intrinsic worth alone. He maneuvered to get his songs performed by vaudeville headliners and incorporated into stage productions. He approached music publishing on a businesslike basis and used whatever means were available to get his work before the public. While his songs were well suited to the turn-of-the-century market, Harris was among the first to promote his successes by "plugging" them in the manner later characteristic of Tin Pan Alley. "Charles K. Harris remains a convincing proof," Sigmund Spaeth contends, "of the fact that one can become an enormously popular songwriter without ever writing a really good song."

Following the unprecedented triumph of "After the Ball," a host of publishing firms sprang up, mostly headed by youngsters operating on a financial shoestring and the philosophy that songs are not only born, they are made. One of the first of the new breed of music publishers was Frank Harding, who took over his father's firm on the Bowery in 1879. Before Harding most of the country's song hits came from print shops, music stores, or establishments specializing in serious music and instruction books. Not only did Frank Harding feature popular music, but he also pursued the notion that composers had to be coddled into writing successful tunes. His office became a hangout for lyricists and musicians who gathered there to drink, play poker, and talk. But they also composed songs for Harding, sometimes in exchange for several rounds of drinks.

The firm of T. B. Harms, after several minor hits, enjoyed an important success in 1883 with Frank Howard's "When the Robins Nest Again." Early in that decade Willis Woodward & Company had offices in the Star Building on Thirteenth Street and Broadway. The struggling house of Witmark moved to 32 East Fourteenth Street in 1888. Six years later, Joseph W. Stern & Company, a new firm, opened on Fourteenth Street, and nearby located another new company—Howley, Haviland. By the middle 1890s Union Square, New York's entertainment center, contained the largest concentration of song publishers in the country. Close at hand were Tony Pastor's theater, the Union Square Theatre, the Academy of Music, as well as numerous burlesque houses, dance halls, saloons, and restaurants. From all over the nation songwriters with tunes to sell poured into the Fourteenth Street district, for even Charles Harris had shifted his home office from Milwaukee to Union Square.

Firms were often formed on the strength of a single hit, while the established companies aggressively competed for composers, lyricists, and pluggers. Many of the Tin Pan Alley men had been salesmen in some other field earlier. From morning until late at night hawkers stood in front of the publishing houses waiting for singers and producers to come along. When they did, the drummers would crowd around in an effort to entice them into the company's studios, where they could hear samples of the firm's wares. If sales talk alone proved ineffective, strong-arm tactics might be used to hoist the show people inside. In the early evening song pluggers began their rounds of theaters, night spots, restaurants, beer joints and brothels—any place where a song might be placed. Vaudeville remained the ideal vehicle for the introduction of new tunes, since performers would carry the number over a circuit that would eventually touch every major city in the nation and many of the smaller ones, stimulating sheet music sales along the way. A song might be kept in an act for several years, assuring it a lengthy popularity. Burlesque seldom introduced new tunes, but was an important media for helping songs stay familiar.

Show people were openly courted by pluggers. A box of cigars, an occasional beer, some inexpensive bauble, or an invitation to dinner might go a long way toward winning a performer's favor. Later on, vaudeville headliners and Broadway stars were plied with cold cash. Yet orchestra leaders, singing waiters, and piano players were encouraged to use the firm's songs with incidental gifts. Even the trainers of dog acts came to expect a small token before they selected tunes for accompanying music.

As the plugger made his rounds he customarily carried a batch of "chorus slips" (sheets of paper with a song's refrain printed on them) under his arm. If he found a genial crowd, he would pass out the slips and urge the group to join in singing. He also coaxed orchestras into playing his selections, often by outbidding rivals. If a song failed to go over, it was frequently reworked for another try. A later practice was to plant a representative in a theater audience when his firm's newest song was featured on the bill. As the orchestra began the tune, the plugger would stand, as if spontaneously. With the spotlight on him, the salesman would sing several verses of the number, until it became implanted in the minds of the audience. When boy singers proved most effective at this sort of advertising, publishers began a raid on synagogues and church choirs. Al Jolson was among those abducted.

Any public gathering might become the field of the song plugger—picnic grounds, parades, river excursion boats, medicine shows, carnivals, and baseball fields. Several publishing firms on good terms with each other banded together to rent a piano for a six-day bicycle race in Madison Square Garden; pluggers played each company's tunes between the scheduled band selections. Melodies were vended on the sidewalks in front of theaters before show time, on the midway at Coney Island, and in department stores. Candidates for office often hired a three-piece band to attract crowds for their speeches. After tipping the musicians to make sure they played a firm's music, pluggers would sing at the tops of their voices when the number came up, overriding the noise of the spectators.

Another effective method of promoting songs was initiated in 1894, when lantern slides were made to dramatize "The Little Lost Child," the first song by Edward B. Marks (formerly a button salesman) and Joseph Stern (a necktie salesman). In keeping with the sorrowful narratives of the day, "The Little Lost Child" was based on a newspaper report and tells of a bewildered waif picked up by a policeman and brought to the station house. There the officer, himself a lonely man, discovers that the child is his own daughter! Marks and Stern went into partnership with this tearjerker and had a photographer set up his camera in a Brooklyn police station to illustrate its story. An actual police officer and a child actress were induced to pose for the slides, while the photographer's wife played the little girl's mother. Each picture contained words of the lyric, so that audiences could sing along. The set was originally exhibited during an intermission in a Union Square theater and met with such profitable results that other publishers immediately took up the idea. Song slides were soon being shipped all over the country, as manufacturers sprang up overnight. Marks and Stern repeated their success in 1896 with "My Mother Was a Lady." The writers were sitting in a German restaurant when they overheard a waitress being insulted by some patrons. As the woman broke into tears, she exclaimed that they would not dare to treat her in such a manner if her brother Jack were present. Then she added, "My mother was a lady."

Meanwhile T. B. Harms had discovered a tremendous market in Broadway show tunes. M. Witmark and Sons became a pioneer in 1893 by moving their offices out of the Fourteenth Street area up to West Twenty-eighth Street. It was the vanguard of a general trend. Music publishing had become increasingly dependent on show business, and as the theaters and restaurants moved uptown, so did the publishers. Twenty-eighth Street represented an even larger concentration of music firms by 1900 than Fourteenth Street had a few years before.

The music business thrived on cheap rentals. As the publishers huddled together along Twenty-eighth Street, the shabby rooms of the once-dignified brownstone houses were partitioned off into small cubicles. In each was placed a secondhand piano, untuned. Nearby were rehearsal rooms and practice studios set up by music teachers and theater people. On hot summer days windows were thrown open in the hope that a breeze would waft in from the Hudson or East rivers. Outside, between Broadway and Sixth Avenue, the sounds of composers and perspiring song demonstrators could be heard mingling with the tap of dancing feet, the blare of instruments, and the noise of vocalizing. To keep competitors from stealing their melodies, songwriters sometimes placed folded newspapers between the strings to mute their pianos.

Just how Tin Pan Alley got its name is a matter of some debate. The most often repeated version is that Monroe Rosenfeld was preparing an article on popular music for the New York *Herald*. Besides being a prolific creator and purloiner of tunes (his publisher, Edward Marks, once called him a "melodic kleptomaniac"), Rosenfeld had a consuming fondness for horses, girls, and poker, and often turned to journalism to cover gambling debts or finance his latest flame. On the prowl for a salable story during the summer of 1903, Rosenfeld dropped in on composer-publisher Harry von Tilzer. He found his crony picking out a tune on his paper-muted, upright piano. Rosenfeld supposedly observed: "That piano sounds like a tin pan. Matter of fact, this whole street sounds like a tin pan alley." Truth or legend, the term caught on, and before long the entire popular music industry in the United States had become known as Tin Pan Alley.

As the music business scrambled for identity and profit, the progression of songwriters grew geometrically. A few gained national recognition. Among the most beloved figures on early Tin Pan Alley was Paul Dresser. Born in Terre Haute, Indiana, on April 2, 1857, Dresser was slightly older than Charles K. Harris. He was fifteen years older than his brother, novelist Theodore Dreiser, who kept the family name. At sixteen Paul was wandering the streets of Indianapolis looking for work when he noticed Hamlin's Wizard Oil show. This consisted of a covered wagon carrying a lecturer, who told people about the wonders of the patent medicine, and an entertainer to draw the crowd. Dresser showed the manager what he could do and was hired on as a medicine-wagon minstrel. In 1886, while employed as an end man for Billy Rice's Minstrels, he wrote his first published ballad, "The Letter That Never Came," inspired by one of his own unhappy love affairs. Like most of the popular songwriters of his day, Dresser reflected a thoroughly naive attitude on life. Yet unlike many of his associates, Dresser was sincere, he believed in the sentiments he put into his songs. Theodore Dreiser, whose own work was brutally naturalistic, described his brother's temperament as "a compound of agile geniality, unmarred by thought of a serious character. He was...warm and genuinely tender and with a taste for simple beauty which at times was most impressive—simple, middle class romance, middle class humor, middle class tenderness." And out of this middle class simplicity, Dresser's songs emerged.

In 1887 the firm of Willis Woodward, whose speciality was sentimental ballads, released Dresser's "The Outcast Unknown." The song was only a modest success, but Pat Howley, then an employee of Woodwards', was convinced that the composer had uncommon talent and should give up acting in order to devote himself fully to song writing. Dresser was easily persuaded and within a year had composed for Woodward the plaintive, but enormously successful "The Convict and the Bird." A convict, doomed to spend his life in prison, is visited by a bird, which alights on the window sill and sings of sunshine and freedom. "Come to me each day, come to me, I pray," the prisoner pleads of the bird. Then one day the bird comes to sing, but there is no one to hear him. The convict lies dead in his cell. Three years later, Dresser returned to prison tragedy in "The Pardon Came Too Late," one of his best sellers.

When Pat Howley left Willis Woodward to launch his own publishing venture in collaboration with F. B. Haviland, he took Dresser with him as staff composer. Most of Howley, Haviland and Company's early success came from the sale of Dresser ballads. Their first big release, "Just Tell Them That You Saw Me," appeared in 1895. Dresser got the idea for the song from an encounter with a girl whose life seemingly had been wrecked by a hopeless love affair. His song told of a casual meeting between a man and a girl he had known in his hometown. "Is that you, Madge?" the man asks, for the girl has obviously come upon bad times. "Don't turn away from me," he implores. She asks that he take home only a single message: "Just tell them that you saw me....I'm coming home some day. Meanwhile, just tell them that you saw me." The phrase became such a favorite greeting in the 1890s that a manufacturer sold lapel buttons bearing the expression in bold letters.

Reminders of the Civil War occasionally crept into Dresser's songs, like "He Fought for the Cause He Thought Was Right," "The Blue and the Gray," and "There's No North or South To-day." The Spanish-American War prompted the jingoistic "Our Country, May She Always Be Right," while memories of home inspired his masterpiece, "On the Banks of the Wabash" (1897), which Indiana eventually adopted as its state song. "The Curse of the Dreamer" in 1899 grew out of the composer's tragic marital life. In the early nineties Dresser had wed burlesque queen May Howard. The musician was soon made aware that his wife was incapable of fidelity, although he chose to ignore her extramarital entanglements. When she deserted him and their child for another man, Dresser incorporated his bitterness into a ballad, "The Curse." A brief reconciliation was followed by a final desertion. The composer now rewrote "The Curse," adding a happy ending and calling it "The Curse of the Dreamer."

Dresser has often been considered the late nineteenth-century counterpart of Stephen Foster. Although he lacked formal training in music, the man from Indiana possessed a gift for melody that had broad appeal. Dresser had rebelled against his family's strict religious orientation and had run away from the seminary his father had sent him to, yet his ballads extolled many of the era's pious attitudes on home, family, and goodness. A huge man, weighing over three hundred pounds, the composer would inveterately burst into sobs at the sound of a touching song, particularly one of his own. He wrote most of his tunes at a folding organ in one of two Broadway hotels he made his home. Generous to a fault, his basic tenderness poorly equipped him to face a life of tribulation.

The songwriter's worth to his publisher was officially recognized in 1901, when the firm was renamed Howley, Haviland, and Dresser. Yet within a year the sale of his ballads was slipping badly. The half million dollars he had earned at the height of his career had been squandered on extravagant living. By 1904 business was so bad that Pat Howley left the company, and a year later Haviland and Dresser were driven into bankruptcy. The composer now went into publishing for himself, opening a two room office on Tin Pan Alley. Times had obviously passed him by. Dresser struggled to put up an impressive front, arriving each morning at his office conspicuously dressed in frock coat and high silk hat. But the air of failure was unmistakable. Old friends turned away; others felt only pity.

He had one more success—"My Gal Sal," published in 1905, about a prostitute Dresser had lived with as a young man in Evansville. The song was introduced in vaudeville later that year by Louise Dresser, whose career the composer had given an important lift. In gratitude she had taken Dresser's name. "My Gal Sal" sold several million copies, but its writer was not alive to enjoy the rewards. He died of a heart attack in his sister's home on January 30, 1906.

Another songwriter who helped fill the coffers of Howley, Haviland and Company in its heyday was black composer Gussie L. Davis. His first hit, "The Fatal Wedding" (1893), told the morbid story of a wedding interrupted by the appearance of the groom's wife and baby. The baby dies in its mother's arms, and the father commits suicide. There is a double funeral, after which the two women decide to live together. The ballad that brought Davis fame, "In the Baggage Coach Ahead," was published three years later. The composer had once been employed as a Pullman porter. As he was going through the train's cars on a trip, he came upon a child weeping bitterly. When Davis asked what was wrong, the child sobbed that its mother was in the baggage coach ahead—in a coffin. A fellow porter wrote a poem about the incident, which Davis later found and set to music. He sold the song outright to Howley, Haviland and Company for a few dollars. Imogene Comer used the number for three years in her vaudeville act, and for three years the sheet music sale reaped a fortune for the publishers, but nothing for the writers.

More financially astute was Carrie Jacobs Bond, one of the few women associated with the commercial music business. Widowed in Chicago, she was left practically penniless with a small son to support. She had earlier had some luck with writing children's songs and now turned again to song writing. Her first collection, *Seven Songs as Unpretentious as the Wild Rose*, contained "I Love You Truly" and "Just A-Wearyin' for You," both of which became popular with the American public. She moved to New York, but the dignified, sentimental songs she wrote there were largely ignored. Returning to Chicago, she experienced years of struggle, illness, and poverty. Most of her work was considered too arty for general appeal. The few pieces she sold were grudgingly purchased at a rate of twenty-five dollars each. With the help of a neighborhood druggist, Mrs. Bond bought equipment and supplies and converted her parlor into a publishing office. The frail little woman wrote her own songs, designed their title pages, and arranged for recitals to introduce them. To the surprise of the music industry, her tunes proved tremendously popular and sold millions of copies. "The End of a Perfect Day," very different from other Tin Pan Alley successes, was among Mrs. Bond's best sellers. She died at the age of eighty-four in Hollywood, honored and wealthy.

Greater concern for art was exhibited by Ethelbert Nevin, whose "The Rosary" proved one of the best loved selections in American song literature, achieving one of the largest sales ever enjoyed by a copyrighted piece of music. Nevin was born near Pittsburgh in 1862. He studied both piano and composition in Germany and made his debut as a pianist at a recital in Pittsburgh, December 10, 1886. Despite ill-health, he achieved a brilliant success, although a personal quality clearly marked his playing. He returned to Germany in 1891 and spent most of the next six years there. His piano suite, *Water Scenes*, was published in 1891; "Narcissus," the fourth of these five pieces, became his most popular piano selection. A sensitive, delicate man, Nevin possessed a lyric gift of remarkable grace and charm. The Boston Music Company issued "The Rosary" in 1898. Set to a poem by Robert Cameron Rogers, the song—according to journalist-historian Mark Sullivan—stands out in the record of popular music "like a solitary tall lily in a garden rather given to marigolds and zinnias." Nevin shows subtle craftsmanship in his writing, although his style is simple. The melody effectively combines the emotions of love and religious devotion. "The Rosary" was first sung publicly in Madison Square Garden Concert Hall by Francis Rogers on February 15, 1898. "Mighty Lak' a Rose," another pleasing song that sold thousands of copies, was written by Nevin in 1901, the year of his death.

But while "The Rosary" earned itself a prominent place on the family piano and Mrs. Bond's "I Love You Truly" became a tradition at weddings, vaudeville performers remained loyal to the sentimental ballad. In 1891 English songwriter Charles Graham attended a play on Fourteenth Street called *Blue Jeans*, in which a farmer turned a picture of his daughter toward the wall because the girl had run away from home. Graham was so touched by the scene that he composed the song "The Picture That Is Turned Toward the Wall," which he sold to M. Witmark and Sons for fifteen dollars. The

Witmarks put the number away in a file of unpublished tunes, where it was forgotten. Andrew Mack, an Irish tenor, dropped into the publisher's office one day looking for a new song for his vaudeville act. When nothing in the catalogue appealed to Mack, the Witmarks let him look through their file of unpublished material. The tenor happened upon "The Picture That Is Turned Toward the Wall," immediately recognized its potential, and made a success of it. Another Graham hit was "Two Little Girls in Blue," about two sisters who marry brothers. The sisters are separated when the couples quarrel, a separation that becomes permanent. The story is told by a heartbroken old man to his nephew, much like "After the Ball."

Most of the ballads of the nineties were waltzes, since that became the standard expression of sentiment. "She May Have Seen Better Days" was a favorite in 1894, followed four years later by "She Is More to Be Pitied Than Censured," which closes with the verdict "that a man was the cause of it all." Village life was still idealized in lyrics, while well-behaved children were sacrosanct. H. W. Petrie's "I Don't Want to Play in Your Yard" (1894) combines both themes:

> *I don't want to play in your yard,*
> *I don't like you any more,*
> *You'll be sorry when you see me*
> *Sliding down our cellar door.*
> *You can't holler down our rain-barrel,*
> *You can't climb our apple tree,*
> *I don't want to play in your yard*
> *If you won't be good to me.*

Not all of the decade's waltzes were of the melancholy, melodramatic genre. "The Band Played On," inspired by one of the German brass bands that roamed the streets of New York City, told of Matt Casey, who "hired a hall" and "formed a social club that beat the town for style." The song first appeared in the New York *World*, and within a matter of days virtually the whole town was whistling the tune. Newspapers soon began printing sheet music as supplements to their Sunday editions as a circulation stunt. "The Sidewalks of New York," beginning "East side, West side, all around the town," was another of the gayer waltzes of the nineties, along with "Sweet Rosie O'Grady," a great favorite with vaudeville performers. The bicycling fad then sweeping the country was mirrored in "Daisy Bell," better known perhaps as "A Bicycle Built for Two" and introduced by Tony Pastor. Among the more uninhibited songs of the 1890s was "Ta-ra-ra-bom-de-ay," a nonsense number popular throughout the entertainment world.

By the mid-1890s commercial music, even in waltz time, was definitely loosening up a bit, both in words and melody. A bubbling spirit pervaded "My Best Girl's a Corker" and "Elsie from Chelsea" (both 1895). Unsanctified relations between men and women still could be mentioned only if there was a moral, as in "She Loved Not Wisely But Too Well" (1894). But during the next decade such reserve was partially abandoned. By 1907 the suggestion was, "Be good, very, very good...If you can't be good, be careful." Double-entendre came creeping into popular songs, as well as gentle references to sex. "Mary Took the Calves to the Dairy Show" (1908), "This Is No Place for a Minister's Son" (1909), and "If You Talk in Your Sleep, Don't Mention My Name" (1910) were all considered fairly suggestive.

Most of this loosening resulted from the influence of the so-called "coon songs," which emerged from Tin Pan Alley about 1895. Usually dealing with the black who had come North and to the city, the "coon songs" were syncopated and employed wording that was more alive—normal conversation, dialect, slang—none of the stilted phrasing of the sentimental ballads. If the ballads represented the mask of tragedy, the "coon songs" provided an essential reason why the decade became known as the Gay Nineties. The songs were often simply urbanized versions of the more energetic minstrel tunes, acquiring added verve from their ragtime rhythm. The first "coon song" to become popular was "All Coons Look Alike to Me" by black vaudeville performer Ernest Hogan. The song is *not* suggesting that each black looked like every other black; its heroine is simply explaining why she is rejecting her persistent suitor—because all suitors seem alike to her. Later that same year—1896—Barney Fagan, a former blackface minstrel and acrobatic dancer, wrote a highly successful "coon song" entitled "My Gal Is a High-Born Lady."

For the next several years catchy tunes featuring black characters and dialect were much in vogue. "What! Marry Dat Gal?" was a comic number popular at the turn of the century, and May Irwin—a buxom vaudeville "coon shouter"—made the "Bully Song" a national favorite. Sexual innuendoes were obvious in "Dar's No Coon Warm Enough for Me," "A Red Hot Coon," "Hottest Coon in Dixie," and "The Warmest Colored Gal in Town." One of the most exuberant of all "coon songs" was "A Hot Time in the Old Town Tonight," which Theodore Roosevelt adopted as the official song of his Rough Riders and therefore became the most popular band number during the Spanish-American War. "I've Got a White Man Workin' for Me" and "She's Gettin Mo' Like the White Folks Ev'ry Day" (both 1901) suggested the city black's economic rise and greater sophistication, while "Bill Bailey, Won't You Please Come Home?" (1902) lamented an age-old marital problem. "Come Along, My Mandy, Sweet as Sugar Candy" (1907) was another "coon song," as was the Sophie Tucker warhorse, "Some of These Days" (1910).

The "coon songs" unquestionably helped perpetuate the minstrel show stereotype of the black people, depicted as whites saw them after a generation of freedom. Instead of calico patterns, the black woman now wants silks and satins, she uses calcimine to help make her fair, and has given up "darky songs" for operatic arias. The caricature is ridiculous, for the black is not taken seriously and is seen as basically irresponsible. The black has become more worldly, is usually full of anticipation regarding his future, occasionally is disappointed, as in the song "The Best I Get Is 'Much Obliged to You' " (1907). Yet while the "coon songs" helped sustain an unfortunate image of the black, they possessed an earthiness and a vitality that offered much to commercial music, going a long way toward pulling popular songs in America out of the sentimental doldrums they had wallowed in for so long. Although it would be years before the two-four rhythms of the "coon songs" would replace the waltz, the late nineties found the more maudlin ballads losing ground.

There were other tunes dealing with minority groups that contributed gusto to the output from Tin Pan Alley. Most of them were humorous songs about the Irish, Germans, Italians, or Chinese. These numbers were not only popular with vaudeville comedians, but were often sung in the rowdier urban dives. "If you wanted to put a song over in New York in the nineties," Edward Marks recalls, "you had to make them sing it in the late joints; the tingle tangels, as we called the minor German beer halls on the East Side; the back rooms of saloons like O'Flaherty's Harp, where you were invited to join a quartet or put up your dukes."

Vaudeville singer Maggie Cline made a sensation of John W. Kelly's "Throw Him Down, McCloskey" (1890), a vigorous ballad about a boxing match. As the powerful Maggie swung her arms and bellowed the lyrics, stagehands in the wings hurled to the floor whatever prop they could get their hands on, much to the public's delight. "When Hogan Paid His Rent," "Come Down, Mrs. Flynn," and "Down Went McGinty" were other popular Irish tunes of the period. The latter recounted a series of awful misfortunes that befell the impulsive McGinty. The Irishman fell down a coal hole, broke his bones, went to jail, and jumped into the sea—all of which, in reality, would be pitiably tragic. But in the 1890s the theme of the song was looked upon as a joke. "It is unlikely that it would have been," Arthur Loesser argues, "had the hero not been Irish." Certainly happenings described with a brogue or accent seemed far funnier than they might otherwise have seemed. "Swim Out O'Grady" (1894) depicted a sailor who tumbles into the sea and sees his ship sail off without him. Humorously O'Grady has one rendezvous after another—with a mermaid, a codfish, a whale, and a seal. Many of these tunes had simplistic choruses so that audiences could join in singing. "Has Anybody Here Seen Kelly?" was a highly spirited number that invited group participation. The song told of Michael Kelly, an immigrant Irishman, who arrived with his sweetheart from County Cork. The two became separated during a St. Patrick's Day parade in New York City. From atop a perch the sweetheart addresses the marchers:

> *Has anybody here seen Kelly? K-E-double L-Y.*
> *Sure his hair is red, his eyes are blue,*
>   *and he's Irish thro' and thro'.*

Whereupon "five hundred Kellys" left the parade to answer the girl's call.

Other songs about the Irish were in the light ballad tradition. In 1899 Chauncey Olcott, a successful singer, actor, and composer, wrote the enduring "My Wild Irish Rose." Eleven years later he collaborated with Ernest R. Ball, who had already written "Will You Love Me in December As You Do in May?" and "Love Me and the World Is Mine," on another Irish classic, "Mother Machree." The two worked together again in 1912 on "When Irish Eyes Are Smiling," followed in two years by "A Little Bit of Heaven, Sure They Call It Ireland." These songs soon found a place in the repertoire of John McCormack and every other Irish tenor, both in vaudeville and on the concert stage.

Irish ballads also became favorites of college singing groups and barbershop quartets. Since the gentle womenfolk controlled the family parlor, most males often did their singing elsewhere—restaurants where there was often only a battered piano for accompaniment, drinking places, even the barbershop. In barbershop singing the first tenor sang above the melody, the second tenor carried the tune, while the other two voices provided the harmony. Although some of the lyrics sung by men's gatherings were on the ribald side, most of the songs preferred were exceedingly sentimental. Perhaps the most celebrated of all tunes with singers of close harmony was Harry Armstrong's "Sweet Adeline" (1903). "Down By the Old Mill Stream" and "In the Shade of the Old Apple Tree" evidenced great popularity, however, around 1906.

The turn of the century found the tune factories of Tin Pan Alley responding to new events and problems. "Good-Bye, Dolly Gray" was written in 1900, as troops were starting off to put down the Filipino insurrection, the first time that American soldiers had left the hemisphere to wage war. "Meet Me in St. Louis, Louis," a lively waltz reminiscent of the old days, obviously referred to the World's Exposition of 1904. Women and children were now employed in great numbers in factories, sometimes supplanting men, a point that was made in "Everybody Works But Father" (1905). "In My Merry Oldsmobile" announced the growing importance of the automobile, while "He'd Have to Get Under—Get Out and Get Under" (1913) referred to a familiar incident in motoring during the days before wayside garages were common. Disasters were still recorded in song. The Iroquois Hotel fire in Buffalo in 1903 inspired laments, while the sinking of the Titanic in 1912 produced even more, including one in Yiddish. The city remained suspect and viewed as the hub of wickedness. "Heaven Will Protect the Working Girl" (1909), Marie Dressler's best known stage number, not only warned of the city's evil ways, but burlesqued the stage melodrama.

A village maid was leaving home, with tears her eyes were wet,
Her mother . . . says to her: "Neuralgie dear, I hope you won't forget
The city is a wicked place,
And cruel dangers 'round your path may hurl."

The mother's foreboding indeed came true—in the person of a natty city villain. The country girl "supposed he was a perfect gent," but was disillusioned at dinner one night in a "table d'hote so blithe and gay," when he said to her, "After this we'll have a demi-tasse!" Whereupon Neuralgie, remembering her mother's warning and alert to peril, declaimed:

"Stand back, villain, go your way! Here I will no longer stay,
Although you were a marquis or an earl;
You may tempt the upper classes with your villainous demi-tasses,
But Heaven will protect the working girl."

There was a lingering nostalgia for the farm and village: "When the Harvest Days Are Over, Jessie Dear" (1900), "When the Frost Is on the Pumpkin" (1904), "When the Morning Glories Twine Around the Door" (1905). "In the Good Old Summer Time" (1902) became one of the most popular "gang" songs, although it was a rendition by Blanche Ring that made the tune such a huge success. "Put On Your Old Gray Bonnet" (1909), "Moonlight Bay" (1912), and "When You Wore a Tulip" (1914) were other big hits that recounted old memories. Love was still seen in innocent terms and as the key to individual happiness. In spite of mounting divorce statistics, the sentiment of "Dearie" (1905) was expressed time and again:

Dearie, my dearie, nothing's worth while but dreams of you,
And you can make ev'ry dream come true;
dearie, my dearie!

Songs of gladness were common, as in every age. Three of the lasting ones from the 1910 period were "Smiles," "The Sunshine of Your Smile," and "I'm Forever Blowing Bubbles."

Many songs became commercial successes because of their identification with a particular performer. A classic example is "Come Down, Ma Evenin' Star" (1902), which was forever associated with Lillian Russell after she introduced it in *Twirly Whirly*. Blanche Ring made "I've Got Rings on My Fingers" (1909) a big hit, and Elsie Janis did the same for "Fo' De Lawd's Sake, Play a Waltz" (1911). Vaudeville and the revue still served as a major vehicle for the sale of sheet music. "Oh, You Beautiful Doll," "Cuddle Up a Little Closer," "Put Your Arms Around Me Honey, Hold Me Tight," and "I Wonder Who's Kissing Her Now?" were all favorites from the stage.

In 1905 Tin Pan Alley was paying out a half million dollars a year to star performers. Competition for their allegiance was keen. Successful acts might be given free rehearsal rooms or have their hotel bill paid by a publisher's representiative. Noted singers were promised a new wardrobe or a glittering gem, if they would but sing the firm's songs. By 1910 it was obvious that things had gotten out of hand. Vaudeville performers and musical comedy stars were using the material that brought them the highest take, regardless of quality or suitability.

Piano players were now beating out Tin Pan Alley's tunes for hours on end in nickelodeons, and song pluggers were already taking good advantage of recorded music—first by means of the player piano, then through cylindrical discs. Around the turn of the century recorded numbers could be heard with earphones in penny arcades. Sheet music covers for the selections available were prominently displayed. By 1901 the Victor Talking Machine Company, the Edison Speaking Machine Company, and Columbia Records (which grew out of the Bell patents) had all been formed. Steady improvement in recording techniques and sound reproduction soon made the phonograph an important source of home entertainment. The earliest records were mostly of vaudeville skits, with some musical selections by singers, bands, and whistlers. Orchestral accompaniment to vocal numbers began in 1906, after an unsuccessful attempt a few years before. Orchestras had to be kept small and loud, while wind instruments recorded far better than strings. By 1910 the family was singing less and listening more.

The gaslight era was coming to a close. The story ballad was almost a thing of the past, and the stepped-up tempo of popular music had come to play an increasingly important role in the accelerated lifestyles Americans were pursuing. More attention was being given to accompaniment, and harmony was about to become a consideration. Lyrics still tended toward the "moon-June-spoon" genre, but there were hopeful signs of change. Three-quarter time morality was giving way to a blustering syncopated hedonism, and motherhood was evolving toward mammyhood. Father was treated less as a joke, nor was he the reprobate he once was in commercial music. Popular songs continued to offer pleasant avenues of escape—plenty of wish fulfillment, vicarious sex, and whoopee—escapism which suggested a little relaxation beside the noble path of respectability.

Jewish names were becoming more prominent in the music business, as the publishers gravitated uptown toward Forty-second Street, again following the theaters. The dingy offices with rolltop desks and pockmarked upright pianos were replaced with more imposing accommodations by the firms that found their way to great fortunes. In 1900 a sheet music sale of two million copies was phenomenal. By 1910 a five-million-copy sale had been reached several times. "Meet Me Tonight in Dreamland" achieved it in 1909; "Down By the Old Mill Stream" and "Let Me Call You Sweetheart" both made it a year later. A total of over two billion copies of sheet music crossed the counters in 1910 alone. Customers could now buy current hits conveniently in five-and-ten cent stores, while department stores were purchasing unpublished songs from struggling musicians for a few dollars, printing them on advertising giveaways, and handing them out to customers.

As commercial music became big business in the first years of the twentieth century, two songwriters stood out above all others: Harry von Tilzer and Gus Edwards. What Charles K. Harris had been to the 1890s, Harry von Tilzer was to the early 1900s. He carried the sentimental tradition into the new century, but in an up-to-date format. He was surely among Tin Pan

Alley's most prolific composers and dominated one of its major publishing houses. Von Tilzer was born in Detroit, Michigan, on July 8, 1872. His brother, Albert, also became a songwriter of merit. Harry first tasted the excitement of show business when the family moved to Indianapolis and his father opened up a shoe shop beneath a loft in which a theatrical stock company gave performances. The lad soon spent hours in hotel lobbies, hoping to catch a glimpse of one of the performers. At fourteen von Tilzer ran away from home, joining a tumbling act with the Cole Brothers Circus. He later attached himself to a traveling repertory troupe, learned to play the piano without formal instruction, and began writing songs. Along the way he changed his name from Harry Gumm, which he felt lacked magnetism. Tilzer was his mother's maiden name; "von" was affixed in an effort to add "class." He met musical comedy star Lottie Gilson in Chicago, who was impressed with his song "I Love You Both" (1892) and encouraged him to pursue songwriting in New York.

The youth worked his way east as a groom for a trainload of horses and arrived in the big city with $1.65 in his pocket. He took a job as a saloon pianist and began turning out songs. Some of his numbers got published; a few were sung at Tony Pastor's Music Hall. "My Old New Hampshire Home" (1898) and "I'd Leave My Happy Home for You" (1899), a novelty "coon song," were both smash hits, each selling over a million copies. The former song became a favorite of vaudeville tenors, the latter a *tour de force* for Blanche Ring. Von Tilzer had sold these songs outright to a neighborhood print shop for fifteen dollars apiece. The printer made a fortune from them, while von Tilzer became a recognized name on Tin Pan Alley.

Although Harry von Tilzer was probably better equipped musically than most of his predecessors, he composed largely by instinct. Melody was the thing for him; of orchestration or serious music he knew nothing. But he possessed versatility within his own field and demonstrated uncanny shrewdness in predicting and shaping public taste. He agreed to write the music for "A Bird in a Gilded Cage" (1900), one of his biggest successes, on the condition that the verse make it perfectly clear that the unhappy girl in the song, whose "beauty was sold for an old man's gold," was the millionaire's wife, not his mistress. The melody, incongruously, was written in a brothel. Von Tilzer supposedly tried the song out on the girls, some of whom burst into tears upon hearing it. "If *these* ladies weep real tears over my song," the writer decided, "I have composed a hit." Indeed he had. Within a year after its publication the ballad had sold two million copies.

"A Bird in a Gilded Cage" was published by the recently organized firm of Shapiro, Bernstein, and Von Tilzer. Its success prompted the composer to break with his partners and go into business on his own. In 1902 von Tilzer left Union Square and set up offices on Twenty-eighth Street. Within a year he had four hits: "The Mansion of Aching Hearts," "On a Sunday Afternoon," "Down Where the Wurzburger Flows," and "Please Go 'Way and Let Me Sleep." Their combined sheet music sale exceeded five million copies. The drinking song "Down Where the Wurzburger Flows" became such a staple in Nora Bayes' vaudeville act that for years she was known as "The Wurzburger Girl." Von Tilzer tried to repeat the triumph a year later with another tribute to beer called "Under the Anheuser Busch," but the results were comparatively modest.

The writer-publisher soon became identified as "Mr. Tin Pan Alley." He was the prototype of the commercial composer, able to turn the mood, fad, or expression of the moment into a hit song. Late in his life von Tilzer claimed to have written eight thousand songs, about two thousand of which had been published. He produced his tunes on virtually an assembly line basis and proved successful in many diverse styles. "Wait Till the Sun Shines, Nellie" (1905) became a favorite "gang" song. "What You Goin' to Do When the Rent Comes 'Round?" (1904) was a popular "coon song," while "Good-By, Eliza Jane" was a ragtime adaptation. He wrote a "mammy song," "I Want a Girl Just Like the Girl That Married Dear Old Dad"; an Irish ballad, "A Little Bunch of Shamrocks"; and a nostalgic tune about the Southland, "Down Where the Cotton Blossoms Grow." His methods of plugging these numbers were as varied and timely as the topics themselves, and the total sales of his songs are estimated into the hundreds of millions.

Von Tilzer's last hit came in 1925 with "Just Around the Corner." He went into early retirement, realizing that the vogues of Tin Pan Alley had left him behind. He spent his last years living in the Hotel Woodward, recalling the good old days on Twenty-eighth Street to anyone who would listen. He died in his hotel room, January 10, 1946.

The career of Gus Edwards was more closely bound up with vaudeville. Born in Germany in 1879, Gustav Edmond Simon was brought to the United States at age eight. His family settled in Brooklyn, and the boy went to work in his uncle's cigar store. He soon discovered Union Square and spent evenings roaming about the section trying to find ways of sneaking into the shows. At fourteen he was hired by Lottie Gilson for five dollars a week as a singing stooge in her act. Young Gus would sit in the balcony until Miss Gilson had finished singing a ballad, then rise from his seat and repeat the refrain. He later worked as a boy stooge for stars like Maggie Cline and Imogene Comer, gaining enough attention that Tin Pan Alley eventually released a number called "A Song in the Gallery."

While plugging songs for the house of Witmark, Edwards was discovered by a vaudeville agent and booked into an act called the Newsboy Quintet. One of the bills featuring the Newsboys had the Four Cohans as headliners. Young George Cohan took a liking to Edwards and gave him some pointers on writing songs. Later Paul Dresser invited Edwards to use a piano at the Howley, Haviland offices for his early attempts at tune making. His first song, "All I Wants Is My Black Baby Back," was introduced by the newsboy act in 1898. Since Edwards knew no music, a friend wrote the notes down on paper for him. May Irwin performed his "I Couldn't Stand to See My Baby Lose" the following year, and Howley and Haviland published "I Can't Tell

Why I Love You, But I Do" with fair success.

Edwards wrote a number of songs with Will Cobb for variety shows and musical comedy and was then employed by M. Witmark as a staff composer. In 1905 he formed the Gus Edwards Music Publishing Company, which quickly enjoyed two hits—"Sunbonnet Sue" and the Anna Held specialty "I Just Can't Make My Eyes Behave," both with lyrics by Cobb. Edwards supplied several tunes for the Ziegfeld *Follies* and had continued success with songs for vaudeville, especially numbers for schoolroom sketches. He often wrote, directed, and starred in these acts. Among the child stars introduced by Edwards were Eddie Cantor, George Jessel, Groucho Marx, Ray Bolger, and Eleanor Powell. "School Days" in 1907 was perhaps the composer's biggest hit, although "By the Light of the Silvery Moon" two years later was a close contender.

In 1928 Edwards temporarily retired from the vaudeville stage and went to work for Hollywood. He returned to variety in the early 1930s, but vaudeville was expiring and Edwards' songs were no longer fashionable. He died in Los Angeles in 1945, after six years of poor health.

The Tin Pan Alley of Harry von Tilzer and Gus Edwards was changing rapidly in the years just before World War I. The competitive struggle between the publishing giants was taking a toll on the smaller firms. The Witmarks had gone into business in 1886 on the strength of brother Isidore's timely "President Grover Cleveland's Wedding March," which they ran off on a tiny printing press. Six years later the house of Witmark regarded itself as the leader among American music publishers. By 1914 the possibilities for such an immediate rise were considerably less. The illiterate composer who picked out his tunes on a piano with one finger so that someone else could write them down, was gradually yielding to the trained musician who knew what he was doing and approached songwriting with some subtlety. The simple A part, B part song form was starting to give way to the more modern and psychologically satisfying AABA form. The A theme, since it is used three times, makes a deeper impression on the memory, while the B section, called a release, offers contrast. By returning to the A material for the conclusion the tune is rounded out, leaving the listener with a sense of completeness.

Gradually the music business was evolving into a profession. A copyright law was passed in 1909, providing for the payment of a two-cent royalty for each piece of music used on phonograph records and piano rolls. Although publishers felt the fee was too little at the time, the arrangement soon proved a major source of income. The American Society of Composers, Authors, and Publishers (ASCAP) came into existence in 1914, largely through the leadership of Victor Herbert, for the purpose of collecting royalties more effectively. A court case instituted against Shanley's Restaurant on Broadway, whose orchestra had played excerpts from Herbert's *Sweethearts* without authorization, tested the validity of ASCAP's demands that fees be paid for performing copyrighted music in public. After setbacks in the lower courts, the Supreme Court in 1917 handed down a decision in favor of ASCAP. "If music did not pay, it would be given up," Justice Oliver Wendell Holmes declared. "If it pays, it pays out of the public's pocket. Whether it pays or not, the purpose of employing it is profit, and that is enough."

Of the young composers who helped liberate American popular music from turn-of-the-century cliches and formulas, none was more formidable than Irving Berlin. While a Berlin ballad was a clear descendant of the sentimental tune, its melodic character was so personal, its lyric expression so hauntingly beautiful that it became a different order entirely. Polished and versatile in his style, Berlin stood between the old and the new, offering songs that were simple, yet distinguished by an instinctive craftsmanship.

Irving Berlin was born Israel Baline, in the Russian town of Temun, May 11, 1888. The Balines came to America when Israel was four to escape anti-Semitic persecution from the Cossacks. The family settled on the lower East Side of New York City, where the father found work as a supervisor of kosher meats and supplemented his income as a synagogue cantor. When Israel was old enough, he sold newspapers on the streets. At fourteen he ran away from home. Most of his meals were earned by singing sentimental ballads for pennies in saloons around the Bowery. For a time he worked for Harry von Tilzer as a song plugger at Tony Pastor's Music Hall and in 1906 took a job as a singing waiter in a Chinatown cafe.

His first published lyric, "Marie from Sunny Italy," appeared in 1907, the music for which was written by the cafe pianist, Nick Michaelson. Berlin tried writing melodies the next year, picking out the tune for "Dorando" on a piano at the Seminary Music Company for a staff arranger to transcribe and harmonize. In 1909 he wrote a take-off on opera entitled "Sadie Salome, Go Home," which Fanny Brice sang with success—her initial attempt at a song in Yiddish dialect.

Berlin had already produced several syncopated numbers when he wrote "Alexander and His Clarinet" in 1910. Not happy with the results, he put the tune away. He reworked it a year later for the annual Friar's Club *Frolics*, calling it "Alexander's Ragtime Band." The song was performed without notice at the Columbia Burlesque House on Broadway, but won ovations later in 1911 when "coon shouter" Emma Carus used it in her vaudeville act in Chicago. Ethel Levey (George M. Cohan's first wife) and Sophie Tucker began singing the number, and before the year was over it had taken the country by storm, selling a million copies within the first months of publication. More important, "Alexander's Ragtime Band" was instrumental in bringing the ragtime craze on Tin Pan Alley to its peak—a corruption, to be sure, of pure ragtime, but a significant commercial idiom nonetheless.

At twenty-three Irving Berlin found himself all at once the focus of the American music industry. While romantic ballads like "All Alone," "Remember," "Always," and "What'll I Do?" ultimately proved his forte, he added to the ragtime mania with "That Mysterious Rag," "Everybody's

Doin' It," and "The International Rag." Suddenly everyone seemed to be trying to write ragtime, and there were attempts to "rag" nearly every song, including "The Star-Spangled Banner" and "Rock of Ages." Two of the better Tin Pan Alley efforts were Lewis F. Muir's "Waiting for the Robert E. Lee" (1912) and Shelton Brooks' "The Darktown Strutter's Ball" (1917). Although the emphasis on syncopation produced a flurry of trivia, it did inject a permanent vitality into the writing of popular music.

And in the midst of the ragtime craze the nation went dance mad. Before "Alexander's Ragtime Band" social dances like the waltz, the polka, and the schottishche were fairly taxing physically and consequently were pretty much reserved for the young. Ragtime made dancing simpler; the new dances required little more than walking around the room clutching a partner. Anyone who could march could now dance. As the happy sounds of ragtime quickened the pulse of popular music, it also made the feet of listeners restless. Even senior citizens participated in the passion for dancing that by 1913 was sweeping the country. The first night clubs opened up, tea-time dancing was begun, and restaurants and hotels introduced dancing during meal hours. Already there had been the two-step and the cakewalk, but with the ragtime frenzy came the one-step and a whole list of new dances reading like an index for a zoo: the Fox Trot, the Grizzly Bear, the Bunny Hug, the Turkey Trot, the Camel Walk, the Lame Duck, the Snake, the Kangaroo Dip, and so on.

It was considered unseemly at the time for partners to dance too close to one another, and restaurant bouncers often tapped patrons on the shoulder if they got nearer than nine inches. Newspapers and moralists grew disturbed as the dance mania continued. The New York *American* lamented that "New York and Newport society are just at present manifesting a craze for the disgusting and indecent dance known as 'Turkey Trot.' " Ragtime was condemned as "degenerate music," "filthy," "vulgar," "suggestive," "negger music." The *Musical Courier* stated: "It is a well-known physiological fact that a superior race may not mingle with an inferior without causing degeneration, debasement." Some physicians argued that dancing was bad for health, while others insisted it was good exercise and definitely therapeutic. A number of important people broke their legs attempting the new dances. Even the Pope came out against the tango, yet the venerable John D. Rockefeller hired a private instructor to teach him the dance. Yale University declared the tango taboo at its 1914 junior prom, but Harvard loftily announced that the tango would be permitted at its prom.

As the controversy raged, new dance floors opened daily, and cabaret performers discovered a lucrative trade in instruction. The Bunny Hug and Grizzly Bear were danced in Harlem and at Sherry's and almost every place in between. Businessmen started taking off early for a turn or two around the floor of the nearest dance parlor. Eventually the practice began cutting into working hours, and one prominent editor fired fifteen of his girls for doing the Turkey Trot during their lunch hour.

Any number of performers were lifted to stardom by the craze, but Vernon and Irene Castle emerged as the dancing idols. The couple were clean-cut, married, young, and dignified in their steps. Even the righteous found it difficult to object to them too strongly. More than anyone else the Castles set the styles, invented new steps, and made dancing look like the fun it was. There was a Castle walk and Castle House, a school for ballroom dance. Women began imitating the streamlined Irene's mode of dress and bobbed hair.

In 1914 the Castles starred in the ragtime revue *Watch Your Step*, Irving Berlin's first complete musical. The show was a great success and marked jazz's entrance onto the Broadway stage. Not all of *Watch Your Step*'s songs were syncopated; its best remembered number was the homespun ballad "Play a Simple Melody." The song introduced a technique Berlin would use many times later. The composer wrote for it two different melodies and two different sets of lyrics for the chorus—each of which was sung independently first, then both melodies and their lyrics were combined contrapuntally. Irene Castle's gowns for the show, created by Lucille, were sensational. The dancer swirled about the stage in one number wearing a blue chiffon gown, twelve yards around the bottom, with flowing sleeves edged with bands of gray fox. Over this was a cloak of blue and silver brocade, with a full skirt and tight bodice laced on the left side with emerald green and chartreuse satin ribbons.

The ragtime dance mania was spread in part by the phonograph, for fox trots, tangos, and the rest poured from the record presses, propelling fledgling companies into an established industry. Between 1913 and 1915 Victor's assets jumped from $13,000,000 to over $22,000,000. When the craze hit, music publishers were temporarily caught short of material, since for years they had been primarily interested in ballads people could sing. The music companies quickly thumbed through their files for the names of black piano players whose songs had been snubbed earlier. Publishers suddenly wanted tunes that were danceable. Words became secondary to rhythm, and many lyrics were frantically thrown together with no pretense of logic. "In the ragtime songs," Mark Sullivan maintained, "the words were merely a series of ejaculations, the music a sequence of panting gasps." More attention was given to orchestration and arrangement, however, than ever before.

But the dance fad died about the time the United States entered World War I. Vernon Castle was killed on an air training base outside Fort Worth, Texas, during the war, and the dissemination of New Orleans jazz in the 1920s gave rise to different dance patterns. Ragtime had captured some of the sunny, muscular spirit of pre-World War I America and reflected much of the bustle and commotion of the growing American city. Although the ragtime of Tin Pan Alley lost its identity around 1917, much of it would be absorbed into later commercial adaptions of jazz.

The United States entered World War I still comparatively naive and unsophisticated. This was evident from the songs that were popular as the nation drifted toward preparedness. Imbued with Wilsonian idealism, most

Americans in 1917 found the cause something to sing about. War songs not only became commercial, but a significant force in military and civilian morale. The war was neither so mechanized nor so all-embracing that song material was effaced. The young men not drafted into the Army served as a cheering section for those boarding ships for France. With the declaration of war, neutrality songs like "I Didn't Raise My Boy to Be a Soldier" made way for rousing tunes like "Goodbye, Broadway, Hello France," "You're in the Army Now," "We're All Going Calling on the Kaiser," and "When Yankee Doodle Learns to 'Parlez Vous Francais.'" There were soldier songs like "K-K-Katy," "There's a Long, Long Trail," the English "Pack Up Your Troubles in Your Old Kit Bag," the British marching song "Tipperary," and several versions, often unprintable, of "Mademoiselle from Armentieres." Irving Berlin wrote a delightful number about army life, "Oh, How I Hate to Get Up in the Morning," while stationed at Camp Upton, New York. Sentimental songs included "Your Country Needs You Now," "So Long, Mother," and "A Soldier's Rosary," while the ideals of the war were summed up in "Fighting for the Cause of Humanity."

The music business flourished during the war, even though show business fell off considerably. Judging from most of the songs, the World War would seem to have been a joyous pilgrimage. There were rare glimpses of confusion, as in Joseph Woodruff's "After the War Is Over Will There Be Any 'Home Sweet Home'?" Yet "The World Is Waiting for the Sunrise" in January, 1919, suggested hope. Hints of the intense post-war disillusionment could be heard in "I'm Always Chasing Rainbows" (the tune filched from Chopin) and "Let the Rest of the World Go By." An amusing afterthought to the war was "How Ya Gonna Keep 'Em Down on the Farm?"—a question that seemed more serious in the decade ahead.

Like the nation as a whole, American music publishers found their world much changed after the war. The country discovered itself faced with prohibition, and many could empathize with Harry Ruby when he asked, "What'll We Do on a Saturday Night—When the Town Goes Dry?" The sale of illegal liquor brought the speakeasy and a more free-wheeling music. The major publishing companies were no longer concentrated along a single street, and several of them would soon become subsidiaries of motion picture studios. Audiences, values, kinds of songs, and means of distribution were all about to change. The radio revolutionized the industry by cutting down on the length of time a success could remain popular. Song hits at the turn of the century might enjoy a lifespan of three years or longer. With radio the time would be cut to months. More and more songs were written to be performed, as phonograph records grew in importance. Tunes must now appeal to the broad middle class. The music business had always been sensitive to fads, but the market became increasingly fickle.

Tin Pan Alley rose out of the expansive spirit of late nineteenth-century America and mirrored the nation's pulse as it entered the new century. Its publishers enjoyed few of the traditions and dignities associated with book or magazine publishing, and the methods they developed were fundamentally determined by business efficiency. Yet the songs themselves serve as a resume of the nation's nostalgia and intimate much about American attitudes. Tin Pan Alley's tunes became a cherished part of the popular culture, one which Europe borrowed and admired, and at times approached the altitudes of art.

CHAPTER

VIII

The Blues and Classic Ragtime

The Civil War left the South in turmoil and destruction, blacks were no longer slaves, but they still were not free. To test their emancipation many of the former slaves fled the plantations, roaming the countryside in search of pleasure, work, and personal identity. Uneducated for the most part, blacks were poorly equipped for the new challenges thrust upon them, and much suffering resulted. The rumor that each family would receive "forty acres and a mule" from the government proved unfounded, while the Thirteenth and Fourteenth Amendments to the federal Constitution soon stood as mocking gestures. Disillusioned, frightened, feeling abandoned and exploited, the former slaves had many reasons for despair. As in the past they voiced their anxieties in song, and antecedents to the blues served as an emotional safety valve during painful years of social adjustment. "The blues," Paul Oliver explains, "acted as a catalyst for the blinding anger, humiliation and frustration that sought to demolish the moral codes and spirit of a man, and the act of artistic creation brought satisfaction and comfort both to him and his companions."

The search of a dispossessed race for a home was echoed in the blues. Blacks still comprised distinct, isolated communities within white society. Much of their culture remained exclusive, not intended to be understood by whites. Alienation from the majority was in large measure accepted, allowing the blacks to imbue their dispossession with realism and a universal significance that would eventually serve as a melancholy symbol for the alienation of modern man. Gradually the poignant sounds of black music expanded and overflowed into the American mainstream, each wave striking a sympathetic chord with successive layers of urban discontent.

Although the latter part of the nineteenth century was a period of great upheaval for Southern blacks, most of them remained tied to the soil. In 1890 eight out of ten blacks still lived in rural districts, many working as sharecroppers or tenant farmers for white overlords. Industry was slow to penetrate the South and even slower to touch the black. Farming exhausted land with outmoded equipment was rewardless and difficult. By the turn of the century the boll weevil had taken a disastrous toll on the cotton economy, and lack of incentive often gave rise to deliberate idleness. An air of happy indolence remained the black's principal barrier against white wrath, but beneath the facade lay subsistence survival and misery.

As black people worked their plots, they cried out much as they had during slavery—with field chants and hollers, frequently utilizing the West African call-and-response pattern. With the demise of the plantations the black farmer customarily labored alone or with his family, a solitude rarely present in slave times. Eventually work songs were improvised to pass the hours, their rhythm corresponding with the labor itself. Melodies were frequently appropriated from white surroundings—fragments of hymns, scraps of dance music, tunes heard whistled by landlords or neighbors. Slowly white ingredients were fused with the black heritage and personal traits and hardships of the singer into an amalgam expressive of the rural South, a primitive form of country blues.

These field songs were unaccompanied, except for the sound of tools like axes and hammers, and were sung in a voice that was sometimes strident, sometimes guttural and throaty. There was much humming and moaning, with a great use of falsetto. The work songs, like the later blues, tended to be private, almost a musical form of talking to oneself, an inner monologue that was occasionally interrupted by grunts and references to the task at hand. The rhythm was monotonous, since it was functional, confined by repetitive labor. Lyrics were simple and frank, yet often concerned a cogent or dramatic theme. There was frequently excitement and tension; images tended to be exaggerated.

As agricultural problems in the South grew worse, many blacks looked elsewhere for employment. Some found jobs on the railroads or on construction gangs, while others toiled as stevedores, roustabouts, or in lumber camps. Work songs accompanied all kinds of manual labor, but many of the earliest recorded deal with prison life. Ballads describing work also emerged. "John Henry" became one of the most widespread songs in the American folk repertoire, appearing in innumerable versions. Its hero was a black railroad worker of tremendous strength and pride, who killed himself attempting to prove that the steam drill could not replace a hard-working hammer man. "Steam is only steam," he says, "but I'm John Henry, and I'm a natural man."

The emancipated blacks lamented many things: boll weevils, bedbugs, poverty, prison, racial oppression, the cruelty of a loved one, storms, individual misfortune. Their forlorn songs were bathed in loneliness, emptiness, and an ageless pain. Blacks of the late nineteenth century initially voiced despair in an effort to lighten their work load, yet they often digressed onto purely personal matters. As the blues evolved, they came to express themselves more directly and plaintively.

Another precursor to the blues was the spiritual, or as Harry T. Burleigh once said, "the blues and spirituals are first cousins." With the end of slavery blacks were no longer forced to attend white churches, and they began to form their own. Denominations like the African Methodist Episcopal Church appeared. The preaching in these black churches was essentially of the uninhibited, hell-fire-and-damnation genre, from which the shouting blues drew its inspiration. "Sermons" were more music than oratory. Singing was of the foot-stomping, hand-clapping variety, with much tone-sliding and improvisation. The lining-out method was customarily used in black churches, in a manner closely akin to the call-and-response system. Many of the spirituals, such as "I'll Soon Be Done with the Trouble of the World," convey, like the blues, feelings of sorrow and hopelessness, although spirituals are generally more expressive of the group than the individual. Black spirituals tended to be highly dramatic—sometimes strongly rhythmic, sometimes sad and slow. The tunes of these spirituals were sometimes interchangeable with those of the work songs.

But there were two distinct currents in the development of the Negro spiritual after the Civil War. One tended to retain the folk character of the blacks and included primitive survivals. The other transmogrified the spiritual into forms and techniques assimilated from European art music. The first was confined to a sort of underground existence, cultivated chiefly in rural areas among blacks only slightly concerned with middle class values, and attracted little attention from the majority. The second spread rapidly through white America and by the close of the century had become hailed as a native music of considerable distinction.

The less Negroid spirituals won their first big acclaim in 1871, when the Jubilee Singers from Fisk University, a black college founded right after the Civil War in Nashville, Tennessee, toured the North in an effort to raise funds for their school. After a slow start their concerts met with tremendous success. In Boston the nine students performed the "Battle Hymn of the Republic" to an audience of over 20,000 and were given a prolonged ovation. The Jubilee Singers were led by George L. White, Fisk's white music teacher and treasurer, and sang in harmony "Swing Low, Sweet Chariot," "Go Down, Moses," "Nobody Knows the Trouble I've Seen," and other spirituals carefully cast in the European mold, sandwiched in between pieces like "Home, Sweet Home," "There's Moonlight on the Lake," and "Old Folks at Home." The group was well received largely *because* it sang music that was comfortable to the ear of white listeners, and as educated young men and women they wanted to perform songs that genteel audiences would find respectable and dignified. Consistent with racial attitudes of the day, the Jubilee Singers desired nothing more than acceptance by white society and consequently fashioned their art and appearance after middle-class models. The singers returned to Nashville in 1878, after a European tour, having earned over $150,000. Already singing groups from Hampton and Tuskegee Institutes had taken to the road, following Fisk's example, and white choirs and glee clubs shortly adopted their repertoire.

The spiritual may be considered an archaic form of blues since it represented the black's attempt to escape frustration and grief through religion. Although the blues was born in the fields and river bottoms of the southern plantations, blues as a distinct form did not emerge until almost the turn of the century, probably from the Mississippi delta region. This country blues was sung for pleasure by a single individual to the accompaniment of a guitar or banjo, generally played in near unison with the voice. Blues songs could be heard in evenings around cabins, at dances, picnics, and other social gatherings, and in black communities throughout the delta area. Migratory workers and singers wandering about in search of employment helped spread verses throughout the Deep South and standardize the blues form, but regional differences clearly persisted. Some of the better singers began earning an occasional dollar performing at roadside honky-tonks; others found their way into black sections of southern towns, where they cried out their sorrowful songs on street corners, in eating places and night spots.

The country blues was created by men at leisure, yet it maintained the strength and intensity of the work songs from which it partially evolved. Because of the Mississippi caste system, this music was in large degree isolated from southern white music, and Samuel Charters feels it represents the American survival most closely related to the West African song styles. The form of the country blues was fluid enough for spontaneous expression, encouraging the singer to voice changing moods and intimate feelings. Lyrics were harshly realistic and directly related to everyday life. Like the work songs, country blues was almost a sung speech. The delta vocal style tended to be hard and unrelenting, producing rough, growling tones, although the falsetto was frequently employed for contrast. Blues singers elsewhere moaned, hollered, murmured, or declaimed. "Blue" notes were produced by sliding up to tones. The melodic range in country blues was limited, while accompaniment was simple, initially limited to tonic, subdominant, and dominant chords, used in a prescribed arrangement.

"Breaks" at the end of each line permitted improvisation on the accompanying instrument and time during which the singer could interject asides, such as "Oh, Lawdy!" The field blues song "Black Woman" illustrates this, along with the informal conception of the early rural blues and the impression that the singer is talking to himself.

Well I said come here Black Woman,
Ah-hmm, don't you hear me cryin', Oh Lordy!
Ah-hmm. I say run here Black Woman,
I want you to sit on Black Daddy's knee, Lord!
M-hmm, I know your house feel lonesome,
Ah don't you hear me whoopin', Oh Lordy!
Don't your house feel lonesome,
When your biscuit roller gone,
Lord help my cryin' time don't your house feel lonesome.

While the blues repeatedly speak of gloom, most songs of the genre are ultimately optimistic; their burden of woe is offset by an almost exultant affirmation of life, love, sex, and hope. By singing of his condition, Oliver concludes, the blues singer "brings relief to his heart and order to his disturbed thoughts, though many a blues indicates that the singer has come close to moral and mental disintegration." Occasionally there is laughter in the blues, although it is not of the easy kind. Sometimes it is flagrantly bawdy; at other times it is laughter through tight lips.

Since blues songs accepted the world on its own terms, were fully erotic, and were often sung by those who had turned their backs on religion, they were commonly called "devil songs." It was aural music and essentially transitory. The country blues singer was constantly drawing new lyrics from personal experiences and investing stock phrases and favorite verses with new meaning. Melodies also changed slowly.

By 1900 increasing numbers of blacks were finding urban jobs and moving into towns and cities. With them came wandering entertainers and country blues singers who performed wherever there was money to be made. Eventually "string bands" (consisting of fiddles, banjos, guitars, mandolins, and basses) and "jug bands" (using ordinary crockery jugs, harmonicas, banjos, mandolins, kazoos, and washboards) were formed, sometimes acompanying the blues singers. Rural blacks flocked to the smaller towns on Saturdays, where musicians congregated on shady corners, in local dives, and frequently played for dances in the evening. Gradually the country music mingled with the more commercial city music of the day, and both styles began to change.

In the years before World War I itinerant country singers of considerable reputation began appearing in the larger southern towns. From the delta came Charley Patton, born on a farm outside Edwards, Mississippi, in Hinds County. Patton sang both rural gospel songs and the amoral country blues, seemingly unconcerned with the conflict between the two points of view. The bond between the blues and the spiritual, however, was evident in the singing of Blind Willie Johnson, a ragged itinerant evangelist who roamed the streets of New Orleans. His "Dark Was the Night" is a somber chant, sung without words to guitar accompaniment, while the earthy vibrato of Blind Willie's voice explains much regarding the birth of the blues. Although "Lord, I Just

Can't Keep from Crying" is decidedly a spiritual, its mood of lament is close to the rural blues.

From Texas came Blind Lemon Jefferson, one of the most individual figures of the early blues. Lemon was born in 1897 near the small market town of Wortham, in central Texas. He was born blind, the youngest of seven children. He began playing the guitar and singing as a young adolescent and shortly learned that this was a good way for a blind boy to earn money. By 1912 he was coming into Wortham to sing, sitting outside the feed store or dry goods store and performing for people who walked by. Soon he was playing for parties, country suppers, and dances throughout the area. Around 1917 Lemon took a train for Dallas, where he lived for almost ten years, although he frequently sang in the cotton centers south of the city.

Lemon wore glasses over his eyes and was obese even as a child. He sang all kinds of songs, and his blues covered practically every aspect of the life he knew. While there was much folk material in Lemon Jefferson's music, he was not as restricted to his country background as Charley Patton. There was always a strongly personal emphasis in Lemon's songs. The blind youth was obviously filled with desire and tormented by sexuality. His blues were dominated by thoughts of women and references to his "brown," his "rider," or his "pigmeat."

Earning a living in Dallas was difficult; Lemon was unknown there and raising money for room and board was a constant concern. For a time he supplemented his income by wrestling, his blindness adding novelty to his billing. Most of his evenings were spent in the red-light district, where he played and sang for enough money for liquor and a girl. Sensitive about his blindness, he refused to let anyone lead him and eventually bought a car and hired a driver. Around 1922 he married, but life in the north Dallas slums remained a hard, chaotic one, and he and his wife soon drifted apart. He began to travel more and in 1925 was asked to come to Chicago and record for Paramount Records.

Blind Lemon's records included field songs, hymns, prison chants, and vaudeville tunes, but his sexual blues were the most intense and successful. The "Black Snake Moan," one of his best songs, was a crying sexual lament.

Um-um, black snake crawling in my room.
Um-um, black snake crawling in my room.
Yes, some pretty mama better get this black snake soon.

Uum, what's the matter now?
Uum, what's the matter now?
Yes, some pretty mama better get this black snake soon.

Well, I wonder where this black snake's gone.
I wonder where this black snake's gone.
Lord, that black snake, mama, done run my mama home.

By now Lemon was leaning toward the city blues. He traveled extensively, singing in a high, crying voice, with his guitar whining behind him. Although many of his recordings sold well, he received little in royalties. He had become a dirty, dissolute man, interested in little besides prostitutes and liquor. In February, 1930, Lemon Jefferson was found dead in a Chicago street, having frozen to death in a snow storm. A drift of snow covered his body; his guitar lay beside him.

Huddie Ledbetter performed with Blind Lemon a few times in Texas and spent a number of years working in the blacklands east of Dallas. Born near the Texas-Louisiana state line about 1885, Lead Belly, as he was familiarly known, was sentenced in 1918 to thirty years hard labor in the Texas penitentiary on two counts, murder and assault to murder. While Lead Belly learned a great deal about the blues tradition singing in the Dallas saloons and brothels with Lemon Jefferson, his style remained more authentically folk than the blind musician's, in part because of his long confinement in prison. Lead Belly preferred work songs, hollers, black ballads, and the "talkin' blues" to more commercial forms of music, and his guitar picking approximated the breaks and riffs of the later jazz instrumentalists.

Until 1912 the blues was almost entirely an unwritten tradition. That year black musician W.C. Handy published his "Memphis Blues" and created a national taste for commercial blues. Originally composed in 1909 as a campaign song for Edward H. Crump, reform candidate for mayor of Memphis, the tune was a local success as soon as Handy's band played it. Called "Mister Crump," it was requested time and again at the street rally where Handy introduced the number. Published first as an instrumental cakewalk, the "Memphis Blues" did not really become widely popular until words had been added and minstrel performer "Honey Boy" Evans had been talked into using it in a New York engagement. The song was republished in New York with lyrics in 1913, and its composer shortly became known as the "father of the blues." The music Handy wrote was far more related to Tin Pan Alley than to the country blues, but he helped lift the blues out of the rural South and make it an urban phenomenon.

Handy was born on November 16, 1873, in Florence, Alabama, nine miles from the Muscle Shoals Canal. His father and grandfather were both Methodist ministers, who looked upon professional musicians as downright disreputable. As a child Handy used to listen to the laborers sing on his maternal grandparent's farm and later attended a public school that boasted a music teacher from Fisk University. The teacher drilled his classes in singing by note and taught them selections from the European masters. In 1892 Handy organized a quartet that earned its way to the Chicago World's Fair by singing in churches, serenading on street corners, and entertaining on trains—only to find that the Fair had been postponed. Handy then spent some time in St. Louis before securing a job as cornet soloist with Mahara's Colored Minstrels. He remained with minstrelsy until 1903, except for two years when he taught music at the black college in Huntsville, Alabama.

Mahara's show played mostly northern cities, since there was more money to be made there, and Handy eventually became the bandmaster for the troupe.

The future composer had an interest in the music of his people, but his knowledge was limited, his attitude somewhat opportunistic. Handy claimed to have heard a man plucking a guitar and singing the blues on the Mississippi delta as early as 1895, music he said that reflected the "sadness of the ages." In 1903 he became leader of the Knights of Pythias Band in Clarksdale, Mississippi, which played mainly Tin Pan Alley hits. During a white society dance in nearby Cleveland, Handy was asked to play some black music. He responded with a slow drag he had learned with Mahara's, but that did not seem to be what the crowd wanted. Eventually three local blacks were brought in who played rough, spontaneous music on guitar, mandolin, and bass viol and earned more in tips than Handy's men had been paid for the whole evening.

The musician moved to Memphis in 1905, where he taught and organized his own band. Social life in Memphis was active. There were many dances, and from the honky-tonks along Beale Street came the sounds of guitars, pianos, and singing, well into the night. Once established in the city, Handy opened a music publishing business with a young lyricist and singer named Harry Pace. The success of his "Memphis Blues" led the bandleader to turn seriously to composition. The "St. Louis Blues," his masterpiece, appeared in 1914, followed shortly by the "Joe Turner Blues" and the "Beale Street Blues." By 1918 Handy's fame had become sufficiently great that the former cornetist moved his expanded publishing firm to New York, where a blues craze was replacing the ragtime fad just dying out. Both black and white songwriters had turned their pens to the blues, while dozens of singers along Broadway were moaning the "miss-my-man" fabrications Tin Pan Alley was cranking out.

Handy himself was somewhere between the black folk tradition in music and the purely commercial variety. His claim that he "aimed to use all that is characteristic of the Negro from Africa to Alabama" in writing his blues is an obvious overstatement. His work was essentially derived from the "coon song" and cakewalk type of popular music, even though the composer seems to have been aware of the strengths of authentic blues. Certainly the "St. Louis Blues" is a long way from the field shouts and work songs of the Mississippi delta; its introduction is a tango, taking advantage of the current tango vogue.

Hart Wand's "Dallas Blues" and Arthur Seals' "Baby Seals' Blues" were published the same year the "Memphis Blues" was published. The first was writttten by a white, the second by a black. The city blues was rapidly evolving, closely tied to the popular entertainment world. Unlike its rural predecessor, the city blues was planned, its texts and music arranged in a precise form. The "classic" blues pattern consists of twelve bars and three lines. The second line is a repetition of the first, almost as if the singer is waiting for another thought to come to mind. The third is a contrasting statement or response.

Woke up this morning, feeling sad and blue,
Woke up this morning, feeling sad and blue,
Didn't have nobody to tell my troubles to.

The repeated phrase emphasizes the sentiment the singer wants to express, carrying over into later instrumental jazz as the "riff." There is a "break" at the end of each line, during which the singer can interject spoken asides like "Yes, man" or "Oh, play it," while the call-and-response structure is continued through the voice's "call" and the instrumental "response." The singer employs a relaxed singing style and frequently alters tones into "blue" notes by scooping or slurring. There is also free use of such vocal effects as falsetto, whining, moaning, shouting, and growling.

The city blues was generally more sophisticated in tone than its rural counterpart and made much greater use of group accompaniment, played in the idiom of a small jazz band. Lyrics concentrated on love, usually telling about the fickleness or departure of a lover. Whereas most of the better known country singers had been men, who were free to wander about, most of the "classic" blues performers were women. By the time the city blues emerged, black theaters had come into existence, and the "classic" blues singers either toured with black minstrel and vaudeville shows or played dingy honky-tonks and roadhouses. Despite its commercial purpose, the city blues remained personal, a musical soliloquy acting as a catharsis whereby life became bearable again. The audience was really irrelevant to what the singer had to say, although even white listeners found they could share much of the vocalist's misery. The movement toward performance, Imamu Amiri Baraka, formerly LeRoi Jones, argues, "turned some of the emotional climate of the Negro's life into artifact and entertainment. But there was still enough intimacy between the real world and the artifact to make that artifact beautiful and unbelievably moving." The "classic" blues represented a balance between the city and the country, the white world and the black, separation and integration.

Undoubtedly the most renowned of the early blues entertainers was Gertrude "Ma" Rainey. Born in 1886 in Columbus, Georgia, she was the daughter of black minstrel people. When she married Will Rainey at fifteen, she was already singing professionally with a company of the Rabbit Foot Minstrels, which Rainey managed. The show toured the towns and whistle stops of the South first by wagon, later by rail. Its bill featured jungle scenes, wrestlers, comedy acts, jugglers, and vaudeville musicians. In the larger towns the troupe played in theaters, in the smaller ones in a tent, which roustabouts raised in a field while a brass band paraded the streets advertising the minstrels' arrival. Young Gertrude Rainey shortly became one of the featured performers. She sang about love affairs gone wrong, bad luck, and trouble—all of which her audiences understood well.

Before long "Ma" Rainey was loved and imitated in black communities all through the South and Midwest. She dressed in sequined gowns, ostrich feathers, costume jewelry, and resplendent wigs; although she was a short and heavy woman, she came to symbolize glamor. At the same time she became something of a mother image for the rootless urban blacks who heard her; when she sang she became Mother Earth. Her voice was huge and somber, with a mellow richness that gave deep feeling to every phrase. Her singing was at once monumental and simple, and often she combined tragedy with humor, the one tempering the other. Unlike the country singers, "Ma" Rainey was aware of her expressive abilities, more calculated in her style. She broadened both the melodic and textural qualities of the blues and turned folk material into dramatic works of art, without becoming falsely sophisticated.

"Ma" Rainey toured for almost thirty-five years, eventually going on the black vaudeville circuit. She drew her material from a variety of sources, and among her best numbers are "See See Rider," "Traveling Blues," "Shave 'Em Dry," "Levee Camp Moan," "Cell Bound Blues," and "Slow-Drivin' Moon." Her accompaniment ranged from tub, jug, and washboard band to horns, piano, banjo, and drums. Hers was vigorous, vital music, with lyrics that were frank and left little to the imagination. Her first records were not made until 1923, when she was past her prime, but they are treasures nonetheless.

Around 1910, on a stopover with the Rabbit Foot Minstrels in Chattanooga, Tennessee, "Ma" Rainey discovered a huge twelve year-old girl with the most amazing voice she had ever heard. Since the child's parents were both dead and she was living in appalling poverty, Gertrude Rainey invited her to join the troupe, promising to teach her to sing the blues. The girl was Bessie Smith, soon to be called "Empress of the Blues." Bessie listened backstage while "Ma" Rainey brought the house down night after night, and during the day "Ma" would sit by the piano and coach Bessie as the girl rehearsed her own numbers. Gertrude Rainey was just twelve years older than her protege, but she quickly became a mother to the girl. Born in Chattanooga, probably on April 15, 1898, Bessie felt she had never had a home, that she was nobody's child. The hard, loveless life she endured as a child left its indelible mark on Bessie, but prepared her well for singing the blues. Even in early grammar school she had shown histrionic ability and at the age of nine had sung at Chattanooga's Ivory Theater.

After about a year with the Rabbit Foot Minstrels, Bessie left to go on her own. She sang for a while at the "81" Theater in Atlanta, before going with a troupe called the Florida Cotton Pickers for TOBA. Theatre Owners' Booking Agency was the black vaudeville circuit, which included the larger towns of the South and Midwest. Managed by whites, TOBA was referred to by black performers as "Tough on Black Asses," since payment was often pitifully small. Bessie also worked in tent shows—part vaudeville, part minstrelsy—and freelanced in Gulf Coast cabarets, dance halls, and waterfront saloons, singing such famous "Ma" Rainey hits as "See See Rider" and "These Dogs of Mine." Bessie was learning how to use her deep contralto voice, learning those broad, tragic nuances that separated the "classic" blues singers from the ballad stylists of the day. Frank Walker, later her promoter, remembered hearing Bessie in 1917 and how he was impressed with her "deep moaning blues" even then. By the time she was fourteen the singer had blossomed into a young woman—a tall, handsome woman. In contrast to "Ma" Rainey, Bessie Smith would prefer simple dresses, her hair swept back, and a single strand of pearls at her neck. But more than anything else, Bessie knew how to deliver a song, knew how to express herself so that word, meaning, and sound became one.

At the end of World War I, the singer was touring with her own show, called the *Liberty Belles*, boasting a chorus of girls as large as Bessie herself. The show was a success and spread its star's fame throughout the South. In 1920 Bessie went to Atlantic City for a long engagement and found there black audiences more sophisticated than those she had known earlier. Vast numbers of blacks had moved into northern cities during the War, attracted by industrial wages, but they were often filled with nostalgia for the South and home. The blues spoke to them, echoing their dislocation, loneliness, insecurity, and bitterness in a time of great social unrest. Bessie Smith played the black cabarets of the North in the early Twenties and became particularly popular on Philadelphia's South Side. In 1923 she married Jack Gee, a Philadelphia policeman, and made the city her home.

Until 1920 none of the blues had been recorded. Mamie Smith (no relation to Bessie) made the first blues disc in August, 1920, when she recorded "That Thing Called Love" and "You Can't Keep a Good Man Down" for Okeh. The next year her "Crazy Blues" sold for months at the rate of 8000 copies a week. Soon record companies were combing the country for girls who could sing the city blues. By the middle of the decade the combined annual sale of records for the black market totalled nearly six million copies, selling in phonograph shops, bars, drug stores, barber shops, cigar stands, and black businesses of every description. By then the country blues singers were being discovered and recorded, but the younger urban blacks especially preferred the more commercial forms. In the South the country blues discs sold considerably better, again to a black market. Record firms eventually began advertising that any of their items could be purchased by mail, and in the rural areas the mail-order business proved quite profitable.

Bessie Smith cut her first disc on February 16, 1923. She had auditioned earlier, but with no success. Record producers had judged her style too uncouth for the urban market. She arrived at the Columbia Records studio in New York seeming very much the country girl. Director Frank Walker, who had admired her years before, remembered her that day as "tall and fat and scared to death." When she sang "Downhearted Blues" into the big recording horn, she was obviously restrained and nervous. It took five takes before Walker and his crew were satisfied. Clarence Williams accompanied Bessie on the piano. The next day the singer recorded Williams' "Gulf Coast Blues" for the other side. The record was released without fanfare and proved a sensation, selling almost a million copies. But this was just a start. By the end of the year Bessie had her recording technique firmly under control. Her style seemed effortless, while her personal phrasing and embellishments added much to the emotional thrust. She was shortly the prize attraction of the "Race" division of Columbia Records, ultimately recording over 160 sides. Her sales before the Depression ran to nearly ten million copies, purchased mostly by blacks. Within the next few years Bessie Smith would become the highest paid black performer in the country, booked solidly at $1500 a week.

Despite the vicissitudes of her personal life, her level of performance remained unsurpassed. She made a triumphal tour of the South with TOBA and was soon traveling with her own show, *The Harlem Frolics*, playing New York, Chicago, Philadelphia, Boston, as well as the larger southern cities, but still mainly to black audiences. While her music remained outside the mainstream of American culture, it was closer to meshing with it than any black music before it. For black migrants Bessie's songs were a reminder of their roots, and they crammed theaters wherever she sang. Although her reputation was made mainly from records, the singer considered live performance the true artistic challenge. She always closed her shows alone, walking slowly to the footlights, accompanied by the pounding of a drum, sometimes augmented by muted brasses. Oran "Hot Lips" Page once backed up Bessie on the trumpet and found her powerful delivery astonishing. "Man," he recalled, "she could sing over and drown out the loudest swing band going." She would stand in the spotlight singing four or five of her hits, swaying gently to the beat, never using a microphone. Sometimes she would walk slowly around the stage, with her head slightly bowed. Either way she commanded the attention of her audience completely, and her numbers were greeted with "amens," then deafening applause. Photographer Carl Van Vechten, who heard Bessie often, described her as "a woman cutting her heart open with a knife until it was exposed for us all to see, so that we suffered, as she suffered."

Her records find her a mistress of vocal inflection—her diction careful, her technique instinctively perfect. Her sense of pitch is dramatic and accurate, her control without parallel. The voice is strong, even harsh, but always with a bewitching natural beauty. At her best Bessie combined sound musicianship with a vigorous folk art. Among her best recordings are "Jail House Blues," "Reckless Blues," "Young Woman's Blues," "You've Been a Good Old Wagon," "Cemetery Blues," and "Careless Love." Like "Ma" Rainey, she frequently returned to the subject matter of the country blues emphasizing the less attractive aspects of life. "Yellow Dog Blues" uses much black slang, including terms like "easy rider" and "southbound rattler." "Black Water Blues" contains memorable images of the Mississippi floods; the song is moving yet never sentimental. In partnership with Louis Armstrong, Bessie cut a version of the "St. Louis Blues" that is as classic as the song itself. At the Columbia studios she also collaborated with Fletcher

Henderson, Coleman Hawkins, Charlie Green, and especially Joe Smith.

In 1927 Bessie Smith was at the peak of her career. Already she was having emotional problems, however, and had taken heavily to the gin. She had become an embittered woman who had lost her way in the sudden climb to fortune and fame. Outside she was ribald and tough, argumentative and aggressive. She adored noise and fights and squandered money with the abandon of an exhibitionist. Inside she was frightened and confused, unable to relate the woman in the spotlight to the misused girl from the Chattanooga slums. At times she was tender and gentle, full of compassion, even sentimental: In the summer of 1926 she walked out on a tour when she heard that Frank Walker's son was ill. She presented herself at the Walker's Long Island home and informed Mrs. Walker that she intended to take over the cooking and cleaning until the two year-old boy was out of danger. Another side was egocentric and temperamental, and she generally treated coworkers with aloofness, imperiously demanding they call her "Miss Bessie." Undoubtedly she harbored resentment that the white community and even the more urbane blacks ignored her. And as the conflict within grew, she devoured bottles of gin to forget, a tumblerful at a time. Her drinking sprees became notorious, and there were times when she had to be propped against a chair on stage to get her through her numbers.

Bessie's reputation began to slip almost simultaneously with the decline of the city blues. As trouble set in, "the Empress" turned more often to Tin Pan Alley tunes like "Alexander's Ragtime Band" and "Hot Time in the Old Town Tonight" and to lyrics that were downright salacious. Her two part "Empty Bed Blues" in 1928 was one of her best-selling records, largely because of its pornographic imagery, yet the song is full of an almost terrifying loneliness. "Kitchen Man" is the cry of a wealthy woman who had "servants by the score." Its sexual message is anything but subtle, as the woman implores Dan, her kitchen man, not to leave her household and describes his talents in the "kitchen."

His jelly roll sure is nice and hot,
Never fails to touch the spot,
I can't do without my kitchen man.

His fine feathers are rolled so sweet,
How I love his young pig meat,
I can't do without my kitchen man.

Oh how that boy does open clams,
No one else is gwina touch my hams,
I can't do without my kitchen man.

When I eat his doughnuts tall I leave him just the hole,
Any time he wants them he certainly can use my sugar pole.

His boloney's certainly worth a try,
Never fails to satisfy,
I can't do without my kitchen man.

Bessie made a Warner Brothers short in 1929, *St. Louis Blues*, and went on tour with a new show, *Midnight Steppers*. But with the Depression fewer of the singer's followers could afford to hear her in person, and the film was never released. Besides, with hard times people wanted lighthearted entertainment, not the frustrations of the blues. The old road shows were barely paying their way now. Suddenly Bessie's blues seemed to take on a more autobiographical note, as she recorded "Gin House Blues," "Me and My Gin," and the unforgettable "Nobody Knows You When You're Down and Out." In 1930 her marriage broke up, and soon Bessie was barnstorming her way southward, singing the blues in tumbledown theaters, carnivals, and third-rate cabarets. To get jobs she resorted to bawdy potboilers and even a "mammy" getup. At one of her last recording sessions, Bessie sang one of her own compositions, the "Shipwreck Blues." Its implications were chilling.

It's cloudy outdoors as it can be.
That's the time I need my good man with me.
It's rainin' and it's stormin' on the sea.
It's rainin' and it's stormin' on the sea.
I feel like somebody had shipwrecked for me.

The gin had taken its toll, for the voice, while still exciting, was now badly worn.

Columbia terminated the singer's contract in 1933. Her last New York appearance came three years later, at a Sunday afternoon jam session at the Famous Door. She sang a few numbers, wearing an old, beat-up fur coat, then disappeared. She went back on the road, playing many of the small southern towns she had known as a girl. But TOBA was no more, and Bessie herself had become an anachronism in an age of radio and smoother, more sophisticated songs.

In the fall of 1937 she was singing with E. S. Winsted's *Broadway Rastus Show*. The show played Darling, Mississippi, on Saturday night, September 25; Bessie finished her act singing "This Is My Last Affair." After the show it rained. Bessie and a friend left for the next stop in a pink Packard, while the rest of the troupe followed in a bus. Early in the morning they were driving along Route 61, about ten miles outside Clarksdale. Bessie had her arm resting on the open car window. Suddenly they came over a rise—a truck on the road was coming toward them. The Packard and the truck collided; Bessie's arm was almost torn off at the elbow.

The death of Bessie Smith had all the elements of tragedy and high drama and has been told many times. Truth has become immersed in a sea of untruth. Dave Oxley, the tent show's drummer and also bus driver for the troupe, stated in an interview for the Tulane Jazz Archives that his bus came upon the scene about an hour and a half after the accident. Bessie was unconscious and probably dead then from loss of blood. Since there was no ambulance for blacks in Clarksdale, an undertaker in Memphis had been called. Oxley contends that Bessie was dead by the time the ambulance arrived. Other accounts hold that a white doctor happened onto the accident. While the doctor was bandaging Bessie, his car was struck from the rear. Now the passengers of the third car lay mangled across the road. The highway was little traveled at that hour, and it was a long time before someone appeared who could get help. Several ambulances finally arrived. Bessie and her driver were taken to the Clarksdale hospital, but officials in the emergency ward insisted they could not treat blacks. The pair were then moved to a combination hospital and funeral home, where Bessie died later that day, after her arm had been amputated. Still another version maintains that Bessie was admitted at the white hospital, but died in the waiting room while the injured whites were treated first. Certainly the singer's death has been the vehicle for much black hostility and racial propaganda, often exploited for sensational purposes. She was buried at Mount Lawn Cemetery in Philadelphia, October 4, 1937.

The city blues reached its summit in Bessie Smith. There were other great "classic" blues singers—Ida Cox, Bertha "Chippie" Hill, Clara Smith, Sippie Wallace, and more, but Bessie's artistry towered above them all. No one else had her rich, full voice; no one else could match her control or tragic intensity. In Bessie's blues there was no pretense. Even when her material was mediocre, she was able to make it into a personal expression. She combined the honest intimacy of the country blues with the more complex style of band-blues and set the standard for many who came later.

Unlike her contemporary Ethel Waters, who sang sweeter songs, Bessie remained largely unknown to the white public of her day. In the late Twenties, toward the end of the Harlem Renaissance, she was welcomed into a number of intellectuals' parties in New York, but the great Bessie Smith cult came later. Bessie's blues spoke of many things that had been lost—lost love, lost freedom, lost happiness, lost human dignity. As the urban majority came to discover its own losses, the music of black blues singers struck a responsive chord. The blues of Bessie Smith might be boisterous or funny, gentle or angry and were often told through a veil of irony and an imagery familiar only to blacks. But underneath was a universal truth—a rock-bottom outpouring of human emotions—that elevated her art into a timeless expression.

The classic blues singers were mostly vaudeville and show business performers, and most of their numbers eventually came to be composed by New York songwriters. But it was in the tent shows and black theaters of the South that the blues and early jazz met. From there the city blues branched off in two directions—either staying with jazz in its purer forms or taking the route of popular music.

Ragtime was another black music directly associated with popular entertainment and a major ingredient in the flowering of jazz. Classic ragtime is written piano music, although itinerant black musicians doubtlessly were playing a similar music in the saloons and brothels of the South long before Scott Joplin and the other ragtime composers began writing their works down. In its classic form ragtime contains much of the charm, elegance, and primness of late Victorianism, and yet some of the boisterous quality typical of the folk songs and dances of frontier America. It is a combination of the European and black ancestry—European in construction and harmony, black in its melodies and syncopated melodic lines. Ragtime was the first black music to achieve wide commercial popularity in the United States, eventually exercising a profound influence on the shape of popular song and popular dance styles. Classic ragtime is fairly difficult, full of melodic and harmonic complexities. While the ragtime composers were indebted to the syncopated plantation melodies and banjo "jigs" of early minstrelsy and their work bore a relationship to the cakewalks and "coon songs" of the late nineteenth century, their collective method was far more cultivated, essentially that of the concert composer.

Since classic ragtime was predominantly European in construction, its development could take place only after its composers had been given an opportunity to study and express themselves outside the black community. Also, ragtime was primarily pianistic, and the piano was one of the last instruments to be mastered by black performers. Therefore the first of the classic rags did not appear until almost the turn of the century. Unlike European music, however, ragtime is syncopated throughout; that is, the normally weak beat is accented, which lends a vigorous, cheerful air to the music. In ragtime the root positions are generally changed every measure or two, while the faster tempos and many notes leave little room for the inflective freedoms permitted in the blues. The left hand in ragtime is customarily cast in a supporting role and rarely engages in syncopation. A quasi-rondo pattern is generally followed, intended to be played with meticulous precision.

Like the barrelhouse pianists, the first ragtime piano players were anonymous drifters, who played in riverside dives and cheap eating places along the Mississippi, sometimes just for tips. W. C. Handy heard one of these "piano thumpers" on a visit to Memphis during the late 1880s. "As I was walking down Beale Street one night," the musician remembered, "my attention was caught by the sound of a piano. The insistent black rhythms were broken first by a tinkle in the treble, then by a rumble in the bass; then they came together again. I entered the cheap cafe and found a colored man at the piano, dog tired. He told me he had to play from seven at night until seven in the morning." Since few of these early ragtime pianists could read music, their style was often unique. During the Columbian Exposition of 1893, black piano players like "Plunk" Henry converged on Chicago to work along the Midway, and it was here that the general public first heard ragtime music. The exposure widened in the decade ahead at the world's fairs in Omaha, Buffalo, and St. Louis. On January 23, 1900, ragtime pianists from all over the country gathered at Tammany Hall in New York for the Ragtime Championship of the World Competition.

The first ragtime piano number was published in 1897, probably William Krell's "Mississippi Rag." Krell was a white bandleader from Chicago, who had traveled up and down the Mississippi and frankly acknowledged his debt to the black piano players he had encountered in waterfront cabarets. That same year black pianist Thomas M. Turpin composed the "Harlem Rag," the first full-fledged ragtime piece published by a black.

Although by now rags were being played in the cities on the East coast, Sedalia, Missouri, became the fountainhead of classic ragtime, while Scott Joplin emerged as ragtime's most creative and consistently inspired composer. Joplin was born in Texarkana, Texas, in 1868. His father, a former slave, was a railroad worker from North Carolina who played the violin and had performed for plantation dances before the Civil War. His mother was a freeborn black from Kentucky who worked as a laundress and played the banjo and sang. One of Joplin's brothers played the guitar. The family occasionally performed at weddings and parties and became well known in the Texarkana area. By the time Scott was seven he had taught himself to play a neighbor's piano. His father managed to scrape together enough money to buy an old-fashioned square grand, and young Scott's ability at the instrument soon became a source of local pride. An old German musician heard the boy and agreed to give him free lessons in piano and theory. He also introduced Scott to the music of the European masters, and for a time it seemed the youth was on his way toward becoming a concert pianist.

A quiet, introverted boy, Joplin left his family shortly after his mother died and wandered around Texas, Louisiana, and the Mississippi River area, playing in honky-tonks, gambling halls, brothels, and cafes for low wages and absorbing the "jig piano" style from the self-taught musicians in the towns where he worked. At seventeen he arrived in St. Louis, where he played in the sporting-house district along Chestnut and Market Streets for the next eight years. He met other musicians at "Honest John" Turpin's Silver Dollar Saloon, which became sort of the unofficial headquarters for black musicians awaiting employment, while day in and day out music poured into the youngster's ears. Sometimes he filled engagements in nearby towns like Hannibal, Carthage, and Sedalia, occasionally traveling as far as Cincinnati and Louisville.

Joplin joined the throng of ragtime pianists at the Chicago World's Fair in 1893 and for a time led a small orchestra there. He also worked various jobs in the Chicago tenderloin district. When the fair closed, he returned briefly to St. Louis, then found himself in Sedalia for almost a year, where he began writing music of his own. He alternated between Sedalia and St. Louis for some time, but in the summer of 1899 he was playing at the Maple Leaf Club in Sedalia, where he was heard by the Missouri music publisher John Stillwell Stark. Stark recognized the originality and vitality of the pianist's music and offered to publish some of his compositions. Joplin's celebrated "Maple Leaf Rag" appeared later that year.

From the standpoint of form the "Maple Leaf Rag" might almost be a Sousa march. It is in 2/4 tempo and marked "Tempo di Marcia." Elsewhere Joplin instructed "Slow March Tempo" and even cautioned performers, "Notice! Don't play this piece fast. It is never right to play 'Ragtime' fast." Like his later selections, the "Maple Leaf Rag" is a work of considerable polish and one that is technically demanding. Its melody is syncopated, while the rhythm remains steady. The composition is an incredible fusion of folk and cultivated traditions, farmland and town. The "Maple Leaf Rag" sold hundreds of thousands of copies within the first decade of its publication and was widely admired by serious musicians. Composer Charles Griffes honestly respected the piece and often played it at private gatherings.

Since Sedalia was a railroad center, it was more cosmopolitan than most of the heartland cities of its size. While there, Scott Joplin studied advanced harmony and composition at the George Smith College for Negroes and played with a local brass band. With the success of the "Maple Leaf Rag" he was able to leave the honky-tonks, move into a large house, and set himself up as a piano teacher. More important, he could concentrate on composition. He turned out sheaves of rags, composed ragtime waltzes, tangoes, and a ballet. He also wrote an instruction book, in which he argued that syncopations were "no indication of light or trashy music."

The "Maple Leaf Rag" also enabled Joplin to marry Belle Hayden, a widow and the sister-in-law of ragtime composer Scott Hayden. The couple shortly settled in St. Louis, which by 1906 had become the ragtime capital and where Joplin continued to teach and compose. His wife supplemented the family income by running a boarding house. The composer seems to have been driven by an impulse to distill from the light-hearted black folk song heritage a music that would be recognized as art both by the black and white worlds.

The early Joplin rags include such gems as "The Sunflower Slow Drag" (in collaboration with Scott Hayden), "The Entertainer," "Easy Winners," "Elite Syncopations," and "Weeping Willow Rag"—all rich in musical expressiveness. The composer was a master of melodic invention, and his lilting music is brimming with energy. "Joplin creates a lacework of sound," William Schafer and Johannes Riedel explain, "filling in every space with lyrical embroidery." His multi-theme structure and graceful key changes are charming, while the crisp attack becomes infectious. Joplin's rags were essentially written in the romantic tradition of nineteenth century piano music, and without being imitative there are wisps of Chopin and Schubert and Liszt. This was music that white middle class America at the turn of the century could embrace comfortably and might almost be described as "white music—played black."

A concert version of the composer's *A Guest of Honor*, a ragtime opera, was produced in St. Louis in 1905, but the manuscript of this work has been lost. By then Joplin's marriage was in trouble; the break-up had been hastened by the birth of a baby girl who died after a few months. The musician's first wife had little real appreciation of his work and never really fit in with his musical friends. During 1907 Joplin moved to New York, where he began writing with renewed enthusiasm. Tired of the wandering life, he was ready to settle down to serious composition in extended forms. In 1909 he married Lottie Stokes and bought a house on West Forty-seventh Street, which his wife ran as a theatrical boarding house.

Joplin's rags between 1907 and 1908 show a definite advance over his earlier efforts and indicate that the musician, having mastered the ragtime style, was free to develop his art. Among these are the "Gladiolus Rag," "Heliotrope Bouquet" (with Louis Chauvin), "Searchlight Rag," "Rose Leaf Rag," "Pineapple Rag," and "Fig Leaf Rag." Here the composer tended to lengthen his phrase, giving it a more serene legato effect. The essentially bouncy spirit of ragtime had been brought under control. There is a greater dignity, even a grandeur.

During his early New York years Joplin, a solidly built man, was described as a good dresser with a liking for companionship. From 1909 on he moved toward even more complex structures and became increasingly experimental in his writing. "Euphonic Sounds" (1909) is harmonically adventuresome, with shifting tonality, while "Magnetic Rag" (1914) is almost a sonata in form. Both employ the coda. There was much interest in tonality, and a growing preoccupation with quasi-classical forms, which the composer probably did not arrive at deliberately. While these later rags are always ambitious, they are of uneven quality and represent a strange assortment of contradictions.

By 1914 Joplin's obsession with his second opera, *Treemonisha*, had become so consuming that his teaching began to suffer. Many of his pupils left, while others felt neglected. The composer and his wife were forced to move into a smaller house on 131st Street. The second Mrs. Joplin believed in her husband's work so strongly that she descended to running the house as a brothel, and it was in this atmosphere that the musician continued his writing. *Treemonisha*, set on a plantation somewhere in Arkansas, contains some of Joplin's most mature composition, yet it is not so much an opera as what the musician *conceived* an opera to be. Its 230-page piano score was published at Joplin's own expense, and the composer spent months orchestrating the work. He was determined to get his opera staged, but none of the New York managers would have any part of it. The work was finally performed in 1915 without scenery, costumes, or orchestra in a dismal rehearsal hall in Harlem. The composer himself provided the accompaniment on the piano. The drama seemed unconvincing and pale, mustering little public interest. Joplin was heartbroken.

He tried to return to other writing, but his spirit was crushed. Periods of sporadic work alternated with deep depression. His mind began to give way and eventually his physical coordination. In 1916 he was committed to Manhattan State Hospital on Ward's Island. Occasionally he would rally for brief moments, long enough to jot down a few bars of music, before lapsing back into a state of dullness. He died on April 1, 1917, of a brain disease brought on by syphilis.

There were other black pianists composing rags in Missouri, particularly Joplin's proteges Scott Hayden and Arthur Marshall. Tom Turpin, owner of the Rosebud Cafe and several bars in St. Louis' tenderloin district, also made a considerable impact, writing many of the rags played in his cafe. The Rosebud became a rendezvous for ragtime piano players, while Turpin's "St. Louis Rag" (1903) became one of the great classics. Louis Chauvin, who developed under Turpin's guidance, was another important force and a real ragtime virtuoso. But aside from Scott Joplin probably the two most distinguished writers of rags were James Scott and Joseph Lamb.

Scott, a theater organist in Kansas City, published three marches in 1903. His "Frog Legs Rag," three years later, exhibited a far more forceful approach than Joplin's. Scott preferred brief phrases, a faster tempo, and splashes of color. His rags explode with a furious energy. Unlike Joplin his style developed very little, and his later pieces—including "Kansas City Rag," "The Ragtime Betty," "Grace and Beauty," and "Hilarity Rag"—are not appreciably different from the first. Lamb, a white musician from New Jersey, began composing in 1908 with "Sensation" and went on to produce classics like the "Ethiopian Rag" and "American Beauty Rose." He attempted much the same exuberance as Scott and clearly saw ragtime's artistic potential. The best of his rags are graceful, intricate, and melodic, yet Lamb lacked Scott's spontaneity and fire and Joplin's serenity. While James Scott and Joseph Lamb wrote uniformly fine rags, neither possessed Scott Joplin's flexibility.

Around 1906 the Sedalia and St. Louis piano players began to drift away—to Kansas City, Chicago, and New York. By 1910 ragtime had become a national fad, spread by thousands of itinerant pianists, gramophone cylinders, the nickleodeon, and especially the player piano. Even Scott Joplin recorded a number of piano rolls between 1906 and 1909. While white musicians like Benjamin Harney had introduced ragtime to polite New York audiences as early as 1896, black pianists such as Baltimore's Eubie Blake established an eastern school of ragtime early in the new century. By then the cakewalk craze was well underway. Cakewalk contests sprang up from coast to coast, as couples sought to outdo one another in improvising struts and kicks to ragtime accompaniment. Ragtime had become an accepted form of American popular music, made respectable by theatrical performers and dance orchestras.

Syncopated music had its critics, of course. *Musical Courier* found it an abomination, declaring in 1899: "A wave of vulgar, filthy, and suggestive music has inundated the land. . . . Nothing but ragtime prevails." Conductor

Karl Muck said: "Ragtime is *poison*. It poisons the source of musical growth, for it poisons the taste of the young!" But when ragtime spread to Europe, a number of eminent European composers judged it an original musical expression. Debussy's *Golliwog's Cakewalk* and Stravinsky's *Ragtime for Eleven Instruments* and *Piano Rag-Music* were clearly influenced by the American idiom.

Gradually ragtime piano players settled on digital speed, dexterity, and rapid keyboard ornamentation to win a mass audience, while the melodic originality and rhythmic force of the classic rags deteriorated into a ricky-ticky bounce. By 1911, when Irving Berlin's "Alexander's Ragtime Band" was published, classic ragtime was coming to an end, replaced by Tin Pan Alley songs like "Put Your Arms Around Me Honey" and "Ragtime Cowboy Joe." A few of the best ragtime composers would continue writing into the 1920s, but the delicate, rococo sounds of the classic piano rags had been engulfed a decade earlier by the banality of the popular song hacks. Ruined by exploitation and overexposure, ragtime hit something of a dead end in the North. In a freer, more vital form, it was picked up by small instrumental groups in the South and transformed into a major tributary for early jazz.

CHAPTER

IX

Early Jazz

Many emancipated blacks turned to music for a livelihood, playing guitars or banjos and singing on street corners, in dives, and brothels throughout the South and much of the Midwest. Gradually "string," "jug," and "washboard" bands were formed, some performing informally in the back country, the more successful ones traveling from town to town. By the 1880s, as increasing numbers of blacks were migrating into cities, black brass bands had appeared in most of the larger southern towns. The black militia during the Civil War had given blacks an opportunity to play march music, and the breakup of the Confederate army bands left pawn shops with plenty of cheap instruments. Most of these early black brass bands were either independent or sponsored by fraternal societies or social clubs, and were made up of musicians who worked at other trades and played in their spare time. They used trumpets, cornets, valve trombones, and tubas, finding them far more expressive than homemade instruments had been. While the string bands played for dances, the brass bands were first heard mainly at parades, funerals, and celebrations.

Few of these black musicians could read music, and they freely improvised on melodies and preferred a driving, "hot" rhythm. The bands eventually began to "rag" many of the marches and tunes they played, influenced by the rolling blues of the barrelhouse pianists and eventually by the ragtime piano players farther north. To say that jazz originated in New Orleans is a rank oversimplification, since similar music was being played in many southern and midwestern towns and on the riverboats that plied the Mississippi. In Louisiana alone, what would become known as jazz was played all over the state before the turn of the century—in Alexandria, Shreveport, Opelousas, Plaquemine, as well as on the larger sugar plantations at special occasions. But New Orleans was definitely the most *important* city in the birth of jazz and in that regard alone may be considered the cradle of the jazz tradition.

Jazz reflected the American melting pot in its mosaic beginnings. Even in New Orleans there were several kinds of jazz. The city was not only the most cosmopolitan, but remained the most musical city in America throughout the nineteenth century. It had always had a large number of free blacks, and after the Civil War thousands more flocked to the city, known for its tolerance. But there were two Negro populations in New Orleans—the downtown Creoles of French descent and the uptown blacks more recently from rural backgrounds and closer to plantation slavery. The Creole blacks maintained much of the French culture, spoke a French patois, and were often successful businessmen who worked side by side with whites. At the French Opera House they might even hold their own boxes. The Creoles had access to musical instruments early, had learned to read music, and played in a style essentially derived from Europe. Their uptown counterparts obtained these instruments later and played a rougher, blues-colored music that polite society viewed with suspicion. Then, too, before the turn of the century there was a white jazz tradition in New Orleans that was distinct from the black and highly important.

There were always many elements present in the evolving jazz compound, some derived from Europe, some from Africa. The balance varied from the start. With the "white supremacy" legislation of the late nineteenth century, the black Creoles lost much of their social autonomy and were repeatedly forced into jobs nearer their darker half-brothers. The downtown musicians "of color" found they were no longer acceptable at white functions and, for a time, could not play in the homes of rich whites or in military parades. They began moving uptown, sitting in with the black musicians there at parties and picnics, in saloons and dance halls. Enforced segregation, therefore, thrust together the formally trained, European-oriented Creole musicians and the uptown blacks who played mostly by ear. By 1894 these uptown groups were playing a "marchy" kind of music in brisk 2/4 tempo, but the tones and timbres coming from their instruments were very different from the sounds of the earlier, European-style marching bands. Their kind of playing wailed, like a human voice—quite differently from the way brass horns had traditionally been used; this blues-like quality purists called "dirty." "The rough, raw sound the black men forced out of these European instruments." Imamu Amiri Baraka (LeRoi Jones) contends, "was a sound he had cultivated in this country for two hundred years. It was an American sound, something indigenous to a certain kind of cultural existence in this country."

While the black Creoles were a more cultured group, the music of the uptown proletariat possessed greater vitality. The main instrument of the former was the clarinet, conspicuous in French music; the latter preferred the trumpet or cornet. Whereas the Creoles brought operatic melodies, French folk tunes, and quadrilles uptown with them, the less sophisticated Negroes fostered more of African inception. And if the country blues by the 1890s was the most residual expression in Afro-American music, classic ragtime—outside the French sector—was the most strongly European. Yet all of this would eventually be brought together, with myriad shadings, in New Orleans *and elsewhere* in the genesis of jazz.

During the decade before 1900 jazz emerged from a nebulous period full of archaic ideas and entered its classic phase. The first of the great Louisiana jazzmen was Charles (Buddy) Bolden. Born in the uptown district of New Orleans in 1868, Bolden likely witnessed the dances in Congo Square as a child and grew up in the midst of the brass band craze. He became a barber by trade, but also learned to play the cornet. In his youth he opened a barbershop on Franklin Street and published a scandal sheet called *The Cricket*. He was a slender, well-built, strikingly handsome man, with hair between black and red. Sometime in the early nineties he organized his own band and quickly became crowned the "King."

Bolden's band consisted of from five to seven men and included cornet, clarinet, valve trombone, guitar, bass, and drums. The group played in uptown saloons and dance halls, in Lincoln and Johnson Parks, in the pecan grove over in Gretna, for picnics at Lake Ponchartrain, in open-air dance pavilions, on excursion trains, and occasionally for private parties. They played mostly the slow blues, although in more polite company they favored schottisches, lancers (something like quadrilles), and varieties (long numbers made up of waltzes, polkas, and other traditional dance music). Bolden's men did not play from music and got many of their tunes from the street or from gospel hymns and spirituals. Some they picked up from other bands; others they made up. "If You Don't Shake, You Don't Get No Cake," "Make Me a Pallet on the Floor," and "Don't Go 'Way Nobody" were all Bolden specialties.

To start the band Buddy would stomp the ground once to tell his men to get ready; then he would stomp three times, and the group would commence on the fourth beat. To stop them he would stomp again at the beginning of the last chorus. Each member freely embellished the melody, following the lead instrument, which at dances generally became the violin. Bolden's cornet style was one of incredible power, full of emotional impact and self-expression. Legend has it that on a still night his raw, brassy sound could be heard for miles! He preferred to play with an open horn, but sometimes used a rubber plunger or water glass for muted effects. Finesse was not his concern, as Buddy lifted his horn to "call his chillun home." "Old Buddy Bolden blew so hard," Louis Armstrong recalled, "that I used to wonder if I would ever have enough lung power to fill one of those cornets."

Most of the halls where Bolden played were rarely attended by whites and genteel blacks, since they were hangouts for roustabouts, gamblers, and hustlers. The tougher the dance hall, the rougher Buddy's music was. The cornetist was a notorious ladies' man, and he often showed up with two or three girlfriends clutching his arm. As the evening progressed, these admirers sometimes got rowdy, and the scene frequently turned into a general free-for-all. In parks, at some of the lawn parties and street parades, and under more seemly circumstances, white listeners were normally present, particularly after Bolden's reputation became established.

By 1906 he was complaining about headaches, and the pain even began to affect his playing. During a Labor Day parade that year his mind snapped. Not only could he no longer play, he was unable to recognize his closest friends. In April, 1907, Bolden was committed to a mental institution. Toward the end of World War I, he was temporarily released, but was shortly incarcerated again. His medical report for 1921 read: "Approachable, answers fairly well, paranoid delusions, also of grandeur, acoustic hallucinations, also optic, talks to himself. . . . Getting worse." He died in the East Louisiana State Hospital, November 4, 1931. Of the forty-odd documents in the hospital files concerning Bolden, almost half deal with the five dollars necessary for his burial.

During the dozen or so years of Bolden's career, several of the great pioneers of jazz played with his band. Around 1896 he added a second cornet to his group, hiring Willie Geary "Bunk" Johnson. Johnson's style was lighter, more delicate than Bolden's, but he, too, played mostly the blues in the early days. Unlike Bolden, Bunk Johnson eventually made records. His rhythms swing gently, almost joggingly, a synthesis of ragtime and march phrasing. While there is much embellishment of melody, the structure reflects strict canons and discipline. Bunk reached his zenith between 1911 and 1914, when he was playing regularly with the Eagle Band, one of the most popular uptown groups. "You really heard music," Louis Armstrong insisted, "when Bunk Johnson played the cornet with the Eagle Band."

During the daytime the band often played in street parades and for funerals. The tradition of the funeral parade in New Orleans probably dates back to the eighteenth century, when, by French law, blacks were permitted to bury their dead with music—a custom dating from life in West Africa. The early jazzmen continued the custom. The musicians accompanied the funeral cortege to the cemetery, playing hymns, spirituals, or sentimental numbers in a slow, dirgelike cadence. After the interment, as the procession filed away, the snare drums would roll. Then the cornet would sound its high, imperious notes. Before the band was three blocks outside the cemetery gates, it would be tearing into an uptempo rendering of transmuted religious tunes like "Didn't He Ramble" or "When the Saints Go Marchin' In," while the mourners strutted and jigged their way home.

The Creole bands tended to be far less boisterous. John Robichaux had what was considered the best "classy" band and played much sweeter music. Sometimes while Buddy Bolden was blowing hard in Johnson Park, Robichaux would be playing more subdued music in Lincoln Park, not far

away, to a middle class crowd. Initially Robichaux's string band, a smaller
affiliate of his brass band, played for society balls and at fashionable
restaurants and hotels. While his men could play the blues, and often did,
they preferred cakewalks, waltzes, quadrilles, schottisches, and mazurkas.
Robichaux's group were viewed as legitimate musicians, meaning that they
could all read music and did as they played. Working with John Robichaux
from time to time were clarinetists Lorenzo Tio, Sr. and Alphonse Picou and
cornetist Manuel Perez.

Perez, who formed the Imperial Band in 1898, was an improvisor,
although he could read music. He played "a nice loud cornet" and became
one of the early lions of New Orleans jazz. "If I got money, I'd bet on him,"
Albert Glenny, the great string bass player, said years later, "but man I'm
tellin' ya, Manuel Perez was a musician." Some of the men who played with
Perez also worked with Bunk Johnson and perhaps Bolden, for after the turn
of the century Creole musicians regularly substituted in the blues bands,
having learned to play the uptown style. "A fiddler is *not* a violinist," the old
Creole Paul Dominguez told Alan Lomax in disgust, "but a violinist can be a
fiddler. If I wanted to make a living I had to be rowdy like the other group. I
had to jazz it or rag it or any other damn thing."

By the Spanish-American War white musicians had also made a
significant impact on New Orleans jazz. Music played by whites in
approximation of black jazz became known as Dixieland, and the great
pioneer in the Dixieland style was George V. ("Papa Jack") Laine. Born in
New Orleans in 1873, Laine began playing drums as a child. At the end of the
Cotton Exposition in 1885, he bought a cheap field drum and later took
lessons from the proprietor of a cigar stand at Royal and Esplanade. As early
as 1892, he organized his Reliance Brass Band, which played for picnics,
parades, and carnivals, and was leading a Ragtime Band before 1900. Jack
himself usually played the bass drum. "I wasn't idle no time at all," the
musician remembered at eighty-four. "Pretty nigh on every night I had an
engagement to fill out, and it got so that I organized five bands." Besides
being a band leader, Laine became a dynamic entrepreneur, booking his
various groups and splitting his groups for different jobs. Some of these were
string bands; most were big brass bands. For a time he even had a troupe called
Laine's Greater Majestic Minstrels. Although Laine's men played by ear,
white Dixieland was always closer to ensemble ragtime than to Buddy
Bolden's blues. As Laine once observed, "they call it jazz today; in my time it
was ragtime."

Jack Laine's groups played for balls, weddings, open-air functions, prize
fights, funerals, and Mardi Gras parades. The marching band had long been a
tradition in New Orleans, for parades were held there on almost any pretext—
political rallies, fraternal celebrations, holidays, occasions honoring visiting
dignitaries. Much of archaic jazz had centered around these marching bands,
which probably played martial music, traditional tunes and spirituals, even
hymns like "Rock of Ages" and "Nearer, My God, to Thee." Many of these

groups were made up of blacks, and a dozen black bands supposedly took part in the funeral ceremonies for President Garfield in 1881. But the annual Mardi Gras, with its colorful processions, parades, and balls, came to feature music of all kinds. In the years before 1900, as classic jazz was crystallizing, the finely trained Creole bands, the raw bands from uptown, and white bands like Jack Laine's were all in great demand during carnival season. Laine played his first big Mardi Gras parade in 1899 and worked several of the carnival parties. He recalled that his marching bands normally used from twelve to fourteen men, but on occasions included up to eighteen. His indoor groups, on the other hand, generally contained seven pieces.

Yet by the turn of the century there was still another facet to New Orleans jazz. Developing separately, but parallel to the early jazz bands was the barrelhouse piano—different from the ragtime piano originating in the great valleys farther north. Until the 1890s the piano had not been particularly important in the vernacular music of the South, and the instrument was not added to jazz bands until considerably later. The piano was one of the last instruments mastered by black performers, and when they did, their style tended to be more percussive and vocal than florid and pianistic. Whereas ragtime was oriented toward Europe, barrelhouse piano and the boogie woogie style were strongly influenced by the blues, fitting comfortably within the emotional range of black music. Ragtime was structured and formalized; barrelhouse piano and boogie woogie were more spontaneous.

In 1897 New Orleans became the only city in the United States to have a legalized red light district. Following a precedent set by Paris and many Catholic cities in Europe, the Louisiana pleasure center licensed a section of about a dozen square blocks back of the French Quarter, where prostitution and gambling could exist openly. The intention was that by confining vice, it might thereby by controlled. Known as Storyville, after alderman Sidney Story, who drew up the ordinance creating it, the district quickly became a profusion of brothels, gambling houses, and saloons, most of which employed barrelhouse pianists. Some of these were black; some where light-skinned Creoles who had recently lost more exalted jobs elsewhere.

Tom Anderson, the unofficial boss of Storyville, ran a joint called the Arlington Annex and published the *Blue Book*, a guide to the tenderloin district selling for twenty-five cents a copy. There were big cabarets like the 101 Ranch, a hangout for pimps and big gamblers, and Pete Lala's 25 Club, a favorite haunt of musicians and hustlers. The Tuxedo Dance Hall was one of the fanciest places, although there were plenty of cheap honky-tonks catering to river rowdies and card sharks. Brothels ran the gamut from dingy one room "cribs" to luxurious mansions with thick carpets, gilt statuary, and crystal chandeliers. Lulu White's Mahogany Hall, on Basin Street, catered to white businessmen and planters. Lulu herself became known as the "Diamond Queen," since she wore diamonds "every place but in her nose" and flaunted a fine assortment of furs. Mahogany Hall went in for champagne and elegance and boasted a mirror room, oil paintings, and beautiful octoroons who changed dresses several times during the course of an evening. Countess Willie Piazza, another of Storyville's celebrated madams, had a big white piano in the parlor of her establishment and served drinks off silver trays, while Josie Arlington's place was done in plush and tapestries and had leopardskin rugs. All of the better houses had a piano—a sure sign of class—and sometimes featured a blues singer..

All night long the sounds of barrelhouse pianos could be heard coming from the pleasure domes of Storyville. It was a hard life for musicians, with long hours. But the pay was relatively good, even in the cheaper spots, where piano players worked strictly for tips. Some of the pianists became well known, especially Tony Jackson and Jelly Roll Morton. Jackson played at several of the houses, including Lulu White's. His style was essentially ragtime; in fact he participated in the great ragtime contest at the St. Louis Exposition of 1904. He also did some singing, possessing a high tenor voice.

The star of New Orleans pianists, however, was Ferdinand "Jelly Roll" Morton. Born in 1885 in Gulfport, Mississippi, of black Creole parentage, Morton virtually grew up with the pool sharks, pimps, gamblers, and musicians of Storyville. He began taking lessons on the guitar at seven, the piano at ten, and for a time sang with a strolling quartet that specialized in spirituals. He was raised by his "French" grandmother, who turned him out when he decided to become a professional piano player. "A musician is nothing but a bum and a scalawag," she told him. "I don't want you around your sisters. I reckon you better move." And so Jelly Roll joined the sporting life, dreaming dreams of fancy clothes, fine things, and big money.

At fifteen he was playing in the Storyville bars and bordellos. As a child he had followed the brass bands along the street—he was a second-liner, as these music-struck youngsters were called. Sometimes he carried the instrument case of one of his idols. He had cut his teeth on the blues of Bolden and Bunk Johnson. He had lived intimately with the older ragtime pianists, who in New Orleans usually played faster and with more strongly marked rhythms than their counterparts up river. Yet throughout his life Morton was haunted by a Creole heritage he sensed he had defiled. In a real sense Jelly Roll Morton brought together the downtown Creole music and the earthier, uptown style, blended ragtime with the blues, and added dashes of the martial music, spirituals, and Spanish, French, and Caribbean dance music he had experienced since boyhood. "I invented jazz in 1902," Jelly Roll once said, and while this is pure exaggeration, so typical of him, Morton's importance in the evolution of jazz cannot be denied.

Whereas Tony Jackson was a bit pretentious in his playing, Jelly Roll Morton played imaginative barrelhouse. Morton seems to have had great respect for Jackson, even to have been a little in awe of him, but decided to concentrate on "something truly different from ragtime." His approach to piano playing was freer, more jazzlike in its use of melody. Tunes were "dragged out," almost in a blues style, with much embellishment, subtle harmony, and warmth. Blues shadings were achieved by "crushing" adjacent keys, simultaneously sounding notes that were half steps apart from each other. Jelly Roll achieved the blues guitarist's effect of "walking the bass" by rolling his left hand. Rags in his rendition became slower, their rhythms smoother than the St. Louis style. The vigor and lyricism of ragtime, the passion of the blues, and the improvisation characteristic of jazz were reconciled and fused by Morton. While he was among the first masters of form in jazz, his structure was flexible rather than static. His playing had variety, sophistication, depth, spontaneity, feeling. With Jelly Roll Morton barrelhouse piano was lifted to a vernacular art, yet remained free of superficial display.

Although Morton's beat could "really rock the joint," his rhythm tended to swing rather than bounce. Initially he played alone; later he occasionally worked with small bands. Barrelhouse pianists were first used in the dance halls and cabarets of Storyville, not in the sporting houses. They were added to the brothels' entertainment roster, Countess Willie Piazza claimed, because that "was what most of our customers wanted to hear." Some of the larger cabarets used small bands, which played slow drags, "bucket shop," and "bumpy" music to put customers in a good mood. Despite many accounts to the contrary, Dixieland was *not* played in the tenderloin district, because it was too fast and lively. Neither were the old waltzes, schottisches, and mazurkas used, for they were too refined. The music played for dancing in Storyville was essentially stomps, slow drags, and barrelhouse blues.

Jelly Roll Morton became a familiar sight in the streets of downtown New Orleans, for he worked all over the district. He also shot pool, chased women, gambled, and even engaged in some casual pimping. During the day he sometimes stopped in Pete Lala's for a drink and would frequently sit down at the piano and play just for fun. He was a flashy dresser, had a diamond in one tooth, and talked constantly about getting rich. A light mulatto, Jelly Roll prided himself on his prowess with women, but was known to be an unmitigated braggart, an audacious liar, and an egotist of the worst sort. At the same time he could be brutally honest, was full of ideas, demonstrated great originality as a composer, and all in all comprised an incredibly complex personality.

After 1904 Jelly Roll was constantly on the move, using New Orleans only as a base. He played all along the Gulf Coast and went up to Memphis and St. Louis. "I had the bad habit...of being a big spender when I had money," he recalled, and there was "a new girl in every town." As early as 1908 he was in Chicago, eventually filling in at the Elite Club there, and around 1911 went to New York. He made a *second* trip to Los Angeles in 1917, which became his base for the next five years. He worked up and down the coast from Canada to Tia Juana. At one of the places he played, the white owner requested a waltz. "*Waltz?*" Morton replied, "Man, these people want to *dance*! And you talking about waltz. This is the *Roll* you're talking to." In the mid-1920s he was back in Chicago, where he made his finest records— including the "Tom Cat Blues," much in the New Orleans style. He formed his own band, the Red Hot Peppers, and successfully toured the Midwest. His orchestral concept was analogous to his view of the piano; solos and breaks by band instruments closely resembled the way Morton played them in solo. Later recordings were made in New York, but by the late 1920s he was on his way down.

Jazz was changing, and Jelly Roll was suddenly a colorful remnant of the past. With the Depression he was frequently out of work. Morton took it personally and became bitter. It was a conspiracy; a West Indian, he claimed, had put an evil spell on him. In 1938 he was living in Washington, D.C., part owner of a small club and doing badly. He liked to talk about the old days and did for weeks to Alan Lomax, then Folk Music Curator in the Library of Congress. Lomax came to look upon Morton as a "Creole Benvenuto Cellini" and recognized him as a creative musician with a remarkable grasp of the theory behind his synthesis. But the public had long since forgotten him. On July 10, 1941, Jelly Roll died of heart trouble and asthma, a frustrated, penniless man.

Morton related with nostalgia the happy days in New Orleans, where "we had a ball every night." But the Crescent City was far from the be-all of early jazz. There were similar activities over much of the Gulf Coast area and up the Mississippi. Cornetist Charlie Love, for example, was born in Plaquemine, Louisiana, in 1885. His mother, father, sister, and brother were all musicians, and his father even had a band. Love began experimenting with different instruments at the age of five and found that he liked the cornet best. As a child he heard Buddy Bolden play at the Odd Fellows Hall in Plaquemine. Charlie learned to play reasonably well on his own, but his father insisted he know how to read music, sending him down to Donaldsonville for lessons. The boy intermittently spent some time in New Orleans, but did not work there professionally until much later. When he left Plaquemine, he went to Alexandria, where he joined Harry Walker's dance band. Love maintained that there were about eighteen bands (!!) playing nightly in Alexandria at the time. Walker's group frequently played out of town—Shreveport, Opelousas, Oakdale, and elsewhere. Love remembered that some rich men from around Alexandria hired the Williams Brothers Band once for a train trip to New Orleans. The train was full of workers from the sawmill who wanted to sleep, and the men paid the band extra to walk through the cars every fifteen minutes playing "There'll Be a Hot Time in the Old Town Tonight." Love also worked in Algiers and Grand Isle and for several years around Shreveport. He stated that he went to Chicago *from* Shreveport in 1917, then returned to Shreveport, where he played with Jim Miller's band from Houston. He recalled that he worked in Texas for a while, but did not play in New Orleans until 1922.

Lead Belly disliked New Orleans, for he told the Lomaxes: "You go down Rampart Street an' you liable to see anything. You see a man without no legs an' a woman doesn't have a nose. Nex' come a man wid his mouf jes' a hole in he face. Yassuh, you gonna see ev'y diffunt kind o' thing down yonder

on Rampart Street in New Orleans." But the city undoubtedly offers the best
documentation of early jazz and provided the most stimulating environment
for the *blending* of the several jazz traditions. Bass player Albert Glenny, who
began playing around the Spanish-American War era, considered Perez's
Imperial Band the best ragtime band of that time. Although Glenny played by
ear, he remembered performing polkas, mazurkas, and varieties for white
dances, quadrilles and lancers for the colored. After hours, when he had
finished with the string band, Glenny recalled dropping in one of the
Storyville brothels, where he sometimes played the "naked dance"
(apparently a hootchy-kootchy danced in the nude) for better money in tips
than he had earned during the rest of the evening. Glenny's experience
illustrates something of the fusion of styles that took place in New Orleans.
Evidently the early jazzmen were not only flexible in their technique, but
often played several different types of music in a single night. Glenny also had
close acquaintance with brass bands, but preferred string groups because
"you don't have to walk so much."

The widespread borrowing of tunes suggests again a mingling of the
assorted jazz styles. "Tiger Rag," for instance, later claimed and copyrighted
by members of the Original Dixieland Jazz Band, had a long history in New
Orleans. Jelly Roll Morton maintained that he transformed the number from
an old French quadrille. Jack Laine played the tune, calling it "Praline."
Steve Brown remembered it as "Number 2," while Eddie Garland knew it as
"Play Jack Carey." Later jazz classics like "High Society," "Livery Stable
Blues," and "Dixieland One-Step" were frequently old numbers, widely used
under such informal names as "Meatballs" or "Snot."

Buddy Bolden's influence caused younger Creoles like Sidney Bechet and
Freddie Keppard to play in a different style from older heads like Lorenzo Tio
and Manuel Perez. Bechet was a clarinetist who played with Keppard and
later Joe Oliver. With the loss of Bolden, Keppard was crowned king of New
Orleans' cornet players. Fifteen years Bolden's junior, Keppard first learned
the violin, but by the time he was twenty had established himself as a
powerful cornetist. His technique was robust, almost coarse, yet his tone was
beautiful and full of feeling. He could intricately embellish a melodic
passage, and his range was fantastic. At times he played so low his cornet
sounded like a trombone, and in the upper range he could go above high E.
Although he was not able to read music, Keppard associated with Alphonse
Picou and the more polished Creole musicians. He became the leader of the
Olympia Band which reigned supreme in New Orleans until 1912, boasting
such distinguished members as trombonists Joseph Petit and Zue Robertson,
clarinetist "Big Eye" Louis Nelson, and guitarist Willie Santiago. From 1913
until 1918 Keppard was in and out of the city and barnstorming from coast to
coast with the Original Creole Band.

When Freddie Keppard departed for Los Angeles around 1912, he left
behind several strong groups competing for the limelight in New Orleans,
among them were those headed by Jack Carey and Oscar ("Papa") Celestin.

But all came to bow before the band of Edward ("Kid") Ory. Many of the greatest names in New Orleans jazz worked for Ory, while Joseph Oliver, who eventually played cornet for him, became the undisputed heir to the Bolden-Keppard mantle. Ory himself played the trombone. Of Creole ancestry, he was born December 25, 1886, on a sugar plantation near La Place, about thirty miles outside New Orleans. As a child he made a banjo out of a tin bucket and fishing cord and later a guitar from a cigar box. He had gotten interested in music after hearing local brass bands, from La Place and nearby Reserve. During the winter bands came out from New Orleans, and Ory remembered Bolden's passing through on an excursion train to Baton Rouge.

While still living on the plantation, Ory and a group of his young friends started their own band, called the Woodland Band, which played for fish fries and picnics. At first the boys used homemade instruments, but bought real ones later on. They were all self-taught. By the time Ory was ten he had a band of seven pieces and was playing for indoor parties and dances. Later the group played the sawmill towns up and down the road between La Place and Baton Rouge. The boys knew Buddy Bolden numbers like "Make Me a Pallet on the Floor," as well as waltzes and schottisches. Ory was using a valve trombone that he had bought for four dollars; it had some holes in it, which he filled in with soap. He worked in a sawmill for a while, going out with the band on weekends.

From time to time he visited New Orleans and recalled hearing Bolden and John Robichaux both playing on Sundays in Lincoln Park, one in the skating rink and the other in the pavilion. When he was twenty-one, Ory moved to New Orleans, working briefly with a string group at Pete Lala's. After he had earned enough money, he sent to La Place for his band. They rented a wagon and went through the streets with a sign advertising, "New Band in Town." Initially retaining the name Woodland Band, the group was soon playing at dance halls, and later for yacht clubs, lodges, country clubs, and private parties, as well as in Lincoln Park, where there were balloon ascensions on Sunday afternoons. At Lincoln Park the girls began calling Ory "Kid," and the name stuck. The toughest place he remembered working was called the Funky Butt Hall, at Perdido and Liberty Streets, which alternated from dance hall to church. "Why, if you didn't have a razor or a gun," Ory claimed, "you couldn't get in there." There were fights in the hall and out on the sidewalk. "Tough."

Kid's men took part in parades and funerals, particularly those of gamblers and hustlers who had supported their dances. The biggest funeral the group played for was that of a young Storyville pimp named Kirk, who had diamonds "in his garters and all over his mouth." Three bands participated. Ory worked in Storyville mostly during Lent, when everything else shut down. Musicians could generally get a job in the District any time they wanted simply by walking into a place that had no band or pianist. The going rate was a dollar and a half a night, plus tips. "It kept you eating," Ory said.

His band played with better conception and tone than Bolden's had, not so loud and with greater finesse. Gradually the personnel changed. Manuel Perez told Ory about a young string bass player named Eddie Garland, who was driving a wagon at the time, hauling barrels of wine and beer. Garland was from New Orleans, began playing around with homemade instruments before he was nine years old, and became a stalwart of Ory's aggregation. Joseph Oliver joined the group about 1914.

Born in 1885 on Dryades Street, Oliver had been associated with brass bands since he was fourteen. Later he worked as a butler, but also played with several dance bands. He played in some of the Storyville joints, and legend has it that he stood on Iberville Street one night, pointed his cornet across the street to Pete Lala's Cafe, where Freddie Keppard was working, then farther down the street to where Perez was engaged, and blew blues loud and clear. For a time Oliver played with A. J. Piron, who took over the Olympia Band when Keppard left for California, but it was not until after he joined Kid Ory that Oliver became known as "King."

He was a big man with a scar over one eye. His style had fire, yet some of his phrases were exceedingly delicate. He possessed a wide range, and no one had Oliver's endurance. His approach was personal and creative. He specialized in muted effects like the baby-cry, the horse-laugh, and the talking cornet, but more than any of his predecessors was noted for his ensemble playing.

Certainly Joe Oliver did not earn the title of "King" easily, for competition was keen among New Orleans brass bands. On afternoons of important jobs the bands would sometimes advertise by riding around town in topless furniture wagons, playing as they went and stopping at major intersections. There were usually seven pieces—trumpet, trombone, clarinet, violin, guitar, drums, and bass. The musicians sat facing the back of the wagon, with the bass player and the trombonist next to the tailgate. This was obviously to keep the slide of the trombone from interfering with other players—hence the term "tailgate trombone." When two rival bands met, they often stopped for a "cutting contest," each group attempting to outplay the other and win the loudest applause from sidewalk listeners.

It was while Joe Oliver was with Kid Ory that he encountered an enthusiastic teenager named Louis Armstrong. To Louis, Oliver was indeed the King, easily "the finest trumpeter who ever played in New Orleans." The boy was a native of the city, born on July 4, 1900. Everything musical interested him at an early age, and he wanted to become a singer. He even organized a quartet among the neighborhood children, which occasionally earned a few cents by singing in the streets. The boy was fascinated with parade bands, recalled hearing Bolden, but was more impressed by Bunk Johnson, with whom he may have studied. On New Year's Day, 1913, Louis was arrested for firing a pistol he had come across and spent the next year and a half in Waif's Home for Boys. The reform school supported a small band made up of some of the older boys and directed by one of the supervisors.

Louis learned to play the cornet and became a member of the group. When he returned to his family, he formed his own boy's band and was soon playing for dances and picnics. During the week he worked at odd jobs—selling newspapers, delivering milk, collecting bottles; shooting craps also brought in money.

Kid Ory first met Louis during a Labor Day parade. Ory and his men were marching just ahead of a boy's band, and they heard a strong cornet coming from behind them, "nice good solid tone to it." When the group stopped for a beer break, Ory went over to Louis: "You're going to be all right some day, you keep that up." Later Kid saw the boy, wearing short pants, hanging around his musicians in National Park. Armstrong even sat in with the band there a few times. Ory remembered that he had to be pulled up on the stand, since it was higher than he was. Mutt Carey, Ory's cornetist then, loaned Louis his horn, so that the boy could show what he could do.

Armstrong came under Joe Oliver's influence early in 1917. The King had noticed the boy's persistent attention and asked him one evening to come by his house and help his wife with some chores. In exchange Oliver would coach Louis on the cornet. Joe gave the youth an old instrument that he had used for years. Louis prized it with his life. "I can never stop loving Joe Oliver," Armstrong said. "He was always ready to come to my rescue when I needed someone to tell me about life and its little intricate things, and help me out of difficult situations." For Louis he became "Papa Joe." Before long the boy was filling in for his idol any time the King was unavailable. When Oliver left for Chicago in 1918, the eighteen year-old Armstrong was invited to take his place in Ory's band. "Kid Ory was so nice and kind, and he had so much patience," Louis wrote, "that first night with them was a pleasure instead of a drag. There just wasn't a thing for me to do except blow my head off."

Although Armstrong's early work was merely a prelude, his emotional range was always tremendously wide. He often expressed pleasure in working with men who could read music, but his best playing was marked by flexibility and spontaneity, in response to the heat of the moment. His work initially contained many rhythmic embellishments, and his phrasing was a marvel from the beginning. With Armstrong jazz entered a new era. "The New Orleans elders tried to preserve what was basically a nineteenth-century 'romantic' musical tradition in the face of enormous musical and stylistic changes," Gunther Schuller contends in his authoritative study of early jazz. "But one of their own was to cut these ties with finality. Through Louis Armstrong and his influence jazz became a truly twentieth-century language. And it no longer belonged to New Orleans, but to the world."

By the time jazz spread to the North and the West, the African and European lineages had become closely intertwined. There were still several kinds of jazz with much cross fertilization and individual variation. The often made contention that jazz rhythm came from Africa, while jazz melody and harmony came from Europe, Schuller says, is great oversimplification. He finds far more of African derivation in early jazz than previous writers had thought. Improvisation, fundamental to most jazz, was a typically African concept, in contrast to the more structured Western music. Jazz also employed the tendency of West African melodies to revolve around a central tone, evident in the blues and repeated phrases known as a "riff." The African call-and-response format continued with modification, as well as African musicians' emphasis on individuality.

On the other hand, jazz developed largely on instruments associated with European art music. The marching band traditions of the German and Italian immigrants blended with the funeral processions of the blacks, and the early New Orleans rhythm was often very close to European march rhythm. Black Creoles played with relatively untrained black musicians who must have been influenced by their more refined technique, yet at the same time the Creoles unquestionably picked up much of the freer style of the unsophisticated blacks. French and Italian operatic arias, which were once sung and whistled in the New Orleans streets, contributed passion and often actual melodies to early jazz. Jelly Roll Morton, for instance, was particularly fond of playing a ragtime version of the *"Miserere"* from *Il Trovatore*.

But black jazz before 1920 also contained the sensuality of the barrelhouse piano, the syncopation of ragtime, and the tension of the blues. Instrumental blues persisted in using the "breaks" of the classic style, while instruments were often made to sound like the human voice. The cornet essentially took the place of the lead vocalist in classic jazz, while the trombone (low voice) and the clarinet (high voice) embroidered the cornet's melody, blending to make three-part harmony. Morton and Armstrong were both noted singers as well as instrumentalists, and Armstrong's "scat" singing—characterized by explosive rhythmic sounds, verbally meaningless —were highly instrumental in feeling. The rough guttural sounds known as "dirty" tones were common in early jazz, but the "pure" timbres of European singing were also used.

White Dixieland, while it picked up much from the black forms, remained more exclusive. The melodies were smoother, closer to Tin Pan Alley, with fewer sliding notes. Its harmony was "purer," its sonorities not so unorthodox. Dixieland was more joyous than passionate, less expressive than spiritied, more intense rather than warm.

When King Oliver left New Orleans for Chicago, he took clarinetist Jimmie Noone with him. Freddie Keppard had already played from Los Angeles to Coney Island. Kid Ory departed for California in 1919, arriving in Chicago six years later. Joe Oliver sent for Louis Armstrong in 1922, asking him to join his band at the Lincoln Gardens in Chicago as second cornet player. By then most of the better New Orleans jazzmen had either left the city or were about to leave, attracted by bigger money in California, New York, and Chicago. Eddie Garland, Tom ("Papa Mutt") Carey, clarinetist Johnny Dodds, his brother Warren ("Baby" Dodds, the great drummer), cornetist Buddy Petit, trumpeter Henry ("Kid") Rena, drummer Arthur ("Zutty")

Singleton, clarinetist Albert Nicholas, and guitarist Johnny St. Cyr—all of whom had rubbed shoulders with Oliver and Armstrong—joined the exodus out of New Orleans.

The supposition that the Original Dixieland Jazz Band introduced jazz to the North when they opened at Reisenweber's Restaurant in New York City on January 26, 1917 is another of the misconceptions that surrounds early jazz. Tom Brown had brought a five-piece Dixieland combination to Chicago in 1914, playing a highly successful engagement at Lamb's Cafe, featuring numbers like the "Livery Stable Blues." Brown's Band from Dixieland, as it was called, created such a stir that Chicago cafe owners sent to New Orleans for other white groups that could play like them. The Original Dixieland Jazz Band was among the ones that came.

Tom Brown and his brother Steve, also an important musician, were both born and raised in New Orleans. Their father had played with a band during the time that lancers, schottisches, mazurkas, and reels were the popular dance music. As children the Browns had heard German bands playing in the streets and remembered them passing the hat around after they had finished. The boys began trying out musical instruments themselves during their early teens, when a musician-friend of theirs stored some band instruments at their house. Before they knew it, they had learned to play a number of them. Tom eventually settled on the trombone, Steve on the bass fiddle. They bought battered up instruments of their own and found jobs around the city. They played their first Mardi Gras parade about 1905, wearing blue coats borrowed from the state militia and white pants. They worked with big brass bands in outdoor dance pavilions and played between rounds at prize fights. To advertise the fight, the band would stand on different street corners and play. Steve could recall a time standing on Royal Street, near Iberville, with a lot of people around watching the group play. Suddenly he heard someone say, "My God, I've been traveling all around, but I never heard anybody play a bass like that." Brown thought the person was being critical and meant he did not know how to play. "Well, it sounded good to me," Steve said, "so I didn't care."

Eventually the boys made enough money to buy better instruments. They first played schottisches and the old dances, occasionally mixing in lively numbers. Gradually, they came to play more and more in 2/4 time, as the change to the new dances took place. The group the Browns worked with consisted of cornet, trombone, clarinet, bass, guitar, and drums. They would try out a new number, and if it sounded good, they would try to repeat it the same way. Sometimes they would play a number differently each time, until it finally simmered down into one general pattern. They often worked at Seventh and Magazine Streets, playing what they called ragtime. "See, it was the same type of music that Tom played at Seventh and Magazine," Steve insisted, that later "he played in Chicago." The brothers did not work in Storyville, for "our type of music wouldn't be acceptable there." The Browns essentially played Dixieland, whereas the dance halls and dives in the District used "entirely different music than ours." And yet the boys were obviously influenced by black music. "I think hot music originally started right down here in New Orleans," Steve contended, "and it all drifted in here from the plantations." As children the two used to go to dances in the black section, where "they'd have tarpaulins spread over the yard," just to hear the black bands. Steve especially called to mind the Stale Bread Band, headed by Emile August La Coume, Sr., at lawn parties. "But they didn't have what we call or considered the Dixieland combination," he observed. "They had violins and flutes and things like that in their orchestras." For harmony, he said, "we used to love to pass by these Negro churches and hear 'em sing."

Tom Brown formed his own band and had expanded his activities around New Orleans before going to Chicago. Steve left the group in 1913, to follow his trade as a sheet metal worker. He moved to Jackson and by late 1917 had opened his own business in Natchitoches. Steve returned to music in 1920, urged by his brother to come north. When he got to Chicago, he was surprised to find few groups using bass fiddles; almost all of them had tubas. He finally got a job at the Blackstone Hotel. Until he came to Chicago, Brown did not know a note of music, since he had never taken lessons. To get jobs with the larger bands, it became necessary for him to learn how to read. He stayed in Chicago until 1926, then signed a five-year contract with Jean Goldkette's orchestra in Detroit. When Goldkette's group broke up in New York, Brown joined Paul Whiteman. Whiteman's music "was a little different from me," Steve declared, "and I never enjoyed myself playing as much as I did with the Goldkette outfit." Whiteman's music was a bit too symphonic for Steve Brown, whereas with Goldkette "we played practically everything rhythmically."

Goldkette, however, had been greatly influenced by brother Tom, during Brown's initial success at Lamb's Cafe in Chicago. The Brown band had been heard earlier in New Orleans by a vaudevillian named Joe Frisco. Aware of the entertainment value, Frisco soon arranged for Tom Brown to bring his five-piece ensemble north. Jean Goldkette had appeared with a group at Lamb's Cafe right before Tom arrived. Sometime later, Goldkette visited the cafe to hear the band just up from New Orleans. "It made such a profound impression on me," Goldkette wrote, and their music "gave me ideas as to its unlimited possibilities that ... this event changed the entire destiny of my career."

Until Tom Brown's engagement in Chicago, the word "jazz" had not been applied. The music played in New Orleans had never been called that. "Jazz" was a name that came into use in Chicago—initially spelled "jas," then "jass." How the term emerged has long been a subject of debate. Joe Frisco claimed that "jazz" was an obscene word used around Chicago as slang for intercourse. Steve Brown insisted it was taken from a French word, *jaser*, meaning to pep up. But the list of explanations is long and varied and highly speculative.

Tom Brown's Band from Dixieland attracted so much attention in

Chicago that local band leaders began offering his players more money to work for them. Some of his men were quite good, particularly Ray Lopez, who played the cornet with his left hand. A number of Brown's men quit, forcing Tom to send down to New Orleans for replacements. In 1916 he took his group to New York, although his success there was never very good.

When the more famous Original Dixieland Jazz Band came to Chicago, they were incorporated, so that they had to stay together as a unit. The group consisted of Eddie Edwards, trombone; Alcide ("Yellow") Nunez, clarinet; Henry Ragas, piano; Johnny Stein, drums; and Nick La Rocca, trumpet. Edwards and La Rocca, about the same age as the Brown brothers, began playing a little later and had frequently heard Tom and Steve play for dances in New Orleans. About 1910 Edwards' uncle, a violinist, fashioned his nephew a tin mute for his slide trombone, patterned after a French horn mute owned by an orchestra member at the French Opera House. The mute was false in some positions and had to be lipped either sharp or flat. La Rocca's father had come to New Orleans from Italy in 1876, and Nick's first job was as an arc light attendant at the French Opera House. He was a great admirer of the Sousa band, worked for a while with Jack Laine, and learned much from listening to Ray Lopez.

What would become the Original Dixieland Jazz Band left New Oreans on March 2, 1916, and arrived in Chicago the next day. Their train was late because of a severe snow storm. None of the youths had brought along an overcoat, for the weather at home had been warm. They walked down Wabash Avenue in zero weather, sporting new straw hats. Between them they might have had forty dollars. They went to work for the Schiller Cafe, playing from nine at night until five in the morning. One evening a patron at Schiller's became so emotionally involved in their music that he twirled a walking cane around his head and let it fly, hitting several people. "Jazz her up fellows," he shouted, "jazz her up!" That, according to Edwards, was the origin of the term.

Business was good at the Schiller Cafe, but hours were long. After three months the Dixieland musicians hired a lawyer and left. They worked a month at Del' Abe, where crowds were modest, then moved to Casino Gardens. They stayed at the Gardens until January, 1917. Actors and entertainers had repeatedly advised the "jass" band to try New York. "New York is the place," they were told. Eddie Edwards, organizer for the group, began sending off letters, trying to find an engagement there. Nick La Rocca did not particularly want to go; he was making forty dollars a week, more money than any of them had made before, and preferred to keep on in Chicago. Larry Shields, who had replaced Nunez as clarinetist, had come north with Tom Brown and strongly resisted the notion of going to New York, having just experienced Brown's failure there. Tony Sbarbaro was now drummer for the group.

Early in 1917 the Original Dixieland Jazz Band, as they now called themselves, received a contract to work at Reisenweber's Restaurant off

Columbus Circle, on a one month trial basis. Their fee would be $850 a week. They opened on a bitter cold evening in late January and stayed almost two years. It was the right spot at the right time, and the Original Dixieland Jazz Band made headlines from coast to coast. A month later the band cut the first jazz record, "Livery Stable Blues" and "The Original Dixieland One-Step," issued by Victor on its popular listing early the next year. It was when these numbers were recorded that several of the old New Orleans tunes were copyrighted by La Rocca and members of his group. "I don't blame 'em," Steve Brown said, "I would have done the same thing." The recordings of the Original Dixieland Jazz Band sold into the millions, given impetus by the wartime excitement, eventually breaking the sales figures of Caruso and the Sousa Band. Their records, even more than their triumph at Reisenweber's Restaurant, helped turn jazz into a national phenomenon.

More than any of their predecessors, the Original Dixieland Jazz Band took advantage of publicity and realized the value of promotion. The band's success in New York was much greater than it had been in Chicago and far beyond anything the musicians had enjoyed at home. A New Orleans *Times-Picayune* editorial in 1918 even went so far as to disown the five young men who were causing such a commotion up north, claiming that their city had had no part in producing the raucous new "jass." Certainly their music was typical of only one strand of the music played in New Orleans, that stemming from Jack Laine, and reflected recent modifications there. The use of a piano in Dixieland groups, for example, had been rare before 1916. Unlike the blues bands, the rhythm of the Original Dixieland Jazz Band tended to be fast and staccato. While they occasionally played softly and slowly, most of their music was an accelerated, somewhat boisterous ragtime. Yet there was freedom and feeling, if not deep warmth. "Jazz is not eye music," Eddie Edwards emphasized; "you don't read it. It is not ear music; you're not playing from ear. It is rather music from the heart, so therefore there can be no set type, because there's so much individuality in jazz music, as performed by the player."

Eastern playboys sometimes annoyed the band by asking to sit in with them. The only times Edwards recalled this was permitted was when Charlie Chaplin, Vernon Castle, and Harold Lloyd sat at the drums. Local bands began coming into Reisenweber's to listen to the Dixieland Jazz Band rehearse, and the group was soon imitated far and wide. Unfortunately many of its competitors cared little for   esthetic values and often sought attention by playing as noisily as possible. New York bandleaders and vaudeville houses were shortly scouring the South for any dance band musician who could blow a flatted seventh. The wartime draft took away some of the men, making rivalry all the more keen.

Although many of the jazzmen who ventured up from the Delta stayed only a few weeks, other groups equalled or surpassed the Original Dixieland Jazz Band's success. The New Orleans Rhythm Kings, one of the finest white bands to come north, made their first recordings in Chicago in 1921. Led by trumpeter Paul Mares, the Rhythm Kings went in for more solo work than Nick La Rocca's group and featured two outstanding soloists, clarinetist Leon Roppolo and trombonist George Brunis. Their rhythm, while syncopated, was much smoother than that normally used by the Original Dixieland Jazz Band.

Black bands from the South had appeared in vaudeville theaters and tent shows across the country prior to the big jazz furor in Chicago and New York. Freddie Keppard and the Original Creole Band had played an extended run at the Winter Garden in New York and had even turned down an offer from Victor to record in 1916. Keppard's explanation was simple: "We won't put our stuff on records for everybody to steal." Fate Marable, a hot pianist from St. Louis, had been working Mississippi excursion steamers between New Orleans and St. Paul for some time. Louis Armstrong eventually gave up his position with Kid Ory's band to join Marable's aggregation on board the *Dixie Belle*, remaining with him for almost two years. By the time Tom Brown achieved his success at Lamb's Cafe, black musicians were already playing obscurely on Chicago's South Side. Manuel Perez is thought to have arrived in the city before 1916, playing an engagement at the Deluxe Cafe.

But the exodus of black musicians out of New Orleans was quickened by the closing of Storyville during World War I. Some sailors on leave had gotten involved in a fight in the District, and two of them were killed. Josephus Daniels, Woodrow Wilson's Secretary of the Navy, asked city authorities to clamp down on vice in all forms, with the result that the police began a series of raids on the whorehouses and gambling dens. Suddenly the cry rang out that a nation fighting to save the world for democracy could not knowingly tolerate immorality. Under pressure from the Navy Department, the New Orleans mayor introduced an ordinance putting an end to Storyville. The law went into effect at midnight, November 12, 1917.

Liquor splashed like water the night Storyville closed. Parties were given all over the District, and practically everything was on the house. As midnight approached, an air of nostalgia swept over downtown New Orleans, as the bordellos and gambling joints prepared to retire. Young Louis Armstrong watched the scene in amazement; "I have never seen such weeping and carrying on," he wrote. From the open doors of the bars and sporting houses came the last sounds of the barrelhouse pianists. Here and there, one of the girls could be heard on a crying jag. As the hour drew near, the bands came out of the cabarets and dance halls, one after the other, and formed a line. Slowly they marched through the streets. And finaly, when the end came, they joined in "Nearer, My God, to Thee," as one giant brass band on its way to the graveyard.

A gentle breeze stirred the leaves of the palm tree in front of Josie Arlington's house. From out of the shuttered cribs came the prostitutes. Some of them walked out of Storyville, carrying mattresses on their shoulders; others loaded their belongings into wagons. The big brothels carted away the beds, padded the mirrors, and folded the towels. Some of the madams auctioned off their finery; Countess Willie Piazza sold her famous white piano for practically nothing. The Countess was bitter. "The countryclub girls are ruining my business!" she fumed. Over on Basin Street, Lulu White's pretty quadroons were packing their things. A red light flickered and went out.

Basin Street was felt to have such a bad connotation that it was broken up and renamed. Later, the name was restored to part of the downtown segment. Many of the Storyville establishments reopened within a few weeks in other areas of the city. Lulu White, who was wealthy enough to retire, moved to Bienville Street, but her house there fared poorly. Opportunities for musicians in the whorehouses and underground cabarets were never so great, encouraging those who had lived by playing "bumpy" music in the tenderloin district to seek better jobs and excitement where the wages were good—up the river, Chicago, California, Texas, Kansas City, New York, in the growing black sections of practically any industrial center. The economy of New Orleans had been ailing for several years, and business even in Storyville had undergone a decline during the last years. Similarly, over in the Quarter the French Opera House was experiencing hard times that were lean enough to prevent the theater from being rebuilt when it burned in 1919. While quality jazz would continue in New Orleans after World War I, salaries there simply did not keep pace with those available in cities enjoying more dynamic financial conditions. New Orleans jazz by 1920 was little publicized, and not much of it was recorded.

The first significant recordings by black jazzmen were made in 1922, by King Oliver's Creole Jazz Band, although Kid Ory had cut some sides in California a year earlier. It was no accident that the American public was introduced to jazz by Dixieland groups rather than their black counterparts. There was the racial issue, more explosive than ever, plus the fact that the music played by the Original Dixieland Jazz Band was a far more commercial style than that produced by the blacks. Jelly Roll Morton insisted that the Dixieland initially heard in New York was no more than a white imitation of Freddie Keppard's band. Larry Shields, the clarinetist of the Original Dixieland Jazz Band, is known to have been an admirer of Sidney Bechet, and other members of the group were remembered hanging around the 101 Ranch and other Storyville cabarets listening to black musicians. "Oliver makes something positive, even gay, out of a painful reality," Wilfrid Mellers observes; "the Dixieland Band, purging away both the passion and the irony, leaves us with the inane grin of the black-faced minstrel." The music of the New Orleans Rhythm Kings, with its more relaxed beat, was closer to black music, but the Rhythm Kings' early acceptance came in no small measure from their being white. While most of these Dixieland bands improvised and played by ear, they had arrived at this technique, achieving something parallel to the black music they admired, by fighting through the customs and prejudices of the genteel tradition.

Jazz from birth was a complex group phenomenon, with New Orleans only the most important of its several spawning grounds. As it grew, jazz came to be even more urban centered, where multiple forces interacted. With its spread to progressive cities of the North and West, changes took place almost immediately. Musicians were suddenly faced with the question of unionization; Joe Oliver's band, for instance, had become union members before they went to San Francisco in 1920. New instruments, particularly the piano and saxophone, were shortly added. But in these industrial centers the jazzmen met head-on the temptation to commercialize, scorn from middle class sophisticates, and the cult of respectability. Schuller maintains that "in purely musical terms the earliest jazz represents a primitive reduction of the complexity, richness, and perfection of its African and, for that matter, European antecedents." Once the social implications are put aside, he argues, "we are left with a music which in most instances can hold the musician's attention only as a museum relic." The great middle class audience in post-World War I America wanted an even more polished music than what they heard coming out of the South after 1914. They insisted on music that fit their concept of gentility, at whatever sacrifice to honesty. Jazz had emerged from a racial minority, been perpetuated by the proletariat, and had become associated with vice and debauchery. Welcome as Tom Brown and the Original Dixieland Jazz Band might have been to many, symbolizing for some liberation, pleasure, rebellion, America, and the new, for others they signaled danger. The black bands, playing a more sensual, emotional jazz, were viewed by middle class whites with curiosity at best; for most their music was primitive, uncouth, immoral, threatening. Traditionalists drew themselves up for combat. The opposition was vigorous and persistent, drawing aid from a restless upper-middle class youth. What followed was the most heated battle between the cultivated and vernacular traditions in the history of American music.

America had lost her innocence, yet tried to hang onto it. She had become a world power, but tried to forget. She had raced to become an industrial nation, longing all the while for an agrarian past. She adored the new, rushed to embrace it, but hated change. She loved freedom, yet feared the loss of structure. She prized the individual, but only so long as he was not different. She was a country skilled at doing, afraid to feel. Her people had learned to work, but not to play. Socially and culturally America had reached the divide—sure of much, uncertain of even more. The jazz controversy of the 1920s, with all of its implications, mirrored the nation's anxiety as she crossed the watershed.

BIBLIOGRAPHICAL NOTES

CHAPTER I. THE RISE OF THE SYMPHONY ORCHESTRA

The logical beginning for a study of the development of the symphony orchestra in the United States, and a model of good writing by a cultural historian, is John H. Mueller, *The American Symphony Orchestra: A Social History of Musical Taste* (Bloomington, Ind., 1951). Less distinguished, but helpful, are Margaret Grant and Herman S. Hettinger, *America's Symphony Orchestras* (New York, 1940), and Henry Swoboda (ed.), *The American Symphony Orchestra* (New York, 1967). Fascinating reading, and providing much general information, is David Ewen, *Music Comes to America* (New York, 1947). Ewen's *The Man with the Baton* (New York, 1936) focuses on specific conductors, as does Harold C. Schonberg, *The Great Conductors* (New York, 1967). Both are highly readable. Paul Henry Lang (ed.), *One Hundred Years of Music in America* (New York, 1961), contaises excellent chapters both on the rise of the symphony orchestra and the concert band era.

George P. Upton (ed.), *Theodore Thomas: A Musical Autobiography* (2 vols., Chicago, 1905), is fundamental, written by Thomas just before his death. The second volume consists of a compilation of Thomas' programs. Considerably less valuable, since it contains a number of inaccuracies, is Rose Fay Thomas, *Memoirs of Theodore Thomas* (New York, 1911). Charles Edward Russell, *The American Orchestra and Theodore Thomas* (Garden City, N.Y., 1927), was a Pulitzer Prize winner in its day. Two fine articles on the early Thomas career are Edwin T. Rice, "Thomas and Central Park Garden," *The Musical Quarterly*, XXVI (April, 1940), 143-152, and Abram Loft, "Richard Wagner, Theodore Thomas, and the American Centennial," *The Musical Quarterly*, XXXVII (April, 1951), 184-202. Philo Adams Otis' *The Chicago Symphony Orchestra* (Chicago, 1924), and "The Development of Music in Chicago: An Historical Sketch," *Papers and Proceedings of the Music Teachers' National Association for 1920* (Hartford, Conn., 1921), 109-127, are serviceable.

Walter Damrosch puts his best foot forward, often at Thomas' expense, in *My Musical Life* (New York, 1925), at the same time offering much worthwhile information on his own career and the career of his father. W. J. Henderson, "Walter Damrosch," *The Musical Quarterly*, XVIII (January, 1932), 1-8, is a good summary of the musician's several accomplishments. Henry Edward Krehbiel, *The Philharmonic Society of New York* (New York, 1892), James Gibbons Huneker, *The Philharmonic Society of New York* (New York, 1917), and John Erskine, *The Philharmonic-Symphony Society of New York* (New York, 1943), are all worth consulting. Richard Aldrich, *Concert Life in New York, 1902-1923* (New York, 1941), is a significant collection of detail by a famous critic. Interesting are Richard Schickel, *The World of Carnegie Hall* (New York, 1960), and Ethel Peyser, *The House That Music Built: Carnegie Hall* (New York, 1936).

H. Earle Johnson, *Symphony Hall, Boston* (Boston, 1950), is a solid account that includes a great deal of material on the Boston Symphony Orchestra. A well-written summary of the Karl Muck affair during World War I is James J. Badal, "Prisoner: 1337; Occupation: Conductor, Boston Symphony Orchestra," *High Fidelity*, XX (October, 1970), 55-60. Herbert Kupferberg, *Those Fabulous Philadelphians* (New York, 1969), adds up to both an in-depth study and engaging prose, whereas Ernst C. Krohn, "The Development of the Symphony Orchestra in St. Louis," *Papers and Proceedings of the Music Teachers' National Association for 1924* (Hartford, Conn., 1925), merely sketches the early symphonic activites of the first midwestern city to establish an orchestra.

Olga Samaroff Stokowski, *An American Musician's Story* (New York, 1939), is an important insight into the career of a celebrated Texas pianist and the musical climate she experienced in the early twentieth century. Richard Strauss' two American tours are described in Robert Breuer, "A Case of Hard-Earned Bread," *High Fidelity*, XIV (June, 1964), 42-45 and 108. Edward G. Leuders, "Music Criticism in America," *American Quarterly*, III (Summer, 1951), 142-151, is a superb analysis of shifting attitudes, while Arnold T. Schwab, *James Gibbons Huneker: Critic of the Seven Arts* (Stanford, Calif., 1963), is a scholarly biography of perhaps the most revolutionary critic in the United States at the turn of the century. Significant personal accounts include Henry T. Finck, *My Adventures in the Golden Age of Music* (New York, 1926), Thomas Ryan, *Recollections of an Old Musician* (New York, 1899), William Mason, *Memories of a Musical Life* (New York, 1901), and George P. Upton, *Musical Memories* (Chicago, 1908).

The colorful life of Patrick S. Gilmore is most completely told by Marwood Darlington in *Irish Orpheus* (Philadelphia, 1950), although a superior volume on the age of concert bands, which contains excellent descriptions of Gilmore's grand festivals, is H. W. Schwartz, *Bands of America* (Garden City, N.Y. 1957). The John Philip Sousa story is related in Kenneth Berger, *The March King and His Band* (New York, 1957), and more briefly by Richard Franko Goldman, "John Philip Sousa," *HiFi/Stereo Review*, XIX (July, 1967), 35-47. Sousa's own version, *Marching Along* (Boston, 1941), is one of the more entertaining autobiographies of American musicians. Young readers will enjoy Ann M. Lingg, *John Philip Sousa* (New York, 1954), and Mina Lewiton, *John Philip Sousa, the March King* (New York, 1944). More comprehensive studies include Alberta Powell Graham, *Great Bands of America* (Toronto, 1951), and Richard Franko Goldman's instructive *The Concert Band* (New York, 1946). Delightful glimpses into a popular turn-of-the-century pastime may be found in Frederick Fennell, "Hardy Perennial: Bands in the Open," *Musical America*, LXXXI (July, 1961), 14-17, and Ruth W. Stevens, "Notice! Band Concerts in the Park,"

Music Journal, XIX (December, 1961), 60. William Carter White, *A History of Military Music in America* (New York, 1944), is an informative, specialized account.

A contemporary article, calling for the recognition of native composers, is Walter R. Spalding, "The War in Its Relation to American Music," *The Musical Quarterly*, IV (January, 1918), 1-11.

CHAPTER II. GRAND OPERA AND THE "NOUVEAU RICHE"

The early history of opera in New York, through the beginning of the twentieth century, is voluminously told by Henry E. Krehbiel in *Chapters of Opera* (New York, 1908), a story that the author continues in *More Chapters of Opera* (New York, 1919). Less detailed is Julius Mattfeld, "A Hundred Years of Grand Opera in New York, 1825-1925," *Bulletin of the New York Public Library*, XXIX (Oct., 1925), 695-702; (Nov., 1925), 778-814; and (Dec., 1925), 873-914. Quite significant for insights into post-Civil War opera in America are Harold Rosenthal (ed.), *The Mapleson Memoirs* (New York, 1966), and Luigi Arditi, *My Reminiscences* (New York, 1896).

Irving Kolodin, *The Metropolitan Opera, 1883-1966* (New York, 1966), is the most reliable account of the great New York opera house, although John Briggs, *Requiem for a Yellow Brick Brewery* (Boston, 1969), is considerably more readable. Even more informal is Quaintance Eaton, *The Miracle of the Met* (New York, 1968), while Frank Merkling, John W. Freeman, Gerald Fitzgerald, and Arthur Solin, *The Golden Horseshoe: The Life and Times of the Metropolitan Opera House* (New York, 1965), is a valuable pictorial history. Eugene Bonner, *The Club in the Opera House* (Princeton, N.J., 1949), is a brief study of the Metropolitan Opera Club, with casual reference to artistic events, whereas Quaintance Eaton's *Opera Caravan* (New York, 1957), deals with the experiences of the Metropolitan Opera Company on tour, 1883-1956.

Vincent Sheean's *Oscar Hammerstein I* (New York, 1956), is a brilliant biography, but the impresario's operatic ventures are more fully discussed in John Frederick Cone, *Oscar Hammerstein's Manhattan Opera Company* (Norman, Okla., 1966). Mary Garden recalls the Hammerstein story, much of the Chicago Opera's, as well as her own in *Mary Garden's Story* (New York, 1951), coauthored with Louis Biancolli. Quaintance Eaton's *The Boston Opera Company* (New York, 1965), is an extremely detailed account of that company's five year history. The origins of resident opera in Chicago have been analyzed by Karleton Hackett, *The Beginnings of Grand Opera in*

Chicago (Chicago, 1913), and C. J. Bulliet, *How Grand Opera Came to Chicago* (Chicago, n.d.). The broader story has been told by Edward C. Moore, *Forty Years of Opera in Chicago* (New York, 1930), and more recently by Ronald L. Davis, *Opera in Chicago: A Social and Cultural History, 1850-1965* (New York, 1966). Personal glimpses are offered by Vincent Sheean, *First and Last Love* (New York, 1956), and Arthur Meeker, *Chicago, with Love* (New York, 1955), both of whom spent a great deal of time at the Chicago Auditorium during their student days.

Information on Chicago, San Francisco, Dallas, and New Orleans may be found in Ronald L. Davis, *A History of Opera in the American West* (New York, 1965). More specialized accounts of New Orleans' French Opera House include Harry Brunswick Loeb, "The Opera in New Orleans," *Publications of the Louisiana Historical Society*, IX (1916), 29-41, and Andre Lafargue, "Opera in New Orleans in Days of Yore," *Louisiana Historical Quarterly*, XXIX (July, 1946), 660-678. Fascinating anecdotes abound in Harnett Kane, *Queen New Orleans* (New York, 1949). William G. B. Carson, *St. Louis Goes to the Opera, 1837-1941* (St. Louis, 1946), is interesting, especially since St. Louis was visited by most of the American touring companies by the 1870s, and therefore serves as an important case study of opera in the hinterland.

Giulio Gatti-Casazza, *Memories of the Opera* (New York, 1941), is an indispensable look into the manager's long supervision of the Metropolitan, while Clara Leiser, *Jean De Reszke and the Great Days of Opera* (New York, 1934), Emma Eames, *Some Memories and Reflections* (New York, 1927), John Hetherington, *Melba* (New York, 1968), Joseph Wechsberg, *Red Plush and Black Velvet* (Boston, 1961), Nellie Melba, *Melodies and Memories* (New York, 1926), Ira Glackens, *Yankee Diva: Lillian Nordica and the Golden Days of Opera* (New York, 1963), Geraldine Farrar, *Such Sweet Compulsion* (New York, 1938), Dorothy Caruso, *Enrico Caruso* (New York, 1945), and Frances Alda, *Men, Women and Tenors* (Boston, 1937), number among the biographies and autobiographies of singers containing relevant material on the American operatic scene.

Early native operas are briefly treated in Edward Ellsworth Hipsher, *American Opera and Its Composers* (Philadelphia, 1927), and Ray Ellsworth, "The 1,950 Operas America Forgot," Hi Fi/Stereo Review, XIII (Oct., 1964), 95-99. General surveys of opera in the United States between the Civil War and World War I are contained in David Ewen, *Music Comes to America* (New York, 1947), and Paul Henry Lang (ed.), *One Hundred Years of Music in America* (New York, 1961), while late nineteenth-century developments are covered in Henry C. Lahee, *Grand Opera in America* (Boston, 1901).

CHAPTER III. THE REVOLUTION IN DANCE

Among the general books on ballet in the United States perhaps the most valuable for the historian are Walter Terry, *The Dance in America* (New York, 1956), and Olga Maynard, *The American Ballet* (Philadelphia, 1959). Also useful are George Amberg, *Ballet in America* (New York, 1949), John Martin, *America Dancing* (New York, 1936), Lillian Moore, *Artists of the Dance* (New York, 1938), Margaret Lloyd, *The Borzoi Book of Modern Dance* (New York, 1949), and Olga Maynard, *American Modern Dancers: The Pioneers* (Boston, 1965).

Andre Oliveroff, *Flight of the Swan* (New York, 1932), is an interesting memory of Anna Pavlova, while Paul Magriel (ed.), *Pavlova* (New York, 1947), and A. H. Franks (ed.), *Pavlova: A Biography* (New York, 1956), both provide worthwhile information. Recollections of Pavlova and several other dancers are included in S. Hurok, *S. Hurok Presents* (New York, 1953). Significant on the Russian reforms are Vitale Fokine (trans.), *Fokine: Memoirs of a Ballet Master* (London, 1961), Arnold L. Haskell and Walter Nouvel, *Diaghileff, His Artistic and Private Life* (New York, 1935), and S. L. Grigoriev, *The Diaghilev Ballet, 1909-1929* (Baltimore, 1960).

Walter Terry's *Isadora Duncan: Her Life, Her Art, Her Legacy* (New York, 1963), adds up to the best study of that fascinating American dancer, although Victor Seroff, *The Real Isadora* (New York, 1971), is an important personal account. Enchanting, if not altogether reliable, is Isadora Duncan's *My Life* (New York, 1927), written in a theatrical vein just before the performer's death. Quite worth consulting are Allan Ross Macdougall, *Isadora: A Revolutionary in Art and Love* (New York, 1960), and Ilya Ilyich Schneider, *Isadora Duncan: The Russian Years* (New York, 1968). Walter Terry's *Miss Ruth* (New York, 1969), a more intimate portrait than his book on Isadora, is excellent, as is Ruth St. Denis' *An Unfinished Life* (New York, 1939).

CHAPTER IV. THE GROWTH OF SERIOUS COMPOSITION

Few of the serious composers of the late nineteenth century have received full biographical treatment, although the music journals contain several articles of consequence. Among the best on the New England Conservatives are M.A. DeWolfe Howe, "John Knowles Paine," *The Musical Quarterly*, XXV (July, 1939), 257-267; Carl Engel, "George W. Chadwick," *The Musical Quarterly*, X (July, 1924), 438-453; Allan Lincoln Langley, "Chadwick and the New England Conservatory of Music," *The Musical Quarterly*, XXI

(January, 1935), 39-52; David Stanley Smith, "A Study of Horatio Parker," *The Musical Quarterly*, XVI (April, 1930), 153-163; and "Horatio Parker," *Musical Times*, XLIII (September 1, 1902), 586-592. Somewhat fuller are George W. Chadwick, *Horatio Parker* (New Haven, Conn., 1921), and Isabel Parker Semler, *Horatio Parker* (New York, 1942), as well as William Kay Kearns, "Horatio Parker, 1893-1919; a Study of His Life and Music," an unpublished thesis (University of Illinois, 1965). For information on the lesser New England Conservatives see Arthur Foote, "A Bostonian Remembers," *The Musical Quarterly*, XXIII (Jan., 1937), 37-44; Daniel Gregory Mason, "Arthur Whiting," *The Musical Quarterly*, XXIII (Jan., 1937), 26-36; Burnet C. Tuthill, "Mrs. H. H. A. Beach," *The Musical Quarterly*, XXVI (July, 1940), 297-310; Herbert R. Boardman, *Henry Hadley, Ambassador of Harmony* (Atlanta, Ga., 1932); and John Clair Canfield, "Henry Kimball Hadley: His Life and Works," another unpublished thesis (Florida State University, 1960). Burnet C. Tuthill, "Daniel Gregory Mason," *The Musical Quarterly*, XXXIV (Jan., 1948), 46-57, and Sister Mary Justina Klein, *The Contribution of Daniel Gregory Mason to American Music* (Washington, D.C., 1957), are both worth consulting.

Dvorak's influence on American music is discussed in most of the biographies of the Bohemian composer, among them Jan van Straaten, *Slavonic Rhapsody: The Life of Antonin Dvorak* (New York, 1948). Edward N. Waters, "The Wa-Wan Press, An Adventure in Musical Idealism," in Gustave Reese (ed.), *A Birthday Offering to Carl Engel* (New York, 1943), is excellent, while Arthur Farwell, *A Letter to American Composers* (Newton Center, Mass., 1903), is an important statement of purpose. Outstanding on Henry F. Gilbert are Olin Downes, "An American Composer," *The Musical Quarterly*, IV (Jan., 1918), 23-36, and Elliott Carter, "American Figure, with Landscape," *Modern Music*, XX (May-June, 1943), 219-225. John Tasker Howard's *Charles Sanford Skilton* (New York, 1929), remains the best study of that composer.

Notable on the early American Impressionists are Carl Engel, "Charles Martin Loeffler," *The Musical Quarterly*, XI (July, 1925), 311-330; Edward Burlingame Hill, "Charles Martin Loeffler," *Modern Music*, XIII (Nov.-Dec., 1935), 26-31; and George Henry Lovett Smith, "Edward Burlingame Hill," *Modern Music*, XVI (Nov.-Dec., 1938), 11-16. Felix Borowski, "John Alden Carpenter," *The Musical Quarterly*, XVI (Oct., 1930), 449-468; Olin Downes, "J. A. Carpenter, American Craftsman," *The Musical Quarterly*, XVI (Oct., 1930), 443-448; and John Tasker Howard, "John Alden Carpenter," *Modern Music*, IX (Nov.-Dec., 1931), 8-16, are each excellent. Edward M. Maisel, *Charles T. Griffes* (New York, 1943) is both chatty and informative, while William T. Upton, "The Songs of Charles T. Griffes," *The Musical Quarterly*, IX (July, 1923), 314-328, and Marion Bauer, "Charles T. Griffes as I Remember Him," *The Musical Quarterly*, XXIX (July, 1943), 355-380, are of special value.

Of the general books on American serious music, several are important for this period: Rupert Hughes, *Famous American Composers* (Boston, 1900); Daniel Gregory Mason, *The Dilemma of American Music* (New York, 1928); Claire R. Reis, *Composers in America* (New York, 1947); Katherine Little Bakeless, *Story-Lives of American Composers* (New York, 1941); and more recently Virgil Thomson, *American Music since 1910* (New York, 1970). Interesting sketches may be found in Paul Rosenfeld's *Musical Portraits* (New York, 1920), Rosenfeld's *Musical Chronicle* (New York, 1923), and Lawrence Gilman's *Phases of Modern Music* (New York, 1904). William T. Upton, *Art-Song in America* (Boston, 1930), is often exceptionally strong. Paul Henry Lang (ed.), *One Hundred Years of Music in America* (New York, 1961), contains a slim chapter on the evolution of American art music by Nathan Broder, while John H. Mueller, *The American Symphony Orchestra: A Social History of Musical Taste* (Bloomington, Ind., 1951), makes passing references to performances of American works. Significant background material is provided by Sumner Salter in "Early Encouragements to American Composers," *The Musical Quarterly*, XVIII (Jan., 1932), 76-105.

CHAPTER V. MACDOWELL AND IVES

None of the full-length biographies of Edward MacDowell are particularly serviceable, and all suffer from age. Among the better efforts are Lawrence Gilman, *Edward MacDowell* (New York, 1921); John F. Porte, *Edward MacDowell* (London, 1922); and for young readers Abbie Farwell Brown, *The Boyhood of Edward MacDowell* (New York, 1924). An excellent portrait of the composer may be found in Rollo Walter Brown, *Lonely Americans* (New York, 1929). Neil Leonard, "Edward MacDowell and the Realists," *American Quarterly*, XVIII (Summer, 1966), 175-182, and Irving Lowens, "Edward MacDowell," *HiFi/Stereo Review*, XIX (Dec., 1967), 61-72, are both first rate, perhaps the most valuable of all the MacDowell literature.

Personal remembrances include Marian MacDowell's *Random Notes on Edward MacDowell and His Music* (Boston, 1950); Upton Sinclair's "MacDowell," *American Mercuty*, VII (Jan., 1926), 50-54; Henry F. Gilbert, "Personal Recollections of Edward MacDowell," *New Music Review*, II (1922), 494-498; T. P. Currier's "Edward MacDowell, as I Knew Him," *The Musical Quarterly*, I (January, 1915), 17-51; and part of Hamlin Garland's "Roadside Meetings of a Literary Nomad," *The Bookman*, LXXXI (March, 1930), 44-57. The Columbia years are viewed by Leonard B. McWhood, "Edward MacDowell at Columbia University," in Karl W. Gehrkens (ed.), *Papers and Proceedings of the Music Teachers' National Association for 1923* (Hartford, Conn., 1924), 71-77, and John Erskine, "MacDowell at Columbia: Some Recollections," *The Musical Quarterly*, XXVIII (October, 1942), 395-405. The press dialogue between Nicolas Murray Butler and MacDowell is summarized in Butler's "Columbia and the Department of Music" (New York, 1904), reprinted from *The New York Times*, February 8, 1904.

The compositions are analyzed in William H. Humiston, "The Work of Edward MacDowell," *Papers and Proceedings of the Music Teachers' National Association for 1908* (Hartford, Conn., 1909), 26-45, and Elizabeth Fry Page, *Edward MacDowell, His Work and Ideals* (New York, 1910). O. G. Sonneck, *Suum Cuique: Essays in Music* (New York, 1916) contains a section on MacDowell, while the composer's own *Critical and Historical Essays* (Boston, 1912), consists of lectures MacDowell delivered at Columbia University. Marian MacDowell's "MacDowell's 'Peterborough Idea,' " *The Musical Quarterly*, XVIII (Jan., 1932), 33-38, is an interesting postscript to her husband's life.

For years the best source on Ives was Henry and Sidney Cowell, *Charles Ives and His Music* (New York, 1955), although David Hall, "Charles Ives: An American Original," *HiFi/Stereo Review*, XIII (Sept., 1964), 43-54, serves as a good short account. The traditional interpretation was convincingly shattered by Frank R. Rossiter's *Charles Ives and His America* (New York, 1975), with many of the new views reinforced by Rosalie Sandra Perry in *Charles Ives and the American Mind* (Kent, Ohio, 1974). Definitely worth consulting is David Wooldridge, *From the Steeples and Mountains* (New York, 1974), whereas Vivian Perlis' *Charles Ives Remembered* (New Haven, Conn., 1974) is a fabulous oral history. Invaluable is Ives' *Essays Before a Sonata and Other Writings* (New York, 1961), John Kirkpatrick (ed.), *Charles E. Ives — "Memos"* (New York, 1972). Excellent chapters on the composer may be found in both Wilfrid Mellers, *Music in a New Found Land* (New York, 1965), and H. Wiley Hitchcock, *Music in the United States: An Historical Introduction* (Englewood Cliffs, N.J., 1969). Less useful is the chapter in Virgil Thomson's *American Music since 1910* (New York, 1971).

Articles worthy of use include Henry Bellamann, "The Music of Charles Ives," *Pro-Musica Quarterly* (March, 1927), 16-22; Henry Cowell, "Charles Ives," *Modern Music*, X (Nov.-Dec., 1932), 24-33; Elliott Carter, "The Case of Mr. Ives," *Modern Music*, XVI (Mar.-April, 1939), 172-176; Henry Bellamann, "Charles Ives: The Man and His Music," *The Musical Quarterly*, XIX (Jan., 1933), 45-58; Elliott Carter, "Ives Today: His Vision and Challenge," *Modern Music*, XXI (May-June, 1944), 199-202; Nicolas Slonimsky, "Musical Rebel," *Americas*, V (Sept., 1953), 6-8, 41-42; Frederic Grunfeld, "Charles Ives—Yankee Rebel," *American Composers Alliance Bulletin*, IV (1955), 2-5; and Richard Weerts, "His Name Is Ives," *Music Journal*, XXIV (March, 1966), 46-47, 111-112. Among the best recent efforts are Audrey Davidson, "Transcendental Unity in the Works of Charles Ives," *American Quarterly*, XXII (Spring, 1970), 35-44, and Alfred F. Rosa, "Charles Ives: Music, Transcendentalism, and Politics," *New England Quarterly*, XLIV (Sept., 1971), 433-443. Some general works may prove helpful: Joseph Machlis, *Introduction to Contemporary Music* (New York, 1961); William W. Austin, *Music in the 20th Century* (New York, 1966); Peter Yates,

Twentieth Century Music (New York, 1967); David Ewen, *The Complete Book of 20th Century Music* (Englewood Cliffs, N.J., 1959); and Aaron Copland, *The New Music, 1900-1960* (New York, 1968). David W. Noble offers an interesting historical slant on Ives in *The Progressive Mind, 1890-1917* (Chicago, 1970).

Significant discussions of Ives' music are found in Bernard Herrmann, "Four Symphonies by Charles Ives," *Modern Music*, XXII (May-June, 1945), 215-222; Sydney Robinson Charles, "The Use of Borrowed Material in Ives' Second Symphony," *Music Review*, XXVIII (May, 1967), 102-111; Paul Rosenfeld, "Ives' Concord Sonata," *Modern Music*, XVI (Jan.-Feb., 1939), 109-112; and Aaron Copland, "One Hundred and Fourteen Songs," *Modern Music*, XI (Jan.-Feb., 1934), 59-64. Dominique-Rene de Lerma, *Charles Edward Ives, 1874-1954: A Bibliography of His Music* (Kent, Ohio, 1970), is a handy compilation, while Leonard Bernstein's oral explanation of the Second Symphony, accompanying the Columbia recording (MS-6889), is an ideal introduction to Ives' work.

Brief comment will be found in Paul H. Lang, "Charles Ives," *The Saturday Review of Literature*, XXIX (June 1, 1946), 43-44; Howard Taubman, "Posterity Catches Up with Charles Ives," *The New York Times Magazine* (October 23, 1949), 15, 34-36; Nicolas Slonimsky, "Composers of New England," *Modern Music*, VII (Feb.-March, 1930), 24-27; Paul Rosenfeld, *Discoveries of a Music Critic* (New York, 1936); Robert Layton, "Music in the United States," in Rollo H. Myers (ed.), *Twentieth Century Music* (London, 1960); and Henry Cowell (ed.), *American Composers on American Music* (Stanford University, California, 1933).

CHAPTER VI. THE MUSICAL THEATER

There are several entertaining surveys of the musical stage in the United States, none definitive and most of them weak on interpretation. Among the best are Cecil Smith, *Musical Comedy in America* (New York, 1950); Stanley Green, *The World of Musical Comedy* (New York, 1960); David Ewen, *The Story of America's Musical Theater* (Philadelphia, 1961); and Lehman Engel, *The American Musical Theater* (New York, 1967). Valuable reference books include J. Walker McSpadden, *Light Opera and Musical Comedy* (New York, 1936), and David Ewen, *Complete Book of the American Musical Theater* (New York, 1959). A discerning chapter on the evolution of American musical comedy may be found in Leonard Bernstein's *The Joy of Music* (New York, 1959), pointing out the relationship to opera and operetta especially well. The histories of popular music in America generally contain accounts of the musical stage, most notably Isaac Goldberg, *Tin Pan Alley* (New York, 1961); Sigmund Spaeth, *A History of Popular Music in America* (New York, 1948);

and three highly repetitious volumes by David Ewen, *Panorama of American Popular Music* (Englewood Cliffs, N.J., 1957), *The Life and Death of Tin Pan Alley* (New York, 1964), and *Great Men of American Popular Music* (Englewood Cliffs, N.J., 1970).

Significant background information is provided by Walter H. Rubsamen in "The Ballad Burlesques and Extravaganzas," *The Musical Quarterly*, XXXVI (October, 1950), 551-561. Bernard Sobel's *Burleycue* (New York, 1931) is the standard treatment of American burlesque, although the author's *A Pictorial History of Burlesque* (New York, 1956) offers supplementary illustrations and a more concise text. Well worth consulting is Irving Zeidman, *The American Burlesque Show* (New York, 1967). Strong on narrative is Robert Baral, *Revue* (New York, 1962), while Marjorie Farnsworth, *The Ziegfeld Follies* (New York, 1956), is better on photographs.

A most stimulating, analytical study is Albert F. McLean, Jr., *American Vaudeville as Ritual* (Lexington, Ky., 1965). Douglas Gilbert, *American Vaudeville: Its Life and Times* (New York, 1940), and Joe Laurie, Jr., *Vaudeville: From the Honky-Tonks to the Palace* (New York, 1953), focus more on factual data and specific personalities. Marian Spitzer's *The Palace* (New York, 1969), adds up to a superlative account of the great vaudeville mecca, and Ray Ellsworth, "Culture at the Palace," *HiFi/Stereo Review*, XVII (November, 1966), 66-70, offers interesting highlights. The career of Harrigan and Hart is engagingly recounted by E. J. Kahn, Jr. in *The Merry Partners: The Age and Stage of Harrigan and Hart* (New York, 1955).

Jacques Offenbach, *Orpheus in America* (Bloomington, Ind., 1957), is the composer's diary of his journey to the New World, while Reginald Allen, "Move Over, Verdi!" *Opera News*, XXV (February 4, 1961), 8-13, summarizes the competition light and comic opera posed to grand opera during the late nineteenth century. *The Merry Widow's* impact on the American musical stage is sketched by Bernard Grun in *Gold and Silver: The Life and Times of Franz Lehar* (New York, 1970), a creditable biography. Mrs. Reginald De Koven tells her husband's story, both as a composer of light operas and as music critic, in *A Musician and His Wife* (New York, 1926). Edward N. Waters' *Victor Herbert, A Life in Music* (New York, 1955) is the most scholarly biography of America's first great composer of operettas, although Joseph Kaye's *Victor Herbert* (New York, 1931) is a livelier account. Young readers will find Claire Lee Purdy, *Victor Herbert, American Music-Master* (New York, 1944), of unusual interest. Since Elliott Arnold's *Deep in My Heart* (New York, 1949), is a somewhat fictionalized account of the life of Sigmund Romberg, it proves more readable than substantive.

Parker Morell, *Lillian Russell, the Era of Plush* (New York, 1940), is a sympathetic portrait of a celebrated entertainer of the American musical comedy stage, while Jerry Stagg, *The Brothers Shubert* (New York, 1968), chronicles the Shubert story. The most balanced look at George M. Cohan is Ward Morehouse's *George M. Cohan, Prince of the American Theater* (Philadelphia, 1943), although the performer's own *Twenty Years on*

Broadway (New York, 1924) captures the Cohan personality more intimately.

George Jean Nathan's *Another Book on the Theatre* (New York, 1915) is highly critical in its appraisal of the American musical stage before World War I. David Ewen, *The World of Jerome Kern* (New York, 1960), is an uneven, casual biography, while the perspective of Robert Simon, "Jerome Kern," *Modern Music*, VI (Jan.-Feb., 1929), 20-25, is understandably limited. Richard J. Voorhees, *P. G. Wodehouse* (New York, 1966), touches only slightly on the Englishman's contribution to the American musical stage, but in *Bring on the Girls!* (New York, 1953) Wodehouse and Guy Bolton devote considerable attention to the Princess Theatre experience.

Personal observations include George Blumenthal and Arthur H. Menkin, *My Sixty Years in Show Business* (New York, 1936); Rudolph Aronson, *Theatrical and Musical Memoirs* (New York, 1913); and Edward B. Marks, *They All Had Glamour* (New York, 1944). Fragmentary information may be gleaned from Abel Green and Joe Laurie, Jr., *Show Biz from Vaude to Video* (New York, 1951); Walter Terry, *The Dance in America* (New York, 1956); Leonard A. Paris, *Men and Melodies* (New York, 1959); and George C. D. Odell, *Annals of the New York Stage*, I-XIII (New York, 1927-49).

CHAPTER VII. TIN PAN ALLEY

For a casual inquiry into the popular songs of the period, David Ewen's *The Life and Death of Tin Pan Alley* (New York, 1964) will serve as a readable beginning. Much of the same information may also be found in Ewen's *Panorama of American Popular Music* (Englewood Cliffs, N.J., 1957), *Great Men of American Popular Song* (Englewood Cliffs, N.J., 1970), and *Men of Popular Music* (Chicago, 1944). Sigmund Spaeth, *A History of Popular Music in America* (New York, 1948), is a highly factual account, as are the same author's *Read 'Em and Weep* (Garden City, N.Y., 1926), *Weep Some More, My Lady* (Garden City, N.Y., 1927), *They Still Sing of Love* (New York, 1929), and *The Facts of Life in Popular Song* (New York, 1934). Isaac Goldberg's *Tin Pan Alley* (New York, revised ed., 1961), on the other hand, is full of brisk interpretation, while Hazel Meyer, *The Gold in Tin Pan Alley* (Philadelphia, 1958), is unusually good on the business aspect of American commercial music.

Other general accounts include Douglas Gilbert, *Lost Chords: The Diverting Story of American Popular Songs* (New York, 1942), John Rublowsky, *Popular Music* (New York, 1967), and—for young readers— Elizabeth Rider Montgomery, *The Story behind Popular Songs* (New York, 1958). Excellent on the nineteenth century are Lester S. Levy, *Grace Notes in American History* (Norman, Okla., 1967), *Flashes of Merriment* (Norman, Okla., 1971), and *Give Me Yesterday* (Norman, Okla., 1975). The first five volumes of Mark Sullivan's *Our Times* (New York, 1928-33) contains a great deal of material on the popular music of this era, along with some interesting interpretation. Less fruitful are Maxwell F. Marcuse, *Tin Pan Alley in Gaslight* (Watkins Glen, N.Y., 1959), Margaret Bradford Boni, *Songs of the Gilded Age* (New York, 1960), Philip D. Jordan and Lillian Kessler, *Songs of Yesterday* (Garden City, N.Y., 1941), Arthur Loesser, *Humor in American Song* (New York, 1942), Frank Luther, *Americans and Their Songs* (New York, 1942), and Larry Freeman, *The Melodies Linger On: 50 Years of Popular Song* (Watkins Glen, N.Y., 1951). James J. Fuld's *American Popular Music, 1875-1950* (Philadelphia, 1955) is a valuable reference book.

Charles K. Harris tells his own story in *After the Ball: Forty Years of Melody* (New York, 1926), while *The Songs of Paul Dresser* (New York, 1927) contains an introduction by the songwriter's brother, Theodore Dreiser. John Tasker Howard, *Ethelbert Nevin* (New York, 1935), is authoritative, while Francis Rogers, "Some Memories of Ethelbert Nevin," *The Musical Quarterly*, III (July, 1917), 358-363, provides useful glimpses. Vance Thompson, *The Life of Ethelbert Nevin* (Boston, 1913), is based on the composer's letters and his wife's memories. Isidore Witmark and Isaac Goldberg, *From Ragtime to Swingtime: The Story of the House of Witmark* (New York, 1939), offers fascinating insights into the music publishing business, and publisher Edward B. Marks records a number of his impressions in *They All Sang* (New York, 1934).

Alexander Woollcott, *The Story of Irving Berlin* (New York, 1925), is quite personalized, while David Ewen's *The Story of Irving Berlin* (New York, 1950) is primarily for young readers. Irene Castle's *Castles in the Air* (Garden City, N.Y., 1958) is a charming autobiography. Hughson F. Mooney, "Songs, Singers, and Society, 1890-1954," *American Quarterly*, VI (Fall, 1954), 221-232, is worth consulting, and Katherine Little Bakeless, *In the Big Time* (Philadelphia, 1953), sketches several interesting portraits.

CHAPTER VIII. THE BLUES AND CLASSIC RAGTIME

Many of the works cited for the next chapter also include material that is relevant to the blues and ragtime. Of the studies exclusively on the blues, however, none is more significant than Paul Oliver, *The Meaning of the Blues* (New York, 1963), originally published as *Blues Fell This Morning* (New York, 1961). Oliver's *The Story of the Blues* (London, 1969) is a pictorial history with a fine supporting text, while his *Aspects of the Blues Tradition* (New York, 1968) and *Savannah Syncopators: African Retentions in the Blues* (New York, 1970) offer valuable supplementary information. Samuel B. Charters, *The Country Blues* (New York, 1959), is definitive on the rural blues, although his *The Bluesmen* (New York, 1967) is excellent.

Another important study is Harry Oster, *Living Country Blues* (Detroit, 1969), while William Ferris, Jr., *Blues from the Delta* (London, 1970), and Tony Russell, *Blacks, Whites, and Blues* (London, 1970), are clearly worth consulting. A superlative chapter on the blues may be found in Harold Courlander, *Negro Folk Music, U.S.A.* (New York, 1963), while Imamu Amiri Baraka (LeRoi Jones), *Blues People: Negro Music in White America* (New York, 1963), is both interesting and useful. More general are Eileen Southern, *The Music of Black Americans: A History* (New York, 1971), and John Rublowsky, *Black Music in America* (New York, 1971). John A. Lomax, " 'Sinful Songs' of the Southern Negro," *The Musical Quarterly*, XX (April, 1934), 177-187, provides masterful analysis, while Otto Gombosi, "The Pedigree of the Blues," *Proceedings of the Music Teachers National Association* (Pittsburgh, 1946), 382-389, holds a few interesting thoughts.

C. Robert Tipton, "The Fisk Jubilee Singers," *Tennessee Historical Quarterly*, XXIX (Spring, 1970), 42-48, is a good, concise account. More detailed, but with less perspective, are G. D. Pike, *The Jubilee Singers of Fisk University* (London, 1874), and J. B. T. Marsh, *The Story of the Jubilee Singers* (Boston, 1880). John A. Lomax and Alan Lomax, *Negro Folk Songs as Sung by Lead Belly* (New York, 1936), was a pioneering effort and remains a classic. W. C. Handy's autobiography, *Father of the Blues* (New York, 1941), is a close look at the publishing of commercial blues, while the composer's *A Treasury of the Blues* (New York, 1949) contains several popular blues numbers, along with a readable text by Abbe Niles. Background on Handy's type of blues may be found in George W. Lee, *Beale Street: Where the Blues Began* (New York, 1934). Paul Oliver's *Bessie Smith* (New York, 1961) focuses on the singer's recordings, while Carman Moore's *Somebody's Angel Child* (New York, 1969) and Chris Albertson's *Bessie* (New York, 1972) are more intimate portraits.

The Jazz Archives at Tulane University are rich in oral history. Among the interviews on file there shedding light on the blues are one with Mrs. Cozzy Cary (October 27, 1960), a centenarian gospel singer, and another with Dave Oxley (January 6, 1965), drummer with Bessie Smith's last tour.

The pioneer study of classic ragtime is Rudi Blesh and Harriet Janis, *They All Played Ragtime* (New York, 1966), although Russell Roth, "The Ragtime Revival: A Critique," *American Quarterly*, II (Winter, 1950), 329-339, is worth noting. Of the works coming out of the recent interest in ragtime, Peter Gammond, *Scott Joplin and the Ragtime Era* (New York, 1975), Terry Waldo, *This Is Ragtime* (New York, 1976), and especially William J. Schafer and Johannes Riedel, *The Art of Ragtime* (Baton Rouge, La., 1973) are among the best.

CHAPTER IX. EARLY JAZZ

The accounts of early jazz are full of misconceptions and error. Writers, for instance, have long overplayed the role of Storyville, and the importance of the Original Dixieland Jazz Band in carrying the music to the North has been repeatedly overstated. The traditional view of New Orleans as the solitary incubator of the new music is subject to modification, while the complexity of the jazz amalgam and the social forces surrounding it have been oversimplified and grossly distorted. The Jazz Archives at Tulane University contain scores of taped interviews with early jazzmen, indicating time and again how badly the jazz story has been written and how inaccurately it has come down to us. The attempt in this chapter has been to achieve a better focus and correct at least some of the errors.

The original material included here was drawn from a sampling of the key interviews on file at Tulane. Among the most significant are extensive sessions with Jack ("Papa") Laine (April 21, 1951 and March 26, 1957); Albert Glenny (March 27, 1957); Ed "Montudi" Garland (April 21, 1957); Charles Love (June 19 and June 20, 1958 and December 9, 1959); Tom Albert (September 25, 1959 and May 7, 1962); Kid Ory (under the auspices of *Life* magazine, April 20, 1957); Steve Brown (April 22, 1958); and Eddie Edwards (July 1, 1959). The Steve Brown file also contains letters from Jean Goldkette (December 21, 1955) and Joe Frisco (October 29, 1957 and another with no date) that confirm Tom Brown's success in Chicago.

Gunther Schuller's *Early Jazz: Its Roots and Musical Development* (New York, 1968) is the best analysis by a musicologist. Superior among the general studies are Marshall W. Stearns, *The Story of Jazz* (New York, 1956), and Rudi Blesh, *Shining Trumpets: A History of Jazz* (New York, 1958). Barry Ulanov, *A History of Jazz in America* (New York, 1952), should be read with caution, while Winthrop Sargeant, *Jazz: A History* (New York, revised ed., 1964), fairly remarkable for 1938, when it was originally published as *Jazz: Hot and Hybrid*, is more a look at Tin Pan Alley than the purer jazz forms. Extremely valuable are Martin Williams, *The Jazz Tradition* (New York, 1970), and *The Art of Jazz: Essays on the Nature and Development of Jazz* (New York, 1959) by the same author. Joachim E. Berendt, *The New Jazz Book: A History and Guide* (New York, 1962), Andre Hodeir, *Jazz: Its Evolution and Essence* (New York, 1956), and Hugues Panassie, *The Real Jazz* (New York, 1942), are interesting foreign accounts. Not always accurate are Rex Harris, *The Story of Jazz* (New York, 1955), and Leroy Ostransky, *The Anatomy of Jazz* (Seattle, 1960). Nat Shapiro and Nat Hentoff's *Hear Me Talkin' to Ya* (New York, 1955), which claims to be "The Story of Jazz by the Men Who Made It," must be used with discretion nonetheless, for it reiterates many of the familiar myths. Excellent recent accounts include Donald M. Marquis, *In Search of Buddy Bolden* (Baton Rouge, La., 1978) and William J. Schafer and Richard B. Allen, *Brass Bands and New Orleans Jazz* (Baton Rouge, La., 1977).

Of the books on individual musicians, Alan Lomax, *Mister Jelly Roll* (New York, 1950), Martin Williams, *Jelly Roll Morton* (New York, 1963), Martin Williams, *King Oliver* (New York, 1961), and Albert J. McCarthy, *Louis Armstrong* (New York, 1961), rank high. Well worth consulting are Hugues Panassie, *Louis Armstrong* (New York, 1971), and Robert Goffin, *Horn of Plenty: The Story of Louis Armstrong* (New York, 1947), as well as Armstrong's own *Swing That Music* (New York, 1936) and *Satchmo: My Life in New Orleans* (New York, 1954). H. O. Brunn, *The Story of the Original Dixieland Jazz Band* (Baton Rouge, La., 1960), is a reasonably good narrative that lacks perspective.

Useful reference works include Leonard Feather, *The Encyclopedia of Jazz* (New York, 1955), Al Rose and Edmond Souchon, *New Orleans Jazz* (Baton Rouge, La., 1967), Samuel B. Charters, *Jazz: New Orleans, 1885-1963* (New York, 1963), an index to Negro musicians in New Orleans, and Daniel G. Hoffman, "From Blues to Jazz: Recent Bibliographies and Recordings," *Midwest Folklore*, V (Summer, 1955), 107-114. Among the pictorial studies are Orrin Keepnews and Bill Grauer, Jr., *A Pictorial History of Jazz* (New York, 1955), and Dennis Stock, *Jazz Street* (Garden City, N.Y., 1960), dealing mostly with a later period.

Dave Dexter, Jr., *The Jazz Story from the '90s to the '60s* (Englewood Cliffs, N.J., 1964), Nat Hentoff, *The Jazz Life* (New York, 1961), George T. Simon, *The Feeling of Jazz* (New York, 1961), Francis Newton, *The Jazz Scene* (London, 1959), Nat Hentoff and Albert J. McCarthy, *Jazz* (New York, 1959), Nat Shapiro and Nat Hentoff, *The Jazz Makers* (New York, 1957), William L. Grossman and Jack W. Farrell, *The Heart of Jazz* (New York, 1956), Sidney Finkelstein, *Jazz: A People's Music* (New York, 1948), Dave Dexter, Jr., *Jazz Cavalcade* (New York, 1946), Robert Goffin, *Jazz, from the Congo to the Metropolitan* (Garden City, N.Y., 1944), Frederick Ramsey, Jr. and Charles Edward Smith (eds.), *Jazzmen* (New York, 1939), Wilder Hobson, *American Jazz Music* (New York, 1939), Henry O. Osgood, *So This Is Jazz* (Boston, 1926), David Ewen, *Men of Popular Music* (Chicago, 1944), Stephen Longstreet, *The Real Jazz, Old and New* (Baton Rouge, La., 1956), and Longstreet, *Sportin' House: A History of the New Orleans Sinners and the Birth of Jazz* (Los Angeles, 1965), each contain enticing, if not always reliable information. Russell Roth, "On the Instrumental Origins of Jazz," *American Quarterly*, IV (Winter, 1952), 305-316, is solid, although a bit indirect for this particular period.

Index

257

A NOTE ON THE AUTHOR

Ronald L. Davis was born in Cambridge, Ohio and raised in Dallas. He attended the University of Texas at Austin, where he received his B.A. in anthropology and his M.A. and Ph.D. in American history. He has taught cultural history at Kansas State College at Emporia, Michigan State University, and since 1972 has been Professor of History at Southern Methodist University in Dallas. He has written *A History of Opera in the American West* (1965), *Opera in Chicago* (1966) and edited *The Social and Cultural Life of the 1920s* (1972). He is the director of the DeGolyer Institute for American Studies and the SMU Oral History Program on the Performing Arts.